ELECTIONS
AND THE
POLITICAL ORDER

ELECTIONS
AND THE
POLITICAL ORDER

Angus Campbell
Philip E. Converse
Warren E. Miller
Donald E. Stokes

Survey Research Center
Institute for Social Research
The University of Michigan

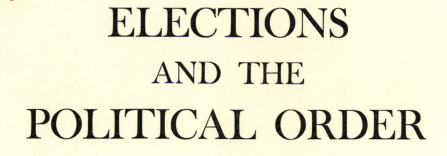
JOHN WILEY AND SONS, INC.
New York · London · Sydney

CI

Copyright © 1966 by John Wiley & Sons, Inc.

Library of Congress Catalog Card Number: 65–27662
Printed in the United States of America

To the memory of
Professor V. O. Key, Jr.

Preface

In many ways this book is a successor to *The American Voter,* in which we collaborated several years ago. Its focus, however, is quite different, although this new emphasis was foreshadowed by the earlier book. *The American Voter,* as its title suggests, "sought primarily to show the influences on individual voting behavior;" yet the final chapters shifted attention "from the voter to the full electorate and from individual choice to the collective decision."

This new emphasis is prominent in our more recent writings, many of which are collected here. The analyses we have undertaken since publication of *The American Voter* have frequently had more to do with aggregate properties of the electorate or with the party system than with the molecular voter. In this type of work, the data of interview surveys have been used not so much to explain individual behavior as to illuminate problems of a wider political order.

Since this emphasis is found in much of our recent work, we felt that it would be worthwhile to assemble a book organized around this theme. The papers collected here were not, however, written originally as chapters of a book, and the devices of ellipsis and redrafting, although liberally used, do not fully conceal these separate origins. If the collection constitutes a coherent whole, it does so because of the degree to which those joining in this program of research have held a set of interests and analytic ideas in common.

As usual our list of acknowledgments is a long one. We especially wish to take note of the contributions to this book of our foreign colleagues, Dr. Georges Dupeux, Professor of Modern History of the University of Bordeaux, Mr. Gudmund Iversen of the Department of Sociology of the University of Oslo, and Mr. Henry Valen of the Institute for Social Research of Oslo, who collaborated in the authorship of four of the ensuing chapters. Our associates at the Survey Research Center provided their usual fine support, in particular Dr. Charles F. Cannell and Dr. Morris Axelrod of the Center's Field Section, Dr. Leslie Kish and Miss Irene Hess of the Sampling Section, and Mrs. Doris Muehl Ginsburg of the Coding Section. Dr. Aage

Clausen served effectively as our principal assistant during the period this research was in process. Ralph Bisco, Julie Crowder, Jon Faily, and Rosemary Pooler also rendered valuable service as research assistants. Our secretaries, Mrs. Betty Jennings, Miss Joyce Johnson, Mrs. Virginia Nye, and Miss Ann Robinson contributed their essential services. Mrs. Bonnie Miller assisted in the editing of the final manuscript.

Our debt to the private foundations which provided financial support for our studies is apparent. The Carnegie Corporation, the Rockefeller Foundation, and the Social Science Research Council independently granted the funds which made the program possible, and we are grateful for their support. Needless to say, they must be absolved of responsibility for anything which appears in these pages.

Eleven of the sixteen chapters of this book have appeared in similar form in earlier publications. We wish to thank the publishers of the periodicals and books in which these chapters were originally printed for their permission to reprint them here. They are the *American Political Science Review,* the Duke University Press, the *Journal of Politics,* the *Public Opinion Quarterly,* and the *Revue Francaise de Science Politique.* Certain elisions and emendations of the original text appear in a number of the chapters for reasons of continuity and brevity.

In dedicating this book to the memory of Professor V. O. Key, Jr., we wish to acknowledge our intellectual debt to him as an imaginative and productive scholar and to express our appreciation of him as an associate and friend. We were fortunate in the fact that he spent the year 1959–1960 with us at the Survey Research Center in Ann Arbor. We remember him with admiration and affection.

Angus Campbell
Philip E. Converse
Warren E. Miller
Donald E. Stokes

Ann Arbor, Michigan
January 1966

Contents

Contents

CHAPTER 1

Introduction

Interest in the vote as a collective event in the total political process has a long history, preceding by many years the advent of what is now called the "behavioral approach" to the study of politics. Public reports of the aggregative vote totals have been available in many of the western democracies for generations, and analysis of these data anticipated many of the demographic descriptions of the vote, which surveys later mapped out in greater detail.

Aggregative analysis has severe limitations, however, and those who attempt to explain the flow of the vote solely on the basis of the statistics which the election apparatus makes available labor at a great disadvantage. They can approach many questions of electoral analysis only indirectly. In the absence of information about individual electors, "indicators" of various types must stand as surrogates for the data which would speak directly, and with unmistakable relevance, to questions of interpretation. The actual evidence at hand is so limited that the scholar is often virtually unrestricted in the interpretation he may choose. He may not be able to subject alternative hypotheses to empirical test because the data that would be necessary for such tests are not available; and, when available, the data perforce pertain only to aggregates in which individuals cannot be identified. This invites the kind of misinterpretation which frequently occurs when relationships between aggregates are taken as the basis for interpreting individual behavior.[1]

Aggregative data, however, permit one to discern cyclical movements in the vote over a period of time and the relation of these movements

---

[1] For a discussion of this problem see W. S. Robinson, "Ecological Correlations and the Behavior of Individuals," *American Sociological Review*, **XV**, 351–357 (1950).

to other simultaneous changes, for example, expansions of the franchise, fluctuations in the national economy, population movements, rising educational levels, or other social changes. The range of such concurrent changes for which adequate data are available is not large, and even though one exploits the regional, state, and even neighborhood comparisons which are possible within the national totals, the total repertoire of variables that one can manipulate will be much more limited and more fallible than one would wish.

The poverty of quantitative evidence available to the student of the aggregative vote is most pronounced in the absence of any direct measure of the motives of the electorate. One must assume that most changes in the collective behavior of the public reflect some change in the underlying motivation of the individual members of the public, whether the change be in birth rate, geographical mobility, purchase of automobiles, or turnout on election day. Collective behavior is undoubtedly influenced by gross measurable changes in the external situations in which people find themselves; a drop in national income will inevitably affect the level of consumer purchases. But people in our society generally have some degree of latitude in their response to circumstances, and their behavior expresses the character of their motives. The problem is to identify what this motivation is. As long as one has only aggregative data at hand one can only speculate as to what moved the individual members of the collectivity, although social theorists have been very inventive in proposing "basic psychological laws" to explain the behavior of society.[2] Science abhors a vacuum, and when no immediate evidence on motives is to be had, it is inevitable that intuitive theories about human nature will be proposed. Subsequent experience may prove these theories to have very limited validity.

The readiness to speculate about the individual's motives is certainly as quick among observers of the vote as it is among students of other forms of social behavior. This is obviously characteristic of the journalistic commentators who have an immediate explanation for each swing of the vote. It is also commonly found in the writings of more serious scholars. An eminently respectable example is the theory propounded some 25 years ago by Professor Arthur Schlesinger. He stated that the major oscillations in the popular vote over the pre-

---

[2] For example, J. M. Keynes in his famous *General Theory of Employment, Interest, and Money* (New York: Harcourt, Brace, 1936) presents a "fundamental psychological law" which is intended to explain certain aggregate relationships between personal income and savings.

ceding century reflected a cyclical movement from a conservative to a liberal mood in the minds of the voters.[3] Professor Schlesinger contended that electoral history since 1841 could be divided into epochs of about fifteen years' duration, which alternated between conservative and liberal governmental policies, resulting from shifts in predominant public sentiment. "Apparently the electorate embarks on conservative policies until it is disillusioned or wearied or bored and then attaches itself to liberal policies until a similar course is run." Professor Schlesinger had no direct measure of the attitudes of the voters who produced these changes in government; he took as a reflection of these attitudes the legislation which was enacted during these successive periods. The "tides of American politics" which he identified were in reality tides in the behavior of Congress; he assumed that they were also tides in the minds of the voters.

At the time Professor Schlesinger wrote this well-known explanation of voting cycles, he and every other student of social change in this country were confronted with the same intellectual problem; what aggregative evidence could be found to represent the motives of the collectivity? No individual data were available, and if one felt impelled to do more than simply identify changes which had occurred, he had to draw on his ingenuity to find some measure which could be plausibly offered in their place. Professor Schlesinger used the votes of Congressmen, making what we shall later argue was a precarious assumption of a close relationship between these votes and the desires of the electorate. Other writers have relied heavily on regional and other geographical comparisons to explain the vote. With no direct evidence of motivation at hand, they have inferred the public state of mind indirectly from aggregative records of public acts.

With the development of survey research, this continuing dependence on aggregative data was broken. The evolution of the techniques of sampling, interviewing, data processing, and the related methodologies opened the door to a new dimension of information about people and society. It became possible to measure the attitudes and motives of the populace by going directly to representative individuals within it, and a broad range of descriptive data which had been inaccessible to the more traditional analysis of election statistics was revealed.

It was natural that the availability of survey data should have led first to an intensive concentration on explaining individual behavior. This was the focus of the early survey studies, whether they dealt with

[3] A. M. Schlesinger, "Tides of American Politics," *Yale Review*, **29**, 217–230 (1939).

consumers, workers, parents, or voters. The individual act was the ulti-mate behavior to be explained, and the analyst typically sought to identify the various types of motivational patterns within a total sample and to indicate their relative frequency. If he went beyond this descriptive level he undertook to demonstrate how the personal and motivational characteristics of individual respondents interacted to produce their behavior. Thus early studies of consumers dealt with the various kinds of stimuli which might lead to a specific pur-chase,[4] the first studies of family planning attempted to assess the influence of sociological circumstances and psychological predisposi-tions on the decisions of married couples to bear children,[5] and the first authentic survey of voting-nonvoting enumerated the reasons given by a sample of Chicago citizens for failing to go to the polls.[6]

There is no doubt that these pioneering studies and their numerous successors had an important influence on research developments in the social sciences in the period following the Second World War. They moved the study of social psychology out of the laboratory into the real world and strengthened its connections with the associated dis-ciplines. The impact of these studies on the general area of behavioral science is increasingly apparent in the literature of this field. Within the realm of political problems, however, the new survey studies seemed unable to answer many important questions concerning the national vote and its function in the total political system. The ap-parent preoccupation with the peculiarities of the individual voter and general disregard for the larger implications of the total vote led to a good deal of impatience among those students of politics who were anxious to see the new behavioral approach applied to the explanation of what Avery Leiserson has referred to as "the functional operation of the collective processes comprising the political system as a whole." [7] Professor Leiserson probably reflected the feelings of many political scientists when he complained in 1958 that "the behavioralists" were overemphasizing the "quantitative analysis of miniscular problems of uncertain relevance to the sweeping institutional complexes of politics."

[4] P. F. Lazarsfeld, "The Art of Asking Why," National Marketing Review, I, No. 1, 32–43 (1935).

[5] P. K. Whelpton and C. V. Kiser (Editors), Social and Psychological Factors Affect-ing Fertility, New York: Milbank Memorial Fund (in 5 volumes), 1946, 1950, 1952, 1954, and 1958.

[6] C. E. Merriam and H. F. Gosnell, Non-Voting, Chicago: University of Chicago Press, 1924, vii–287 pp.

[7] Avery Leiserson, Parties and Politics, New York: Alfred A. Knopf, 1958, p. 371.

Ingenious as survey analysts have been in exploiting their data, the episodic and time-bound character of these early surveys greatly restricted their ability to satisfy interest in the explanation of the collective processes of politics. Scientific analysis is typically concerned with the explanation of differences which occur under varying circumstances. In a single study of a single population the only circumstances which vary are those associated with the individuals or types of individuals who make up the sample, their personal history and their present situation, and these variables provide the basis of most survey analysis. It is not possible in a single study to take account of influences which change through time because there is no variation in time. It is not possible to study the effects of differences in a wider political environment if the study population lives within only one such environment. It is not possible to analyze the interaction of different populations within a structure of political institutions if information is available from only one of the interacting populations. These were the typical constraints on early survey analysts; because of them the early studies were primarily concerned with individual behavior and had relatively little to say about collective events.

Many attempts to find the "relations between collective results and the underlying individual human acts" have been made by social theorists but they have not proved altogether rewarding.[8] The connections between the great aggregative events in which the history of society is recorded and the individual acts of which they are composed are seldom clear. Typically the line of explication has been "downward" from the readily visible collective event to the component acts of individuals. As we have observed, this has led to speculative descriptions of the psychological basis of individual behavior, of which many have remained wholly untested and some have been proved by historical events to be untenable.

The behavioral approach to the study of social behavior is now reaching a point of development which makes it possible to think of bridging the conceptual gap between the individual and society by moving "upward" from the individual act toward the collective event. We are emerging from a period of exploratory soundings of various areas of social life into a period of programmatic research in which highly interconnected, and to some degree identical, inquiries follow

8 Arnold Toynbee has recently expressed the view that our "ignorance of the relations between collective results and the underlying individual human acts is not an ignorance peculiar to us in our time. All human beings who have ever lived so far . . . have been as ignorant as we are on this point."

each other through time. By extending the depth and breadth of their studies, behavioral scientists have greatly increased their ability to bring data gathered from individuals to bear on the explication of the collective acts of society. With the systematic replication of measurements of significant political events, the comparative study of populations in differing political environments, and the integration of information from interrelated levels of the political system, the analysis of political behavior is entering a new phase.

The Chapters Which Follow

We are primarily concerned in this book with the presidential and congressional elections in the United States. We have exploited the data from our program of national surveys covering the period from 1948 to 1960 in an effort to reveal the character of the collective vote which the elections record and to expand our understanding of the part played by the elections in the functioning of the total political system.

We have organized the chapters which follow into four sections. Part I, entitled "The Flow of the Vote," is concerned with stability and change in the national vote. These seven chapters develop a general theory of the vote as a collective event and apply it not only to the elections held during the years of our research program but also to earlier periods in American electoral history. Part II, "Voting and the Party System," deals primarily with the characteristics of competition between parties in the American political system. The four chapters discuss the nature of the party controversy, the relation of ideological positions to the vote, and the special circumstances of party competition in the Southern States. Part III presents three chapters devoted to "Comparative Political Analysis." Parallel studies in Norway, France, and the United States have made possible comparisons of political attitudes and activities in those countries. Two of these chapters are concerned with differences associated with the multi-party and two-party systems, and the third analyzes the phenomenon of the "military hero" as a political figure. Part IV, "Institutional Analysis," consists of a single chapter. This presentation combines information from constituents, legislators, and roll-call records in an analysis of the nature of representation in Congress.

I

The Flow of the Vote

The early applications of the behavioral approach to the studies of voting greatly increased our understanding of the individual voting decision, but it was not until a succession of election studies made it possible to analyze the movements of the vote from one election to the next that the characteristics of the total vote began to be seen more clearly.

These early studies provided a description of the basic political characteristics of the electorate, the extent of their interest in political affairs, the strength of their party attachments, and the level of their information and of their understanding of political issues and events. They also described the way in which the immediate political scene was perceived by the citizenry; they gave a rough measure of the impact on the voters of the personalities and appeals important on the political stage at the moment of decision. They undertook, of course, to relate these descriptive facts regarding the characteristics and the perceptions of the individual members of the electorate to their actual vote.

From these studies of the electorate in specific elections a set of concepts has emerged which provides a basis for the description of elections rather than of voters, of the flow of the vote rather than of a single turnout. Central to this general theory is the concept of the "normal vote," the vote division expressing the standing strength of the competing parties. Short-term political forces are seen as putting pressure on this normal expectation, swinging the vote according to their strength and direction.

This particular theoretical development is, of course, but one illustration of a far more general strategy. Study of other patterns of individual change which cumulate to aggregative variations over time is the first step to be taken in bringing many facets of our national history within range of the tools of behavioral research. For the public

7

record of aggregative variation in social, political, and economic phenomena greatly antedates individual evidence from surveys. The firmer grasp of the underlying individual meaning or range of possible meanings in specified variations in aggregative behavior which can be derived from current study of individuals provides keys to unlock hidden meanings in the past record. At the same time, that record of past aggregative variation, if properly illuminated, can help to interpret the significance of limits in current or "modern" variation.

CHAPTER 2

The Concept of a Normal Vote

Philip E. Converse

In interpreting mass voting patterns, great importance is given to any signs of change that current balloting may betray. Patterns established in the past, even though they may nearly determine the outcome of the election, tend to be taken for granted, while results are eagerly scanned for departures from these patterns. These departures are then taken to represent the unique "meaning" of the electoral message or the beginnings of significant secular trends in partisanship for some segment of the population. Thus, for example, a minority party may lose an election but show "strong gains" in the popular vote. In many contexts, such gains are taken to define the flavor of the election more clearly than the identity of the winning party. Although it remains historically important that the majority party did carry the election, the primary message of the voting may reasonably be construed as a rebuke to the party in power, if not indeed a trend indicating the future rejuvenation of the minority party.

Although such fascination with change is entirely to be commended, it is more difficult to specify, in any particular situation, the actual character of the change. Such a specification presumes some sort of baseline against which the change is registered, and conclusions about the change vary according to the choice of baselines. This ambiguity is a constant source of comfort to official party spokesmen after an election, for a "moral victory" can be claimed on the basis of a rather wide variety of results.

When aggregate statistics are analyzed on some geographic basis, it is customary to choose as a measuring stick for change the most recent prior election which is at all comparable to the current voting in turnout, level of office contested, and the like. This criterion of recency has both virtues and shortcomings. Most notable among its shortcomings, perhaps, is its insensitivity to the possibility that the most recent prior election was itself rather unusual. In that event, any observed change between the two elections may represent not so much a vital new reaction to the partisan scene as an absence of the peculiar forces which had characterized the benchmark election.

The obvious remedy for this shortcoming of a recency criterion in ecological studies is to establish baselines with a more extended time series of election results, through some averaging process. However, when the population is defined geographically, such extended series encounter severe problems because of population movement. Although geographical redistribution of partisans can be of extreme interest from the point of view of local politics, it is a confounding factor when the focus is on the changing reaction of individuals over time in a broader setting. If certain constituencies in Florida have shown dramatic secular trends toward the Republicans in recent years, it is important to determine whether this progression means some fundamental drift in sentiment on the part of native Floridians, or simply the influx of elderly and well-to-do Republicans from the North. In the latter case, the observed change in partisanship would not be an indication of any genuine re-evaluation of the parties; it would, in fact, indicate the stability of the evaluations of both groups over time.[1]

It has been documented that partisan preferences of individuals do tend to survive changes in residence very admirably, even when the voter migrates into strongholds of the opposition.[2] This fact, coupled with high American rates of residential mobility (particularly of the "short-hop" variety),[3] poses a severe dilemma for ecological

---

[1] Many observers have noted that the partisan vote division in most constituencies most of the time tends to shift back and forth between the parties in phase with national shifts in partisanship. This was the thesis developed by Louis H. Bean in *How to Predict Elections* (New York: Alfred A. Knopf, 1948). See also V. O. Key, Jr., *Politics, Parties, and Pressure Groups*, Fourth Edition (New York: Thomas Y. Crowell, 1958, pp. 215–217). When a constituency departs dramatically from such a pattern over a substantial period of time, it is very often found to be a constituency undergoing unusual rates of emigration or immigration.

[2] A. Campbell, P. E. Converse, W. E. Miller, and D. E. Stokes, *The American Voter*, New York: John Wiley and Sons, 1960, Chap. 16, pp. 441 ff.

[3] The Census Bureau estimates that some 20 per cent of the current American population moves from one address to another in the course of a year. However, relatively few of these moves carry out of the area, state or region completely.

analysis. On one hand, there is pressure to work with the smallest geographical units possible, in order to isolate populations that are sufficiently homogeneous to be unlikely to mask real partisan change by compensating internal shifts in preference. On the other hand, the prevalence of short-distance residential changes means that the finer the geographical subdivisions, the greater the personnel turnover of a district between elections. For example, we feel it is necessary to distinguish between central cities and expanding suburbs in aggregate analyses, but such distinctions run afoul of the movement problem in the most distressing fashion. If we are interested in individual change and wish to extract baselines from long time series, we would be on much more solid ground to treat the metropolitan area as a whole, thereby keeping a very large part of the residential movement within the unit of analysis.

Complementary shortcomings are suffered by sample survey techniques. Here the problem of locating homogeneous groupings at differing points in time is relatively minor. If the universe is the nation as a whole, we can locate the set of people of white-collar occupations born in the 1920's in a succession of national samples, regardless of how they may have been geographically redistributed in the interim. On the other hand, sample surveys of the single cross-section variety provide much less reliable historical depth than district voting records, simply because of the unreliability of individual recall of past behavior.

Nonetheless, certain properties observable in data from the lengthening sequence of election studies conducted by the Survey Research Center lend themselves to the development of an operational construct of a "normal" vote, which may be estimated for any segment of the population on the basis of single-wave, cross-section survey data. Such a construct is, of course, primarily an analytic tool rather than a theory or a set of substantive findings. It suggests a means of splitting the actual vote cast by any part of the electorate into two components: (1) the normal or "baseline" vote division to be expected from a group, other things being equal; and (2) the current deviation from that norm, which occurs as a function of the immediate circumstances of the specific election. At the same time, the construct is an integral part of the theoretical view of the electoral process which we have been developing, and it makes possible a number of interesting deductions about the operating characteristics of the process in the current American period. In the following pages we shall first consider the conceptual underpinnings of the construct, and then discuss in nontechnical terms the characteristics of the data which encourage this type of treatment.[4] Finally, we shall illustrate the empirical use of the construct.

Theoretical and Empirical Backgrounds

The voting record of the American public in the last decade has shown unusual partisan fluctuation. If we examine the national division of the two-party vote as measured biennially (the presidential vote and alternately, in off-year elections, the accumulated votes for Congress), we find oscillation which is as strong as any in the past century. Indeed, the movement in a single two-year span from a 42 per cent Democratic vote for President (1956) to a vote for congressional candidates approaching 57 per cent Democratic (1958) almost defines the limits of the range of variation in the national two-party vote division observable in two-party races over the entire last century.

This picture of dramatic short-term variation becomes even more interesting as we discover, in sequences of sample surveys across precisely the same period, a serene stability in the distribution of party loyalties expressed by the same public (Table 2-1). Furthermore, this is not the sort of net stability which conceals gross turnover of individual partisanship over time. "Panel" studies, which involve the re-interview of a national cross-section sample after intervals of two and four years, confirm a remarkable individual stability in party identification, even in this period of extravagant vote change.[5] It is clear that the electoral outcomes of the 1950's were shaped not simply by Americans who shifted their partisanship, but also by large numbers who indulged in what was, from their own point of view, "crossing party lines."

Indeed, the proportion of conscious defectors in our samples since 1952 supplies the numbers necessary in each election to account for partisan swings of the vote. That is, in 1952 and 1956, masses of Democrats expressed themselves as voting "this time" for Eisenhower; in 1956 in particular, the majority showed their continuing Democratic allegiance by returning to the Democratic column after they had made their choice for President. Similarly, Republican defections in 1958 outweighed Democratic defections in the same year, thereby creating

[4] For those interested in details, an extended technical note is presented in the Methodological Note at the end of this chapter.

[5] A panel study conducted by the Survey Research Center which involved interviews in 1956, 1958, and 1960 was supported by grants from the Rockefeller Foundation. Materials from this extended study will be treated in a forthcoming book.

TABLE 2-1

The Distribution of Party Identification in the United States, 1952–1964

	Oct. 1952	Sept. 1953	Oct. 1954	April 1956	Oct. 1956	Nov. 1957	Oct. 1958	Oct. 1960	Oct. 1961	May 1962	Aug. 1962	May 1964
Strong Democrat	22%	22%	22%	19%	21%	21%	23%	21%	26%	25%	23%	24%
Weak Democrat	25	23	25	24	23	26	24	25	21	24	24	22
Independent Democrat	10	8	9	6	7	7	7	8	9	7	7	7
Independent	5	4	7	3	9	8	8	8	10	9	11	10
Independent Republican	7	6	6	6	8	6	4	7	5	4	5	5
Weak Republican	14	15	14	18	14	16	16	13	13	15	16	17
Strong Republican	13	15	13	14	15	10	13	14	11	11	11	11
Apolitical (do not know)	4	7	4	10	3	6	5	4	5	5	3	4
Total	100%	100%	100%	100%	100%	100%	100%	100%	100%	100%	100%	100%
Number of Cases	1,614	1,023	1,139	1,731	1,772	1,488	1,269	3,021	1,474	1,299	1,317	1,465

the vast shift in the two-party vote division between 1956 and 1958. Once again, what is important to the current argument is not the shifting of the vote itself, but the fact that large-scale, and essentially unidirectional, defections occur while the participants continue to think of themselves as adherents to the original party.

Such facts make it useful to consider any particular vote cast by any particular group—the nation as a whole or some subpopulation—as consisting of a long-term and a short-term component. The long-term component is a simple reflection of the distribution of underlying party loyalties, a distribution that is stable over substantial periods of time. In any specific election the population may be influenced by short-term forces associated with peculiarities of that election (for example, a candidate of extreme attractiveness or a recent failure of party representatives in government) to shift its vote now toward the Republicans, now toward the Democrats. Therefore, although we start with a single variable (the vote itself) to be explained in any situation, we now commission two variables: the "normal" partisan division of the vote for the group over a long period of time, and the deviation of the group's vote from that norm in a specific election.

It is easy to see this stable central tendency to group voting patterns, as well as the short-term oscillation of actual votes around this central tendency, in many empirical situations. That is, if we erect time series of votes cast at a national level by politically interesting groups, such as organized labor, Negroes, the aged, and the like, we tend to find with monotonous regularity that sequences of the Democratic portion of the two-party vote behave as follows:

	Election				
	1	2	3	4	5
Group A	78%	70%	72%	82%	74%
Group B	48%	40%	42%	52%	44%
Group C	58%	50%	52%	62%	54%

This is, to be sure, an idealized pattern. Yet the degree to which large masses of empirical data on the votes of social groups approximate this idealized pattern is striking.[6] And such a pattern underscores the

[6] Most departures from such a pattern which can be observed for groups traditionally studied are too slight to be distinguished reliably from sampling error. The most dramatic exception came in 1960 when the Protestant and Catholic votes,

importance of distinguishing between long-term and short-term components, for it is clear in such cases that two radically different explanatory chores are involved. The first has to do with how the partisanship of Group A came to be established in the 70 per cent range rather than in the 40 per cent range of Group B. The second has to do with the dynamics of short-term variations shared across all three groups. The roots of the first phenomenon lie so deep in the past that it is doubtful if the data gathered can help to explain them. The second phenomenon is notable primarily because it lacks continuity with the past; the explanations lie clearly in the present. Other differences between Groups A, B, and C in an earlier day are likely to have some bearing on the first phenomenon, but they are likely to be entirely irrelevant in understanding the second.

The election outcome in the population or subpopulations, then, may be construed as the result of short-term forces acting upon a certain distribution of party loyalties which have characterized the population. For the moment we shall not try to paint in any specific content for these forces, save to observe a general distinction between *forces of stimulation* (which act to increase turnout) and *partisan forces* (which are pro-Democratic or pro-Republican in varying degrees of strength).[7] The hallmark of the short-term partisan force is, of course, that it induces defections across party lines, yet defections which are unaccompanied by any underlying revision of party loyalty. The model does not preclude the possibility that the distribution of underlying loyalties itself may change over time for a population, and the initial phases of such a change might well be marked by defections not yet accompanied by partisan conversion.[8] However, it is empirically clear that in the lengthening period of our observation, vote shifts have not been accompanied by conversion but rather have been followed routinely by actual return to the party of original choice.

Let us imagine that we have subdivided a population on the basis of a continuum of party identification, running from strong Democrats through Independents to strong Republicans. A subdivision of this sort has been common practice in all of our recent election studies.[9] If the distribution of the population in these classes remains

---

after a decade of motion in tandem, diverged sharply. Such an exception, however, poses no theoretical problems; it is encompassed easily in the model which is compelled by the total series of our observations.

[7] For a fuller discussion of such forces see Chapter 3.

[8] For an expanded discussion of these points see Chapter 4.

[9] The primary party identification question is "Generally speaking, do you think

stable over time, large-scale shifts in the vote from election to election must arise from shifting proportions of votes cast within each class of party identifier. Actually, such motion could occur in a number of patterns to produce any given vote. Most of these, however, are rather fanciful. Empirical data over a series of elections suggest that this motion takes a very straightforward form. This key pattern is shown, in a form only slightly idealized from empirical data, in Figure 2-1.

Several broad observations can be made. First, the strains introduced in the behaviors of identifiers of differing party and strength (Figures 2-1a and 2-1b) fairly plead to be quantified in terms of direction and strength, according to the slope of the arrows. This leads immediately to the concept of net short-term partisan forces. As in other realms, the net force cannot be directly measured; rather, it is posited and measured in terms of its observed effects. In this case, the observable effects have to do with the defection rates of classes of party identifiers.

Second, to the degree that empirical data collected over time and under a variety of net forces (pro-Republican and pro-Democratic as well as differing degrees of strength) conform to such regular patterns, it is more a mechanical than an intuitive matter to estimate the characteristics of a "normal" vote, conceived as one in which the behaviors of Republicans and Democrats of differing strengths show no distortion toward either party. The regularity of the patterns means that they may be readily formalized in a limited set of rules. If, for example, we are told that strong Democrats in a particular election turned out to vote in certain proportions and defected at certain rates, we can deduce from this limited information the properties of the two basic sets of forces operating in the election, and thence we can predict with quite gratifying reliability the turnout and defection rates characterizing each of the other classes of identifiers. By interpolation a normal vote can be located within this pattern as one in which the net balance of partisan forces is zero (either because of an absence of short-term forces or because existing partisan forces are in perfect equilibrium), even though within a limited range of time an actual "normal vote" is

---

of yourself as a Republican, a Democrat, an Independent, or what?" Those who classify themselves as Republicans or Democrats are then asked, "Would you call yourself a strong (Republican, Democrat) or a not very strong (Republican, Democrat)?" Those who classified themselves as Independent were asked this additional question, "Do you think of yourself as closer to the Republican or Democratic Party?" Thus a maximum of seven classes are distinguished. These are often collapsed, as in this article, to five or three classes, in response to needs for greater case numbers per class, or under certain circumstances to assure monotonicity.

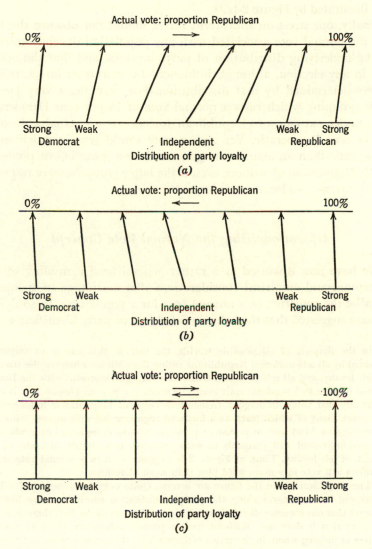

Figure 2-1. Varying strains induced on party loyalties by short-term net partisan forces. (*a*) Strong pro-Republican forces. (*b*) Mild pro-Democratic forces. (*c*) No forces; balance of forces.

never cast.[10] With some oversimplification, this is essentially the situation illustrated by Figure 2-1c.[11]

Finally, our stress on short-term forces should not obscure the fact that the normal vote associated with any population depends entirely on the underlying distribution of party loyalties, and that the actual vote in any election, although influenced by short-term forces, still is largely determined by that distribution. For example, a very Democratic grouping which casts a normal vote of 75 per cent Democratic may, under extreme pro-Republican forces, cast an actual vote only 60 per cent Democratic. Yet such a vote would remain much more Democratic than an actual vote generated by a grouping of predominantly Republican identifiers, even if the latter grouping were responding to extreme pro-Democratic forces.[12]

Operationalizing the Normal Vote Concept

We have now discussed at a rather general level a number of the conceptual and empirical considerations that encourage us to operationalize the construct of a normal vote for a population. In so doing, we have suggested that the behavior of classes of party identifiers varies

[10] In the simplest of all possible worlds, the vote at this zero-point might be generated by all self-confessed Republicans voting Republican, whatever the strength of their loyalty, and all self-confessed Democrats voting Democratic, with the limited handful of pure Independents split evenly between the parties. However, it is clear empirically that voters undergo a tremendous range of idiosyncratic influences on their votes, many of which (such as a husband requiring his wife to vote with him and not against him) lead to persistent pressures toward defection. The probability that any individual will succumb to such pressures is a simple function of the strength of felt loyalty. Thus, as Figure 2-1c suggests, even in a normal vote strong identifiers will vote in a more solid bloc than weak identifiers.

[11] The simplifications in the figure are several. Quite notably, classes of identifiers are arrayed in even spaces along the party identification continuum. We have no assurance that our measure discriminates such equal intervals. In fact, there is reason to believe that it does not. Without such a property, however, there is a severe problem in judging when, in the terms of Figure 2-1c, the arrows are indeed vertical. However, the figure is presented to convey the intuitive notion intended by the "normal vote."

[12] The underlying distribution of party identifications has a strong bearing not only on the partisanship of the actual vote, but upon the amplitude of the deviation which a given short-term force can produce. A grouping such as a cohort of elderly people is likely to have a U-shaped distribution, since party identifications strengthen with age, and is likely to be pushed less far by short-term forces of a given magnitude than a cohort of the very young, which shows a much more bell-shaped distribution of identifications, with few strong identifiers and many weaker ones.

systematically as a function of the level of stimulation accompanying a given election, and as a function of the short-term net partisan forces created by the election. We have suggested further that the normal vote represents nothing more than an interpolation within this patterned variation. To arrive at criteria for this interpolation we must first establish what the more general patterns are.

Short-term stimulation and turnout. It can be shown that in some instances strong partisan forces affect the turnout of different classes of identifiers, increasing the turnout of the advantaged party and depressing the turnout among its opponents. However, these instances are rarer than is commonly assumed, and it is a convenience to treat patterns of turnout as a function of short-term stimulation independently of partisan variation.

We cannot measure the level of stimulation directly. Nonetheless, the overall turnout figure for an election may be taken as a surrogate measure. Thus the relatively high turnout in presidential elections reflects high stimulation, whereas the sharp reduction in overall turnout in off-year congressional elections shows the greatly reduced stimulation. From this point of view, the most cursory inspection of turnout rates produced by different classes of identifiers over the range of elections that we have observed reveals a very clear pattern. When overall turnout is at a peak, as in 1960, Independents and weak identifiers are only moderately less likely to vote than are those who are strongly identified with a party. Thus a graph of the proportion turning out at each step across the party identification spectrum shows almost a straight line under conditions of very high stimulation (Figure 4-4). As we move to elections where turnout has been lower, however, we find that although strong identifiers are somewhat less likely to vote, Independents and weak identifiers are *much* less likely to vote. Hence as turnout declines, our graph shifts from a shallow slope to a V, and the V deepens as turnout declines still further (Figure 4-1). In other words:

> (1) *responsiveness of the turnout rate to the level of stimulation varies inversely with the mean strength of party identification.*

This "responsiveness" may be quantified quite congenially. Instead of erecting a graph election by election for all classes of identifiers, let us graph the variation in turnout for each class of identifier across five elections, as a function of the overall turnout in each election. Since this amounts to a part-whole correlation, it is of somewhat limited interest that these several graphs (five or seven, depending on the number of classes of identifiers we wish to distinguish) all strongly suggest linear relationships.[13] What is important is that the slope of the linear function varies systematically with the strength of identification, being steeper for the least partisan and shallower for the most partisan, as the V-phenomenon would necessitate. Thus the slope of the function estimated for each class of identifier (least squares method) can be seen as a representation of the "responsiveness" of the class to short-term stimulation. And in view of the systematic variation in slope as a function of identification strength, the degree of fit of the empirical observations for each class to its own characteristic linear function is quite remarkable.[14]

Figure 2-2 gathers up the estimated functions for the several classes of identifier in a single graph, illustrating the covariation of slope and strength of partisanship.[15] We note as well that at each level of partisan commitment, Republicans are less responsive than Democrats to the degree of immediate stimulation surrounding the election. Thus the V, which characterizes low-turnout elections, is not per-

[13] It is somewhat more interesting to note that if we set aside the South as a special case, the Southern observations for each class of identifier across elections extend beautifully, in a lower domain of turnout, the line of observations pertaining to the non-South. The degree of fit of all observations to a simple linear function is so excellent where underlying case numbers are at all numerous that isolation of the South and addition of its observations separately to give ten data points for five elections does little to change the optimal function. Indeed, the linear function for each class of identifier has been estimated on the basis of ten observations rather than five among Democrats and Independents.

[14] The fit is poorest where case numbers are fewest (among Republicans), although it remains sufficiently good that one hardly hesitates to estimate an underlying linear function. Among both types of Democrats and Independents, where the South can be represented separately and the total range of variation in the independent variable is about 40 per cent, the observed turnout of the specific identification class departs from that predicted by its linear equation on the basis of overall turnout by less than 0.5 per cent in about one-quarter of the comparisons, and by less than 2.5 per cent in more than two-thirds of the comparisons. Given the known sampling error which must be attached to the observations despite the part-whole structure of the relationship, this degree of fit to the characteristic slope of each class of identifier leaves little to be desired.

[15] The several functions converge quite well upon the point (100,100). The character of the functions toward the opposite extreme is less clear, and we have extended each function only as far as observed values warrant. While we can imagine that Independents might drop completely out of the electorate in elections of 10 to 20 per cent participation, the part-whole character of the relations represented requires as well that the functions for strong partisans "warp" to meet the point (0,0). Within the range of observed variation, however, such warping is not foreshadowed. For the moment, then, we must remain ignorant of patterns of variation when turnout is extremely low.

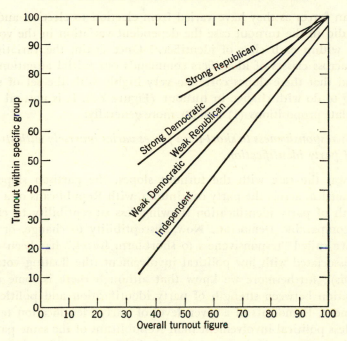

Figure 2-2. Turnout within classes of party identifiers as a function of overall turnout in five national elections.

fectly symmetrical across the party identification continuum: the arm of the V toward the Democratic pole tends to sag (lower Democratic turnout). This lack of symmetry is of both theoretical and practical importance. We shall consider it more systematically in a moment.

Short-term partisan forces and defection rates. Where partisanship and rates of defection are concerned, we have already constructed Figure 2-1 so that it reveals in advance that parallel patterns of variation occur. That is, under the influence of short-term partisan forces, movement toward the advantaged party tends to be slightly sharper (by a percentage metric) in the center of the party identification continuum than it is at the extremes.

Thus it follows that:

(2) *responsiveness of the vote division to short-term partisan forces varies inversely with the mean strength of party identification.*

Because underlying party loyalties in the nation as a whole have remained essentially constant in the last decade, we can take the national division of the two-party vote as an indicator of net short-term partisan forces as they have varied from election to election and plot as we did in the turnout case the dependent variation in the vote division within each class of identifier.[16] Once again, the variation in slope across classes of identifiers commands our initial attention, and we find that these slopes correlate very highly with the set of slopes having to do with change in turnout (Figure 2-2). It is natural to reformulate propositions (1) and (2) more generally:

> (3) *responsiveness to short-term forces varies inversely with strength of party identification.*

As was the case with the turnout slopes, the partisan slopes are asymmetrical across the party continuum, with Republicans of a given strength of party identification showing less susceptibility to change than comparable Democrats. Now, susceptibility to change, or what we have called "responsiveness to short-term forces," has been classically associated with low political involvement (the floating voter hypothesis) ; furthermore we know that although there is some direct correlation between strength of party identification and political involvement, Democrats of a given level of party identification tend to show less political involvement than Republicans of the same partisan commitment, even if the South is excluded from consideration. If we take stock of these partisan differences in involvement, we find that they match almost perfectly the turnout and partisanship slopes for the different classes of identifiers (Table 2-2) .[17] It is hard to imagine that these measures are not reflecting a certain unitary underlying property which affects voting behavior and which, incidentally, leads to some asymmetry between the parties in the current period. We may suggest, then, that:

> (4) *responsiveness to short-term forces varies inversely with the level of political involvement.*

The relationship between propositions (3) and (4) needs some further comment. We tend to view them as relatively independent

[16] The data points in the partisanship case fit linear functions a little more loosely than in the turnout case, indicating both greater scatter and, as will become clear later, an incipient departure from linearity. Nonetheless, the fit remains sufficiently good that estimation of functions requires little apology.

[17] Pearson correlation coefficients computed on the basis of five pairs of observations are not very useful. However, it gives some crude indication of the mutual fit of this triad of measures to note that over the five observations the correlation of turnout and partisan slopes is .97; that of turnout slopes with involvement means is −.98; and that of partisanship slopes with involvement means is −.97.

TABLE 2-2

Some Basic Characteristics of Classes of Party Identifiers
Bearing on Responsiveness to Short-Term Forces

	Turnout * Slope	Partisanship † Slope	Mean ‡ Involvement
Strong Democrats	0.76	0.57	0.81
Weak Democrats	1.05	1.09	−0.01
Independents	1.29	1.21	−0.23
Weak Republicans	0.98	0.75	0.16
Strong Republicans	0.52	0.29	1.18

* Let x be the overall turnout in a specified election, and let y be the turnout of the indicated class of identifier in that election. For five elections (10 observations including South and non-South) the linear function $y = mx + b$ is estimated. The slopes recorded are the m's. A slope exceeding 1.00 means that the change in turnout of the indicated class as a function of election stimulation exceeds that recorded by the population as a whole; a slope less than 1.00 means that change in turnout is less than that of the population as a whole.

† Let x be the national two-party division of the vote in a specified election, and let y be the two-party vote division of the indicated class of identifier in that election. The partisanship slope is the m computed for the least-squares solution of the equation $y = mx + b$.

‡ The mean involvement is based on an index of two questions, in which positions are assigned and a simple integer scoring employed to extract means. The values themselves convey no ready intuitive meaning. While the general ordering of classes of identifiers in terms of mean involvement remains constant from election to election, the measure does show some responsiveness itself to party fortunes. Therefore the means presented are those summed across several elections.

propositions. That is, both political involvement and partisan identification can contribute independently to a reduced responsiveness to short-term forces. It is certainly true that political involvement and strong party commitment tend to occur in combination, and it is likely that the emergence of either in an individual facilitates the development of the other. However, the correlation is mild indeed, and it currently seems fruitful to assume two correlated entities rather than one underlying entity that we happen to be measuring by two rather imperfect means.

Similarly, it seems useful to view the asymmetrical distribution of involvement between the two partisan camps as a mere coincidence of the current period, albeit one which demands empirical recognition. That is, we do not conceive Democrats as less politically involved because the Democratic Party is in any direct way a less stimulating object of affection. The stream of events which led the South to become a one-party Democratic region is of another order entirely. Yet this piece of history is partially responsible for the current asymmetry. Outside the South, the asymmetry stems from the fact that the Democratic Party tends to attract people of lower education on the grounds of the self-interest of "the common man," and since education is quite sharply correlated with political involvement for a totally different set of reasons, this biasing of the Democratic group toward the less-educated brings in its train a less politically involved group. To the degree that we can erect a model in which these involvement differences between the parties are taken into account (perhaps simply in the scale scores assigned to classes of identifiers), we can at the same time succeed in representing these empirical differences between the parties in the current period, at the same time providing a structure to encompass future situations in which these involvement differences favoring the Republicans may be ironed out or even become reversed.

In sum, then, we find that observations from five national elections reveal relatively simple patterns of variation in turnout and partisanship as a function of short-term forces.[18] The key operational question which remains is one of locating, within the pattern of partisan varia-

---

[18] Since we have come to see responsiveness to short-term partisan forces and forces of stimulation as related to strength of party commitment in identical ways, the next logical step might be to unify our turnout and partisanship equations, thereby simplifying and generalizing the exposition. We shall not perform this step for several reasons, both conceptual and empirical. Our data indicate that it is useful to distinguish between nonvoting which occurs because the potential voter has failed to pass the various registration hurdles imposed by state law, or is sick or unexpectedly out of town on election day, and more "dynamic" sources of nonvoting, such as disgust with the alternatives proffered by the parties. If most nonvoting were of the dynamic variety, as is often thought, then it would be important to take joint account of turnout and partisanship. Instead, it seems that the frequency of "dynamic" nonvoting is negligible in high-turnout presidential elections, and becomes important if at all in low-stimulation off-year elections. In the same vein, there is evidence that the character of partisan forces "contaminates" turnout only among the weakest of partisans in elections of lowest stimulation, seen as more "optional" by the citizen. In short, we have ascertained with some care that we commit no violation on the current data by setting turnout aside as an independent problem.

tion, the "zero-point" that represents the rates of defection of the varying classes of identifiers which would be expected under a perfect balance of short-term partisan forces.

Interpolation of the normal vote. Intuitively, we might suppose that a normal vote would be located where comparable classes of identifiers from the two partisan camps show equal defection rates. That is, when there are strong pro-Republican forces, strong Republicans are much less likely to defect than strong Democrats. Similarly, in the election of 1958, when there was reason to suppose that net forces were somewhat pro-Democratic, strong Democrats were less likely to defect than strong Republicans. Hence a perfectly natural point of interpolation for the normal vote is that point at which the defection rates of strong Republicans and strong Democrats (or weak Republicans and weak Democrats) are exactly equal.[19]

In effect, we do pursue this stratagem. The matter becomes somewhat complicated, since the asymmetry of involvement between comparable identifiers of the two partisan camps leaves Democrats slightly more susceptible to defection than Republicans, even when identification strength and strength of partisan forces are equated. However, we shall leave consideration of this complication to a methodological appendix, and shall treat only the idealized case here.

The linear partisanship equations were useful in indicating the fundamental regularity of some of these phenomena, pointing up at the same time the annoyance of partisan asymmetry in involvement. As we have already observed, however, the fit of the empirical partisanship observations to the linear functions was slightly poorer than in the turnout case. And despite the coherence of slope differentials, extrapolation of these functions to extreme values made no particular theoretical sense, as it had in the turnout case. Another mode of organizing the partisanship data provides functions which make sense at extreme values, which produce a better fit with the observations, and which, happily, leave little doubt about an objective location for the normal vote.

Since we have become interested in the relative balance of defection

[19] There is less clarity as to what level of turnout should be presumed "underneath" the normal partisan division. Where the balance of short-term partisan forces truly represents an absence of forces, we should probably expect at best a low average turnout for the type of election being conducted. Indeed, we shall reserve the term "normal vote" for the situation in which turnout is to the low side of average for a presidential election in the current period. Fortunately, as we shall see below, this choice turns out to matter very little save in the instance of extremely Republican or Democratic subpopulations and extreme variation in turnout.

rates for Republicans and Democrats of comparable identification strength under varying short-term forces, let us simply plot this association for our sequence of elections. The new graph, once involvement complications are removed, lends itself to the simple formalization shown in Figure 2-3. The figure is less formidable than it may appear. Suppose we wish to know how different classes of identifiers would behave under moderately strong pro-Republican short-term forces. We need merely follow the appropriate ray from the origin (labeled simply "pro-Republican") , noting the points at which the ellipses for strong and weak identifiers are intercepted. Thus, under these partisan forces, we see that about 3 per cent of strong Republicans will defect as opposed to 6 per cent of strong Democrats, whereas about 12 per cent of weak Republicans as against 27 per cent of weak Democrats will defect. If we wish to reverse the partisanship of the forces, but maintain the same moderate strength, we find the same points mirrored above the natural midline of the figure (labeled $x = y$), for the figure is symmetrical around this midline.

The involvement problem disturbs the symmetry of the actual empirical functions which underlie Figure 2-3. However, this disturbance is slight, and it may be shown to reasonable satisfaction that correction for partisan differences in involvement restores the observations to

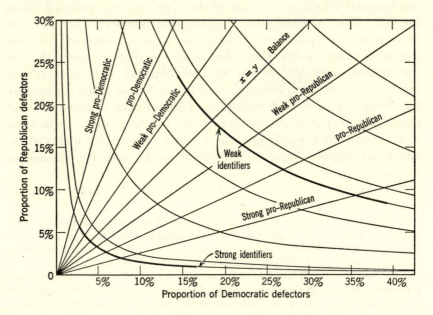

Figure 2-3. Defection rates as a function of short-term partisan forces.

symmetry (see Methodological Note at the end of this chapter). This disturbance aside, the "fit" of the empirical observations to the idealization in Figure 2-3 is exceptionally good. And, of course, to the degree that this presentation "accounts" for all of our data points under differing degrees and directions of short-term forces, there is no possible doubt about the location of the normal vote, which must of course lie along the midline $(x=y)$ of the figure.

From this point it is a simple mechanical matter to establish the actual norms which are used in computing a normal vote. Assuming a presidential election with a turnout somewhat below recent average, the data suggest the following:

	Expected Proportion Voting		Expected Proportion of Two-Party Vote Democratic
	Non-South	South	
Strong Democrats	0.79	0.59	0.957
Weak Democrats	0.71	0.43	0.818
Independents	0.62	0.28	0.492
Weak Republicans	0.76	0.50	0.162
Strong Republicans	0.86	0.72	0.037

The vote division to be expected in the normal case from any particular population group can be computed by applying these norms to the proportions of different classes of identifiers represented in the group. If we take the recent American electorate into consideration in these terms, for example, we find that the sample estimates of the normal vote characterizing the population from 1952 to 1960 have centered closely around 54 per cent Democratic. It is, of course, no coincidence that this figure is a little more than 1 per cent higher than the average national congressional vote for the five elections of this period and is almost identical with such an average if the two elections in which Eisenhower headed the ticket are excluded.

Some Illustrative Applications

Ultimately, of course, our interest lies less in the technical characteristics of the normal vote construct than in the new information which it permits us to extract from our data. We turn, therefore, to a brief illustration of the new types of substantive question which the construct encourages. We shall focus first upon the partisan implications of turnout variation when partisan forces are held constant at the zero or normal point, and second upon the information to be gained by dissecting the actual vote of a subpopulation into its long-term and short-term components.

Turnout variation. It has long been a matter of controversy as to whether the Republican or the Democratic Party tends to profit on balance from a general "non-partisan" campaign to stimulate turnout. If there has been a majority opinion, it has undoubtedly been that high turnout tends to favor the Democrats. Although this would seem on the surface to be a direct implication of our model as well, the matter turns out to be much more complex than appears at first glance. This is certainly true where changes in the strength or direction of short-term partisan forces are overlaid in systematic patterns on changes in the forces of stimulation, as is regularly the case in the alternation between presidential elections and off-year congressional elections. But it is true as well when we rule partisan forces out of the picture entirely.

Table 2-3 is constructed to represent this case. Rates of partisan defection established for the normal case have been applied to a range of levels of overall turnout, in accord with the equations underlying Figure 2-2. Hence the consequences of the differential turnout slopes

TABLE 2-3

Variation in Partisanship of Normal Vote as a Function of Changes in Turnout

	Overall Turnout *				
Hypothetical Population	25%	40%	55%	70%	85%
Preponderantly Democratic	74.7%†	72.8%	71.7%	71.3%	71.1%
Relative Partisan Balance	52.5%	53.4%	53.9%	54.2%	54.4%
Preponderantly Republican	14.3%	20.3%	23.6%	25.2%	26.5%

* The turnout proportion entered has been roughly equated with the proportions usually cited for elections where the base is the "number of eligible adults over 21."

† The cell entry is the per cent Democratic of the expected two-party vote when partisan forces are balanced, for the specified subpopulation and turnout level.

may be examined for three subpopulations of varying partisan coloration.

It is obvious that two dynamic components of the model will come into play as the turnout level declines: (1) "Independent" voters move out of the electorate more readily; and (2) Democrats are more likely to drop out than comparable Republicans. Table 2-3 illustrates the fact that of these two components, the first is notably more powerful than the second. The first component has the effect of strengthening any majority as turnout declines, whether that majority be Republican or Democratic. A subpopulation with a strong Democratic coloration, for example, is made up typically of a large number of identifying Democrats, a lesser number of Independents, and a still smaller number of identifying Republicans. In a high-turnout election, therefore, a substantial proportion of the total Republican votes cast by such a population come not from hard-core Republicans but rather from Independents, even though as a class these Independents are splitting their votes approximately equally between the parties. As turnout declines and these Independents drop out, the Republicans in such a case would suffer *proportionally* heavier losses than the Democrats. Hence low turnout would increase the Democratic majority.

The other component—lesser Democratic involvement—has some effect as well, with Democrats losing strength more rapidly than Republicans as turnout declines. This second effect is, however, much weaker than the first. The Democratic losses with declining turnout become notable only where the Democrats are in a small minority (the Republican subpopulation), and much of this loss is due rather to the first component—the general penalizing effects of low turnout on the minority party. Where this penalty hurts the Republicans instead (the Democratic subpopulation), the effect of lesser Democratic involvement is quite eclipsed, and majority Democrats gain ground despite declining turnout. In the middle, where the majority factor is nearly ruled out, the Democrats do lose ground with declining turnout, but remarkably little.

Perhaps more striking than these differential shifts in partisanship is the general insensitivity of partisanship to large changes in turnout. Partisan change quickens in the ranges where turnout is relatively weak, and it is undoubtedly true that bizarre effects occur quite readily in certain municipal elections where turnout may be as low as 10 to 20 per cent. But where presidential elections involving two national parties in some rough numerical balance are concerned, we see that shifts of 20 to 30 per cent in turnout scarcely make a per cent difference in expected outcome, provided that short-term partisan forces remain in balance.[20] This latter clause is important, of course, since empirically it may well be that higher-turnout elections tend to be characterized by stronger partisan forces. However, it remains of some interest to see that turnout variation unaccompanied by shifts in partisan forces produces little partisan change, save at the most feeble levels of turnout. And although our data do suggest that Democrats are slightly penalized by low turnout *all other things equal,* it is not surprising that practical politicians in some areas swear that quite the opposite is true.

Long-term and short-term partisan components of the vote. As a second illustrative application, let us consider the increase in information which our data may yield if we employ the normal vote construct to break up any particular actual vote into its long-term and short-term components. We are particularly interested in those cases where some independent variable is thought to be correlated with only one of these two components. In any such instance, empirical correlations between the independent variable and the vote may be lacklustre due to the confounding influence of the other component, unless the vote itself has been broken into its components first.[21]

In some cases, of course, we may not know exactly what to expect of the relationship between the independent variable and the two components of the vote. When doubt arises, we may ultimately learn from the data what the contrasting correlations are, provided that we have gained some prior confidence in our analytic tools through work with situations in which theoretical expectations are quite clear. To create this confidence, we shall consider two instances in which our differential expectations are indeed so clear as to be almost trivial, at least from the point of view of the technician accustomed to data of this sort.

First, let us consider a case in which the religion of the voter is related in fair degree to the long-term component of the vote, but is not at all related to the short-term component. Such a situation might have been expected in 1952, when indignation at Democratic corruption, aggravation at the Korean War, and the attractiveness of the

20 Hence our note above that the choice of turnout level for the normal vote, within the rather large range of turnouts presidential elections have produced, was not particularly critical.

21 Since the long-term component of the vote (prior party identification) is always the more powerful of the two terms, predicted relationships are less strongly confounded when the independent variable related to an actual vote has reason to be related only to the long-term component, than when the independent variable has reason to be related only to the short-term component.

Eisenhower candidacy were primary among the short-term forces having strong pro-Republican impact. None of these elements has any obvious religious relevance in the strong sense that Kennedy's Catholicism had in 1960.[22] In short, then, although we know that there are abiding differences in partisanship between Protestants and Catholics, particularly if the South is excepted from consideration, there was little reason to expect that the short-term influences in 1952 would have much differential impact by religious category. And indeed, when the 1952 vote is divided into its components, we find that Catholic-Protestant differences did lie entirely in the long-term component:

Non-South	Long-Term Expected Proportion Democratic, Normal Vote	Short-Term Deviation of 1952 Vote from Expected Vote
Protestants	44%	−13% *
Catholics	64%	−13%

* A negative deviation means a vote more Republican than normal.

In such situations, we may severely question the typical effort to "explain" the Protestant swing to the Republicans in one set of terms relevant to Protestantism, and then to search for another set of terms peculiar to Catholics to explain why the Catholic voters changed in a Republican direction as well. Obviously two groups can move in the same direction at the same time for different reasons, and this possibility must be kept open. Yet when evidence is strong that a certain configuration of forces produced the shift, and when these forces can only be given religious relevance, if at all, through somewhat subtle academic argument, it seems more reasonable to consider that religion was probably irrelevant to the dynamics of the particular vote. The long-term religious differences do indeed require explanation, but the fact that they turn up in the long-term component and not in the short is itself assurance that they have in no sense been caused by the specific features of the 1952 election.

[22] To be sure, analysts interested in predicting the voting trends among sociological groups in 1952 had surmised that Catholics, being more sharply anti-Communist, would evaluate the Korean War in a different light from that of Protestants, or that Stevenson's divorce would cause more Catholic than Protestant indignation. But as usual where hypotheses get somewhat subtle and indirect, the evidence for differential perceptions of this sort by religious category in 1952 is poor indeed.

It is equally easy to find illustrations of the opposite case, in which an independent variable is correlated with the effects of short-term forces, but is not correlated with the long-term component of the vote. We may continue with religious attitudes as independent variables, for we know that short-term forces in the 1960 election had unquestionable religious relevance. However, since Protestant-Catholic differences are "built into" the long-term component of the vote in the current period, we shall set aside Catholics entirely, restricting our attention to Protestants. Among Protestants, we argue, there is little theoretical expectation of correlation between attitudes toward Catholics and the long-term partisan component, but strong expectation of a marked correlation between such attitudes and the *short-term* component of the 1960 vote.

In 1956 we asked our respondents a battery of items having to do with their trust or distrust of political recommendations made by a variety of interest groupings in the population, including both "Protestant groups" and "Catholic groups." Responses to the two groupings can be ordered on an a priori basis to provide a scale of political anti-Catholicism, by placing individuals who distrusted Catholics and trusted Protestants at one extreme, and those who trusted Catholics and distrusted Protestants at the other extreme. For Protestants, of course, the latter extreme is vacant, although there is a fair range of variation from the anti-Catholic extreme through the neutral point to slightly pro-Catholic views (would distrust Protestants, but not Catholics, or would trust Catholics, would not distrust Protestants).

There is no systematic correlation between Protestants arrayed in this fashion and 1956 party preference. Furthermore, if we attempt to relate this 1956 measure to the vote cast by the same respondents in the 1960 election, we again find no regular differences in the predicted direction, despite the strong religious short-term forces in the latter year. The Democratic percentage of the 1960 presidential vote for these respondents reads:

				Slightly
Anti-				pro-
Catholic				Catholic
25%	40%	34%	36%	25%

If, however, we compute a normal vote for each category and then a 1960 deviation from this vote, thereby isolating the short-term component, we find a perfectly monotonic and rather close relationship:

	Anti-Catholic			Slightly pro-Catholic
−23%	−18%	−12%	−11%	+3%

where a negative deviation means a vote more Republican than normal, and a positive deviation means a more Democratic vote. Hence this rather obvious hypothesis shows no results until the dependent variable is broken into components. Then the influence of prior anti-Catholicism among Protestants becomes quite clear.

The important point for our current purposes, of course, is not so much the immediate substance of these data as the utility of the normal vote construct in sharpening our analyses of the meaning of voting change. If citizens approached each new election tabula rasa, then there would be no point in analyzing long-term components of the vote. The stability of party identifications, along with the apparent functional autonomy they gain for many individuals over time, however, has been amply documented. On the other hand, if all channels of political communication were to be shut off, so that citizens were obliged to go to the polls with no new political information to evaluate, there would be no short-term component to analyze.[23] In reality, voting decisions involve a blend of these components, and it is illuminating to be able to split them analytically. The normal vote construct enjoys a theoretical rationale and a sound operational base for this task. And, as is perhaps the true proof of the pudding, when put to use it leads to empirical findings of clear theoretical intelligibility.

Conclusion

For all of these reasons, then, the concept of a "normal vote" which may be expected of some subgroup in the American population, or of the American population as a whole, has increasingly become an integral part of our thinking about the flow of the vote registered across the history of American elections. Within the recent period for which sample survey measurements are available, the actual computation of normal votes under differing circumstances provides baselines which become crucial in assessing the meaning of electoral change, as we shall see most notably in Chapter 5. But even for the prehistory of survey research, where normal vote divisions can at best be crudely esti-

[23] We will consider this contingency in Chapter 8.

mated from the general cast of election returns, the *concept* of an underlying normal vote remains crucial in finding new meaning in old statistics. It is to some of these insights that we now turn.

METHODOLOGICAL NOTE

The problem of asymmetry of involvement. The asymmetry of involvement between comparable identifiers of the two partisan camps means that the empirical "balance point" in defection rates does not represent too accurately what we conceive as the location of the normal vote. One further logical step beyond points made in the text is required to understand why this is so. The fact that turnout varies more sharply among the weakly involved as a function of level of stimulation than it does among voters of stronger political involvement does not of itself assure us that at an individual level involvement is positively correlated with turnout in any specific election. It is quite apparent, both on common-sense grounds and empirically, however, that this is the case. Although it is slightly less apparent on the face of the matter, there is also reason to believe that there is a parallel positive relationship between involvement and party fidelity. This observation, coupled with the partisan asymmetry in involvement, means that if strength of party identification and strength of short-term partisan forces are held constant, Democrats are slightly more likely to defect than are Republicans.

Hence the normal vote cannot be simply conceived as one in which defection rates of comparable identifiers "balance"; rather, this empirical balance point must be expected to be one in which there is already a sufficiently strong pro-Democratic net force to make up for some small involvement-based delinquency in the Democratic camp. Or, correlatively, the normal vote will be one in which, for example, weak Republican identifiers remain slightly more faithful to their party than do weak Democratic identifiers.

Where Figure 2-3 (see text) is concerned, this means geometrically that the hyperbolic tracks best fitting the empirical observations should be slightly displaced from their symmetrical position about the axis ($x = y$). Actually, the displacement of the track for strong identifiers is imperceptible, and the symmetrical equation

$$xy = 15.6$$

seems a perfectly adequate fit. The heavy segment of this track near the origin represents the range which our empirical observations cover.[1] The track sug-

---

[1] The character of the range covered by the elections we have studied has some implications for the partisanship slopes of Table 2-2. That is, for any of the sym-

gested by the data for the pairing of weak partisan identifiers does indeed seem somewhat askew in the direction expected, however (fewer Republican defectors than the proportion of Democratic identifiers would lead us to predict if symmetry is assumed). It is possible to test the source of this asymmetry by controlling differences in involvement between the two sets of partisans, to see what defection rates would be were involvement levels equated. The data points corrected in this fashion do shift in the plane to a good fit with the symmetrical equation

$$xy = 336$$

and this track is represented by the heavy curve farther away from the origin.[2] All of these circumstances contribute to our confidence that involvement differences do account for much of any systematic asymmetry. They also suggest that quite in the spirit of some of our previous generalizations, the effects of involvement differences upon partisan defection are negligible where partisanship is strong, and become notable only among weaker partisans.

---

metrical hyperbolas of Figure 2-3, $dy/dx = -c/x^2$. Therefore, where $x > y, \frac{dy}{dx} > -1$. Now if the symmetrical case pertained, and if we took a large enough sample of elections to arrive at a set of partisan forces averaging to zero, then $\frac{dy}{dx}$ would equal -1, meaning that the rates of change in partisanship with respect to changes in partisan forces would be equal between Democrats and Republicans. In this light, we can see that some of the discrepancy in slope between partisans of comparable identification strength in Table 2-2 is an artifact of our sampling of elections, in that we have oversampled cases in which $x > y$ and $\frac{dy}{dx} > -1$. It is our contention, however, that these partisan discrepancies are not entirely due to the biased set of elections we have observed. That is, while a more balanced sample of elections would reduce the partisan discrepancies materially, they would not erase them completely, due to the underlying differences in involvement.

[2] A comparable correction of involvement differences for strong partisans generates points which differ very little from the original points, and certainly suggests no systematic correction of the original equation. The correction does improve the fit of the observations to the function slightly, however. In general, we might note that the fit of the observed data to the equations is excellent in both cases. If the least distances (nonrectilinear) between the data points and the functions are computed, they average 0.7 per cent for the strong identifiers without any involvement correction, and 0.6 per cent after the involvement correction is made. The matter is less clear for the weak identifiers, where it is evident that the empirical observations require an asymmetrical function. A simple assumption as to the fashion in which involvement-based partisan asymmetry varies as a function of the strength of partisan forces produces an asymmetrical function which fits these skewed points very well. For our immediate purposes, however, it may be noted that the average deviation of weak identifiers from the *symmetrical* function which is optimal when involvement is not corrected is 1.4 per cent. This declines to an average deviation of 0.6 per cent relative to the new optimal symmetrical function when the involvement correction is applied.

Nevertheless, the intrusion of the involvement problem undermines the most mechanical location of the normal vote suggested by Figure 2-3: along the axis $x = y$. The proper normal vote configuration must lie on a ray from the origin $y = mx$, where m is slightly less than unity. There is no very compelling mechanical method, given the paucity of data points, for determining just how much less than unity m should be. Hence an element of the arbitrary or indeterminate cannot be avoided. However, the range of indeterminacy involved is narrow by any lights. That is, if Figure 2-3 has any merit, the available data would make it appear entirely unreasonable to choose an m which lies outside the bounds

$$0.8 < m < 1.0$$

And while there are no clear criteria for locating m within this zone, a shift in m from one of these bounds to the other only produces a shift of 1.2 per cent in the estimation of an expected vote for a representative distribution of party identifiers with turnout level held constant. Such indeterminacy is hardly grave.

To establish the norms presented in the text, we have chosen an m in the middle of this zone. From these data we extrapolated to locate a cutting point which is comparable on the linear partisan equation for Independents.

Computation of a normal vote for a specific population. Once the turnout proportions are applied to the five classes of identifiers in the relative numbers characteristic of the specific population, then these five new proportions may be considered a row vector x, with the column headed "Expected Proportion of Two-Party Vote Democratic" (text) being taken as a five-component column vector y. The normal vote for the group is then simply the vector product xy. A somewhat less cumbersome method gives a very good approximation of the normal vote where the distribution of partisanship is not extremely skewed to one side or the other. Let V be the proportion Democratic of the expected vote; let M be a "mean party identification" for the distribution, where scale scores $(+2, +1, 0, -1, -2)$ have been assigned to the five classes from Strong Democrats to Strong Republicans, respectively. Then

$$V = 0.268M + 0.483$$

the approximation being good to roughly ±1 per cent, where $M < |\,0.8\,|$.

Other sources of indeterminacy. Before concluding our technical observations, it is important to point out that our measurement of party identification is adequate to the model but is not perfect. That is, there is a tiny handful of people in any cross-section of the American population whose professions of general party loyalty largely reflect their current vote intention or most recent vote. While it may be an empirical reality that they have no "general" loyalty, their claims of loyalty, shifting with their actual votes, makes the trend of the division of underlying loyalties shift very faintly over time in periods of Republican or Democratic popularity. In other words it cannot be said that the division of party loyalties has been perfectly stable in the past decade, but only that it has been highly stable relative to the amplitude of variation shown by the actual vote.

Such respondents are so few in the population that the minor undulations which they produce in the division of party loyalties can never be reliably distinguished from sampling error. That is, if we compute an expected vote for each of our eight party identification readings between 1952 and 1960, we find that all of the readings lie within a band of about 4 per cent, although five of those eight readings lie in a narrow 1½ per cent range. Even the extremes of such variation could very reasonably be attributed to sampling error. The fact remains, however, that the most Republican of the eight readings was taken shortly before the Eisenhower landslide of 1956, while the most Democratic reading arose at the time of the 1958 Democratic sweep of Congress. This is probably more than accidental: the undulations do move slightly in phase with current partisan forces, as would occur if a handful of respondents in each year gave as a general loyalty a current vote intention. However, this undulation effect is slight at best, and its main influence in practice is to make for some little underestimation of the impact of short-term forces.

A second source of indeterminacy is of greater substantive interest. Far more often than not, it seems that cues from the world of politics which set up short-term partisan forces have a common valence, an "across-the-board impact" throughout the electorate. Thus, for example, there are not two sides to corruption as a political cue. Adherents of the erring party may defend against such a perception in a variety of ways, attempting to localize it in a wayward individual or maintaining some doubt that charges against the party are true. But the impact of the cue, individual partisanship aside, is unidirectional, favoring one party and disfavoring the other. Essentially the same may be said for a figure like Dwight Eisenhower, who failed to carry a positive valence only among the most extreme Democratic partisans resisting him on party grounds.

From time to time, however, there is an important political cue in an election which by its very nature has an opposite partisan impact for two different segments of the population. The Catholicism of Kennedy in 1960 provides a classic case: this basic cue set up strong pro-Republican forces for Protestants and strong pro-Democratic cues for Catholics at one and the same time. Now the basic model which we have laid out in order to locate a normal vote rests on data which reflect averaging processes at two levels: that of the individual weighing forces and deciding upon a vote, and the necessary averaging across individuals to arrive at aggregated data. Our question is whether, in the two-group conflict case, the cumulation of data across the two groups would still yield a summary data point fitting the model, assuming of course that data from each of the two groups taken separately fit the model initially.

One can readily see that the cumulative estimate of forces operating in the case where two groups experience equal but opposite forces will depend very directly upon the relative size of the two groups. This is the sort of averaging across individuals which is a perfectly satisfactory implication of the model. At the same time, since the cumulation of results from two conflicting groups is a linear combination, one can see as well that if a point P on a hyperbolic track of Figure 2-3 represents the position of (e.g.) weak identifiers within Group A, while data from Group B produce a point Q on the opposite side of the axis $x = y$, the cumulation of the two sets of observations will give a data point which falls not at some intermediary point on the hyperbola, but rather on the chord PQ of the hyperbola. Thus the overall rate of defection summed over the two groups would be slightly higher than what one would have predicted if one had failed to recognize the conflict lines underlying the cumulation. And the possibility is open of somewhat slighter distortion in the estimate of the partisan balance of those forces.

Actually, the location of the data points fitting Figure 2-3 which would be cumulated in the conflict case are a complex function not only of the relative size of the groups, but of the degree of symmetry of the opposing forces around the zero point, the polarization of the forces, the correlation of the differential partisan forces with differences in prior partisanship between the two groups, and the like. Each of these factors, if given extreme values which are totally implausible from an empirical point of view, could introduce some distortion in the location of the cumulated data point; if all of these factors conspired at once in the proper extreme patterns, the distortion would be quite large indeed, representing an indeterminacy up to one part in four for the total likely range of variation in net partisan forces. Within the range of configurations which seem empirically plausible, however, the indeterminacy can be considered less than one part in fifty.

Discrepancies between the predicted and observed levels of defection in such combining problems are greater than are the shifts in the estimation of the net balance of forces on the cumulated groups. That is, factors which affect the location of the cumulated data point most strongly are factors which move the point toward or away from the origin more than "sideways" in a circle around the origin. The defection rate, for example, is most dramatically affected by the correlation of current partisan forces with prior partisan differences between the conflicting groups. That is, if a set of strong partisan forces had differential impact for groups A and B, where A is a Democratic group and B a Republican group, then other things equal the summed defection rates will be high if Group A is being pushed in a Republican direction while

Group B is being pushed in a Democratic direction; the rates will be lower than expected if the short-term forces coincide with prior partisan differences between the groups. But the estimate of the actual net partisan forces is not greatly affected unless other conditions are extreme.

The 1960 data provide a fine example of the good fit of the practical case despite mathematically possible indeterminacy. We have suggested that we would expect a cumulated data point for a given pairing of identifiers in Figure 2-3 based on results from two conflicting groups to fall on the appropriate chord of the hyperbola, and not on the hyperbola itself. However, this is true only if there is no correlation between the partisanship of the force to which the groups are subject and prior differences of party coloration between them. Other things constant, the cumulated data point shifts from the chord toward the hyperbola as some positive prior correlation of this sort is introduced. The point arrives at the hyperbola when the prior correlation is about .20. This is precisely the situation which pertained in 1960 between Catholics and Protestants, and it may not be too much to suggest that this is very likely to be the background situation in any case where cues have broad-scale, short-term "cleavage" impact. Thus the 1960 points, despite their clear base in the summation across conflicting groups, do indeed fit the model perfectly even when cumulated, in spite of the fact that the model had been largely formalized before the 1960 election had occurred.

Hence while there is mathematical room for indeterminacy in such combining problems, the practical effects we are likely to encounter are very limited indeed. This is particularly true if we restrict our use of the model, as in this paper, to a formalization which permits estimation of behaviors which would arise in a hypothetical normal case. For distortions in the estimates of net forces as a result of most of these sources of indeterminacy are at their minima when forces balance to the null case. If our use of the model does not extend to attempts at precise quantification of forces in particular extreme instances, then, the dangers of misleading distortions are slight indeed.

CHAPTER 3

Surge and Decline:
A Study of Electoral Change

Angus Campbell

The study of election statistics has revealed certain impressive regularities in the voting behavior of the American electorate. It has been pointed out by Key [1] that in presidential elections since 1890 sharp upsurges in turnout have invariably been associated with a strong increase in the vote for one party, with little change in the vote for the other. Key also documents the well-known fact that since the development of the two-party system in 1860 the party which has won the Presidency has, with a single exception, always lost seats in the House of Representatives in the off-year election which followed.

The establishment of regularities of this kind through the use of aggregative data typically leaves unanswered the question as to why the regularity exists. We propose in this chapter to demonstrate the manner in which survey data can be used to illuminate the nature of aggregative regularities and to present a theory of political motivation and electoral change which will comprehend both of these seemingly unrelated characteristics of the national vote.

---

[1] V. O. Key, Jr., *Politics, Parties, and Pressure Groups,* Fourth Edition, New York: Thomas Y. Crowell, 1958, p. 638.

This chapter appeared originally in the *Public Opinion Quarterly,* **24** (Fall 1960).

The Nature of Electoral Change

Fluctuations in the turnout and partisanship of the vote in the national elections are primarily determined by short-term political forces which become important for the voter at election time. These forces move the turnout by adding stimulation to the underlying level of political interest of the electorate, and they move the partisanship of the vote from a baseline of "standing commitments" to one or the other of the two parties. In the following pages we will first review a series of propositions which elaborate this general statement and then turn to certain national surveys conducted by the Survey Research Center for relevant empirical evidence.

Short-term political stimulation. Political stimulation in an election derives from several sources: the candidates, particularly those leading the ticket; the policy issues, foreign and domestic; and other circumstances of the moment. The intensity and character of this stimulation vary from one election to the next. There are occasions when none of these components of the world of politics seems important to the electorate, resulting in what we will refer to as a *low-stimulus* election. In other years dramatic issues or events may stir a great deal of interest; popular candidates may stimulate widespread enthusiasm. Such an election, in which the electorate feels the combined impact of these various pressures, we will speak of as a *high-stimulus* election.

The essential difference between a low-stimulus and a high-stimulus election lies in the importance the electorate attaches to the choice between the various party-candidate alternatives which it is offered. If the alternatives are generally seen as implying no important differences if one candidate or the other is elected, the stimulation to vote will be relatively weak. If the alternatives are seen as implying significantly different consequences, the stimulation to vote will be relatively high.[2] It may be assumed that in every election a certain air of excitement is created by the sheer noise level achieved by the mass media and the party apparatus. This type of direct stimulation undoubtedly has some impact that is independent of the particular alternatives which confront the voter and accounts for some of the varia-

[2] Anthony Downs uses the term "expected party differential" to express the degree of importance the voter attaches to the difference between the various party-candidate alternatives offered. See his *Economic Theory of Democracy,* New York: Harper, 1957, Chap. 3.

tion in turnout from one election to another, but for the most part we may assume that the effectiveness of such stimulation varies in a dependent way with the significance the electorate attaches to the particular election decision at issue.

Underlying political interest. The individual members of the electorate differ substantially in their level of concern with political matters, in their responsiveness to political stimulation, and in the salience of politics in their psychological environment. This level of interest is an enduring personal characteristic. We assume that it typically develops during the process of early socialization and, having reached its ultimate level, persists as a relatively stable attribute of the adult interest pattern. It is not simply a function of social or economic background; people of high and low political interest are found at all levels of the electorate.

Party identification. Political partisanship in the United States derives in large part from a basic psychological attachment to one of the two major political parties. As we have seen in Table 2-1, a large majority of the electorate identify with greater or less intensity as Republicans or Democrats, and this identification is impressively resistant to change. To the extent that they so identify, their political perceptions, attitudes, and acts are influenced in a partisan direction and tend to remain consistently partisan over time. Those members of the electorate without party attachment are free of this influence and are consequently less stable in their partisan positions from year to year.

Turnout. Differences in turnout from election to election are brought about by one or both of two causes, either by changes in the other-than-political circumstances which face the electorate on election day, or by variations in the level of political stimulation to which the electorate is subjected from one election to the next. The former factor can have only limited influence. We may assume that bad weather or an epidemic may affect the vote in restricted areas or even nationally on occasion, but such external considerations cannot reasonably be associated with the kind of fluctuation which we know to exist. It is, for example, quite untenable to suppose that the weather or the health of the electorate is always worse in off-year elections than in presidential years. The explanation of these and other fluctuations must lie in the changing motivation of the electorate.

A large proportion of the turnout in any national election consists of people whose level of political interest is sufficiently high to take them to the polls in all national elections, even those in which the level of political stimulation is relatively weak. These "core voters" are joined in a high-stimulus election by additional "peripheral voters," whose level of political interest is lower but whose motivation to vote has been sufficiently increased by the stimulation of the election situation to carry them to the polls. There remains a sizable fraction of the electorate which does not vote even in a high-stimulus election; some of these people are prevented from voting by poor health, failure to meet eligibility requirements, or conflicts of one sort or another. Others do not vote because their level of political interest is so low that no amount of political stimulation will motivate them to vote.

The turnout in any specific election is largely a question of how many of the less interested, less responsive people are sufficiently stimulated by the political circumstances of the moment to make the effort to vote. An election in which a stirring issue or an attractive candidate makes the party-candidate choice seem unusually important may bring these peripheral voters to the polls in large numbers. In an election of lesser apparent importance and weaker total stimulation the participation of these peripheral voters declines, leaving the electoral decision largely to the high-interest core voters. A low-stimulus election is thus not simply a smaller version of a high-stimulus election; in the extent to which the peripheral voters differ from the core voters, the two elections may have quite different characteristics.

Partisanship. The partisan division of the vote in any particular election is the consequence of the summation of partisan forces on the voters. In every election there are superimposed on the underlying orientations the electorate has toward the two parties (party identifications) the contemporary elements of politics which tend to swing voters one way or the other. In a particular election these elements may be relatively weak and have little impact on the electorate. Despite the best efforts of the party publicists, the candidates may have little appeal, and the issues little apparent relevance to the basic interests of the electorate. In such a case the turnout would of course be low, and the division of the vote would approximate the underlying distribution of party identifications. In the absence of strong pressures associated with persons, issues, or circumstances prominent at the moment, party loyalty holds the adherents of the two parties to their respective tickets, and the independent voters divide their vote between the two. In other words, a low-stimulus election tends to follow party lines.

Contemporary events and personalities occasionally assume great importance for the public and exert a strong influence on the vote. The general increase in the motivation to vote in such an election will, as we have said, bring a surge of peripheral voters to the polls. It will also swing the partisan division of the vote toward the party which happens to be advantaged by the circumstances of the moment. It is very unlikely that a political situation which heightens the public's sense of the importance of choosing one party-candidate alternative or another will favor these alternatives equally. The circumstances which create a high-stimulus election may be expected to create simultaneously a strong differential in the attractiveness of the vote alternatives. Increases in turnout will consequently be accompanied by shifts in the partisanship of the vote.[3]

The partisan surge which characterizes a high-stimulus election consists of two components: (1) those peripheral voters for whom the stimulus of highly differentiated party-candidate alternatives provides the needed impetus to move them to the polls and who, depending on the strength of their party identification, are swung toward the ticket of the advantaged party, and (2) those core voters who are drawn from their normal position as Independents or identifiers with the disadvantaged party to the candidate of the party which is advantaged by the political circumstances of the moment. The number of voters who consistently turn out in presidential elections in support of their party's candidates is now sufficiently close to an equal balance between the two parties so that the movement of these two components of the partisan surge will almost certainly determine the outcome of any high-stimulus election.

If a high-stimulus election is followed by a low-stimulus election, the reduction in the general level of political stimulation will result in a decline in the total vote. There will also be a decline in the proportion of the vote received by the party advantaged by the political circumstances of the preceding high-stimulus year. This decline also consists of two components: (1) the dropout of those peripheral voters who had gone to the polls in the previous election, and who had given the advantaged party a majority of their votes, and (2) the return to their usual voting position of those core voters who had moved in the surge year from their normal position to support the advantaged party, the identifiers with the disadvantaged party moving back to the support of that party, and the Independents back to a

---

[3] We omit from consideration in this chapter shifts in the partisanship of the vote which occur in periods of stable turnout. Substantial shifts of this kind can be found in the history of American elections, as for example in the presidential elections of 1928 and 1932, and they pose interesting questions as to how a shift in the absence of a surge in turnout differs from a shift which accompanies a voting surge. We will be concerned exclusively with the latter type of partisan change in the present discussion.

position between the two parties. Those voters whose normal identification was with the advantaged party would, of course, support it in the high-stimulus election; of these, the less-involved peripheral voters would drop out in the subsequent low-stimulus election, and the core voters would continue to support their party.

The cycle of surge and decline. In the normal flow of events in American politics, fluctuations in turnout and partisanship follow the "natural" cycle which we have described. The long-run stability of the system depends on the underlying division of party loyalties. Short-term circumstances may swing large numbers of voters away from their usual partisanship or from a position of independence, but when the smoke has settled these people strongly tend to return to their former position, thus restoring the party balance to its former level. Only in the most extraordinary national crises has this cycle been broken, and a new balance of party strength created. Such elections, in which a basic realignment of party loyalties occurs, are rare in American electoral history.[4] For the most part, fluctuations in the vote reflect the passing impact of contemporary events, and the subsequent decline toward the underlying division of partisanship after these events have lost their salience.

The Evidence

The study of individual change requires data from the same persons at different points in time. Such information can best be provided by a panel study covering the period in which the change took place. It can be obtained somewhat less satisfactorily by asking survey respondents to recall their attitudes or behavior at earlier points in time. Two surveys conducted by the Survey Research Center make available data regarding voting patterns which are relevant to our present concerns. The first of these was a study of the presidential election of 1952, in which a national sample of adults living in private households were asked to report their vote for President in 1952 and to recall their vote for President in 1948.[5] The second was a panel study of a similar national sample, interviewed first in 1956 and again in 1958, being asked on each occasion to report their vote in that year.

[4] A discussion of maintaining, deviating, and realigning elections is presented in Chapter 4.

[5] A detailed report of this study appears in A. Campbell, G. Gurin, and W. E. Miller, *The Voter Decides,* Evanston, Ill.: Row, Peterson, 1954.

1948–1956: A Case of Electoral Surge

The presidential election of 1952 presents a unique opportunity for the study of electoral surge. The election of 1948 had seen one of the lowest turnouts of presidential voters in recent history with only 48.4 million voters. The proportion of eligible voters who turned out lagged far behind the record of peacetime presidential elections prior to the Second World War. In 1952, 61.6 million voters went to the polls, an increase of more than 25 per cent above the total of the previous election. This great surge in turnout was associated, of course, with a tremendous increase in the vote received by the Republican presidential nominee, which far exceeded the increment in the Democratic vote.

The increase in turnout. The movement in the turnout of the vote from 1948 to 1952 was made up of four components. Of our sample interviewed in November 1952, 58 per cent said they had voted in both 1948 and 1952; 6 per cent said they had voted in 1948 but not in 1952; 15 per cent said they had voted in 1952 but not in 1948; and 21 per cent said they had not voted in either election.[6] When we examine the characteristics of these four segments of the electorate we find that the core voters who had voted in both elections and the peripheral voters who had voted in one election but not the other differed very little in respect to those variables which are usually found to be associated with turnout. In education, income, occupation, and sex the two kinds of voter were very similar, although they differed significantly from the persistent nonvoters in all these respects. The characteristic which does discriminate sharply between the core voters and the peripheral voters is their level of political interest.

Several indicators of political interest are available to us from our interviews; the one which is freest from the impact of the specific election we are studying is the respondent's report on his previous voting history. In the 1952 interview our respondents were asked, "In the elections for President since you have been old enough to vote, would

---

[6] There is a clear discrepancy between these reports and the election statistics for 1948 and 1952. Survey reports of turnout are always higher than the proportion of total vote to the total adult population, partly because surveys do not cover the institutional, military, and "floating" populations and partly because some respondents report a vote they did not cast. In the present case, the report of the 1952 vote does not appear to be greatly overstated, but the recall of the 1948 vote is more seriously inflated. The proportions saying they voted in both elections or in 1948 but not 1952 are probably both somewhat high. This introduces some distortion in the relative size of the different components of the vote and some restraints on the uses we can make of the data.

you say that you have voted in all of them, most of them, some of them, or none of them?" We assume that people who vote in all elections, regardless of the highs and lows of political stimulation, must be relatively responsive to political matters, and those who have never voted must be relatively lacking in political interest.

We can also use the respondent's direct statement about his degree of interest in the current campaign. In October 1952 we asked the question, "Some people don't pay much attention to the political campaigns. How about you, would you say that you have been very much interested, somewhat interested, or not much interested in following the political campaigns so far this year?" This question does not give us as clean a measure of long-term interest in political activities as we would like, since it related to the 1952 campaign specifically. The effect of this specific reference almost certainly reduces the range of response we would expect from a more general question, because the impact of current political activities might be expected to raise the interest level of those at the bottom of the range more than those near the top. In other words, the differences we find between the different types of voter would probably be larger if this question were more general in its reference.

When we now compare the levels of interest shown by the four components of the 1956 electorate, we find a very consistent pattern. That part of the electorate which reported voting in both the 1948 and 1952 elections was far more responsive to the stimuli of politics than any of the other groups. This is especially impressive in the report of previous voting: 90 per cent of those who voted in both elections said they had voted in all or most previous presidential elections, as compared to 66 per cent of those who voted in 1948 but not in 1952, 23 per cent of those who voted in 1952 but not 1948, and 6 per cent of those who did not vote in either election. The interest of the 1948–1952 voters in the campaign then current, as expressed by their subjective report, was also higher than that of any of the other groups: 48 per cent of those who voted in both elections said they were "very much interested in the campaign," as compared to 26 per cent of those who voted in 1948 but not 1952, 31 per cent of those who voted in 1952 but not 1948, and 14 per cent of those who did not vote in either election.

On both these measures those people who were responsible for the major part of the difference in turnout between the two elections (the 1952 voters who had not voted in 1948) gave substantially less evidence of high political interest. Although they appear to come from the same strata of society as the more persistent voters, they apparently are drawn from the less concerned and less attentive levels of the stratum to which they belong.

It is clear that the persistent nonvoters, those people whom even the high stimulation of the 1952 campaign could not move to the polls, are not prevented from voting by adventitious considerations of health or weather. For the most part, these people do not vote because their sensitivity to the world of politics is so low that political stimulation does not reach them. As one might expect, they come largely from the low-income and low-education groups. Two-thirds of them are women.

The swing in partisanship. The 1948 election may be taken as the prototype of a low-stimulus presidential election. In the absence of candidates, issues, or circumstances that might have aroused strong public interest in the choice of alternatives, the turnout was low, and the partisanship of the vote was determined largely by the established party loyalties of the voters. Of the total Democratic vote for President in 1948,[7] 74 per cent came from Democratic Party identifiers, 20 per cent from Independents, and 6 per cent from Republican Party identifiers. Of the total Republican vote for President in 1948, 71 per cent came from Republican Party identifiers, 23 per cent from Independents, and 6 per cent from Democratic Party identifiers.

The high-stimulus election in 1952 brought to the polls millions of voters who had not voted in 1948 and shifted the partisanship of the vote of a sizable proportion of those who had. We see in Table 3-1 that the two parties received almost equal support among those people who voted for the same party in both years. Although these consistent core voters made up well over half the voters in 1952, the decisive margin for Mr. Eisenhower was provided by two other groups, those who switched from a 1948 vote for Mr. Truman and those who had failed to vote in 1948. The former group appears to have been considerably larger than the latter, although it is likely that the overstatement of the 1948 vote to which we have referred makes our estimate of the number of new voters in 1952 somewhat lower than it actually was. The Democratic Party also appears to have lost a little ground among the small proportion of 1948 voters who did not vote in 1952, but this figure is subject to the same overstatement, and we may assume that this component of the total shift of votes between 1948 and 1952 was not very significant.

---

[7] All references to voting in 1948 are based on the respondent's recall of this event when interviewed in 1952. Those few individuals who reported having voted for Thurmond or Wallace in 1948 are included in the Democratic vote.

TABLE 3-1

Presidential Votes in 1948 and 1952 as Reported by Survey Research Center Sample in 1952
(N = 1614)

Vote for President in 1948	Vote for President in 1952	Per Cent
Democratic	Democratic	23
Republican	Republican	24
Democratic	Republican	11
Republican	Democratic	1
Democratic	Did not vote	4
Republican	Did not vote	2
Did not vote	Democratic	6
Did not vote	Republican	8
Did not vote	Did not vote	21
		—
		100

We can illuminate the character of these movements considerably if we examine the degree and quality of the customary party identifications of the people in these groups of 1952 voters (Table 3-2). The greatest polarity of party attachment is found among those voters who supported the presidential candidates of the same party in both elections. The fact that the consistent Democratic vote is composed so heavily of Democratic Party identifiers conforms to our supposition regarding the high-stimulus surge. When the political tide is running against a party, it reduces that party to its loyal partisans; the party will lose most of the support it may have received at other times from Independent voters or from defectors from the other party. The advantaged party benefits from this partisan movement, particularly among the Independents and weak adherents of the opposite party who are not strongly held by feelings of party loyalty. This gain is apparent in the Democratic-Republican column of Table 3-2.

The party affiliations of the two groups of 1952 voters who had failed to vote in 1948 provide additional evidence of the interaction

TABLE 3-2

Party Identification of Components of the 1948 and 1952 Vote for President
(in per cent)

Party Identification	1948: Democratic 1952: Democratic (N = 372)	1948: Republican 1952: Republican (N = 385)	1948: Democratic 1952: Republican (N = 172)	1948: Republican 1952: Democratic (N = 17)	1948: Did Not Vote 1952: Democratic (N = 105)	1948: Did Not Vote 1952: Republican (N = 130)
Strong Democrat	48	*	19	(4)	36	5
Weak Democrat	33	4	36	(2)	43	23
Independent	17	23	31	(7)	20	29
Weak Republican	2	28	11	(3)	1	26
Strong Republican	*	45	3	(1)	†	15
Apolitical, other	*	*	†	†	†	2
	100	100	100	†	100	100

* Less than one-half of 1 per cent.
† No cases.
Note. Figures in parentheses are number of persons rather than per cent; number of cases is too small to support reliable estimates.

of party identification and the partisan pressures of a surge year. Those previous nonvoters who came to the support of Stevenson in 1952 were largely Democratic Party identifiers. The high stimulation of the 1952 campaign brought them out of their nonvoting status, but their party loyalty was sufficiently strong to resist the pro-Republican drift of the times. In contrast, the nonvoters who were inspired to vote for Eisenhower came from all party groups. Some of them were indifferent Republicans who had sat out the Dewey campaign; a large number were Independents; there was a sizable number of Democrats, although few of them called themselves "strong" Democrats. None of these people had voted in 1948, but they contributed significantly to the increase in turnout and the Republican surge in 1952.

The fact that only 1 per cent of the electorate in 1952 moved against the Republican tide, from a Republican to a Democratic vote, provides an effective illustration of the nature of a partisan surge. Although the high level of stimulation in 1952 brought some peripheral Democrats to the defense of their party, there was no countervailing Democratic force beyond that of party loyalty to offset the powerful impact of candidates and issues which advantaged the Republican Party. This we believe to be the basic characteristic of a surge election; the conditions which give rise to a sharp increase in turnout invariably greatly favor one party over the other. The political circumstances which create the surge in turnout also produce the shift in partisanship.

1956–1958: A Case of Electoral Decline

One of the most dependable regularities of American politics is the vote decline in off-year congressional elections. The turnout in the off-year elections is invariably smaller than in the presidential elections which they follow, usually by a margin of over 25 per cent of the presidential vote. Almost as dependable is the loss which the party which has won the White House in the presidential year suffers in the midyear election that follows. As we have observed, in every off-year election since the Civil War, with the exception of 1934, the presidential party has lost seats in the House of Representatives.

The vote for President in 1956 totaled 62 million; the vote for congressional candidates in 1958 was 45.7 million, a decline of slightly less than 25 per cent from the vote cast two years earlier. President Eisenhower received nearly 58 per cent of the popular vote in 1956. The Republican candidates for Congress in 1958 received 44 per cent of the two-party vote, and the Republican Party lost 47 of the 200 seats it had held in the House of Representatives.

The decline in turnout. The off-year election of 1958 was a low-stimulus election. Within the framework of the American electoral system the off-year congressional contests must always present the electorate with a less intensely charged situation than the presidential elections which precede and follow. The election of a Congressman cannot have the importance to the average citizen that the election of a President has; the expected consequences of the election of one or the other congressional candidate cannot seem as great. Associated with this lesser significance is the fact that party activities are less intense, and the mass media somewhat quieter in off-year elections. The impact of the typical congressional election is considerably more muted than even the least exciting presidential election.

When we examine the components of the electorate in 1956 and 1958 we find the counterparts of the four segments of the electorate we identified in our 1952 survey. Of our panel interviewed in both 1956 and 1958, 56 per cent said they had voted in both elections, 19 per cent said they had voted in 1956 but not in 1958, 4 per cent said they had voted in 1958 but not in 1956, and 21 per cent said they had not voted in either election.[8]

Comparison of the core voters in 1956–1958 with those who voted only in 1956 reveals differences similar to those we observed in the core and peripheral components of the 1952 electorate. Those 1956 voters who dropped out in 1958 had somewhat more distinctive socioeconomic characteristics than the 1948 nonvoters who went to the polls in 1952. As compared to those who voted in both 1956 and 1958 they were of a somewhat lower status in occupation, income, and education. They were also younger. But these differences were small and very much less impressive than the differences in political interest which distinguished these groups: 92 per cent of those who voted in both elections said they had voted in all or most previous presidential elections, as compared to 60 per cent of those who voted in 1956 but not in 1958, 59 per cent of those who voted in 1958 but not in 1956, and 17 per cent of those who did not vote in either election.[9]

[8] We again have some problem of overreport of voting in the low-turnout election. This has the effect of understating the size and importance of the group of 1956 voters who dropped out in 1958. However, since the 19 per cent of our sample who place themselves in this category are very unlikely to include individuals who actually voted in 1958, we can regard this as a relatively pure group for analytical purposes, remembering that it is somewhat smaller in size than it should be.

[9] The differences in these data from those obtained in 1952 derive in large part from the fact that in this case we are grouping voters according to their performance in a presidential and a congressional election, and in the previous case we were

Involvement in the 1956 campaign, as expressed in the interviews in that year, was also much lower among those parts of the electorate which did not vote in either or both elections: 40 per cent of those who voted in both elections said they were "very much interested" in the campaign, as compared to 21 per cent of those who voted in 1956 but not in 1958, 33 per cent of those who voted in 1958 but not in 1956, and 12 per cent of those who did not vote in either election.

Thus it appears that the people who accounted for the decline in the vote in 1958 were politically similar to the people who increased the vote in 1952. They were in-and-out voters, with a very irregular history of previous voting performance and a low level of sensitivity to political affairs. They appear to form a rather inert reservoir of voters, available for service under conditions of high stimulation but not highly motivated by an intrinsic interest in politics. Activated to vote by the highly charged circumstances of the 1956 campaign, they were not sufficiently moved to go to the polls by the lesser impact of the congressional election. Without them, the core voters who had made up 75 per cent of the vote in 1956 contributed virtually the entire vote (93 per cent) in 1958.

The swing in partisanship. Like the presidential election of 1948, the congressional election of 1958 attracted a relatively low turnout. Without strong national candidates, pressing issues or circumstances to move the electorate, the voting decision was determined largely by the standing party loyalties of those voters sufficiently concerned with politics to go to the polls. The sources of the vote which the two parties commanded in 1958 resemble those from which they drew their vote in 1948, although there was apparently more crossing of party lines in the latter election than there had been in the former.[10] Of the total vote for Democratic Congressmen in 1958, 69 per cent

grouping voters according to their performance in two successive presidential elections. The 1952 data are further influenced by the fact that about one-fourth of those 1952 voters who had not voted in 1948 were too young to vote in that year. Since the 1956–1958 sample is a panel, there is no comparable group in the 1958 data.

[10] A number of factors might be expected to contribute to party crossing in the congressional elections. The personal impact of the Congressman in his district is not likely to equal that of a highly publicized presidential candidate, but it may be rather intense within a more limited range of individual voters. Over time a Congressman may establish sufficient personal contacts to have a visible effect on the vote. The repeated reelection of Congressmen in some districts tends to give them the character of nonpartisan fixtures: they attract cross-party votes which a less well-established candidate on the same ticket would not get. Of course, in those districts where a candidate runs without opposition, members of the minority party must cross party lines if they are to vote at all.

came from Democratic Party identifiers, 20 per cent came from Independents, and 11 per cent came from Republican Party identifiers. Of the total vote for Republican Congressmen in 1958, 65 per cent came from Republican Party identifiers, 26 per cent came from Independents, and 9 per cent came from Democratic Party identifiers.

The substantial shift from the comfortable majority which Mr. Eisenhower received in 1956 to the Republican congressional defeat in 1958 was almost wholly accounted for by two segments of the electorate, that is, those Eisenhower supporters in 1956 who switched to a Democratic vote in 1958 and the considerable number of people who voted for President in 1956 but failed to vote in 1958. The number of 1958 voters who had not voted in 1956 and of voters moving against the tide (Democratic to Republican) was much smaller than the two other groups (Table 3-3).

The similarities between Table 3-1 and Table 3-3 are striking, despite the fact that Table 3-1 compares succeeding presidential elections, and Table 3-3 compares a presidential election with a congressional election. We now find that when we distribute the party iden-

TABLE 3-3

Partisanship of the Vote in 1956 and 1958
(N = 1,354)

Vote for President in 1956	Vote for Congressman in 1958	Per Cent
Democratic	Democratic	22
Republican	Republican	22
Democratic	Republican	2
Republican	Democratic	11
Democratic	Did not vote	6
Republican	Did not vote	12
Did not vote	Democratic	3
Did not vote	Republican	1
Did not vote	Did not vote	21
		100

tifications of the people making up the major components of the 1956–1958 electorate, a table results which closely resembles Table 3-2 (see Table 3-4). We find again that those voters who support the same party through both low-turnout and high-turnout elections consist largely of people who identify themselves with that party. These are the core voters on whom each party relies. They were joined in 1956–1958 by a sizable number of Independent voters, but by very few people who identified with the opposite party.

Those people who fail to vote in a low-stimulus election after having been brought to the polls in a preceding high-stimulus election provide a counterpart to those peripheral voters in Table 3-2 who did not vote in 1948 but did turn out in 1952. We see that they have comparable partisan characteristics. The smaller group, people who had voted for Stevenson in 1956 but did not vote in 1958, had strong Democratic Party attachments and closely resembled the 1948 nonvoters who went to the polls in 1952 to vote for Stevenson. Those 1956 Eisenhower voters who failed to vote in 1958, by contrast, were distinguished by having very few strong identifiers with either party. They include a high proportion of Independents and weak identifiers from each party, just as did the group of people who did not vote in 1948 but who turned out for Eisenhower in 1952. In all likelihood these two groups in 1958 consisted largely of people who had also failed to vote in the congressional election of 1954. They had been brought to the polls as peripheral voters by the stimulation of the 1956 election but dropped out again because of the weaker stimulus of the 1958 election. They contribute the major part of the surge and decline in turnout in these successive elections. Since these people tend to come to the polls more favorably disposed to one party than the other, they contribute to the partisan shift in a surge election, and their failure to vote in the succeeding election tends to reduce the proportion of the vote the previously advantaged party receives.

The other component of the shift in partisanship in both the 1952 and 1958 elections is the core voters who move from support of one party to the other. We saw in Table 3-2 that in 1952 the bulk of these people, moving then from a Democratic to a Republican vote, were Independents and weak partisans, and we see in Table 3-4 that the comparable group, moving in the opposite political direction, had the same characteristics. We assume that the large number of Democrats in the 1958 group were moving back to their "normal" party position after having supported Mr. Eisenhower in the 1956 election. The number of Republican identifiers in this group is larger than we would have anticipated and suggests that the partisan movement in

TABLE 3-4

Party Identification of Components of the Vote for President in 1956 and Vote for Congressman in 1958
(in per cent)

Party Identification	1956: Democratic 1958: Democratic (N = 303)	Republican Republican (N = 294)	Democratic Republican (N = 21)	Republican Democratic (N = 144)	Democratic Did Not Vote (N = 89)	Republican Did Not Vote (N = 159)
Strong Democrat	50	1	(4)	13	41	6
Weak Democrat	31	4	(9)	27	37	17
Independent	15	26	(6)	30	17	36
Weak Republican	3	25	(2)	20	5	27
Strong Republican	*	44	†	8	†	14
Apolitical, other	1	†	†	2	†	†
	100	100	–	100	100	100

* Less than one-half of 1 per cent.
† No cases.
Note. Figures in parentheses are number of persons rather than per cent; number of cases is too small to support reliable estimates.

56

1958 cannot be entirely attributed to a normal decline toward standing party loyalties after the displacement of the vote in a surge year.[11]

Ticket Splitting and the Congressional Vote

A comparison of the vote for President and the vote for Congressman in the ensuing off-year election does not fully describe the movement of voters in this two-year election sequence. Because of the option which the American voter has of splitting his ticket, the relation of the presidential vote to the subsequent congressional vote may be very different from the relation of the vote for Congressman in a presidential year to the vote for Congressman in the subsequent off year. If we examine the consistency with which the 1956–1958 voting groups supported the ticket of the presidential candidate they preferred in 1956, we find convincing support for our earlier observations regarding the characteristics of these groups, and we discover a pattern of change in the congressional votes in the two elections quite different from what we found in the comparison of successive presidential and congressional votes.

Table 3-5 presents the 1956 voting patterns of the core and peripheral voters in the 1956 and 1958 elections. We see again that those voters who withstood the Republican surge in the 1956 election were strongly committed to the support of the Democratic Party, as indicated by their high level of straight-ticket voting. Fewer than 1 in 10 of the voters in the two major Democratic groups, those who voted for Stevenson in 1956 and a Democratic Congressman in 1958 and those who voted for Stevenson in 1956 but did not vote in 1958, split their 1956 vote at the national level. The consistent Republican voters also had a high record of straight-ticket voting, although not quite as high as the consistent Democrats because of the large number of Independents included among them. The other Republican group, the Eisenhower voters who did not go to the polls in 1958, had a notably smaller proportion of straight-ticket voters and a much larger proportion who split their tickets at the national level. We have seen that this group of peripheral voters who came to the polls in 1956 to vote for Mr. Eisenhower was made up of people of heterogeneous party background, including many Independents and a considerable number of weakly identified Democrats. Many of these latter people obviously did not go all the way to the Republican position. Thirteen per cent

---

[11] Losses going beyond the normal decline have occurred in other off-year elections and may be taken to reflect the development of circumstances unfavorable to the presidential party in the first two years of its term.

TABLE 3-5

1956 Voting Patterns of Major Voting Groups in the Vote for President in 1956 and Vote for Congressman in 1958
(in per cent)

1956 Voting Pattern	1956: Democratic / 1958: Democratic (N = 289)	1956: Republican / 1958: Republican (N = 286)	1956: Democratic / 1958: Republican (N = 21)	1956: Republican / 1958: Democratic (N = 140)	1956: Democratic / 1958: Did Not Vote (N = 77)	1956: Republican / 1958: Did Not Vote (N = 143)
Voted straight ticket at national and local levels	68	60	(10)	26	66	46
Voted straight ticket at national level only	20	20	(5)	15	8	17
Split ticket at the national level	7	15	(6)	49	8	24
Did not vote complete ticket	3	1	*	3	13	8
Other	2	4	*	7	5	5
	100	100	*	100	100	100

* No cases.

Note. Figures in parentheses are number of persons rather than per cent; number of cases is too small to support reliable estimates.

of this group (not shown specifically in Table 3-5) voted for Mr. Eisenhower but otherwise supported a straight Democratic ticket.

The 1956 Eisenhower voters who voted for a Democratic Congressman in 1958 present an especially interesting picture of ballot splitting. As we have seen, these core voters consist very largely of Democrats and Independents. Only a quarter of this group voted a straight Republican ticket in 1956, although they all voted for Mr. Eisenhower. A fifth of them voted a straight Democratic ticket except for President, and an additional quarter or more failed to vote a consistent Republican ticket at the national level. They responded to the personal appeal of Mr. Eisenhower as the Republican candidate in 1956, but they did not accept his party. When Mr. Eisenhower was not on the ballot in 1958, these people moved back to their usual party positions.

It is significant that both groups of peripheral voters, those who voted for either Eisenhower or Stevenson in 1956 but did not vote in 1958, contain a number of people who reported that they failed to vote a complete ticket on their presidential ballot. These are the only groups in which such voters appear in any significant frequency. This evidence of limited involvement in the vote is consistent with our earlier picture of the peripheral voter. Having less intrinsic interest in political matters and coming to the polls only when there is strong stimulation to do so, their concern about voting is inherently weak, in contrast to those voters who go to the polls whatever the circumstances.

The decline from the Republican Party's proportion of the presidential vote in 1956 to its proportion of the congressional vote in 1958 was associated with a considerably smaller decline from its congressional vote in 1956 to its congressional vote in 1958. As our data on ticket splitting make clear, the Republican congressional candidates in 1956 received far fewer votes than their standard-bearer, Mr. Eisenhower; they did not in fact achieve a majority of the popular vote. The decline of their congressional vote in 1958 from their congressional vote in 1956 was much smaller than the decline from the high mark of Mr. Eisenhower's vote, and the components of this decline differ somewhat from those of the decline from the presidential vote (Table 3-6).

It is clear that the dropout of the peripheral voters in 1958 had very little effect on the distribution of congressional votes in that year, since, at the same time they were giving Mr. Eisenhower a 2-to-1 margin of their votes in 1956, they were dividing their votes for Congressman about equally between the two parties. We would ordinarily expect

TABLE 3-6

Partisanship in the Congressional Vote
in 1956 and 1958
(N = 1301)

Vote for Congressman in 1956	Vote for Congressman in 1958	Per Cent
Democratic	Democratic	25
Republican	Republican	19
Democratic	Republican	3
Republican	Democratic	6
Democratic	Did not vote	9
Republican	Did not vote	8
Did not vote	Democratic	4
Did not vote	Republican	2
Did not vote	Did not vote	24
		100

this component of the vote to have greater importance than it had in 1958. In most elections that the electorate is strongly motivated to vote, we would expect the congressional vote for the advantaged party to swing along with the presidential vote. It was precisely the failure of this joint movement to occur, however, which made the 1956 election remarkable and resulted, for the first time in over a hundred years, in the election of a President of one party and both houses of Congress of the other. The Republican surge in 1956 was largely an Eisenhower surge.

In the absence of any influence from the dropout of 1956 voters, the major contribution to the rather small decline in the vote received by Republican congressional candidates in the two elections was made by party switchers. There were movements in both directions from one election to the next, but there were twice as many changes from Republican to Democratic candidates as from Democratic to Republican. It is probable that part of the 3 percentage point Democratic advantage in this shift reflects the "coattail" effect which Mr. Eisenhower exerted on the 1956 election.[12] Some of these people were Democrats who had gone over to Mr. Eisenhower in 1956 and had voted his party ticket. But when Mr. Eisenhower was no longer on the ballot in 1958 they returned to their usual party choice.

The fact that the off-year elections typically reduce the congressional strength of the party which has won the Presidency two years earlier is readily understandable within the terms of our description of surge and decline. As long as there is no significant shift in the distribution of standing party attachments within the electorate, the decline in turnout in an off-year election will almost certainly be associated with a decline in the proportion of the vote received by the presidential party. If the partisan pressures of the presidential election have induced any movement toward the winning candidate among the Independents and members of the opposing party, this movement will recede in the following congressional election, partly because of the dropout of voters who had supported the ticket of the winning presidential candidate and partly because of the return to their usual voting positions of those Independents and opposing partisans who had switched during the presidential year.

The one clear reversal of this pattern which has occurred in the last hundred years is instructive. The House of Representatives that was elected with Mr. Roosevelt in 1932 had 310 Democratic members; in the 1934 elections this majority was extended to 319 members, although the turnout in 1934 was approximately 18 per cent lower than it had been in 1932. According to our understanding of the nature of electoral decline, this could not have happened if the basic division of party loyalties was constant during this period. There is substantial reason to believe, however, that the distinguishing feature of American politics in the early 1930's was a realignment in the basic strength of the two parties. The economic collapse associated with the Hoover Administration brought millions of Independents and Republicans into the Democratic Party, not as temporary supporters but as long-term committed adherents. The Democratic gain in the 1934 election reflected a period of political conversion that gradually changed the Democratic Party from the minority party, which it had been since at least 1896, into the majority party of today. Such mass realignments of party identification, however, are very infrequent in

---

[12] Additional coattail influence was undoubtedly felt among those people who voted for Eisenhower and a Republican Congressman in 1956 but did not vote in 1958. For a discussion of the nature of coattail voting, see W. E. Miller, "Presidential Coattails," *Public Opinion Quarterly*, **19**, 353–368 (1955).

American politics; more commonly the distribution of party loyalties remains stable despite the ups and downs of individual elections. Swings away from the basic division of party loyalties in high-turnout elections tend to swing back in the low-turnout elections which follow.

Conclusion

We have presented a theory of the nature of electoral change that is specifically intended to comprehend and explain two well-established regularities of American voting behavior, the highly partisan character of upsurges in turnout in presidential elections and the characteristic loss which the party winning the Presidency suffers in the ensuing off-year elections. We have proposed that fluctuations in turnout and partisanship result from a combination of short-term political forces, superimposed on the underlying level of political interest and on the long-standing psychological attachments of the electorate to the two parties. We have been able to present data from two election sequences, one illustrating electoral surge and the other decline. Additional evidence from other electoral situations would obviously be desirable, but the data in hand give convincing support to our understanding of the dynamics of voting change.

Our discussion has dealt entirely with electoral change within the American political system. We think it likely that the basic concepts which we have relied on in this analysis—political stimulation, political interest, party identification, core voters and peripheral voters, and high- and low-stimulus elections—are equally applicable to the understanding of political behavior in other democratic systems. But it is apparent that political behavior in other societies takes place within different institutional forms than those in the United States, and that they would have to be taken into account if we were to attempt an analysis in those societies comparable to the one presented here.

CHAPTER 4

A Classification
of the Presidential Elections

Angus Campbell

In some way each election is unique. New candidates, contemporary issues, the changing tides of domestic and international affairs—all these contribute to its individuality. Election rules do not differ significantly from year to year, but each election has its own characteristics, and to the voter who focuses on detail rather than generality each election seems like a new experience. We must assume, however, that with all their idiosyncrasies, elections do have common attributes and that these may be used to develop a descriptive model of all presidential elections. We propose to draw on the theory of the flow of the vote which we have presented in the preceding chapters as a basis for a classification of presidential elections.

Our basic assumption is that the standing commitments of the electorate define the "normal" division of the vote, and that fluctuations from this normal vote result from short-term forces which become important in specific elections. Depending on whether the movement of the vote results in the election of the candidate of the majority or the minority party, and on whether this movement is associated with a basic shift in long-term partisan attachments, each election can be

An earlier version of this chapter appeared in A. Campbell, P. E. Converse, W. E. Miller, and D. E. Stokes, *The American Voter*, New York: John Wiley and Sons, 1960, pp. 531–538.

classified as maintaining, deviating, or realigning.[1] We will draw on the four elections for which we have survey data to illustrate these classifications and will refer, but less confidently, to earlier elections in American history for further documentation.

Maintaining Elections

In a maintaining election the pattern of partisan attachments prevailing in the preceding period persists, and the majority party wins the Presidency. If the short-term forces are weak, the total turnout will be relatively low, and the partisan division of the vote will approximate the normal vote. If the short-term forces are strong, the turnout will be high, and the vote will typically swing away from the normal level to the advantage of one or the other candidate. If the short-term forces are advantageous to the majority party, its candidate will receive a higher than normal proportion of the vote. If they are disadvantageous, he will receive less of the vote than normal but may still win the election.

Most presidential elections during the last hundred years have been maintaining elections. If we assume that during the period immediately following the Civil War the majority of the electorate was Republican in its partisan sympathies, that this majority declined to something near an even balance during the 1876–1892 period and was revitalized in 1896, we may conclude that the numerous Republican victories down through the 1920's fall in this category. More recently, the later Roosevelt elections maintained a Democratic majority which had been established in the New Deal elections of the early thirties. Of the elections within the scope of our research program, two may be classified as maintaining. The elections of 1948 and 1960 differed greatly in important respects, but they both returned the candidate of the majority party to the White House.

The 1948 election. The most striking feature of the presidential election in 1948 was the extraordinarily low turnout, only 51.5 per cent of the total citizenry. This was the smallest presidential vote since the establishment of the two-party system, except for the two elections immediately following the advent of women's suffrage. It was obviously a year in which the electorate was not greatly moved by the circum-

---

[1] The reader will recognize that this classification is an extension of V. O. Key's theory of critical elections. See V. O. Key, Jr., "A Theory of Critical Elections," *Journal of Politics*, 17, 3–18 (February 1955).

stances, issues, or personalities of the moment; the balance of forces on the electorate appears to have approximated that represented in Figure 2-1c. Mr. Truman was elected with slightly less than half the popular vote. Mr. Dewey received 45 per cent of the vote, and the remaining portion was divided between Thurmond (States' Rights Democrats) and Wallace (Progressives.)

Our understanding of the nature of the presidential elections leads us to expect that the vote in an election with an abnormally low turnout will demonstrate the following characteristics:

1. The dropout of voters will be sharpest among those members of the electorate who are least strongly party-identified, that is, the Independents and weak identifiers. The strong identifiers will be sustained by the high level of political involvement associated with their party identification.

2. Among the strong party identifiers defections to the opposite party, resulting primarily from idiosyncratic influences, will be few in number and will balance between the two parties. The absence of short-term forces, which produces the low turnout, also removes the stimulus to defection from accustomed party loyalties.

3. Among the weak party identifiers there will also be idiosyncratic defections, more numerous than among strong identifiers but balanced between the two parties.

4. Those Independents who vote will divide their vote equally between the competing parties.

5. The partisan division of the total vote will approximate the "normal vote" determined by the standing strength of the competing parties at the time.

We see in Figure 4-1 the extent to which our data regarding the vote in 1948 conformed to these expectations. Unfortunately we did not measure party identification in our 1948 survey, and we must draw on data from our 1952 survey to construct this figure. We asked the respondents in our 1952 survey to recall their vote in 1948, and we can combine this statement with their party identification as stated in 1952.[2] When this is done we find that our expectations are generally

[2] This substitution of data gathered in 1952 for data which should ideally have been recorded at the time of the 1948 election involves us in two assumptions, neither of which is above criticism. In taking the 1952 statement of party identification in place of a 1948 statement, we are assuming that none of our respondents changed his identification during this period. We know this is not entirely true, although our evidence gives some assurance that such changes are infrequent. More serious is the

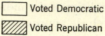

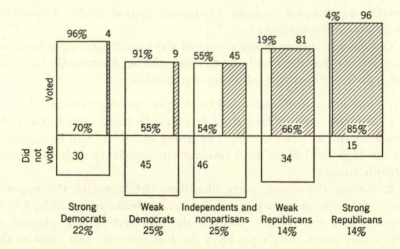

Figure 4-1. The vote of partisan groups in 1948. (The data in this figure are based on recalled 1948 votes given by the respondents of the Survey Research Center's 1952 election study. Votes for Wallace and Thurmond are grouped with the Democratic votes.)

supported, the deviations apparently being related to the inadequacies of our reports based on memory. The configuration of turnout is as anticipated, and the sharpness of the drop in turnout of the weakly identified groups is especially impressive when compared with the slope of turnout in the higher turnout elections which followed 1948. The strong identifiers did indeed adhere to their parties, although it is noteworthy that the 4 per cent of defections on both sides is per-

acceptance of our respondents' recall of their 1948 vote four years after the event. We know there is a tendency for reminiscent reports of earlier voting decisions to overstate the vote of the candidate who won the election, and we find some indication of this "bandwagon" inflation in the present case. The 1952 sample reported having given Dewey only 42 per cent of the vote, when in fact he received 45 per cent. This discrepancy is not large but it is sufficient to distort Figure 4-1 slightly. We also know that errors of recall are most likely to occur among those people whose interest in the event being recalled is the weakest. Consequently we would expect the distortions of reported 1948 vote to occur primarily among the weakly identified and Independent voters rather than among the strong identifiers. As we see in Figure 4-1, it is precisely these groups which depart moderately from our expectations.

ceptibly higher than we find among strong Republican partisans in the Eisenhower elections when the short-term advantages of the Republican Party eliminated even the infrequent idiosyncratic defections. Defections were more numerous among the weak identifiers, as predicted, although much less frequent than in the elections which followed. The balance of these defections was not as close as expected, there being a larger proportion of weak Republicans reporting voting Democratic than weak Democrats reporting voting Republican.[3] The Independent voters split their votes in about an even division, with a slight inclination toward the Democratic candidate. Both of these minor discrepancies appear to reflect the Democratic bias in the recall of the 1948 vote by respondents who were questioned in 1952.

Although it would appear from Figure 4-1 that the Democratic vote in 1948 exceeded normal expectations, this is entirely a function of the overstatement of the Democratic vote by our 1952 respondents. If we consider the actual election statistics and assume that those voters who supported Thurmond or Wallace were largely Democrats, we find that the combination of their votes and those for Mr. Truman approximates the proportion of the total vote which we take to represent the "normal" Democratic strength. The minority party was not able to swing the Independent vote or capture any advantage from defecting voters in 1948, and the majority party was maintained in power.

The 1960 election. The Democratic Party was still the majority party in 1960, and it elected its presidential candidate. The election was thus also a maintaining election, although it differed substantially from the election of 1948. The characteristics of this election are discussed in detail in the ensuing chapter; we need only note two distinguishing attributes, the high turnout and the great discrepancy between the vote of the Democratic candidate and the vote for the congressional candidates who ran with him. It is obvious from these characteristics of the vote that short-term forces played a much stronger role in 1960 than they had in 1948. The general level of voter stimulation was high, as demonstrated by expressions of interest in our interviews as well as by the election statistics. The partisan direction of these forces is indicated by the fact that Mr. Kennedy failed by several percentage points to achieve the normal expectation of a Democratic presidential candidate.

[3] Because the total number of weak Republicans is much smaller than that of weak Democrats the actual number of transfers in one direction or the other is about equal.

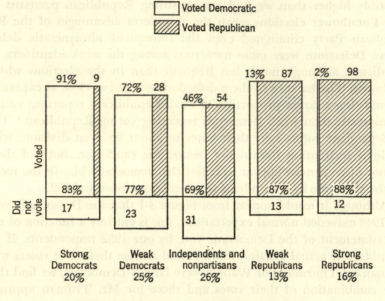

Figure 4-2. The vote of partisan groups in 1960.

When we compare Figure 4-2, showing the voting record of the partisan groups in 1960, with Figure 4-1, in which comparable data from 1948 are presented, we see first, the source of the substantial increase in turnout, and second, the location of the swing away from the normal vote toward the Republican candidate. It is clear that although all the party identification groups increased their turnout from the abnormally low levels of 1948, the increment was proportionately smallest in the strongly partisan groups and greatest in those groups with the weakest party commitment.[4] It is also apparent that it was the weakly identified Democrats who are most susceptible to the impact of short-term forces in 1960.[5] The Independent vote was split about equally between the two candidates. The total movement away

---

[4] The reported turnout in our 1960 study was somewhat inflated by the fact that our 1960 sample was based primarily on the survivors of a panel which had been selected in 1956. The losses from this panel over the four-year interval were somewhat larger among the uninvolved members of the sample than they were among the involved, resulting in an upward bias in the proportion of self-reported voters in 1960.

[5] We return to a consideration of these Democratic defectors in Chapter 5.

from the normal vote was not large (as we shall see the movement in 1952 was much larger), but it very nearly cost the Democratic Party the Presidency.

Deviating Elections

In a deviating election the basic division of party loyalties is not seriously disturbed, but the influence of short-term forces on the vote is such that it brings about the defeat of the majority party. After the specific circumstances that deflected the vote from what we would expect on the basis of party disappear from the scene, the political balance returns to a level which more closely reflects the underlying division of partisan attachments. A deviating election is thus a temporary reversal which occurs during a period when one or the other party holds a clear advantage in the long-term preferences of the electorate.

The election of Woodrow Wilson in 1916 is an obvious example of a deviating election. There seems little doubt that during the period of the Wilson elections the electorate was predominantly Republican. Wilson attained the White House in 1912 with a minority (42 per cent) of the total vote, as Roosevelt and Taft split the Republican Party. His incumbency and the public emotion aroused by the darkening shadow of the First World War apparently provided the additional votes he needed in 1916 to reach the narrow plurality that he achieved over his Republican opponent. According to Key, the Democratic gains of 1916 were due principally to "a short-term desertion of the Republican Party by classes of British origin and orientation." [6] The temporary character of the Democratic victory began to become apparent in the 1918 elections when the Republican Party won control of both the Senate and the House of Representatives. In 1920 and the two following elections, the minority status of the Democratic Party was again convincingly demonstrated.

A similar situation occurred forty years later when, during a period of Democratic ascendancy, the Republican Party nominated General Dwight D. Eisenhower as its presidential candidate. These two elections fell within the coverage of our research program, and we can consider them in the light of our extensive survey data.

The 1952 election. In November 1952, 62.7 per cent of the adult citizenry went to the polls, an increase of some 27 per cent over the

6 V. O. Key, Jr., *loc. cit.*

total turnout four years earlier. They made the event further memorable by overturning a Democratic Administration which had been in office for twenty years, the longest unbroken period of party supremacy since the Republican Administrations of Lincoln and his successors. Mr. Eisenhower received over 55 per cent of the popular vote, and the Republican Party won both houses of Congress. This dramatic increase in turnout and the shift in the vote are illustrated in Figure 4-3.

The essential fact which emerges from Figure 4-3 is that in 1952 the number of people in the electorate who identified themselves as Democrats outnumbered those who called themselves Republicans by a ratio of three to two, and that the Eisenhower majority was assembled within this distribution without basically changing it. The impact of the combination of political forces which were important in 1952 was felt throughout the spectrum of party identification (see Figure 2-1a). Normal Republicans held solidly to their party with only minor defections, even among those who called themselves "weak Republicans." A clear majority of the Independent voters supported Mr. Eisenhower, and serious inroads were made among those groups who ordinarily voted Democratic. The political circumstances of the moment were very unfavorable to the Democratic Party and resulted in its

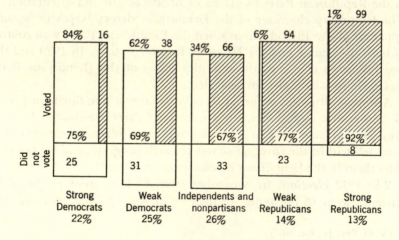

Figure 4-3. The vote of partisan groups in 1952.

defeat, but they did not alter the underlying majority which it held in the standing partisan commitments of the electorate.

The Republican victory in 1952 was accomplished by a temporary movement of normal Democrats and nonpartisans toward the Republican candidate. The extent to which this was a movement toward the candidate and not toward the party is dramatically demonstrated by the high rate of ticket-splitting reported by these voters. Three out of five of those Democrats and Independents who voted for Mr. Eisenhower in 1952 were not willing to support the rest of the Republican slate. Subsequent events, beginning with the 1954 election when the Democratic Party again took both houses of Congress, made it clear that the election of 1952 deviated from normal expectations during a period of Democratic majority.

The 1956 election. Mr. Eisenhower was re-elected to the Presidency in 1956 with a slightly higher majority (57 per cent) than he had received four years earlier. The distribution of party identification was almost precisely the same as it had been in 1952, and the contribution of the various party groups to Mr. Eisenhower's total vote closely resembled that of the previous election. This small increment in his support appeared to come largely from those voters who had no consistent partisan identification.[7] (See Figure 4-4). The separation which the voters made between Mr. Eisenhower and the Republican ticket was clearly demonstrated as the Democratic candidates won both houses of Congress, the first time since 1848 that a split of this kind had occurred. This was accomplished by an even larger proportion of ticket-splitting by Democrats and Independents than was observed in 1952. Three out of four of these people who voted for Mr. Eisenhower rejected the party whose ticket he headed.

This increasing discrepancy between the vote for Mr. Eisenhower and the vote for his fellow candidates foreshadowed the failure of the Republican Party to bring about a basic shift of party loyalties during

[7] We find it especially interesting that the swing of the Independent vote to Eisenhower was larger in 1956 than it had been in 1952. Although we expect the nonpartisan voter to be more easily moved by short-term political forces than voters whose loyalties hold them to their party, it is also true that the nonpartisans are less involved in politics and less alert to political stimulation. Their votes are more likely to be influenced by experiences and events of an idiosyncratic character than are those of the voters who are concerned with political affairs. Apparently it took four years for the Eisenhower appeal to have its full impact on these relatively inattentive nonpartisan voters. We are reminded of our earlier finding that the preferences for Eisenhower among the even less involved nonvoters was very much greater in 1956 than they had been in 1952 (see A. Campbell et al., *op. cit.*, p. 111).

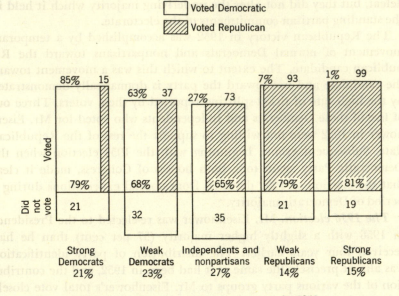

Figure 4-4. The vote of partisan groups in 1956.

the Eisenhower years. The congressional elections of 1958, in which the Democratic Party won 58 per cent of the popular vote, made the Republican weakness apparent. As the Eisenhower period drew to a close, it became clear that Mr. Eisenhower had attracted a tremendous personal following in his two elections, but his administration had not produced a significant realignment in the distribution of partisan attachments. The Democratic Party remained the majority party and in 1960, when the Eisenhower appeal was no longer a factor, it was re-instated in power.

The two Eisenhower elections were deviating elections; our survey data from 1952 and 1956 may provide a key to an understanding of the other elections of this type that have occurred in American history. The most striking fact about the flow of the vote in the 1952 election (and again in 1956) was the universality with which the various segments of the electorate moved toward the Republican candidate. It was not a situation in which some groups became more Republican than they had been in 1948 but were offset by other groups moving in the other direction. There was virtually no occupational, religious, regional, or other subdivision of the electorate which did not vote more strongly Republican in 1952 than it had in 1948.

The second impressive fact about these two elections was the relative insignificance of policy issues in the minds of the voters. There were no great questions of policy which the public saw as dividing the two parties. In 1952 the voters were thinking about the "mess in Washington," the stalemate in Korea, and General Eisenhower's heroic image. In 1956 they were no longer concerned with the Truman Administration or the Korean situation, but they were even more devoted to Mr. Eisenhower than they had been in 1952.[8] It would appear that the flow of the vote from the Democratic majorities of the previous twenty years to the Republican victories in the 1950's was a response to short-term forces which had little policy content and did not set interest group against interest group, class against class, or region against region.

It is our belief that it is this absence of great ideological issues which provides the basic quality of these deviating elections. Professor Charles Sellers concludes from his application of these concepts to the full range of presidential elections since 1789 that the "essential ingredient" of such elections is the presence of a "popular hero" candidate.[9] He points out that all the presidential elections displaying some aspects of temporary surge featured a military hero, Eisenhower, Harrison, Washington, Grant, Taylor, and Jackson.[10] The fact that so many of these elections have been dominated by persons of military background dramatizes their lack of ideological content. If Mr. Eisenhower may be taken as an example, the public image of these gentlemen has little to do with great issues of public policy. With certain notable exceptions, which we will consider shortly, the dramatic swings of turnout and partisanship during the last hundred years do not give the impression of an aroused electorate taking sides in a great debate on national policy. On the contrary, these swings in the vote appear to grow out of some immediate circumstance which is exploited by a candidate blessed with unusual personal appeal. Public interest in these events and persons is translated into political action, with a movement toward the party which happens to be in a position to profit from the situation. The movement is unidirectional because the circumstances which produce it are not seen as favorable by one section of the electorate and unfavorable by another. They tend rather to create a generally positive or negative attitude throughout the elec-

[8] A comparison of public perceptions and attitudes in these two elections is presented in A. Campbell et al., *op. cit.*, Chap. 19.

[9] Charles G. Sellers, Jr., "The Equilibrium Cycle in Two-Party Politics," *Public Opinion Quarterly*, 29 (Spring 1965).

[10] Sellers classifies the 1916 election as a realigning election; we include it with the deviating elections.

torate, resulting in the almost universal type of shift which we observed in 1952. The movement is temporary because the circumstances and personalities with which it is associated pass from the scene without having introduced a new dimension of party position around which the electorate might become realigned.

Realigning Elections

Key has pointed out that there is a third type of election, characterized by the appearance of "a more or less durable realignment" of party loyalties.[11] In such a realigning election, popular feeling associated with politics is sufficiently intense that the basic partisan commitments of a portion of the electorate change, and a new party balance is created. Such shifts are infrequent. As Key observes, every election has the effect of creating lasting party loyalties in some individual voters, but it is "not often that the number so affected is so great as to create a sharp realignment."

Realigning elections have historically been associated with great national crises. The emergence of the Republican Party and its subsequent domination of national politics were the direct outgrowth of the great debate over slavery and the ultimate issue of secession. The election of 1896 divided the country again as the East and Midwest overcame the Populist challenge of the South and West. According to Key, "The Democratic defeat was so demoralizing and so thorough that the party made little headway in regrouping its forces until 1916." It might be argued that the Democratic Party did not in fact hold a clear majority of the electorate at the time of the Cleveland elections, but the election statistics make it clear that whatever hold it did have on the voters was greatly weakened after 1896.

The most dramatic reversal of party alignments in this century was associated with the Great Depression of the 1930's. The economic disaster which befell the nation during the Hoover Administration so discredited the Republican Party that it fell from its impressive majorities of the 1920's to a series of defeats, which in 1936 reached overwhelming dimensions. These defeats were more than temporary departures from a continuing division of underlying party strength. There is little doubt that large numbers of people who had been voting Republican or had previously not voted at all, especially among the younger age groups and those social and economic classes hardest

[11] V. O. Key, Jr., *loc. cit.*

hit by the Depression, were converted to the Democratic Party during this period.[12] The program of welfare legislation of the New Deal and the extraordinary personality of its major exponent, Franklin D. Roosevelt, brought about a profound realignment of party strength which has endured in large part up to the present time.

Key has pointed out that the shift toward the Democratic Party which occurred in the early 1930's was anticipated in the New England area in the 1928 election. It is difficult to ascertain whether the changes in these successive election years were actually part of the same movement. Since the shifts in New England were highly correlated with the proportions of Catholic voters in the communities studied, it would not be unreasonable to attribute them to the presence of Governor Alfred E. Smith at the head of the Democratic ticket in 1928. Had the Depression not intervened, the New England vote might have returned to its pre-1928 levels in the 1932 election. It may be recalled, however, that the Smith candidacy had not only a religious aspect but a class quality as well. It may well be that New England voters, having moved into the Democratic ranks in 1928 for reasons having to do with both religious and economic considerations, found it easy to remain there in 1932 when economic questions became compellingly important.

It is worth noting that the nationwide shift toward the Democratic Party during the 1930's was not fully accomplished in a single election. Although Mr. Roosevelt's margin of victory in 1932 was large (59 per cent of the two-party vote), it was not until 1936 that the Democratic wave reached its peak. The long-entrenched Republican sympathies of the electorate may not have given way easily in the early years of the Depression. Had not Mr. Roosevelt and his New Deal won the confidence of many of these people during his first administration— or even his second—there might have been a return to earlier party lines similar to that which occurred in 1920. From this point of view we may do well to speak of a realigning electoral era rather than a realigning election.

The total redistribution of party attachments in such an era does not necessarily result from a unilateral movement toward the advantaged party. The far-reaching impact of the crises which produce these alignments is likely to produce movements in both directions as individual voters find their new positions in the party conflict. It is also likely to increase the political polarization of important segments of

[12] The sources of the Democratic gains during the 1930's are discussed in Campbell et al., *op. cit.*, Chap. 7.

the electorate, usually along sectional or class lines. We know that this happened during the 1930's as the Depression and the New Deal moved working-class people and certain minority groups toward a closer identification with the Democratic Party and middle-class people toward the Republican Party. Which party gains more from this sort of reshuffling depends on the relative size of the groups affected and the solidarity with which their membership moves.

The fact that the different regional and class divisions of the electorate become associated with the competing parties helps the shifting of loyalties develop into a lasting realignment. When an entire group polarizes around a new political standard, the pressures associated with group membership tend to hold the individual members to the group norm. Attitudes having the strength of group support are likely to be more stable than those which are merely individual. The development of the Solid South after the period of Reconstruction, when the expression of Republican sympathies became tantamount to sectional treason, is an illuminating case in point.

We may note finally that in contrast to those elections in which deviations from the normal vote were only temporary, the realigning elections have not been dominated by presidential candidates who came into office on a wave of great personal popularity. It is significant that neither Lincoln, McKinley, nor F. D. Roosevelt was a military figure, and none of them possessed any extraordinary personal appeal at the time he first took office. The quality which did distinguish the elections in which they came to power was the presence of a great national crisis, leading to a conflict regarding governmental policies and the association of the two major parties with relatively clearly contrasting programs for its solution. In some degree national politics during these realigning periods took on an ideological character. The flow of the vote was not a temporary reaction to a heroic figure or a passing embarrassment of the party in power; it reflected a reorientation of basic party attachments brought about during critical periods in the nation's history.

Conclusion

The ultimate significance of an election victory or defeat is often difficult to assess at the time. The immediate implications for the contending candidates are apparent, but the fuller meaning of the vote may not become clear until the succeeding elections have given a prospective within which it may be judged. The basic element in the long-term trend of the vote is the underlying division of party loyalties. If a substantial majority of the electorate are held by long-established commitments to one or another of the competing parties, the vote will oscillate from election to election around this party balance. If the circumstances in a particular election excite the electorate sufficiently, the oscillation may be large enough to dislodge the majority party temporarily from power. If the circumstances are so drastic as to force a new orientation of party positions, a period of realignment of partisan attachments may be induced, and a new balance of party strength created.

CHAPTER 5

Stability and Change in 1960: A Reinstating Election

Philip E. Converse, Angus Campbell
Warren E. Miller, Donald E. Stokes

John F. Kennedy's narrow popular vote margin in 1960 has already earned this presidential election a classic position in the roll call of close American elections. Whatever more substantial judgments historical perspective may bring, we can be sure that the 1960 election will well demonstrate to a reluctant public that after all is said and done every vote does count. And the margin translated into "votes per precinct" will become standard fare in exhortations to party workers that no stone be left unturned.

The 1960 election is also a classic in the license it allows for "explanations" of the final outcome. Any event or campaign stratagem that might plausibly have changed the thinnest sprinkling of votes across the nation may, more persuasively than is usual, be called "critical." Viewed in this manner, the 1960 presidential election hung on so many factors that reasonable men might despair of cataloguing them.

Nevertheless, it is possible to put together an account of the election in terms of the strongest forces that influenced the American electorate in 1960. We speak of the gross lines of motivation which gave the election its unique shape, motivations involving millions

This chapter appeared originally in the *American Political Science Review*, 55 (June 1961).

rather than thousands of votes. Analysis of these forces is not intended to explain the hairline differences in popular vote, state by state, which edged the balance in favor of Kennedy rather than Nixon. But it can indicate quite clearly the broad forces which reduced the popular vote to a virtual stalemate, rather than any of the other reasonable outcomes between a 60-40 or a 40-60 vote division. And it can thereby help us to understand in concise terms why even a feather thrown on the scales in November 1960 could have spelled victory or defeat for either candidate.

Surface Characteristics of the Election

Any account of the election should not only be consistent with the obvious characteristics as they are filtered clear from raw vote tallies in the days after the election, but should as well organize them into a coherent pattern. These characteristics are, of course, the ones that have nourished post-election speculation. In addition to the close partisan division of the popular vote, the following items deserve mention:

1. *The remarkably high level of turnout.* Although estimates of turnout vary systematically according to the figures chosen to describe the potential electorate, all such estimates converge to suggest that the proportion of Americans going to the polls in 1960 was remarkably high for the current period. These figures show turnout in 1960 running from 1½ to 2 percentage points above comparable estimates for the 1952 election, which had been the high-water mark of voter participation since the First World War.

2. *Stronger Republican voting at the presidential level.* On balance across the nation Nixon led Republican tickets whereas Kennedy trailed many other Democratic candidates, especially outside of the Northeast. These discrepancies in the partisanship of presidential voting and ballots at other levels were not, of course, as striking as those in 1956.

3. *The stamp of the religious factor in 1960 voting patterns.* While the Kennedy victory was initially taken as proof that religion had not been important in the election, all serious students of election statistics have since been impressed by the religious axis visible in the returns. Fenton, Scammon, Bean, Harris, and others have commented on the substantial correlation between aggregate voting patterns and the relative concentration of Catholics and Protestants from district to district.

Of these surface characteristics, probably the last has drawn most attention. Once it became clear that religion had not only played some part but, as these things go, a rather impressive part in presidential voting across the nation, discussions hinged on the nature of its role. It could safely be assumed that Kennedy as a Catholic had attracted some unusual Catholic votes, and had lost some normally Democratic Protestant votes. A clear question remained, however, as to the *net* effect. The *New York Times,* summarizing the discussion late in November, spoke of a "narrow consensus" among the experts that Kennedy had won more than he lost as a result of his Catholicism.[1] These are questions, however, which aggregate vote statistics can but dimly illuminate, as the disputed history of Al Smith's 1928 defeat makes clear. Fortunately in 1960 the election was studied extensively by sample surveys, permitting more exact inferences to be drawn.

The national sample survey conducted by the Survey Research Center in the fall of 1960 had features which give an unparalleled opportunity to comment on the recent evolution of the American electorate. The fall surveys were part of a long-term "panel" study, in which respondents first interviewed at the time of the 1956 presidential election were re-interviewed.[2] In the fall of 1956 a sample of 1,763 adults, chosen by strict probability methods from all the adults living in private households in the United States, had been questioned just before and just after the presidential election. This initial sample was constituted as a panel of respondents and was interviewed again in 1958 and twice in connection with the 1960 presidential election.[3]

[1] *New York Times,* November 20, 1960, Section 4, p. E5.

[2] Results of the 1956 survey, considered as a simple cross-section sample of the nation, are reported in A. Campbell, P. E. Converse, W. E. Miller, and D. E. Stokes, *The American Voter,* New York: John Wiley and Sons, 1960. There are natural difficulties in any attempt to retain contact with a far-flung national sample over periods of two and four years, especially in a population as geographically mobile as that of the current United States. Of the original 1,763 respondents interviewed twice in 1956, nearly 100 had died before the 1960 interview. Others had been effectively removed from the electorate by advanced senility or institutionalization. Of the remaining possible interviews, numbering somewhat over 1,600 people, more than 1,100 were successfully re-interviewed in the fall of 1960. The 1956 social, economic, and political characteristics of the 1960 survivors show almost no sign of deviation from the characteristics of the larger pool of original 1956 respondents. Therefore, although attrition may seem substantial, there is no evidence of alarming bias.

[3] The 1960 sample design provided not only contact with the 1956 panel which, due to aging, no longer gave an adequate representation of the 1960 electorate, but also a set of additional interviews filling out an up-to-date, cross-section sample of all adult citizens living in private households in 1960. Both the panel and cross-section bodies of data contribute, where appropriate, to materials in this article.

These materials permit the linking of 1960 and 1956 voting behavior with unusual reliability.

The Evolution of the Electorate, 1956–1960

The difference in the presidential election outcome between 1956 and 1960 might depend on either or both of two broad types of change in the electorate. The first is of a nonpolitical nature. The electorate had physically changed over time. That is, some adult citizens who voted in 1956 were no longer part of the eligible electorate in 1960 because of death or institutionalization. On the other hand, a new cohort of voters who had been too young to vote in 1956 were eligible to participate in the 1960 election. Even in a four-year period, these physical changes alone could account for shifts in the vote. In addition, changes in the electoral vote, though not in the nationwide popular vote margin, might result from voters' changing their residences without changing their minds.

The second is that there are obviously genuine changes in the political choice of individuals eligible to vote in both elections. Such citizens may enter or leave the active electorate by choice, or may decide to change the partisanship of their presidential vote.

The contribution of these two types of change to the shift in votes from a 1956 Eisenhower landslide to a narrow 1960 Kennedy margin— a net shift toward the Democrats of almost 8 per cent—can be analyzed. Somewhat less than 10 per cent of the eligible 1956 electorate had become effectively ineligible by 1960, with death as the principal cause.[4] Older people naturally are the most numerous in this category. The party identification expressed in 1956 by these "departing" respondents was somewhat Republican relative to the remainder of the sample. Nonetheless, these people cast a vote for President which was about 48 per cent Democratic, or 6 per cent *more Democratic* than the vote of the 1956 electorate had been as a whole. Although this appears to be a contradiction, it is actually nothing more than a logical consequence of existing theory. The high Republican vote in 1956 depended on a massive defection to Eisenhower by many people identified with the Democratic Party. Since the strength of party at-

[4] Throughout this chapter the "eligible electorate" is taken to consist of those noninstitutionalized citizens over 21. Negroes disqualified in many parts of the South, for example, are included in this bounding of the electorate, as well as those who had moved too recently to have established new voting residences in 1960.

tachment increases with age, and since defections are inversely related to strength of party identification, it follows that 1956 defection rates were much higher among younger citizens than among older.[5] The data make it clear that the group of older people voting for the last time in 1956 had cast a much straighter "party vote" than their juniors. Only about 5 per cent of these older Democrats had defected to Eisenhower, as opposed to about a quarter of all Democrats in the electorate as a whole. So both things are true: this older group was more Republican than average in party identification but had voted more Democratic than average in 1956. If we remove them from the 1956 electorate, then, we arrive at a presidential vote of about 60 per cent for Eisenhower among those voters who went to the polls again in 1960. Hence the elimination of this older group from consideration increases the amount of partisan change to be accounted for between 1956 and 1960, rather than decreasing it.

Comparable isolation of the new cohort of young voters in 1960 does very little to change the picture. Little more than one-half of this new group of voters normally votes in the first election of eligibility; [6] furthermore, in 1960 its two-party vote division differed only negligibly from that of the nation as a whole. Therefore if we analytically remove this group of new voters, we see that the vote among the remainder of the electorate is nearly unchanged. By way of summary, then, this physical change between the 1956 and 1960 electorate does not explain the 1956–1960 change in vote; if anything, it extends the amount of change to be otherwise explained.

We may further narrow our focus by considering those people eligible in both 1956 and 1960 who failed to join the active electorate in 1960. A very large majority of these 1960 nonvoters had not voted in 1956, and represent Negroes in the South as well as persistent nonvoters of other types. Among those who *had* voted in 1956, however, the vote had been rather evenly divided between Eisenhower and Stevenson. As with the older voters, removal of this group leaves an active 1956–1960 electorate whose vote for Eisenhower now surpasses 60 per cent, broadening again the discrepancy between the two-party divisions in the 1956 and 1960 votes. The final fringe group, which we can set aside analytically, is constituted of those citizens eligible to have voted in 1956 but who did not participate, yet who joined the electorate in 1960. The fact that young voters often "sit out" their first

[5] Our theoretical understanding of this net of relationships is suggested in A. Campbell et al., *op. cit.*, pp. 161–167.

[6] Participation rates by age in 1960 follow rather nicely the rates indicated in A. Campbell et al., *op. cit.*, Fig. 17-1, p. 494.

presidential election or two indicates part of the composition of such a group. Once again, however, these newly active citizens divided their ballots in 1960 almost equally between the two major candidates, and the residual portion of the 1960 electorate changes little with their removal.

By this point we have eliminated all the fringe groups whose entry or departure from the active electorate might have contributed to change in the national vote division between 1956 and 1960. We come now to focus directly on the individuals who cast a vote for Kennedy or Nixon in 1960 *and had voted for President in 1956* (Table 5-1). As we see, removing the fringe groupings has had the total effect of increasing the net shift in the vote division between the two years from 8 per cent to 11 per cent. If we can explain this shift it will be clear that we have dealt with those broad currents in the electorate which brought the 1960 election to a virtual stalemate.

Naturally, the most interesting features of Table 5-1 are the cells involving vote changers. In a sequence of elections such as the 1956–1960 series it is tempting to assume about 8 per cent of the Eisenhower voters of 1956 shifted to Kennedy in 1960, since this was the net observable change between the two years. Much analysis of aggregate election statistics is forced to proceed on this assumption within any given voting unit. However, we see that the net shift of 11 per cent in the vote of the active 1956–1960 electorate in fact derived from a gross shift of 23 per cent, over half of which was not visible in the national totals because of countermovements that canceled them.

TABLE 5-1

1956–1960 Vote Change within the Active Core of the Electorate

1960 Vote for	1956 Vote for		
	Stevenson, Per Cent	Eisenhower, Per Cent	Total, Per Cent
Kennedy	33	17	50
Nixon	6	44	50
	39	61	100

Note. Since we usually think of vote shifts in terms of proportions of the total electorate, percentages in this table use the total vote as a base, rather than row or column totals.

A traditional analysis of these vote changers would specify their membership in various population groupings such as age and occupation, union membership, race, and the like. However, results of this sort in 1960 are so uniform across most of these population groupings that they seem to reflect little more than national trends, and change seems at best only loosely connected with location in any of these specific categories. If we took the fact in isolation, for example, we might be struck that union members voted almost 8 per cent more Democratic in 1960 than in 1956. However, such a figure loses much of its interest when we remind ourselves that people who are not labor union members also shifted their votes in the same direction and in about the same degree between 1956 and 1960. Such uniform changes characterize most of the standard sociological categories.

There is, of course, one dramatic exception. Vote change between 1956 and 1960 follows religious lines very closely. Within the 6 per cent of the active 1956–1960 electorate who followed a Stevenson-Nixon path (Table 5-1), 90 per cent are Protestant and only 8 per cent Catholic. Among the larger group of Eisenhower-Kennedy changers, however, only 40 per cent are Protestant and close to 60 per cent Catholic. In the total vote in 1956 and 1960, Protestants show almost no net partisan change. Eisenhower had won 64 per cent of the "Protestant vote" in 1956; Nixon won 63 per cent. Meanwhile the Democratic proportion of the two-party vote among Catholics across the nation skyrocketed from a rough 50 per cent in the two Eisenhower elections to a vote of 80 per cent for Kennedy. These gross totals appear to substantiate the early claims of Kennedy backers that a Catholic candidate would draw back to the Democratic Party sufficient Catholics to carry the 1960 election. Furthermore, it appears that Kennedy must have gained more votes than he lost by virtue of his religious affiliation, for relative to Stevenson in 1956, he lost no Protestant votes and attracted a very substantial bloc of Catholic votes.

The question of net gains or losses as a result of the Catholic issue is not, however, so simply laid to rest. The data cited above make a very strong case, as have the aggregate national statistics, that religion played a powerful role in the 1960 outcome. The vote polarized along religious lines in a degree which we have not seen in the course of previous sample survey studies. Moreover, the few interesting deviations of other population groups in the 1960 vote, to the degree that they are visible at all, seem with minor exceptions to reflect the central religious polarization. That is, where a group exceeded or fell below the magnitude of the national shift to the Democrats, it is usually true that the group is incidentally a more or less Catholic group. The central phenomenon therefore was religious; the question as to its net effect favoring or disfavoring Kennedy remains open.

In a strict sense, of course, the answers to this question can only be estimated. We know how the election came out, with Kennedy a Catholic. We cannot, without major additional assumptions, know what the election returns might have been if Kennedy had been a Protestant and all other conditions remained unchanged. We can make an estimate, however, if we can assume some baseline, some vote that would have occurred under "normal" circumstances. A number of such baselines suggest themselves. We might work from the 1956 presidential vote, as we have done above (42 per cent Democratic); or from the more recent congressional vote in 1958 (56 per cent Democratic); or from some general average of recent nationwide votes. But it is obvious that whichever baseline we choose the answer will be determined accordingly. If we choose the 1958 vote as a baseline, it is hard to argue that Kennedy could have made any net gains from his religion; if we choose the 1956 presidential vote, it is equally hard to argue that he lost ground on balance.

Indeed, the most cogent arguments documenting a net gain for Kennedy—those accounts which appear to express the majority opinion of election observers—used the 1956 presidential vote quite explicitly as a baseline. Yet the second Eisenhower vote seems the most bizarre choice for a baseline of any which might be suggested. The vote Eisenhower achieved in 1956 stands out as the most disproportionately Republican vote in the total series of nationwide presidential and congressional elections stretching back to 1928. In what sense, then, is this extreme Republican swing plausible as a "normal vote"? Its sole claim seems to be that it is the most recent presidential election prior to 1960. Yet other recent elections attest dramatically to the extreme abnormality of the 1956 Eisenhower vote. In the 1954 congressional elections the nation's Democrats, although they do not turn out as well as Republicans in minor elections, still fashioned a solid majority of votes cast. The fall of 1958 witnessed a Democratic landslide. Even in 1956, underneath Eisenhower's towering personal margin, a Democratic popular vote majority appeared at other levels of the ticket, exceeding that which Kennedy won in 1960. Finally, if 1956 is taken as a normal baseline and if it is true that Kennedy did score some relative personal success in 1960, how can we possibly explain the fact that other Democrats on state tickets around the nation tended to win a greater proportion of popular votes than he attracted?

It seems more reasonable to suggest that Kennedy did not in any sense *exceed* the "normal" vote expectations of the generalized and anonymous Democratic candidate; rather, he fell visibly below these expectations, although nowhere nearly as far below them as Adlai Stevenson had fallen. This proposition is congruent not only with the general contours of election returns in the recent period, but with the great mass of sample survey data collected in the past decade as well. Indeed, we have already seen (Chapter 2) that a "normal" vote of the sort which might be expected in the current period for a generalized Democratic candidate running in the absence of any notable pro-Democratic or pro-Republican short-term forces would be about 54 per cent of the two-party vote. This figure falls much closer to the vote achieved by the sum of President Kennedy's congressional running mates across the land than it does to his own vote, which fell some 4 per cent short of this expectation.

Hence our calculations of the normal vote as a representation of the basic voting strength of the two parties, although hypothetical, seems a much more defensible baseline from which to assess the peculiarities of the 1960 election than is any other actual past vote, affected as such votes are by other short-term Democratic or Republican tides.

Using such a baseline we can draw into a coherent pattern the several surface characteristics which seemed intriguing from the simple 1960 vote totals. It should be emphasized that in so doing we take the existing division of deeper party loyalties for granted, examining only the 1960 *departure* of the vote from this division. This is proper simply because the fact that the Democrats enjoyed a standing majority was in no way a consequence of the personal duel between Kennedy and Nixon, but rather was a majority created long before either candidate became salient as a national political figure, and long before most of the campaign issues of 1960 had taken shape.

With this perspective, then, we can consider some of the forces which drew the 1960 vote away from its normal point, and subsequently can locate the 1960 election more generally in the stream of American political history.

Short-Term Forces in the 1960 Election

Popular vote tallies show that Kennedy received 49.8 per cent of the two-party vote outside the South and 51.2 per cent of the popular vote cast in the South. The vote outside the South is almost 1 per cent more Democratic than our estimates of the normal vote for this portion of the nation. In the South, however, the Democratic deficit relative to the same baseline approaches 17 per cent. Naturally some short-term forces may balance out so that no net advantage accrues to either party. But the comparisons between our baselines and the 1960 vote suggest that we should find some short-term forces which gave a very slight net advantage to Kennedy outside of the South, and yet which penalized him heavily within the South.

As in all elections that attract wide public attention, a number of short-term forces were certainly at work in 1960. A comprehensive assessment of these forces cannot be undertaken here. However, there can be little doubt that the religious issue was the strongest single factor overlaid on basic partisan loyalties in the 1960 election, and we have focused most of our present analysis in this area. And since we can calculate the normal vote to be expected within different religious categories, we can put this information to use in estimating the net effect of Kennedy's Catholicism upon his candidacy.

The Catholic vote. As we have observed, the vote division among Catholics soared from a 50-50 split in the two Eisenhower contests to an 80-20 majority in the 1960 presidential vote. However, it is hard to attribute all of this increment simply to the Kennedy candidacy. In the 1958 election, when there were mild short-term economic forces favoring the Democratic Party, the vote among Catholics went well over 70 per cent in that direction. Ever since our measurements of party identification began in 1952, only a small minority—less than 20 per cent—of Catholics in the nation have considered themselves as Republicans, although a fair portion have typically styled themselves as Independents. Most of what attracted attention as a Republican trend among Catholics during the 1950's finds little support in our data, at least as a trend peculiar to Catholics. To be sure, many Democratic Catholics defected to vote for Eisenhower in 1952 and 1956. But so did many Democratic Protestants; and as data in Chapter 2 have suggested, there is little evidence that Catholics responded more dramatically to the short-term forces of these elections than did other groups. Thus we doubt that the short-term personal "pull" exerted on Democrats generally by Eisenhower had a different strength for Catholics than for Protestants. The myths that have arisen to this effect seem to be primarily illusions stemming from the large proportion of Democrats who are Catholics. Their loss was painful to the Democratic candidate in the two Eisenhower elections. But they were at the outset, and remained up to the first glimmer of the Kennedy candidacy, a strongly Democratic group.

Calculating the normal vote to be expected of Catholics, we find that one would expect at least a 63 per cent Democratic margin among Catholics. The difference between 63 per cent and the 80 per cent which Kennedy achieved can provisionally be taken as an estimate of the increment in Democratic votes among Catholics above that which the normal Protestant Democratic presidential candidate could have expected.

We can readily translate this 17 per cent vote gain into proportions of the total 1960 vote, taking into account levels of Catholic turnout and the like. On such grounds, it appears that Kennedy won a vote bonus from Catholics amounting to about 4 per cent of the national two-party popular vote. This increment was, of course, very unequally divided between the South and the rest of the nation, owing simply to the sparse Catholic population in the South. Within the 1960 non-Southern electorate, Kennedy's net gain from the Catholic increment amounted to better than 5 per cent of the two-party vote. The same rate of gain represented less than 1 per cent of the Southern popular vote.

The anti-Catholic vote. Respondents talked to our interviewers with remarkable freedom about the Catholic factor during the fall of 1960. This is not to say that all respondents referred to it as a problem. There were even signs that some Protestant respondents were struggling to avoid mention of it, although it was a matter of concern. Nonetheless, nearly 40 per cent of the sample voluntarily introduced the subject in the early stages of the pre-election questionnaire before any direct probing on our part. Since this figure certainly understates the proportion of the population for whom religion was a salient concern in 1960, it testifies rather eloquently to the importance of the factor in conscious political motivations during the fall campaign.

These discussions of the Catholic question, volunteered by our respondents, provide us in the next chapter with more incisive descriptions of the short-term anti-Catholic forces important in the election. Our interest here, however, is to estimate the magnitude of anti-Catholic voting in terms of Democratic votes which Kennedy would have otherwise won. In such an enterprise, our material on the political backgrounds of our respondents is most useful.

We focus, therefore, upon the simple rates of defection to Nixon among Protestants who were identified in 1960 with the Democratic Party. As Figure 5-1 shows, this defection rate is strongly correlated with the regularity of attendance at a Protestant church. Protestant Democrats who, by self-description, never attend church and hence are not likely to have much identification with it, defected to Nixon only at a rate of 6 per cent. This rate, incidentally, is just about the "normal" defection rate which we would predict for both parties in the equilibrium case; it represents the scattered defections which occur

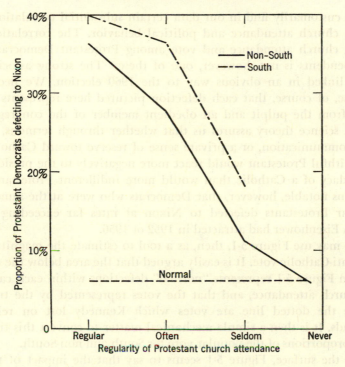

Figure 5-1. Defections to Nixon among Protestant Democrats as a function of church attendance. (The number of Protestant Democrats who "never" attend church in the South is too small for inclusion.)

for entirely idiosyncratic reasons in any election. Therefore, for Democrats who were nominal Protestants but outside the psychological orbit of their church, the short-term religious force set up by a Catholic candidacy had no visible impact. However, as soon as there is some evidence of identification with a Protestant church, the defection rate rises rapidly.

Although Protestant Independents are not included in Figure 5-1, they show the same gradient at a different level of the two-party vote division. The few Protestant Independents not attending church split close to the theoretically expected 50-50 point. Then the Nixon vote rises to 61 per cent in the "seldom" category; to 72 per cent for the "often" category; and to 83 per cent for the Protestant Independents attending church regularly. This increment of Republican votes above the normal division for Independents matches remarkably the increment of Republican votes above the "normal" figure of 6 per cent in the case of the Democrats.

We customarily find in our data certain substantial correlations between church attendance and political behavior. The correlation between church attendance and vote among Protestant Democrats and
Independents is not, however, one of these.[7] The strong associations
seem linked in an obvious way to the 1960 election. We need not
assume, of course, that each defection pictured here represents a ser-
mon from the pulpit and an obedient member of the congregation.
Social science theory assures us that whether through sermons, informal communication, or a private sense of reserve toward Catholicism,
the faithful Protestant would react more negatively to the presidential
candidacy of a Catholic than would more indifferent Protestants.[8] It
remains notable, however, that Democrats who were at the same time
regular Protestants defected to Nixon at rates far exceeding those
which Eisenhower had attracted in 1952 or 1956.

We may use Figure 5-1, then, as a tool to estimate the magnitude of
the anti-Catholic vote. It is easily argued that the area below the dotted
line in Figure 5-1 represents "normal" defections within each category
of church attendance, and that the votes represented by the triangle
above the dotted line are votes which Kennedy lost on religious
grounds. It is then a simple mechanical matter to convert this triangle
into proportions of the popular vote for South and non-South.

On the surface, Figure 5-1 seems to say that the impact of the religious factor was very nearly the same, North and South, because the
Southern gradient of defection is only slightly higher than the non-
Southern gradient. If we think of the impact of short-term forces *on
individuals* as a function of their party and religious loyalties, this conclusion is proper. Indeed, as we consider in later analyses the impact
by different types of Protestantism, it may well be that the character
of the impact will show no remaining regional difference whatever.
However, to construe Figure 5-1 as suggesting that the *magnitude* of
the anti-Catholic effect was about the same in votes cast in North and
South is quite improper. The differences between the regions turn out
to be substantial.

We must consider first that less than two-thirds of the active non-

---

[7] Re-examination of earlier data shows a faint residual relationship between Republican voting and church attendance among Democratic Protestants which is not
statistically significant. In 1956, the rank-order correlations involved were about .05
both within and outside the South. On the other hand, the comparable coefficient for
Independents in 1956 was negative, $-.04$. The text ignores these variations as probably inconsequential.

[8] This is simply a special case of more general propositions concerning group identifications discussed in A. Campbell et al., *op. cit.*, Chap. 12.

Southern electorate is Protestant whereas within the South the electorate is almost completely (95 per cent) Protestant. Second, Protestants are more faithful church-goers in the South than outside it. Quite specifically, we find that over half of the Southern presidential vote is cast by Protestants who go to church regularly whereas less than 20 per cent of the vote outside the South comes from regular, church-going Protestants. Finally, of the minority outside the South who are Protestant and attend church regularly, only a small proportion are Democratic identifiers: Republicans clearly predominate in this category. In the South the situation is reversed, with regular Protestants being far more often than not Democratic identifiers.

This conjunction of regional differences means that the defecting votes represented in Figure 5-1 are of vastly different sizes, South and non-South. It turns out that outside the South regular, church-going Protestants who are Democrats cast only about 5 per cent of the total non-Southern vote. Within the South, however, regular church-going Protestants who are Democrats contributed over 35 per cent of the total Southern vote. Thus it is that the anti-Catholic impact in the South turns out to involve a much larger share of the votes than elsewhere. The anti-Catholic vote in the South fulfills our search for a short-term force of strong net Republican strength in that region.

Summing up these apparent anti-Catholic votes as proportions of the total vote in the South, the non-South, and the nation as a whole, we can compare them with our estimations of the bonuses received by Kennedy from Catholics. Table 5-2 shows the balance sheet.

It should be stressed that these calculations refer to the popular vote and not to the electoral vote. Our samples do not permit the state-by-state estimates which would make a translation into the terms of the electoral college possible.

However this may be, it is impressive the degree to which the surface characteristics of the 1960 election become intelligible even when viewed simply as the result of an "ancient" and enduring division of partisan loyalties overlaid by a short-term cross-current of religious motivation. Usually a national vote as close to normal as the 1960 case would be a relatively low-turnout election. That is, a vote near normal suggests either weak short-term forces or else a balance of stronger forces creating conflict in individuals and thereby lowering their motivation to vote. It is rare that forces strong enough to compel indifferent citizens to come out and vote do not also favor one party over the other quite categorically.

In 1960, however, the motivational picture underlying the vote was somewhat different. Strong forces and counterforces were indeed in

TABLE 5-2
Offsetting Effects of the Catholic Issue, 1960 Democratic Presidential Vote

Area	Per Cent of Two-Party Vote in Area
Outside the South, Kennedy's "unexpected" . . .	
Gains from Catholics	5.2
Losses from Protestant Democrats and Independents	−3.6
Net	+1.6
Inside the South, Kennedy's "unexpected" . . .	
Gains from Catholics	0.7
Losses from Protestant Democrats and Independents	−17.2
Net	−16.5
For the *nation as a whole,* Kennedy's "unexpected" . . .	
Gains from Catholics	4.3
Losses from Protestant Democrats and Independents	−6.5
Net	−2.2

evidence, but these did not create much conflict within individuals. The reason is clear: to the degree that religious motivations were engaged, forces were conflicting between groups rather than within individuals.

Catholics, predominantly Democratic, were exposed to strong unidirectional short-term forces motivating them to get out and vote for Kennedy. Protestants, particularly those both religiously devout and Republican, were exposed to unidirectional forces in just the opposite direction. Where populations fitting these latter specifications were concentrated geographically, as in the north central heartlands of the country, there was indeed a surge of turnout carrying beyond the high national norm for the year. Similarly, in the preponderantly Democratic southern enclave of relative Catholicism represented by the State of Louisiana, there was a surge in turnout remarkable for the South and for the nation as well. Elsewhere in the South, the Protestant but relatively secularized populations of the few cosmopolitan states like Florida and Virginia voted at rates much closer to those of the moderate 1956 turnout. Among Protestants of the "Bible-Belt" South, turn-out kept pace with the national increase, however, and often exceeded it.

Thus a large portion of the national population did indeed vote at high rates in response to unidirectional short-term forces; but summed nationally, these forces tended to cancel each other out, and the result was a vote division that did not depart greatly from the normal.

Other surface characteristics of the election are equally intelligible in these terms. Despite his position as majority candidate, Kennedy very nearly lost and tended to run behind his ticket. In the Northeast, where concentrations of Catholics are greatest, his relation to the rest of the ticket was not generally unfavorable. The penalty he suffered becomes visible and consistent in the Midwest, where Catholics are fewer and Protestant church attendance is more regular. In the South, and for the same reasons, the differences between the Kennedy vote and that of other Democrats become large indeed. Everywhere, if one compares 1956 vote statistics with 1960 statistics, the course of political change is closely associated with the religious composition of voting units.

There was some relief even outside the more committed Democratic circles when the Kennedy victory, slight though it was, demonstrated that a Catholic was not in practice barred from the White House. Yet it would be naive to suppose that a Catholic candidate no longer suffers any initial disadvantage before the American electorate as a result of his creed. Not only did Kennedy possess a type of personal appeal which the television debates permitted him to exploit in un-usual measure, but he was also the candidate of a party enjoying a fundamental majority in the land. Even the combination of these circumstances was barely sufficient to give him a popular vote victory. Lacking such a strong underlying majority, which Al Smith most certainly lacked in 1928, it is doubtful that the most attractive of Catholic presidential candidates in 1960 would have had much chance of success. It remains to be seen how far the experience of a Catholic President may diminish the disadvantage another time.

The 1960 Election in Historical Perspective

In a publication which appeared a few months prior to the 1960 elections,[9] we posed the question of "how long a party can hope to

9 A. Campbell et al., op. cit., Chap. 19.

hold the White House if it does not have a majority of the party-identified electorate." We had identified the two Eisenhower victories as "deviating elections," in which short-term forces had brought about the defeat of the majority party. We had not found any evidence in our 1952 or 1956 studies that these short-term forces were producing any significant realignment in the basic partisan commitments of the electorate. We felt that unless such a realignment did occur, "the minority party [could] not hope to continue its tenure in office over a very extended period."

Our subsequent studies have shown that the eight-year Eisenhower period ended with no basic change in the proportions of the public who identify themselves as Republican, Democrat, or Independent. If there had been an opportunity in 1952 for the Republican Party to rewin the majority status it had held prior to 1932, it failed to capitalize on it. The Democratic Party remained the majority party, and the 1960 election returned it to the Presidency. It was, to extend the nomenclature of the preceding chapter, a "reinstating" election, one in which the party enjoying a majority of party identifiers returns to power. The 1960 election was remarkable not in the fact that the majority party was reinstated but that its return to power was accomplished by such a narrow margin.

It may be argued that the deficit the Democratic presidential candidate suffered from his normal expectation did not derive from damaging circumstances which were specific to the 1960 election but from a progressive weakening in the willingness of some Democratic partisans to support their ticket at the presidential level. It has been suggested that some voters who consider themselves to be Democrats and customarily favor Democratic candidates at the lower levels of office may have come during the Eisenhower period to have a perverse interest in favoring Republican candidates for President, either because of notions of party balance in government, because of local considerations in their states, or simply out of admiration for Eisenhower.

Important differences no doubt exist between voting at the presidential level and voting for a Congressman. Our studies have shown, for example, that the popular vote for lesser offices is a more party-determined vote than the vote for President and varies around the normal equilibrium vote figure within a much narrower range than does the presidential vote.[10] However, the supposition that Kennedy failed to win a normal Democratic majority because of a cadre of

---

[10] The relationship between votes for President and votes for lesser offices is discussed in Chapter 11 of this book.

Democrats who are covertly Republican in their presidential voting is not supported by our data.

Table 5-1 has already demonstrated that the overall shift in partisanship of the vote between 1956 and 1960 cannot be explained as a simple unilateral movement of erstwhile Eisenhower Democrats. The election did not depend, as was often supposed, on the number of Eisenhower Democrats whom Nixon could retain as "covert Republicans." Our panel materials show that if Nixon had been forced to depend only upon the Eisenhower Democrats whom he retained, he would have suffered a convincing 54-46 defeat, assuming that other Democrats had continued to vote for Kennedy. He did not suffer such a defeat, because he drew a new stream of Democratic defections nearly sufficient to put him in the White House.

The patterns of short-term forces in the 1960 election were independent of those shaping the 1956 election, then, in the sense that they affected a new set of people, on new grounds. There were Democrats susceptible to Eisenhower in 1956; there were Democrats sensitive to religion in 1960; the two sets of people do not intersect much more than one would expect by chance. In short, there is little evidence that the two Eisenhower elections had created a set of Democrats peculiarly disposed to vote for a Republican presidential candidate.

CHAPTER 6

Religion and Politics: The 1960 Election

Philip E. Converse

I'm so confused this election year. [How is that?] I'm a Republican and a Catholic, and religion and politics are important to me. I'll have to make a decision, looks like I'll have to go against my church. [Is there anything you like about the Democratic Party?] Well, no . . . it is just like religion. [How do you mean?] Politics is something wide and deep—no end to it—you get it in your system so deep. [Is there anything you like about the Democrats?] No, there isn't. I am Republican Committeewoman for this district.

[Is there anything about Kennedy that might make you want to vote for him?] No, there is not. The only thing he is a Democrat. I could not vote for him for that reason. I *couldn't*. On the other hand he is a Catholic—oh, dear! Why does it have to be that way?

The respondent was atypical. She was a Catholic woman in an otherwise Baptist family, living in a border state in the American heartlands. Well above average in education, political interest, and sophistication, she was serving as a local Republican Party official. Yet the facts that made her situation atypical also trapped her at the center of those cross-currents which lent the 1960 presidential election prime interest. That she was unusually active in politics, that she was unusually devout in religion, merely gave her plight dramatic heightening. But it was in essence the same simple conflict of group loyalties felt, at a lower pitch, by millions of other Americans in 1960. In this chapter we propose to record the basic characteristics of this conflict of loyalties as it emerged in 1960 and to examine a few of the phenomena attendant on it.

96

Some Basic Estimates of the "Religious Effect" in 1960

An insulation between political and religious orders has been fervently sought by most elites in the United States for a long time. Many sophisticated observers were torn between the desire to see free access to the Presidency regardless of creed and an apprehension that the candidacy of John F. Kennedy would bring back currents of religious intolerance. Although motives varied, there was a remarkable show of consensus in an attempt to stifle religion as an issue in the campaign. The two candidates as well as the vast majority of top leaders of the dominant political and religious groups pled as one with the American public to maintain a reasonable separation between the two orders. Indeed, few matters could have reached this degree of importance and at the same time have aligned so many prominent people of divergent viewpoints on the same side of the fence.

Nevertheless, it has become clear that religion played a powerful role in shaping voting behavior in the 1960 election. This force generated differences quite beyond the customary, long-standing ones between the major religious groups in the United States. We emphasize this point in Figure 6-1a by reviewing the recent history of presidential and congressional votes cast by Catholics and non-Southern white Protestants against the backdrop of biennial estimates of the normal

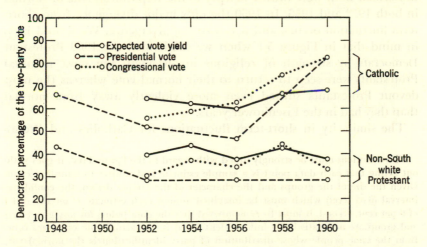

Figure 6-1a. Vote trends among Catholics and non-Southern white Protestants.

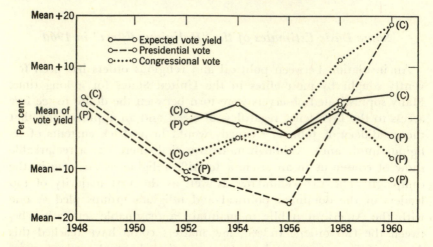

Figure 6-1b. Vote trends among Catholics and non-Southern white Protestants, with expected vote differences removed.

vote expected for each group.[1] The point of Figure 6-1a is quite simple. Although the normal votes to be expected of the two groups differ greatly, the flow of actual votes cast by each group, relative to their respective normal votes, is remarkably similar. To underscore this fact, Figure 6-1b reproduces the data in Figure 6-1a, with the basic and long-term Protestant-Catholic difference in normal vote artificially removed. Both groups appear to have cast a 1948 presidential vote close to normal. Both were drawn sharply to the Republican side of normal in both 1952 and 1956. In 1960 the only major divergence from short-term fluctuation occurs, and it is a strong divergence. We should keep in mind that in Figure 5-1 when we subdivided the 1960 Protestant Democrats by strength of religious involvement, the most nominal Protestants were seen to return to their normal vote whereas the most devout Protestants shifted even more violently away from normal than they had in the Eisenhower years.

The similarity in short-term fluctuations for Catholics and Protes-

[1] Two cautions must be strongly urged with regard to the figure. First, it goes without saying that each data point is a sample estimate and subject to sampling error. Given the size of the groups and the character of the sample design, the confidence interval (0.05 level) which must be imagined around each estimate is on the order of 6 per cent. Second, it must be remembered that the data points for any given year and group are not statistically independent. That is, the actual vote estimates come from the same people whose distribution of party identification is the normal vote estimate.

tants between 1948 and 1958 is, to be sure, no surprise. As we have seen in Chapter 2, such motion in tandem seems to be the rule for most politically relevant groups in all the elections we have studied. With the sole dramatic exception of Catholics and Protestants in 1960, short-term forces appear to have had little differential impact along lines of the more commonly studied social cleavages in this period. Where such patterns as those presented in idealized form in Chapter 2 emerge and persist over considerable periods of time, one can conclude that whatever the sociopolitical mechanisms were that first drew Group A toward the Democrats and Group B toward the Republicans, group members are currently reacting primarily (though not exclusively) as Republicans or Democrats. They remain, of course, members of the nonparty group. If the nonparty group becomes politically salient in any particular election, then loyalties to the nonparty will be in competition with loyalties to a party, where the two are in conflict. Given the notorious lack of attention paid by group members to public debate, even on the more complex issues that directly affect the group, most members most of the time will not have a strong sense of the political relevance of the nonparty group. In such periods, traces of differential response to the changing political scene by members of the nonparty group will be weak indeed. The overriding result will be, for example, that Catholic Democrats will evaluate politics in a manner which is almost indistinguishable from that of Protestant Democrats, but which differs very notably in all the common ways from the evaluations of Catholic and Protestant Republicans.

When, however, circumstances arise that make this nonparty group politically relevant and that are so obvious that no member can fail to see them or to assign them portent, then the nonparty loyalties are going to compete with party loyalties with some visible effect. This is the case in 1960. But it remains a competition, and a competition which, when strengths of loyalty are equated, will fall more often than not to party loyalty, simply because it is the more relevant.

The important conceptual point, however, is not the manner in which loyalties are weighted to arrive at a given decision, but rather the fact that over time party loyalties develop a functional autonomy. They become coordinate for the voter with loyalties to nonparty groups, even loyalties that any student of history knows to have antedated the adoption of the party in an earlier generation.[2] The re-

---

[2] We say "coordinate" and not "equal in weight." The weighting depends on the instance. By "coordinate" we mean simply that the party is not conceptually set off in a "means-realm" while the nonparty group monopolizes some "goal-realm."

spondent whose remarks introduced this chapter reflects admirably this conflict of coordinate loyalties, and in this regard is typical of our respondents who commented on the religious question in 1960 ("[Politics] is just like religion . . . it is something wide and deep—no end to it—you get it in your system so deep. . . .").

In sum, then, any analysis of the relation between nonparty social groups and politics in general, or the 1960 Catholic-Protestant case in particular, should not confuse the following components:

(1) *The long-term partisan component.* The distinctive division of party loyalties which characterizes the nonparty group over periods of time, even though the political relevance of the nonparty group is faint or passes unperceived, must have originated at some point more or less deep in the past. It is likely to be either a direct consequence of group membership, or at least a consequence of other life situations once correlated with group membership. In the Catholic-Protestant case, the literature abounds in historical surmises which are well known. Since this basic difference stretches back into what is, for us, prehistory, we cannot hope to improve on these surmises with our data.

(2) *Certain maintaining mechanisms.* A variety of phenomena may be classed here. The functional autonomy of party loyalties, which maintains political differences even in periods when the perceived political relevance of the originating group is low, obviously falls in this category. It is true as well that turnover in personnel between generations creates maintaining problems in the degree that the basic level of partisanship of the group departs from a 50-50 division. If the group is relatively homogeneous in partisan terms, and if the transmission of the dominant party loyalty from parent to child ever fails, then some other mechanisms such as a differential birth rate giving more offspring to families of the dominant party, or a differential recruitment of the ensuing generation such that the occasional intergenerational partisan changes favor the dominant party very disproportionately, are required to keep the partisan level of the group from drifting slowly toward a 50-50 division.[3]

---

[3] Evidence that such differential recruiting phenomena occur in the current era for Catholics and Protestants has been remarked on by Gerhard Lenski in *The Religious Factor* (New York: Doubleday, 1961, pp. 126–128) and by B. R. Berelson, P. F. Lazarsfeld, and W. H. McPhee in *Voting* (Chicago: University of Chicago Press, 1954, pp. 61–69). These phenomena are clear in national data as well. It is easy to forget,

(3) *Short-term partisan forces.* The response to transient election circumstances which do not materially affect the abiding division of party loyalties in the group.

Despite our great interest in all of these phenomena, this discussion is restricted to the third. That is, we are interested here in the impact of the Kennedy candidacy in drawing partisans of differing religious beliefs to deviate from their normal political responses. Provisionally we locate the Kennedy candidacy as a short-term force, since it is still too soon to tell in any reliable way if these vote shifts have affected party loyalties. It is always entirely possible, of course, that the 1960 shifts will turn out to have more durable consequences. There is a slight oscillation in 1960 in the more stable vote yield measure toward and away from the Democrats on the part of Catholics and Protestants, respectively (Figure 6-1a or 6-1b), that might herald such change. However, we have watched such oscillations before, even dwarfed as they have been by the actual vote swings, expecting them to be the seeds of more permanent change. They have never developed into any permanent change strong enough to be disentangled from sampling error, and hence we have come to be more cynical about them.[4]

Whether the impact of the Kennedy candidacy turns out to be permanent or transient, however, the strategy of analysis is the same. We still wish to dissociate the current impact from more ancient differences. Therefore as we push our investigations *within* the primary religious groups we shall continue to take into account deviations in 1960 from prior partisanship. To avoid any possible contamination from the 1960 oscillations in basic party loyalties, we shall employ 1958 measures of party identification for our panel people as the indicator of such prior partisanship.

For those who like to visualize these matters of force and impact, Figure 6-2a summarizes the effects of Kennedy's candidacy in creating a conflict of coordinate political and religious loyalties, and Figure 6-2b is the comparable picture for the same people categorized by the

---

however, that these recruiting differences must be extremely strong in a case like the Catholic one, or the group will lose ground nonetheless. In national data or in the Lenski data, although the differential seems intuitively to be remarkably strong, it remains insufficient to maintain the Catholic group at its current level of distinctiveness, if the total story is actually told by the simple fourfold father-child, party-party, table.

[4] Subsequent data suggest that this cynicism was justified. As of early 1964, the lasting impact of the Kennedy candidacy on the basic party loyalty of Catholics was slight indeed, amounting at most to a percentage point or two.

same measures (1958 party identification, a 1960 measure of religious identification) for the 1956 election. As we see, there is no reliable slope associated with religion in the 1956 vote, once party is considered; in 1960 the religious measure exerts a very systematic distortion on the original slope.[5]

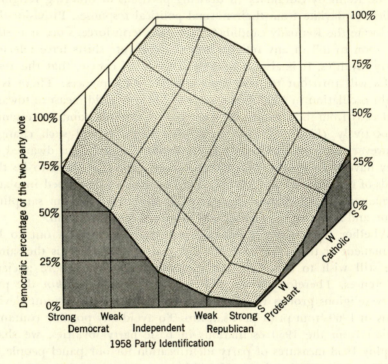

Figure 6-2a. 1960 presidential vote by party identification (1958) and by religious identification (1960).

Inside the Catholic Vote

Differential lines of impact of the Kennedy candidacy within the Catholic community are somewhat hard to trace because the size of the group does not permit very elegant subdivision. And, since normally less than 20 per cent of Catholics consider themselves uncondi-

[5] It should be remarked that two points on each surface (1956 and 1960) suffering from inadequate numbers of cases (less than 10) have been artificially smoothed in a manner which seems dictated by the character of the surface around them. This smoothing, however, does not involve any of the four critical corner points.

tional Republicans, the biting edge of any analysis is further dulled. However, we can draw a few brief observations about the way different types of Catholics responded to the 1960 situation.

The ethnic subcommunities. Kennedy was not only a Catholic candidate, but an Irish Catholic candidate. Since it has often been ob-

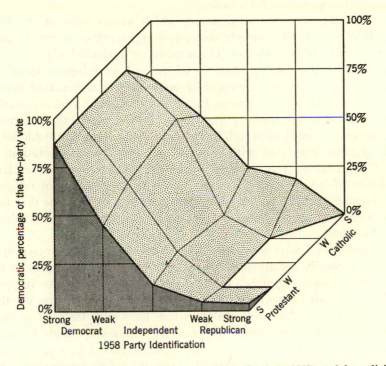

Figure 6-2b. 1956 presidential vote by party identification (1958) and by religious identification (1960).

served that lines of the old ethnic communities have been dissolving in favor of broader religious communities, it is of interest to consider the interplay between the ethnic factor and the religious factor among Catholics in 1960. We can examine not only the contrasts between Irish and non-Irish Catholics, but we have enough cases to get at least a rough idea as well of the 1960 response in a third logical subset, that of the Irish non-Catholics (Protestants).

The degree of socio-economic assimilation of the Irish Catholic community into the mainstream of American life is well recognized. Almost three-quarters of the Irish Catholics in our 1960 sample were of third generation or more, as opposed to one-third of the non-Irish Catholics.[6] Combining samples from the 1950's to maximize cases, the Irish Catholics appeared to have an educational background and occupation level which (1) compared quite well with that of non-Southern, non-Irish white Protestants; (2) exceeded that of Irish Protestants, even with the South set aside; and (3) exceeded very notably that of non-Irish Catholics.

At the same time, on all measures which were employed, the Irish Catholics in the 1960 sample showed stronger religious involvement than did non-Irish Catholics. These measures include both reports of church attendance and professions of strength of religious identification. Lenski has noted a pattern of lower church attendance among the less "Americanized" citizens, Protestant or Catholic, whose families have arrived in this country more recently.[7] Although these patterns are present in our data as well, Irish Catholics remain visibly higher in church attendance even with controls on status or on generations in the United States. And although none of the differences between Irish and non-Irish were extremely large across these measures of religious involvement, they would certainly render it difficult to argue that relative socio-economic assimilation has made inroads on Irish Catholic religious faith.

So much for background. The Irish Protestant political reaction in 1960 was totally indistinguishable, both North and South, from the reactions of other groups of white Protestants. The same negative attitude toward Kennedy is reflected, and in the same degree, whether we look at vote shifts recorded between 1956 and 1960, or at their 1960 deviations from normal vote patterns. Although it might be maintained that an ethnic attraction was counterbalanced by a particularly intense intracommunity religious cleavage, it is as easy to presume that the now-remote ethnic factor had no weight, and the religious factor operated at what was, for Protestants in 1960, normal strength.

On the other hand, there is some indication that Irish Catholics were more affected by the Kennedy candidacy than were non-Irish Catholics. The differences are not great, and case numbers are too small for definite conclusions. However, Irish Catholics who had voted for Eisenhower in 1956 were more likely to join the movement to Kennedy in 1960 (Table 6-1). The deviation toward the Democrats of the 1960 Irish Catholic vote (N of 49) from levels which would have

---

[6] The Protestant Irish contingent is almost without exception of very ancient vintage.

[7] Lenski, op. cit., pp. 41 ff.

TABLE 6-1

Vote Change among 1956–1960 Presidential Voters for Irish and Non-Irish Catholics

	Irish Catholics			Non-Irish Catholics	
	Steven-son	Eisen-hower		Steven-son	Eisen-hower
Kennedy	52%	37%	Kennedy	42%	39%
Nixon	0	11	Nixon	1	18
		100%			100%
Number of cases		(37)			(178)

Each fourfold table is percentaged to its corner, rather than along rows or columns.

been expected in the light of their 1958 expression of party identification is in absolute terms larger than that for non-Irish Catholics, though not statistically significant by usual standards (a Democratic increment of 19 per cent, as opposed to 14 per cent among non-Irish Catholics). Some, but not all, of this absolute difference is removed if we take into account the fact that Irish Catholics before the Kennedy candidacy were more strongly involved as Catholics. It seems that among strongly identified Catholics, the Irish, non-Irish difference in reaction disappears; it is rather among people weakly identified with the religion that the ethnic difference seems to have its fullest impact. Irish people weakly identified with Catholicism were nonetheless more likely to deviate to a vote for Kennedy whereas the non-Irish weakly identified show no reliable impact whatever (N of 45). Although insufficient case numbers leave these observations on the thinnest empirical base, the pattern of absolute differences has the same flavor as many others observed in comparable situations and may be worth some credence.

Perhaps the most intriguing difference, however, is the fact that Irish Catholics contributed disproportionately to the minor shift toward the Democrats in party loyalties between 1958 and 1960 (see the Catholic vote yield, Figure 6-1a). If there is to be any lasting impact of the Kennedy candidacy on the Catholic community, it may well be that it will register primarily among Irish Catholics.

Although it is plausible to suppose from these data, then, that the ethnic factor contributed some extra "push" to Catholics in 1960, there is of course no question but that its role was entirely over-whelmed, like an eddy in a torrent, by movements along broader religious lines.

Types of religious involvement. It is of at least anecdotal interest that the two Catholics in our survey who swam against the Catholic tide in the 1956–1960 period, voting first for Stevenson and then switching to Nixon, were rather peculiar Catholics. Neither was a regular church attender (as opposed to 70 per cent of all Catholics) and neither was Irish Catholic. One showed signs of positive psy-chological identification with the Catholic community despite irregu-lar church attendance, and her defection clearly sprang from her multiple memberships. She was a Negro woman of unusual education, reared in a Baptist home, who had married a Catholic and had ac-cepted his faith. She expressed positive interest in "seeing what a Catholic would do" as President, but she voted for Nixon out of sharp racial reaction to Lyndon Johnson. The second case, a skilled worker in New York City, was not only a rare churchgoer but also indicated complete disinterest in the Catholic community on every measure. The candidacy of a Catholic was simply irrelevant to him: he re-ported an immediate distrust of both Kennedy and Nixon and before the election was thinking of voting "no" for President. After the elec-tion he reported a Nixon vote, since Kennedy had finally impressed him as the less sincere of the two men.

It has been apparent throughout this discussion that the differential impact of the Kennedy candidacy formed along lines of religious in-volvement. The more religiously devout Protestant Democrats were more likely to cross party lines to vote Republican than were the less religiously faithful Protestant Democrats; the more involved Catholics were more likely to shift their vote to the Democratic column in 1960 than were the more peripheral Catholics. If we view the election as a conflict of loyalties, it is not surprising, of course, that ultimate decisions rested on the relative intensity of these loyalties.

However, it is interesting to dissect the involvement phenomenon into components which give some better understanding of the under-lying relation between these influences. For example, in his study of religious subcommunities in Detroit, Lenski maintained empirical con-trasts between "associational involvement" in the religious group—frequency of attendance at formal worship services—and "communal involvement," measured by the degree to which the individual's pri-mary relations (close friends and relatives) are limited to persons of his own religious group.[8] Such a procedure gives obvious entree to

8 Lenski, *op. cit.,* pp. 21 ff.

bodies of theory concerning the interplay of primary and secondary group relations.

Over the course of our panel study between 1956 and 1960 we used two measures which reflect religious involvement in somewhat the same differential manner. The first measure, report of church attendance, is equivalent to the Lenski gauge of associational involvement. The second measure differs operationally from Lenski's communal measure, although it bears some conceptual similarities.[9] It attempts to measure the sense of proximity and common interest which individual members feel vis-à-vis the group.[10]

The parallel between the empirical results gathered by this measure and the communal involvement measure employed by Lenski are very striking. Thus Lenski finds, for example, that Jews in Detroit rank lowest of the major religious categories in church attendance and the highest in communal involvement; at a national level, Jews in our samples similarly show the lowest church attendance and by far the highest community identification. Similarly, church attendance is very high among Catholics relative to white Protestants, as is true nationally. But, as Lenski remarks, Catholics and white Protestants are at the same levels on the communal measure, and nationally they are indistinguishable in terms of our identification measure. Indeed, we have been unable to find any basic discrepancy between the patterns produced by the Lenski measures and the ones we have used.[11] It is

[9] Although we collected data in 1960 on the religious homogeneity of the immediate family, which formed part of the Lenski measure of communal involvement, these data are not employed here. It might be observed that Lenski's measure is somewhat more useful in a polyglot metropolis than it is in a national sample, where ecological distance rather outstrips social distance as a factor in inhibiting cross-group primary contacts. We are currently working with estimates of relative density of various groups drawn from our repeated samplings in the same areas over time, and it will be interesting to see how this ecological variable interacts with other measures discussed here.

[10] The two questions employed were: "Would you say you feel pretty close to Catholics in general or that you don't feel much closer to them than you do to other people?" and "How much interest would you say you have in how Catholic people as a whole are getting along in this country? Do you have a good deal of interest in it, some interest, or not much interest at all?" In the Protestant case, the group object referred to was the denomination, unless the respondent labeled himself simply a "Protestant." For large areas of the country the broader referent would make little sense. Naturally this changes the focus of the questions and reduces comparability with the Lenski procedure for Protestants.

[11] It is true, however, that the intercorrelations generally between our two involvement measures on different groups run higher than those which Lenski reports, although the patterns of these intercorrelations across groups, once again, seems similar. This simply means that it should be harder to get differential results between our two measures.

likely that there is some degree of functional equivalence between our community identification measure and the results of the Lenski procedure.[12]

Table 6-2a permits us to examine the differential impact of the

TABLE 6-2a

**Political Preferences of the Catholic Community
by Two Types of Religious Involvement**

The 1960 Presidential Vote Deviation

Identification with the Catholic Community	Church Attendance			
	Regular	Often	Seldom, Never	Total
High	22% (83)	14% (12)	— (6)	23% (101)
Medium-high	21% (82)	12% (17)	— (10)	20% (109)
Medium-low	14% (69)	11% (14)	6% (19)	12% (102)
Low	9% (37)	— (4)	4% (24)	3% (65)
Total	16% (271)	7% (47)	10% (59)	

The cell entry in each case is the increment in the Democratic proportion of the two-party 1960 presidential vote over the expected vote for each cell computed in Table 6-2b. Each deviation is positive, indicating that the vote generated by each cell was more Democratic than expected in 1960. Only cells with more than ten cases have been entered. Bizarre distributions and votes in these small cells account for some of the apparent anomalies which arise if one compares internal entries for various rows or columns with the summaries for the rows or columns. Case numbers are indicated in parentheses under each entry.

[12] A third simple measure of identification was included in the 1960 study in order to parallel the party identification measure by asking the respondent whether he considered himself a "strong or not very strong Catholic." This measure seems to go more directly to an underlying sense of involvement, in that the associational measure and the community identification measure each correlates more strongly with it than they do between themselves. We have used it in this text where we have wished a simple and summary discrimination, as in Figure 6-2a.

Kennedy candidacy as a function of these two measures of religious involvement. The dependent variable here again is not the vote itself, but the deviation of the actual 1960 vote from the vote division which might have been expected (short-term forces aside), given the distribution of party loyalties expressed in 1958 by individuals within each cell. As we see, both variables make some independent contribution to differences in impact. Although there are several means of drawing the comparison, they all suggest that the impact tends to run more strongly along lines defined by community identification rather than those of church attendance. This difference conforms with comparisons drawn by Lenski for Detroit.

In Table 6-2b we have reproduced the 1958 base from which the 1960 deviations were extracted, since a comparison of the two tables is illuminating. We note immediately that in 1958 the gradients of party preference as a function of both involvement measures were entirely degenerate: either there was no relationship at all or a non-monotonic progression which summed to a weak positive relationship. On the basis of 1956 data we had once surmised that such seedy patterns as were present at that time in the Catholic instance must

TABLE 6-2b

**Political Preferences of the Catholic Community
by Two Types of Religious Involvement**

The 1958 Base

Identification with the Catholic Community	Church Attendance			
	Regular	Often	Seldom, Never	Total
High	71%	53%		67%
Medium-high	64%	68%		65%
Medium-low	70%	73%	67%	70%
Low	47%		75%	59%
Total	67%	63%	66%	

The cell entry in each case is the proportion of the two-party Democratic proportion which could be expected in the respective cross-partitions on the basis of the distribution of party identifications professed in 1958. This entry is what we have called the normal vote or the vote yield for the group. Only cells with more than ten cases have been entered, although the missing entries are of course included in the summary totals for the marginals.

reflect the late stages of a decline in group political relevance.[13] This impression is now lent considerable weight by an abbreviated time series which we can erect for Catholics during the 1950's, representing a rank-order correlation between these measures of religious involvement and basic partisan loyalties: [14]

	1952	1956	1958
Church attendance x party identification	.05	.02	.00
Community identification x party identification	—	.09	.03

As Table 6-2a indicates, the events of 1960 dramatically resuscitated the correlation between involvement terms and at least momentary partisan choice.

Yet it is noteworthy that the apparent erosion of these intragroup correlations prior to 1960 had occurred while the basic partisanship of Catholics as a whole seemed to be remaining at its high Democratic level. Let us suggest that when a social group is in its early stages of political relevance, there is a structure of intragroup correlations which betrays the lines of impact of whatever forces are leading the group to political distinctiveness. The most generic correlation in the structure, and from one point of view the least illuminating, is the inevitable association between member involvement and susceptibility to the political norms which the group is advocating. If in a later phase the political relevance of the group has declined, this structure of intragroup correlations begins to lose its clarity. It is worn away by all the forms of turnover which characterize the terms of the relationship. There is, for example, slow turnover in the membership of the group, occasionally by conversion but more often by population replacement; turnover as well in the political opinions of some members of the group, shifting now for non-group reasons; and turnover in the involvement of some members in the group itself, once again for reasons unrelated to matters political. If we were to use what is known of certain political maintaining mechanisms which are irrelevant to group peculiarities, and certain probabilities of social interaction which are quite independent of political controversies per se, it should be possible to model a total process in which intragroup correlations erode much faster than the partisan distinctiveness of group members relative to other population groups.

[13] P. E. Converse, *Group Influence in Voting Behavior*, unpublished doctoral dissertation, The University of Michigan, 1958. See Chapter 3.

[14] The Kendall tau-beta was used. See H. M. Blalock, *Social Statistics*, New York: McGraw-Hill, 1960, pp. 321 ff.

A new relevance for the group will give life to such patterns again, as in the 1960 case for Catholics. Whether correlations form more directly along lines of associational involvement or communal involvement may depend on the character of the stimulating political term, or on the structural peculiarities of the group in question, or both. For 1960 Catholics, the restoration seems to be picked up more clearly by the community identification variable.[15] Whether the restoration in this case will be entirely transient or will endure for some further period depends, as we have argued, on the degree to which underlying party loyalties turn out to be affected.

Catholic values concerning barriers between church and state. One of the most curious tables to come out of the panel analysis is worth a brief report. In 1956 we had attempted to secure, from members of various nonpolitical groups, a measure of the degree to which they felt it was legitimate for their group to engage in direct political activity.[16] This "legitimacy" variable tended to correlate with group identification and with the tendency to accept group political norms. At the time, however, we expressed reservations as to the causal status of such relationships, since the values expressed could be quite superficial relative to the underlying behavior dynamics. One of the sole characteristics which suggested utility was the fact that members of religious groups, like Catholics, were less likely to consider group intervention in politics legitimate than were union members and Negroes.[17]

We repeated this measure on our 1960 panel of Catholics to see what would happen at a moment when many Catholics were deeply influenced by the unusual presidential candidacy of a group member.

[15] It should be called to the reader's attention that the stronger discrimination of the community identification variable in Table 6-2a is a phenomenon quite independent of the fact that some residual correlation between the community term and partisanship remained in 1958 whereas there was none for church attendance. Since the deviations are extracted from precisely these 1958 patterns, the fact of independence should be immediately clear.

[16] The two questions posed were: "How do you feel about Catholic organizations trying to get Congress to pass laws that Catholics are interested in? Do you think it's all right for them to do that, or do you think they ought to stay out of that?" and "How do you feel about Catholic organizations trying to help certain candidates get elected? Do you think it's all right for them to do that, or do you think they ought to stay out of that?" Respondents answering that such intervention was all right on both counts were considered "high legitimates" whereas those against both were "low legitimates."

[17] A. Campbell, P. E. Converse, W. E. Miller, and D. E. Stokes, *The American Voter*, New York: John Wiley and Sons, 1960, pp. 321–322.

TABLE 6-3

Change in Beliefs as to the Legitimacy of Catholic Political
Activity among Catholics, 1956–1960

1960	1956			1960 Total
	High Legitimacy	Mixed Reaction	Low Legitimacy	
High legitimacy	38%	16%	9%	20%
Mixed reaction	10	17	14	14
Low legitimacy	52	67	77	66
	100%	100%	100%	100%
1956 Total	32%	25%	43%	100%
Number of cases	(82)	(64)	(112)	(258)

The turnover in the table and the shift in the marginals were as sharp
and yet as systematic as any we have seen to date in panel analysis
(Table 6-3). Of the original set of Catholics who had defended the
propriety of Catholic intervention in *both* legislative lobbying and
candidate support, a majority had moved in 1960 to outright repudia-
tion of both types of intervention!

This sudden expression of a desire for high barriers between church
and state gives an interesting reflection of the apprehension brought
to the Catholic community by the 1960 religious controversy. In 1960
the proportion of Catholics denying the propriety of both forms of
intervention (66 per cent) actually cannot be distinguished from the
proportion of non-Southern white Protestants (64 per cent) who make
the same double rejection for *Catholic* organizations. On the other
hand, of course, there is little sign that such apprehension served to
diminish the volume of political shifting to Kennedy among Catholics.

The Anti-Catholic Reaction among Protestants

Whatever the entreaties of the most reputable political and religious
elites, it is clear that American Protestants in 1960 were remarkably
preoccupied by the fact that Kennedy was a Catholic. In our pre-
election questionnaire during the campaign, we avoided introducing
the matter directly on a number of grounds. Despite our reticence,

however, nearly half of the white Protestant respondents themselves introduced "the Catholic question." Given the normal dispersion of interest displayed by the American public in the face of nondirective questioning in past elections, this focus on Catholicism amounts to an obsession. The "silent" religious issue showed a salience which put it in the class of the most central and widely debated issues of past elections, such as Korea or corruption in 1952. When one reflects that some Protestants must have felt sufficient inhibition to avoid the subject, these comparisons take on even greater significance.

Not all Protestants introducing the subject were unequivocally negative. About 1 per cent of the white Protestants offering comments did so to defend the right of a Catholic to be President or to deny indignantly the relevance of the issue. Another rather large group made remarks with some edge of ambiguity, such as "I know the fact he's a Catholic shouldn't bother us." Although comments of this order seem to reflect no more than a superficial bow to social values on the part of a person deeply influenced in spite of himself, they were coded as intermediate reactions. Despite this leniency in classification, over three-quarters of white Protestants who introduced the subject were coded as unequivocally negative.

These hostile reactions can be divided into the elaborated and the unelaborated. The latter were numerous: "I just don't like Catholics"; "I just can't see a Catholic for President." Where elaborations were given, they were sufficiently diverse to give support to most of the current theories of prejudice. A Kentucky man had disliked Catholics since the day when, at a Cincinnati hiring hall, the Catholic doling out the jobs had asked Catholics in the hall to raise their hands first. Another man reported having heard Kennedy charge in a campaign speech that Catholics heretofore had been excluded from high government jobs, and that if elected, he would personally remedy that in a hurry. The modal elaborations expressed alarm at papal control of American policy. These comments varied widely in sophistication from moderate discussions of a Catholic's primary commitment to his faith to dark beliefs that Catholicism lay somewhere on the road to Communism.

If we consider a priori the social distribution which this antiCatholicism should take, we can develop some delightfully conflicting expectations. On the one hand, we now have a large literature which indicates that verbal expressions of intolerance—political, religious, racial—show a strong inverse correlation with education. It is worth remembering, of course, that these data rarely involve discriminatory acts, and we are always subject to the possibility that education, in communicating certain social values concerning intolerance, builds in inhibitions in verbal responses which may be more or less disengaged from underlying evaluations and actions. However this may be, the education correlate would lead us in two directions in looking for any sharp anti-Catholic reaction: downward to the more anomic, alienated strata of the urban status hierarchy, and outward toward the provincial hinterland.

On the other hand, it was no great trick to predict that the anti-Catholic reaction would follow lines of church attendance, as we have seen to be the case. More generally, it could be argued that Kennedy's Catholicism would be most repugnant to those members of the society most vitally bound up in the dominant values of the dominant Protestant community. The local Protestant minister is of course the prototype here, but one may think more generally of the "pillars of the community," particularly where the effective community is exclusively Protestant. Here we are talking not of people socially adrift, as before, but of the social activists who are themselves the anchors. We are at the opposite end of the status continuum. These are the people who are most aware of, and have the greatest stake in, the ascendance of Protestant values, for they, far more than the great masses, are the keepers of the flame.

The more elite anti-Catholicism could find justification, if not initial motivation, in concerns over the separation of church and state and the anomalous position of an American Catholic in these regards. The low-status anti-Catholicism would occur despite rather than because of these highly valued barriers, since there is a great deal of evidence to make us believe that such abstract considerations go largely unappreciated where education is weak. That is, for the poorly educated, anti-Catholicism would be a free-floating animus toward a dimly perceived outgroup, an animus which could receive free political expression simply because of a failure to compartmentalize between religion and politics.

Since differential reactions seemed plausible along both of the dimensions which we have broadly outlined, it was plausible as well to suppose that the anti-Catholic response would be greatest at their intersection. That is, in the sparsely populated cells representing the low-status, poorly-educated people who are nonetheless faithful or active in the Protestant community, we anticipated the sharpest anti-Catholicism. By the same token, we expected such signs to be weakest or nonexistent among well-educated people least involved in Protestantism. The cells on the more populated diagonal—high-activist and high-education, or low-activist and low-education—would then be expected to fall in intermediate positions.

Across the grossest subdivisions of the white Protestant population, voluntary anti-Catholic references showed a distribution which seemed indeed to follow education lines (Table 6-4). That is, hostility was expressed more freely among blue-collar Protestants than among white-collar; among farmers than among nonfarm people; and at all levels, more frequently among white Protestants in the provincial and poorly educated South.

Although we should not lose sight of these broad facts in the more detailed probing which follows, they tell a story which is mildly misleading. In the first place, the volunteering of anti-Catholic remarks turns out to be much less tightly correlated with education than Table 6-4 would lead one to deduce. In the South, there is a fair relationship, with 30 per cent of the college respondents, 43 per cent of the high-school respondents, and 48 per cent of the grade-school white

TABLE 6-4

Anti-Catholic Commentary Volunteered by White Protestants during the Pre-election, 1960, Interviewing, by Region and Occupation

	Occupation of Head of Household		
	White Collar	Blue Collar	Farm Operator
Non-South:			
Clear negative references	22%	32%	32%
Ambiguous references	12	10	23
No references	66	58	45
	100%	100%	100%
Number of cases	(231)	(284)	(60)
South:			
Clear negative references	35%	46%	57%
Ambiguous references	17	6	8
No references	48	48	35
	100%	100%	100%
Number of cases	(185)	(158)	(49)

Protestants proffering anti-Catholic comment. But outside the South, the correlation is sparse indeed, the comparable gradient running 22 per cent, 29 per cent and 28 per cent. If we focus on the urban status hierarchy outside the South (Table 6-5), we find a remarkable picture, one which indicates rapidly why the non-Southern correlation with education is so slight. The incidence of such commentary is very markedly curvilinear, with anti-Catholicism being expressed most frequently at the high and low extremes of the status continuum. There is perhaps the shadow of such a pattern in the South, with professional people slightly more likely to register anti-Catholicism than the business and managerial stratum. From this point, however, the incidence of Southern comment increases rapidly as status decreases, so that the global impression is one of linearity.

Table 6-5 appeared to argue even more eloquently than expected, of course, for a distinction into two types of anti-Catholic reaction. By this account the clerical stratum in the middle would be too well educated on the one hand to indulge in the more ignorant forms of reaction yet too little bound into the active leadership of the Protestant community to resist strongly the advent of a Catholic President. We know, for example, that professional people outside the South are in extreme disproportion among regular Protestant church

TABLE 6-5

Anti-Catholic Commentary Volunteered by Non-Southern White Protestants during the Pre-election, 1960, Interviewing, by Head's Occupation

	Occupation of Head of Household				
	Prof. and Semi-Prof.	Business and Managers, Officials, Proprietors	Clerical and Sales	Skilled and Semi-Skilled	Un-skilled
Clear negative references	28%	28%	16%	28%	47%
Ambiguous references	7	18	10	9	14
No references	65	61	74	63	39
	100%	100%	100%	100%	100%
Number of cases	(78)	(85)	(68)	(202)	(51)

attenders, with business and managerial people also disproportionately represented, and the remainder of the occupational hierarchy showing fairly weak status differentials in attendance. Therefore it seemed a simple matter to forge the empirical links between church attendance and the anti-Catholic response among business and professional people to complete the picture.

We were chagrined, therefore, to discover that outside the South there was no correlation between church attendance and the anti-Catholic responses *within the business and professional strata.* Below these strata, from clerical workers downward, the correlation is strong, but at the top it simply does not exist. This is true whether we measure involvement in the Protestant community by the associational criterion (church attendance) or by the community identification terms, or by a reasonable combination of the two. Indeed, in absolute terms (differences not statistically significant), we tend to find that the anti-Catholic reaction is actually stronger among the less religiously involved, even though these less involved people turn out to be the more highly educated.

We have dealt up to this point with volunteered reactions to Kennedy's Catholicism during the pre-election interviewing. We may also bring to bear the behavioral criterion, as measured by the deviation of a group's 1960 presidential vote from the one expected on the basis of the 1958 distribution of partisanship. The verbal criterion suffers because of possible inhibition of comments along systematic social lines. The behavioral criterion suffers a weakness in the possibility that some deviations in 1960 voting in one or another social group might have been touched off by concerns other than the Catholicism of the candidate. It is gratifying, therefore, that across all the comparisons we have drawn, these two criteria give the same results. That is, where partitions of the population show significant differences in incidence of anti-Catholic responses, they show comparable differences in the magnitude of deviations away from a Democratic vote in 1960.[18]

---

[18] We have encountered only one exception, which is neither surprising to the observer nor disturbing to the current analysis. Examination of aggregate vote statistics from the rural Midwest leads to the strong impression that a farm revolt toward the Democrats in 1960 on economic grounds was largely stifled *at the presidential level* by rural anti-Catholicism. And indeed, we do find that the deviation away from the Democrats in 1960 was much less strong than the incidence of anti-Catholic references would have suggested given the norms set for the comparison by the other groupings studied to date. Although case numbers are once again limited, it may be noteworthy in this connection that the only major positive deviation we have encountered among Protestants—a vote *more* Democratic than normal—occurs among farmers who seldom or never attend church (a positive deviation of 11 per cent, as opposed to a negative deviation of 8 per cent among more regular church attenders).

thus, for example, the curvilinear distribution of anti-Catholic responses along the status continuum outside the South is duplicated by a curve of 1960 vote deviations (a negative deviation means motion away from the Democrats):

	Deviation	*N*
Professional and semi-professional	−16	88
Business and managerial	−10	80
Clerical	0	79
Skilled and semi-skilled	−12	227
Unskilled	−10	65

Similarly it is true that for clerical people and below, church attendance correlates handsomely with a strong deviation away from the Democrats. For the business and professional community outside the South, however, there is no such correlation.

Table 6-6 summarizes these data for both regions and both types of religious involvement. If we start at the bottom of the table, we find a pattern of deviations within the South which fits our original predictions. That is, the impact of anti-Catholicism is indeed strongest where low status combines with high religious feeling and is mildest where status is high and religious involvement is low. Outside the South, however, the pattern is different, as most clearly exemplified by the church attendance quarter of the table. Here status differences account for little or nothing even within the set of regular church attenders, although there is a trend in the predicted direction. And there is a clear reversal among Protestants attending church only irregularly: low-status people registered little or no anti-Catholic impact, but that impact remains high in the business and professional community.

The reader is warned that the division of the status hierarchy in Table 6-6 leans more toward the post hoc than we like. Normally on both conceptual and empirical grounds the division into blue-collar and white-collar is indicated. In this case, however, the step change between business-professional people on one hand and clerical people on the other is large, in terms of the capacity of measures of religious involvement to explain differences in anti-Catholic impact. At the same time, it goes without saying that this division of the occupation hierarchy isolates much more incisively the "pillars of the community" which we originally had had in mind. It is a distinction which seems to reflect local prominence and local power.

This being so, we are naturally interested to see whether differences

TABLE 6-6

1960 Deviations of Presidential Vote Partisanship from 1958 Expectations of White Protestants by Region, Head's Occupation, and Two Types of Religious Involvement

Head's Occupation	Church Attendance	
	Regular, Often	Seldom, Never
Non-South:		
Professional or business	−11%	−13%
	(107)	(58)
Clerical or blue collar	−15%	−2%
	(171)	(183)
South:		
Professional or business	−25%	−16%
	(70)	(34)
Clerical or blue collar	−36%	−13%
	(110)	(68)

	Identification with Protestant Community	
	High	Low
Non-South:		
Professional or business	−13%	−12%
	(63)	(97)
Clerical or blue collar	−17%	−5%
	(130)	(217)
South:		
Professional or business	−24%	−15%
	(68)	(38)
Clerical or blue collar	−32%	−20%
	(111)	(68)

The cell entry in each case is the decrement in the Democratic proportion of the two-party 1960 presidential vote relative to the two-party vote proportion which could have been expected on the basis of the distribution of party identifications shown by individuals in the cell in 1958. Case numbers for each cell are indicated in parentheses under each entry.

in the type of community have some bearing on the observed patterns. As always, we encounter limitations in case numbers here which make any elegant subdivisions precarious. However, we can draw some impressions from a crude trichotomy of the non-Southern sample into large urban concentrations (over 100,000 in population), towns and small cities (2,500 to 100,000), and villages and rural areas. Such a division suggests strongly that the non-Southern pattern which surprised us tends to be confined to the metropolis. As we move outward into smaller towns and rural areas, the patterns seem to shift from the deviant case toward the Southern, or originally expected pattern. It never becomes the case outside the South that business and professional people who are religiously uninvolved show less anti-Catholic impact than lower-status people peripheral to religious activity. This part of the expected pattern emerges only in the South. Nonetheless, it does seem to be true that the incidence of anti-Catholicism in the professional and business community comes to depend more and more reliably upon religious involvement once out of the non-Southern metropolis. For such higher-status people in the metropolis, the less involved were actually more likely to deviate away from the Democrats than were the high church attenders. If we express this reversal as a negative difference in deviations, we find the following progression moving out of the metropolis:

	Deviation [19]	N
Non-Southern metropolis	−9	59
Non-Southern small cities, towns	+3	56
Non-Southern villages and rural areas	+7	52
The South	+9	104

We do not feel that we are rigging a case here in locating the South as a whole at the bottom of the ordering. In part this is so because of the profoundly small-town and rural character of the South. More to the point, however, the order is correct if we consider it less a ranking of population concentrations by size alone, than an order reflecting the proportion of Catholics in the given population. For it is primarily

[19] Deviation here represents the subtraction of the 1960 vote deviations for high church attenders from the same statistic for the low church attenders, all within the white Protestant business and professional strata. Thus Table 6-6 shows high church attenders from these strata deviating 25 per cent away from the Democrats in 1960, with low church attenders deviating only 16 per cent. The difference of 9 per cent is entered above.

in the non-Southern metropolis that Catholics have moved into positions of political power and have made progress toward greater economic equality with members of the Protestant community. In some smaller cities in certain subregions outside the South this evolution has occurred as well, although it has been spotty. In rural areas outside the South, or in the South as a whole (New Orleans excepted), Catholics have been sparsely represented indeed.

The broad picture suggested, then, is this. By and large across the nation where Catholics are either absent or reside in dispersed minorities, the pattern of the anti-Catholic impact was more or less as originally predicted. However, the contribution of education was somewhat mild, and was generally eclipsed in these areas by differences linked to religious involvement: the reaction was to Catholics *as a religious outgroup,* and anti-Catholicism strongly reflected prior religious involvement. Where Catholics were remote and the individual was lukewarm about his Protestantism, the impact tended to be less.

On the other hand, where Catholics reside in large numbers and have come to compete for some of the forms of secular power, the anti-Catholic reaction fell much less clearly along lines of religious involvement in a narrow sense. This was particularly true of the upper middle-class in the non-Southern metropolis, where the Catholic advancement has been most notable. Here, despite the highest education level, the Protestant business and professional community responded in a manner which suggests a threat along a broad front, not simply a challenge to religious orthodoxy. Of course, as soon as the perceived world is split into Catholics and Protestants, the upper strata do not stand alone in the metropolis as suffering some broad secular threat from Catholics; the lower strata have experienced economic competition of this kind for a long time. It is therefore noteworthy when we discover that although outside the South generally the anti-Catholic deviation in 1960 among lower-status irregular church attenders was slight indeed (Table 6-6, entry of −2 per cent), this figure breaks into a significantly negative deviation in the non-Southern metropolis (−11 per cent) and slightly positive, statistically insignificant deviations for the same types of low-status, religiously indifferent people in cities, towns, and villages.[20] As is the case for the upper strata, the lines of

[20] As these signs of anti-Catholic reaction in the non-Southern metropolis accumulate, the reader is cautioned against concluding that there was a "Republican swing" in these urban areas. Such a conclusion would directly contradict what we know to be true, whether we look at aggregate voting statistics or the total structure of our own data. We must remember that these heightened deviations away from the Democrats in 1960 in the metropolis are small and are confined to white Protestants. They

religious involvement predict the anti-Catholic deviation least effectively for the lower strata in the non-Southern metropolis as well. The fact remains, however, that the most striking departure occurs in the business and professional community here, a departure the more striking in a sense because it is forced to work "uphill" against an advanced education.

These findings have an odd ring when couched against theories of the urban metropolis as a melting pot, the focus of secularism and cosmopolitanism. In general, of course, there remains some mild progression of increasing religious involvement as we move from the metropolis to the rural, and with it, some progression of religious intolerance as well. The broad pattern of findings does little to repudiate the view that religion per se is a more focal area of life in the provinces than in the largest urban centers.

But the wrinkles in the pattern serve to remind us of the proposition that intergroup contact does not, in and of itself, reduce intergroup tension: under many common circumstances it can lead to broadened competition. Lenski and others have recently challenged the older view of the city on grounds that the religious subcommunities remain more distinct and vital in metropolitan life than has been commonly supposed. By and large the data we have presented support this view. Subcultural boundaries based on religion do appear to have maintained considerable tone in the metropolis where the groups involved have lived for some time in contact. But the data suggest as well that the mainsprings of antagonism in the contact situation are themselves secularized in a sense. They come to pivot less uniquely upon religious feeling and broaden out across other areas where, of course, competition is occurring. Whatever its original source, the friction becomes less directly religious than subcultural in the broadest sense of the word.

Conclusions

It is worth some effort to keep the 1960 presidential election in perspective. However fascinated we may be by the x-ray of sociopolitical cleavage it provides, we ought not exaggerate the degree to which

---

ignore the strong Catholic movement to the Democrats in precisely these areas as well as a general Democratic trend among Negroes and Jews. Furthermore, they are deviations from an expected vote and not shifts from 1956 voting patterns. Actually some of the smaller deviations away from the Democrats represented here would look like actual gains in Democratic strength *relative to 1956*. Suffice it to say that we are looking now at small underlying wrinkles in the texturing of the 1960 vote and not at the whole cloth.

it has set American politics asunder along religious lines. Even the 1960 data themselves would contest this most strongly: despite our interest in the exceptions, the fact remains that Protestant Democrats were more likely to behave as Democrats than as Protestants, and Catholic Republicans were more likely to behave as Republicans than as Catholics.

It mattered, of course, that Kennedy was not running on a "Catholic platform" and Nixon was not running as a Protestant. Although there were attempts from the sidelines to inject issues which would underscore the religious difference—for example the birth control question—such efforts were artificial and had little popular repercussion. The 1960 contest did not take shape because religious tensions in the society were coming to a head at this particular moment. Rather, the fact that Kennedy emerged when he did was, from a religious point of view, purely accidental. Whatever bitter religious struggles have been moved to the political arena to plague pluralistic democracies, the 1960 election in the United States was of another order. In a sense, it was at most a flash of lightning which illuminated, but only momentarily, a darkened landscape.

To have supposed that this time the dark landscape would not show represented in part wishful thinking and in part a basic misunderstanding of the kinds of discriminations made by a relatively ill-informed electorate. Generally these discriminations strike the intellectual as superficial. It happens that some are socially divisive and some socially integrative. One which is most obviously divisive is the contrasting group memberships of the candidates. This fact in all its simplicity and primitive meaning was among the first to be disseminated about Kennedy.

Even in the heat of the campaign, however, integrative mechanisms could be witnessed. The oft-disparaged mass media must be accorded a prime role here in its communication of other discriminations, some equally superficial but less divisive in cast. There is strong reason to believe, for example, that most of the public had no idea who Kennedy was until the spring of 1960, and that a very large portion first learned of his existence when he was nominated for the Presidency. The initial reactions of Protestant Democrats were particularly interesting, as best we can piece them together from our early interview materials. One subset of Protestant Democrats learned that Kennedy was a nominee without learning that he was a Catholic. These respondents were often well along in the time-honored processes of taking the unknown candidate of one's own party to the bosom before word of the Catholic background reached them; the reaction was one of betrayal. Other Protestant Democrats learned at the outset that their party had nominated a Catholic and were in high dudgeon at the fact. Word of Kennedy's Catholicism traveled fast enough so that by mid-September most Protestant Democrats "knew" and were in considerable torment. One can suppose that had no further information been conveyed to the public, through either a truncation of the campaign or an absence of powerful mass media, the anti-Catholic reaction registered in the 1960 Protestant vote would have been greater.

But gradually the mass media—and the television debates in particular—filled in an image of Kennedy. They did not modify cleavages by convincing Protestants that Catholicism per se was not bad. But they did present a great deal of other information about this man. He was not only a Catholic but was as well (in the public eye from interview material) quick-witted, energetic, and poised. These are traits valued across religious lines and act at the same time to question some of the more garish anti-Catholic stereotypes. Although in totality such perceptions may seem superficial, they are real to the participants, and the fact that such perceptions compete with some success against the initial cognition of the candidate's group membership reveals how superficial this stereotyping can be. Bit by bit, as religiously innocuous information filled in, the Protestant Democrat could come to accept Kennedy primarily as a Democrat, his unfortunate religion notwithstanding. Vote intentions angled away from group lines toward party lines.

We must therefore keep perspective on the significance of the voting act itself. Even though we may try to estimate with some precision the impact of the Kennedy candidacy on the two religious groups, there is no conversion formula to translate these statistics into terms of day-to-day local intergroup antagonism. To the degree that the voter has minimal information, so that beyond basic party loyalties the question devolves to "other things equal, whom do you choose—a member of your own group or a member of some other," the impact registered in the vote is perhaps unduly large.

On the other hand, to the degree that the stark group difference becomes imbedded in a broader process of political choice, a process laden with components irrelevant to the religious cleavage, the primitive power of the group term is muffled. That it is thus imbedded, not only in this election situation but in other situations characteristic of the American scene as well, is a fact of the first water where the overall stability of the system is concerned. Yet the spontaneous burst of hostility which greeted the simple fact of other-group membership is, at the same time, a warning that in the mass electorate the potential for social friction on these bases is far from dead.

CHAPTER 7

Party Loyalty and the Likelihood of Deviating Elections

Donald E. Stokes

In voting research, as any branch of inquiry, knowledge is advanced as much by seeing new problems as by solving old ones. Contemporary voting studies have answered many questions that could only be guessed at a few years ago. Yet any such cumulation of findings brings to the fore a number of "second-generation" problems that could hardly be stated except in terms of the theoretical ideas evolving out of current work. This has especially been true in the voting studies as interest has extended from the population of voters to a population of elections; concepts that could explain a good deal about individual choice inevitably spawned additional questions about elections as total social or political events. This chapter states such a "new" question or problem and draws from historical evidence a preliminary answer, although a sure answer waits for evidence that is not at hand.

The problem can be described briefly as follows. By measuring a limited set of political orientations (among which party loyalty is preeminently important) we are able to state with increasing confidence what the behavior of the American electorate would be in any given election if the vote were to express only the influence of these basic dispositions. But, as we have seen in the preceding chapters, the election returns also reflect the public's reaction to more recent and transitory influences that deflect the vote from what it would have

This chapter appeared originally in the *Journal of Politics*, 24 (November 1962).

been had these short-term factors not intruded on the nation's decision. Therefore, we think of any national election as an interplay of basic dispositions and short-run influences. Yet the freedom of these "disturbing" influences to modify the effects of long-term dispositions is not well understood. Their capacity to do so is not of trivial importance; there have been few presidential elections in the last hundred years that we could not imagine having gone to the loser, had the right combination of short-term factors appeared in time. And yet each election is not merely tossing the coin again; like all strong prejudices, the electorate's basic dispositions have a tremendous capacity to keep people behaving in accustomed ways. The freedom of short-run influences to deflect the vote has an obvious bearing on how well long-standing party loyalties are able to explain a total election outcome. Plainly a closer estimate of the ease with which short-term electoral tides may run to one party or the other would tell a good deal about the importance of party identification in a predictive theory of elections.

The Role of Basic Partisan Dispositions

No element of the political lives of Americans is more impressive than their party loyalties. Our research has amply demonstrated how early partisan identifications take root and how widely they are found in the adult population. Despite the grip of political independence on our civics texts, most Americans freely call themselves Democrats or Republicans when asked, and most of those who say at first that they are Independents will concede some degree of party loyalty under the gentlest urging. If we think of the electorate as spread out along a dimension extending from strong Democrat through Independent to strong Republican, not more than a tenth of the public sees itself at the point of full independence.

In view of the fact that very few Americans have any deep interest in politics, it is a mild paradox that party loyalties should be so widespread. A partial key to this puzzle is that these identifications perform for the citizen an exceedingly useful evaluative function. To the average person the affairs of government are remote and complex, and yet the average citizen is asked periodically to formulate opinions about those affairs. At the very least, he has to decide how he will vote, what choice he will make between candidates offering different programs and very different versions of contemporary political events. In this dilemma, having the party symbol stamped on certain candidates, certain issue positions, certain interpretations of political reality is of great psychological convenience.

Because of this evaluative function, party identification should not be regarded as a simple disposition to vote out of habit for one party or the other. To be sure, there *is* some totally unadorned persistence voting. But for most people the tie between party identification and voting behavior involves subtle processes of perceptual adjustment by which the individual assembles an image of current politics consistent with his partisan allegiance. With normal luck, the partisan voter will carry to the polls attitudes toward the newer elements of politics that support his long-standing bias.

Undoubtedly this perceptual process is seen most melodramatically in popular response to the personal qualities of the presidential candidates. For the millions of Americans identified with a particular party, the candidate bearing the party symbol tends to become more of a lion, his opponent more of a wolf. To take an example that will not excite modern passions, we may suppose that anyone judging the candidates according to the dominant values of American culture, rather than in purely partisan terms, would have found Grover Cleveland a more estimable man than James G. Blaine in the campaign of 1884. Yet we can be sure that the public's actual response to these new presidential personalities was colored almost completely by its prior partisan loyalties, as the small vote swing from 1880 to 1884 suggests.

Therefore, the capacity of party identification to color perceptions holds the key to understanding why the unfolding of new events, the emergence of new issues, the appearance of new political figures fails to produce wider swings of party fortune. To a remarkable extent these swings are damped by processes of selective perception. Because the public so easily finds in new elements of politics the old partisan vices and virtues, our electoral history, as so much else, shows that *plus ça change, plus c'est la même chose.*

And yet the nation's response to a changing political world is not wholly governed by fixed party loyalties. Some elements of political reality not agreeing with these loyalties will get through the perceptual screen raised in the partisan voter. A war, a sharp recession, a rash of scandal will leave their mark on all shades of partisans, though the mark will not be deep enough to change the votes of more than some. What is more, as Chapter 6 has just shown us, other identifications will at times lead the voter to perceive political objects in a way that contradicts his partisan bias. As they become relevant to politics, identifications of a racial or national or religious or class nature may counter the perceptual effects of long-term partisan loyalties in large segments of the electorate.

This interplay of basic orientations and transient factors underlies the voters' decisions on election day. What is the relative weight of these influences in determining the total vote? What is the freedom of short-term forces to modify the influence of basic dispositions? Current measurements of partisan dispositions indicate that the Republicans could expect about 46 per cent of the vote if the nation expressed only its fixed party loyalties at the polls. Yet as a minority party the Republicans won popular majorities in 1952 and 1956. How probable were these deviating elections in view of the country's underlying partisanship? Given the distribution of party identification found today—or any other distribution of party loyalties—what is the likelihood that the minority party will win?

The Probability of Deviating Elections

Putting the question this way inevitably implies some sort of probability model, and one will be made explicit here in terms of an idealized conception of electoral history. Under this conception the electoral process will be regarded as repeatedly sampling a universe of short-term forces. At each election a sample of such forces is drawn, and the two-party division of the vote deflected according to the strength and partisan direction of the forces that have fallen in the sample.[1] The sum of the forces in the samples drawn in 1956 and 1960 favored the Republicans, although not all the terms contributing to these sums were pro-Republican, especially in the latter year. Each of the samples that might possibly be drawn would deflect the two-party division of the vote by some given amount in a given direction; hence, over all the possible samples that might be drawn (that is, over all possible configurations of short-term influences) these deflections define a sampling *distribution*. We would naturally take the mean or expected value of this distribution to be zero or, if its values are to be mapped into percentages of the two-party vote, we would associate this mean with the division of the vote expected from party

[1] Presumably successive samples are not drawn entirely independently, since some short-run influences carry over from one election to the next, as Eisenhower's appeal carried over from 1952 to 1956. The lack of full independence does not bias the estimates we will obtain below, although it does have the interesting consequence of making the *conditional* probability of a deviating election, given the immediate electoral past, somewhat different from the unconditional probabilities we seek.

identification. To do anything else would be to assume that over all possible configurations of short-term factors the electoral process will deal more kindly with one party than the other.[2] The more difficult problem, the one that holds the key to the probability of a deviating election, is to reach an estimate of the *variance* of this sampling distribution.

The connection between the variance of such a distribution and the probability of a deviating election can be brought out by a simple figure. Figure 7-1 shows three such idealized distributions, drawn over a scale representing the Republican percentage of the two-party vote for President. Each distribution has the same mean—46 per cent, in accord with our empirical estimate of the expected Republican vote in the present era. And each distribution has the form of a normal probability function.[3] These three hypothetical distributions differ only as to their variances: the variance of *A* is of intermediate size whereas the variance of *B* is small and of *C* large. As is true for any continuous probability function, the probabilities associated with these distributions are interpreted by areas under the curves. Thus for a given distribution the probability of the Republican Party winning a majority of votes is represented by the shaded area under the curve that is to the right of the point of equal division. Because of the differences in the variances, the size of this area (and the probability of the Republicans winning) is very different for the three distributions. In the case of distribution *A*, roughly a third of the total area under the curve lies to the right of 50 per cent; in the case of *B* about a tenth;

[2] Some may think such an assumption warranted. In view of the maintenance of effective two-party competition since the Civil War, can we not say that the electoral process has been unexpectedly kind to the minority party? Two points should be made in this connection. First, because our attention here is fixed on deviating elections we have excluded those rare elections in which the strength of the minority party is restored by a change in the underlying distribution of party identifications, as it was not in the Eisenhower or Kennedy elections. Second, our computation of an expected division of the vote has already discounted the majority party's strength in certain respects. In particular we have allowed for the fact that the historical circumstances that give a party a majority of party identifiers usually attract to it a number of people who are only marginally interested in politics and relatively unlikely to vote. Certainly the wave of new recruits to the Democratic Party during the Great Depression and the Roosevelt New Deal included many people of this type who are infrequent voters today. Our method of computing expected strength at the polls has already applied this penalty to the Democrats.

[3] The assumption of normality is not gratuitous but is well supported by the form of the empirical distributions to be examined below. The test of normality applied to these distributions is described in M. G. Kendall, *Advanced Theory of Statistics* (London: Charles Griffin, 1948, Vol. 2), p. 105.

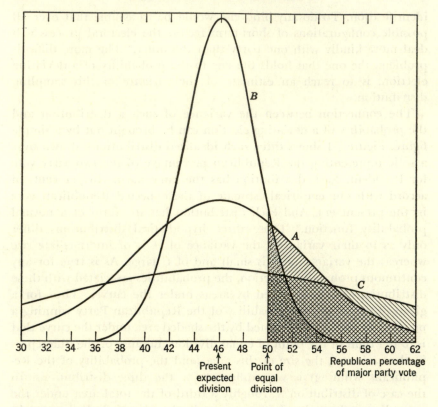

Figure 7-1. Relation of variance of theoretical distributions to probability of a deviating election.

of *C* not much less than half. Interpreting these areas as probabilities, we would say that the chance of a deviating election under *A* is about .3; under *B* about .1; and under *C* almost .5. Therefore, the meaning of the 4 per cent difference between the expected Republican share of the vote and an equal division would be grossly different according to which of these distributions has the closest fit with the real world. Undoubtedly *B* and *C* are extremes. The electoral process does not give the minority party a trifling chance of winning; neither does it treat each election as a fair toss of a coin. Reality lies somewhere between.

Just where is a question on which the historical record is not moot. To be sure, exact estimates cannot be made because here, as so often is true, significant measurement is hampered by the extreme niggardliness with which history has furnished cases of an event that involves a whole political system, as the choice of an American President does. Nevertheless, the evidence of history can be used to fix an upper bound for the variance of our theoretical distribution and, hence, for the probability of a deviating election.

Seen in terms of our model, past deviations of the vote about some central value are deflections of the party division by successive samples of short-term forces. The central value we would use for any given election if past measurements of basic dispositions were available would, of course, be the division of the vote expected on the basis of the distribution of party loyalties at that time. But with these measurements forever lost, a conservative alternative is to take the mean value of the party division in the period, say, from 1892 to 1960 and to attribute *all* the variation of the vote about this central value to the work of short-run factors.[4] This procedure is conservative in the sense that it tends to inflate the variance estimate we seek and, with it, our estimate of the probability of a deviating election.

The details of this procedure are suggested by Figure 7-2a, in which the Republican proportion of the two-party vote in the elections from 1892 to 1960 is distributed along a percentage scale.[5] The mean of this distribution is roughly 51 per cent, and its variance is obtained by calculating the deviation of the party division from this central value in each election year. The division in 1928, for example, was about 8 per cent more Republican than the mean. The theoretical normal probability distribution we have fitted to this empirical distribution is drawn above the scale.

Calculating deviations about the mean *for the whole period* tends to exaggerate the magnitude of short-term influences on the vote. If we had for each election an expected value based on the distribution of party loyalties at the time, the average deviation would be somewhat reduced. For example, the expected Republican share of the vote in the late 1920's undoubtedly was higher than 51 per cent and the deflection due to transient factors in 1928 less than 8 per cent. Of course we cannot recover the true expected values with any precision, but our estimates can be improved by assuming that the realignment

[4] The choice of 1892 as a starting point was prompted by the fact that the variability and cyclical pattern of the vote in the first generation following the Civil War differed a good deal from what they have been since.

[5] Corrected figures are used for the two-party division of the vote in 1912 and 1924 to take account of the fact that a third party in each of these years cut deeply into the strength of the losing major party. The details of these corrections, which are based on the two-party division of the congressional vote, are available from the author on request.

of party loyalties brought on by the Great Depression divides the whole period into an era of Republican dominance, extending from 1892 to 1928, and an era of Democratic dominance from 1932 to 1960. This assumption leads naturally to the use of a separate mean for each era and the measurement of deviations from these more historically realistic central values.

The consequence of this change is suggested by Figure 7-2b, which shows the empirical distribution for the period of Republican dominance. The central value from which deviations are measured is now

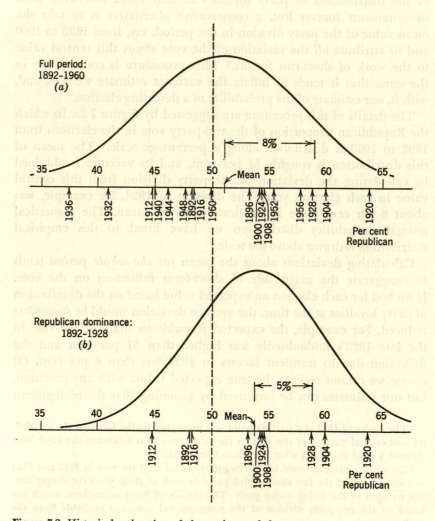

Figure 7-2. Historical estimation of the variance of the two-party vote for President.

about 54 per cent rather than 51 per cent. The magnitude of the deviations is, on the average, reduced. In 1928, for example, it is reduced from 8 per cent to about 5 per cent. Because of this average reduction, the effect of breaking the whole period in two is to lessen the variance of the vote attributed to short-term factors and, with it, the estimated probability of a deviating election. As a result, this refinement—or any other that is faithful to historical realities—leaves undisturbed the upper bound for the probability of a deviating election obtained by the original procedure. It will indeed be clear presently that this refinement has little effect on our probability estimates.

When the variance of our theoretical sampling distribution is estimated from these historical data, it turns out not to look very different from the first of the three hypothetical distributions drawn in Figure 7-1. The accompanying estimate of the probability of a deviating election is about .28 if deflections of the vote are measured in terms of the mean of the whole period and slightly less if they are measured in terms of the separate means for the eras of Republican and Democratic dominance. Therefore, under the assumptions of the model, the probability is less than three in ten that a minority party, faced at a given election with an expected deficit of 4 per cent, can poll a majority of votes; the chance of a deviating election occurring under the present division of party loyalties is very much less than even.[6]

However, the uses of this simple apparatus extend beyond existing conditions. Having fixed the variance of our theoretical sampling distribution, we may use the model to estimate the probability of a deviating election if the expected division of the vote were other than that derived from the distribution of party loyalties found in the 1950's and early 1960's. These estimates under other assumptions about the departure of the expected division of the vote from 50 per cent are given in Table 7-1. The table presents estimates based on both procedures for establishing the variance of the sampling distribution, although the two sets of estimates diverge very little.

A word should be said about the Electoral College. A popular majority is not the same as a majority of Electors, and if a deviating election is defined as one in which the minority party captures the White House, we need to consider the impact of the Electoral College.

---

[6] This conclusion depends, of course, on the assumption that the average fluctuation of the party division will not differ substantially from what it has been from 1892 to 1960.

TABLE 7-1

Estimated Probabilities of a Deviating Election

Difference between expected vote and 50 per cent	0	1	2	3	Present ↓ 4	5	6	7	8
Estimates using mean for whole period	.50	.44	.39	.33	.28	.24	.20	.16	.13
Estimates using separate means for eras of party dominance	.50	.44	.38	.32	.27	.23	.18	.13	.10

It should frankly be said that the relation between popular and electoral votes introduces some additional uncertainty into our problem. Any close examination of this relation in the modern period of party competition shows that it has been somewhat variable.[7] On the other hand, such an examination gives little support to the idea that the Democrats have to win more than a popular majority to capture the Presidency, despite the familiar lore on this point. If anything, the reverse is true, although the points of discrimination in the popular and electoral vote are very close. How nearly these points coincide can be seen by ignoring all extreme values and confining our attention to the five closest elections in the past seventy years, those of 1892, 1896, 1916, 1948, and 1960. When this is done the Republican proportion of the popular vote associated with 50 per cent of the electoral vote is found to be 50.4 per cent. A fair judgment of the historical evidence is that the variability of the relation between popular and electoral votes gives our estimate of the probability of a deviating election a limited additional degree of error without biasing the estimate either for or against the Republicans.

Conclusion

If the supporting argument runs true, the estimated likelihood of a deviating election bears out the importance of partisan dispositions in a predictive theory of elections. At the state or local level party

[7] These comments on the Electoral College are based on the regression of the electoral vote on the popular vote in the period from 1892 to 1960.

loyalties are so frequently all-important in deciding whether a Democrat or Republican will win that they can hardly be overlooked. Most lesser political units of the American commonwealth are one-party or modified one-party areas. But at the national level, especially in presidential elections, party allegiance is sometimes felt to be a limited tool of analysis. The view of some observers is that everything depends on the sample of short-term forces drawn in a particular election, and that nothing of real value is to be learned by measuring the electorate's long-term partisan dispositions. From this it is only a short step to the idea that party allegiance is a purely nominal attachment of slight motivational significance to the voter, at least in choosing a President.

No one who has taken a careful look at the data of voting research can still believe that party identification is of slight significance for *individual* behavior. But voting in presidential elections is not completely determined by party allegiance, and so long as it is not we may ask how likely the electorate is to give a majority of votes to the minority party. If the likelihood proved high, party identification would lose a good deal of its efficacy for the prediction or explanation of a total election outcome, even though it remained a variable of great power for predicting or explaining individual voting choice. Therefore, the probability estimate given here is implicitly a judgment about the appropriate framework for analyzing the national election decision, a judgment confirming the importance of party identification in carrying one candidate to the White House and returning the other to some lesser office or private life.

CHAPTER 8

Information Flow and the Stability
of Partisan Attitudes

Philip E. Converse

The low level of public information about politics has been documented with monotony ever since sample survey techniques developed
several decades ago. Although the critic of public opinion studies is
fond of citing Pareto, De Maistre, LeBon, and other anti-democrats
of the nineteenth century to show that "we knew this all along," it
is worth remembering that these elite theorists represented but one
side of a debate, and it was, furthermore, a debate that they lost. It is
ironic that enough data to document their premises about "the common
man" have come along only after the conclusion argued from these
premises—that mass democracy was not viable—has lost a good deal of
its impact.

This irony has been compounded by a second prime finding of
public opinion studies. Not only is the electorate as a whole quite
uninformed, but it is the least informed members within the electorate
who seem to hold the critical balance of power, in the sense that
alternations in governing party depend disproportionately on shifts
in their sentiment. In one form of accounting, of course, the stable
vote has equal weight with the shifting vote in any given election.
Nonetheless, it is easy to take the stable vote for granted. What commands attention as the governor of party success at the polls, and
hence administrations and policies, is the changing vote. And "shift-

This chapter appeared originally in the *Public Opinion Quarterly,* **26** (Winter 1962).

ing" or "floating" voters tend to be those whose information about politics is relatively impoverished.

Although most major investigations of voting behavior have converged on this finding in one vocabulary or another, the evidence mustered in support has not been striking. Of course any data would be disillusioning if one imagines that an electorate is definitively split into two segments, one made up of fairly informed voters who never shift parties, and the other of uninformed voters who account for any electoral change. This is, of course, not the intended picture. There are very highly informed voters—should Walter Lippmann be cited?—who shift parties at occasional junctures. And there are as well myriads of extremely uninformed voters who have never crossed party lines. Instead we think at most in terms of potentials and probabilities; susceptibility to party shifting seems higher for some types of voters than for others, and in any given shift between two elections, the hypothesis argues that the less involved and less informed voters are disproportionately represented.

Even with such an amendment, however, proof of the hypothesis has generally been rather weak. Indeed, a recent intensive review of the major voting studies asserts that none of the published data has adequately supported the notion of a "floating voter," much less any hypothesis as to his character.[1] Part of the problem has been that the dependent variable (vote shifts from election to election) is a dynamic one whereas most studies have either been single-interview studies or panels nestled in a single campaign period. On common-sense grounds, individuals who vacillate in forming their voting decisions during the campaign period are likely to contribute disproportionately to such interelection voting shifts as do occur, and the Lazarsfeld Erie County study in 1940 showed that these waverers tended to be the less involved and less informed.[2] However, the authors hesitated to generalize the finding to interelection vote changes. More recent studies have asserted the more inclusive version of the hypothesis quite baldly, basing the judgment in the clearest cases upon recall of a previous vote.[3] The data shown, however, usually consist of weak correlations at best.

[1] H. Daudt, *Floating Voters and the Floating Vote: A Critical Analysis of American and English Election Studies*, Leiden, Holland: H. E. Stenfert Kroese N. V., 1961.

[2] P. Lazarsfeld, B. Berelson, and H. Gaudet, *The People's Choice*, New York: Columbia University Press, 1944, pp. 69 ff.

[3] Almost all the major studies might be cited. A partial list that indicates variety of national setting and emphasizes interelection partisan change, as well as campaign vacillation, includes M. Janowitz and D. Marvick, *Competitive Pressures and Demo-*

In our own sequence of Survey Research Center studies we have also been impressed with the amount of presumptive evidence for the general hypothesis, once again without definitive long-term panel tables. It has been a standard static finding, for example, that more involved voters are more strongly identified with one of the major parties and hence could be supposed to have a higher probability of remaining faithful to it over time. A similar mild correlation exists between indices of political involvement and recall of party fidelity in voting. Voters who split their tickets have been found to be less politically involved than straight party voters.[4] A relatively strong negative correlation emerged between a scale measuring sophistication of political conceptions and the crossing of normal party lines in the 1956 presidential vote, although here once again the evidence of interelection shifts in party is presumptive.[5]

Belief in the broad hypothesis has been stronger than actual evidence might warrant in part because of obvious measurement problems, all of which act in the direction of weakening positive results. For example, if we try to establish the fact of a vote shift from the individual's recall of his next prior vote, we are at the mercy of the accuracy of his report. The same theory which predicts that the less involved are more susceptible to party change suggests that the less involved will also give less accurate accounts of past political behavior. For simple psychological reasons, we would expect them to distort past behavior in the direction of current preference. Such distortions build in a false impression of stability; and if they are more frequent among the less involved, then they act to weaken empirical results in the most direct way.

Similarly the frailties of involvement measures can affect the clarity of findings.[6] People usually shift parties in a state of what is, for them,

cratic Consent: An Interpretation of the 1952 Presidential Election (Ann Arbor, Mich.: University of Michigan Institute of Public Administration, 1956); R. Milne and H. Mackenzie, Marginal Seat, 1955 (London: The Hansard Society for Parliamentary Government, 1958); A. Girard and J. Stoetzel, "Le Comportement Electoral et le Mecanisme de la Decision," Le Referendum de Septembre et les Elections de Novembre 1958 (Paris: Librarie Armand Colin, 1960).

    [4] A. Campbell and W. E. Miller, "The Motivational Basis of Straight and Split Ticket Voting, American Political Science Review, 51, No. 2 (1957).

    [5] A. Campbell, P. E. Converse, W. E. Miller, and D. E. Stokes, The American Voter, New York: John Wiley and Sons, 1960, p. 264.

    [6] It must be noted, of course, that the hypothesis has its greatest interest when the independent variable is political comprehension or political information rather than political involvement per se. We tend to use involvement as a surrogate for comprehension because it is more readily measured, and because it is a fair assumption that

TABLE 8-1

The Association between Stability or Change in Presidential Voting over Time and Political Information Level, 1956–1960
(in per cent)

Information Level *	Voted Twice and for Same Party (N = 712)	Voted Twice but Shifted Parties (N = 207)	Failed to Vote in One of Two Elections † (N = 220)	Twice a Nonvoter † (N = 201)
High	49	33	19	11
Medium	32	32	35	17
Low	19	35	46	72
Total	100	100	100	100

* By and large, knowledge of the more obvious items of political information turns out to show cumulative scale properties for a cross section of the national population. This is a preliminary measure based on a scaling of items concerning such knowledge about the 1960 presidential candidates as the region from which they came and knowledge about which party controlled the 1960 Congress.

† The table is restricted to individuals who were eligible to vote in both the 1956 and 1960 elections, where the eligible include all noninstitutionalized adult citizens over twenty-one.

relative political excitement. Such a transient surge of excitement, if it occurs among people who normally pay little attention to elections and still less to politics outside the campaign, has little to do with political involvement as a durable, year-to-year concern about things political. Yet it is likely that such excitement registers in our measures as involvement and further blurs findings concerning the floating voter.

Two- and four-year longitudinal studies of the national electorate have served to confirm such methodological suspicions and to throw more light on the character of interelection vote shifts. Table 8-1, employing panel information for the 1956 and 1960 presidential elec-

---

there is a high correlation between involvement (motivation to attend to information about matters political) and breadth of comprehension about what is going on in politics. One of the better estimates of this relationship is presented in Campbell et al., *op. cit.*, p. 252. The uninvolved voter is, by and large, the uninformed voter, and we shall presume this loose equation frequently in the course of this paper.

tions, lends rather clear support to the standard floating voter hypothesis. The final column, involving persistent nonvoters, has no bearing on vote change in this period and is inserted merely as an informative anchor to the table. The voters in the two central columns fashioned the shift in the national vote division, 1956–1960, and they compare quite poorly in political information with the stable partisans of the first column. A similar table employing a summary measure of durable political involvement expressed over the entire four-year period gives very comparable results.

The broad normative implications of the floating voter hypothesis have been frequently discussed. It is less our purpose here to repeat these discussions than to suggest a refinement in the hypothesis itself. Although this modification does not render earlier treatments obsolete, it does have some interesting implications of its own. This modification can be seen as a simple logical deduction from the general view of mass voting phenomena as developed in the preceding chapters.

In order to make this deduction apparent, let us restate our general view. We have argued that if no other factors intervened in a systematic way, the two-party division of the popular vote at a national level would remain constant from election to election, reflecting nothing more than this underlying division of loyalties. Usually, however, perturbations or oscillations of the actual vote around this underlying division are fashioned by forces associated with the immediate election—such transient factors as Eisenhower's great personal attractiveness to the public, or Kennedy's Catholicism.[7] In other words, identification may be seen as an inertia or momentum component which determines the partisan direction of any individual decision *unless there are short-term forces in the immediate situation acting with sufficient strength in an opposite partisan direction to deflect the momentum and shift the behavior.*

If we wish to locate the floating voter in the general scheme, it is worth pursuing the Newtonian metaphor one step further. Quite obviously, the oscillations of the actual vote around the constant baseline are, by the hypothesis, attributable disproportionately (although not completely, of course) to shifts in short-term evaluations on the part of less informed voters. Now "mass" is not entirely wild as an analogue for information level, in the sense that the highly informed voter operates with a large storage of political lore, and the

---

[7] It is not hard to see this model as a special case of what Lewin discussed as "quasi-stationary social equilibria." See Kurt Lewin, in Dorwin Cartwright, editor, *Field Theory in Social Science* (New York: Harper, 1951, pp. 202 ff.).

uninformed voter is characterized by a poor retention of past political information. Our repeated observations of the staggering differences in information level in the electorate are, then, observations of the great differences in this "mass" from voter to voter.[8] And *the probability that any given voter will be sufficiently deflected in his partisan momentum to cross party lines in a specified election varies directly as a function of the strength of short-term forces toward the opposing party and varies inversely as a function of the mass of stored information about politics.* The latter part of this proposition is, of course, no more than a restatement of the floating voter hypothesis.

A Puzzle and a Prediction

As we have already implied, our data permit us to determine for any of the elections that we have observed which citizens were defecting and hence were responsible for the departure of the national vote division from its underlying constant baseline. Furthermore, our general argument would predict that the magnitude of the correlation between party identification and the actual vote for any election, being an index of the gross amount of defection from party, should vary within the population as a direct function of political comprehension or involvement. In the 1952 and 1956 presidential election data we were able to observe some faint variation of this sort, although the relationship was more ragged than anticipated. Subsequent methodological demonstrations have provided one answer as to why this pattern of variation is not stronger.[9]

Accepting the fact that there is a partially obscured relationship is, however, where our puzzle begins. For if the relationship was

[8] From a psychological point of view, any cognitive modeling of these propositions could rapidly capitalize on the many hypotheses concerning the development of structure and interconnectedness as the mass of information increases. For our purposes here, however, the spare notion of mass itself suffices. An explanation of this rule, employing our general theoretical framework, has been presented in Chapter 3.

[9] Not only is it true that less involved people recall their prior votes with greater distortion, but they also are relatively labile in their responses to items concerning current partisan identification. If we look at turnover tables on measures of party identification drawn from the same respondents after a two-year interval, subdivided into thirds on political involvement, we find that despite no significant changes in the marginals, the correlation (Pearson product-moment) for the most involved third is over .9, is over .8 for those only moderately involved, and is in the .7 range for the weakly involved. Hence the reports of the least involved hide instability in voting, for even the underlying loyalties "float" quite considerably.

ragged for presidential materials in 1952 and 1956, the picture was even murkier for the 1958 congressional elections. Here, if we subdivided the lower end of the involvement continuum somewhat more finely, it appeared that the expected relationship was actually reversed; the least involved were less likely to have departed from their party in the 1958 voting than were the somewhat more involved!

Now we know several interesting distinctions between presidential and off-year congressional elections. For example, the oscillations of the actual vote over time around the constant term reflecting the underlying division of party loyalties seem weaker in amplitude in congressional voting than in presidential voting (see Figure 10-1). This phenomenon has led to one of the most reliable rules of thumb in the game of mass voting statistics; that is, the party which has won the Presidency in any given quadrennial election is almost certain to lose ground in Congress in the ensuing off-year election. This rule has been broken only once since 1860, although it has remained an "empirical rule" without solid theoretical explanation.

An explanation of this rule, employing our general theoretical framework has been presented in Chapter 3. This explanation has resolved quite well one of the older riddles facing the political scientist. However, it would not in itself lead us to expect any reversal of the gradient of magnitude of the party-vote correlation in the off-year election. Nor does it explain (although intuitively the reason may be apparent enough) why it is that even in presidential years when floating voters go to the polls the congressional vote is more nearly a party vote, with less crossing of party lines by individual voters than is the accompanying presidential vote.[10]

We would have no difficulty guessing that the congressional vote in a presidential year is more nearly a party vote in large measure because the flow of information about the congressional candidates is a good deal weaker than that for the two presidential candidates. Voters go to the polls primarily to vote for President in a presidential year,

---

[10] The clearer "party vote" at the individual level contributes to the phenomenon of a two-party congressional vote showing oscillations of a smaller amplitude even in years of presidential elections. In the presidential year, the congressional vote summed nationally tends to fall between the baseline set by the constant loyalty term and the direction in which the actual presidential vote has swung. Another major source of this muffled variation is the simple aggregation of voting units at the congressional level. In some races, an attractive Democrat induces Republican defections whereas in others a more attractive Republican wins an unusual vote. Cumulation over three-hundred-odd congressional races will find many local swings of the vote balancing one another out. For a further discussion of these relative oscillations and their sources, see Chapter 11.

and have been supplied by the media with a great deal more information about the presidential candidates. Democrats who were seduced to an Eisenhower vote in 1956 had a choice at lower levels of the ballot, either to continue with a straight Republican ticket or to switch back to their normal Democratic choices. Some Democrats chose one way and some the other, and the inevitable result was a national congressional vote less extremely Republican than the Eisenhower vote, yet more Republican than a straight party vote would have been.

The same conditions of low information mark the off-year congressional voting as well. Indeed this is the source of turnout reduction in what we have called the "low-stimulus election." In a presidential election the public is so massively bombarded by information about the two presidential aspirants that only a remote and indifferent citizen could fail to absorb some meaningful items of information about each candidate. The actual flow of information about local candidates for the national Congress, on the other hand, is extremely weak.[11]

The short-term forces mentioned above that either reinforce partisanship or deflect the voter from his normal partisan course obviously depend on the flow of current information. Something of a ceiling is set on the strength of these forces by the volume of information flow. Other things equal, both the individual rates of defection from party and the amplitude of the vote oscillations will be limited if the flow of information is weak. If the flow of information is strong, no particular prediction is safe, in the sense that the partisan valences of the incoming information may be so varied that net pressures toward change are weak, or in the sense that other canceling processes may arise between individuals whose current reactions polarize. If the flow of information is weak, however, very potent limits on defections and vote oscillation are established. And, most important, if there is no new information input at all, there will be no defection and no oscillation; the vote will be a pure party vote. The latter deduction is more interesting than might appear.

11 In 1958, when there was no presidential ballyhoo to occupy newspaper space, we initiated an analysis of newspaper content relating to local congressional candidates campaigning for re-election. The project was rapidly dropped because examination of newspapers even after the campaign was well under way showed that information about such candidates was printed only sporadically and then was usually buried in such a remote section of the paper that the item would go unheeded by all but the more avid readers of political news. It is no wonder that data that we have collected over the years show a large portion of citizens who fail to be aware of their congressional candidates as individuals at all.

The ultimate information intake of the voter is limited in two directions: (1) by the volume of output of the formal and informal systems of political communication in the society, and (2) by the voter's motivation to attend to political communications, once some flow exists. As we have seen there is systematic variation in output volume between presidential and off-year elections as well as between various levels of office. There is obviously systematic variation across individuals in the motivational term as well. Quite specifically, there is a strong correlation between the mass of stored political information and the motivation to monitor communication systems for additional current information. The highly involved voter draws a much larger sample of the current information flow than does the uninvolved voter.

We can see at once, then, that the very uninvolved voters, who we have come to expect will tend to "float" politically, present us with something of a paradox in this regard. On the one hand, such voters show a high susceptibility to short-term change in partisan attitudes *provided that any new information reaches them at all*. On the other hand, when the flow of information through the society is weak, these are the individuals who are *most* likely to experience no new information intake, and hence are individuals *least likely to show changes in patterns of behavior*, if indeed they are constrained to behave at all.[12]

It should be stressed that our propositions do little to disturb the basic floating voter hypothesis associating "mass" with partisan stability. If we order voters on a continuum of increased stored "mass," we have only to imagine that the gradient of current information intake, although positively sloped as well, increases less steeply than the stored mass itself, in order to preserve the flavor of the basic prediction.[13] The modification occurs at the lower end of the involve-

---

[12] One might wonder why individuals with no new relevant information should ever stir themselves to vote, but it is clear that they do, although quite naturally at lower rates of turnout. Party loyalties, along with generalized values concerning citizen duty, appear to be sufficient stimuli. A concrete example is the Nebraska woman who considered herself a strong Republican and voted with some regularity. Probed in 1960 as to her political perceptions, she displayed no awareness of any current political issues or figures. The lone shred of political content came when she was asked what she disliked about the Democratic Party: "I've never liked them ever since they got rid of Prohibition way back. I don't just know what the parties have been up to lately."

[13] This is a crude simplification for the sake of brevity. In the more elaborated model that underlies the discussion the partisanship of different communications and communication channels is taken more explicitly into account. These, along with some commonplace psychological propositions, threaten if anything to "overaccount" for increasing stability rather than to "underaccount" for it.

ment continuum. That is, let us suppose that along the abscissa of a coordinate system respondents are arrayed in terms of enduring political involvement, and that this array is a very good surrogate for arrays in terms of (1) current information intake and (2) mass of stored information from the past. If stability of partisan attitudes were to be plotted along the ordinate, then our propositions would predict a very sudden "step change" at the lowest levels of involvement, from perfect stability where information input is zero, dropping precipitously to a minimum just above the zero point. Beyond this minimum, of course, stability would increase as a function of involvement.

Since we obviously have not monitored all the intake of political information for our respondents during any political campaign, empirical tests to which we might put these predictions are certain to be crude. However, we have traditionally asked our respondents after each campaign whether or not they had listened to any political broadcasts on radio or television, or had read any political articles in newspapers or magazines. Although such questions fail to cover the sector of informal social communication about politics, they do cover the major mass media and should provide a rough index of intake during the campaign, an index superior for our purposes to traditional measures of political involvement.

We wished to avoid the body of data which had first stimulated our thinking so we returned to data collected from an entirely independent sample of the nation in connection with the 1952 election. For measures of stability of partisan attitudes we employed two rather different indices. The first had to do with the rate of turnover between the statement of vote intentions prior to the election and the actual voting behavior. A high correlation would indicate high stability of intentions, a lower correlation relative instability. Since the ultimate voting act consisted in a Republican vote, a Democratic vote, or a failure to vote, it was inconvenient to consider any respondents who were unclear as to their vote intention before the election. Thus a three-by-three table could be constructed, and a rank-order (tau-beta) correlation computed for it within subsets of the population, according to whether no media were used or some higher number. Since there might be some question as to the effect of differences in proportions of nonvoters upon the correlation, a comparable coefficient was also calculated for the two-by-two table reflecting constancy or change in choice of candidates. These are obviously not independent tests.

The second portion of the test had to do with the correlation between party identification and final vote. For the theoretical reasons given above, a low rate of defection from party (a high party-vote

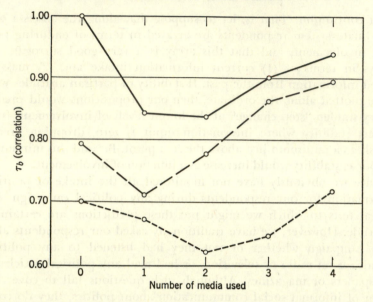

Figure 8-1. Measures of attitude stability, by number of mass media that respondent monitored for political information during the 1952 campaign. *Key:* The solid line represents the 2 × 2 table, party intention by party choice. The dashed line represents the 3 × 3 table, vote intention by vote. The dotted line indicates party identification by vote.

correlation) should reflect high attitude stability whereas a low correlation should reflect relative instability under the short-term forces of this particular election. The second test once again is not independent of the first, having been performed on the same units of analysis. However, their distribution is somewhat different for the two tests, and in this sense some weight is added by the second set of computations.

Despite the crudity of the measures the accompanying chart indicates that the predicted curve did indeed emerge very clearly.[14] Furthermore, the same phenomenon has been visible at other points in our data. For example, it can be shown that the relatively small portion of the population that failed to see any of the television debates between Kennedy and Nixon in 1960 was made up of voters less likely to have revised their voting intentions before the final decision than were

[14] Although the minimum in the test involving party identification is farther to the right than predicted, it must be remembered that the measurement difficulties described above—the tendency of the most weakly involved to bring their statements of party loyalty into line with current vote—would affect this particular test in this fashion. The other tests are true panel tests.

people who watched the debates. The rank-order correlation between vote intention and vote in the two-by-two case for nonwatchers whom we had interviewed before the debates was .96, but for the watchers it was .89. In the three-by-three case, taking into account intentions as to whether or not one would vote, the correlation was .88 among nonwatchers but only .64 among watchers. Although the first of these two comparisons is relatively weak, further investigation shows that the only nonwatchers who changed their choice of candidate between the predebate period and the election fell in a subset of nonwatchers who distinguished themselves by indicating to our interviewers that they had not watched the debates because of some mechanical barrier (they worked a night shift, their television set was broken, and the like). Some of these people may have heard the debates on the radio; in any event, they stand as the most involved subset that can be isolated among nonwatchers. Among the remaining majority of nonwatchers (who either said that they were too uninterested in politics to watch the debates or else failed to give a reason for their inattention), there was no change at all in vote intention, the correlation thereby being 1.00 in the two-by-two case (N of 52 voters). As indicated, this second subset of nonwatchers was the less politically involved of the two, and by the simple floating voter hypothesis should have been the more unstable. Thus throughout these debate materials in 1960 we find evidence of the newly predicted reversal; the more remote the respondent was from the flow of information represented by the debates, the more stable his vote intention, despite the general correlation within the large set of watchers (80 per cent of the population) between partisan stability and political involvement.

In sum, then, our predictions are confirmed in several bodies of data. And their parent propositions serve to explain our initial puzzles. That is, we can now understand why in the off-year congressional vote the gradient of correlations between party identification and vote should show some reversal, with the least involved being more likely to follow normal behavior patterns than the more involved who do manage to pick up some new information from the weaker flow. Of course, the original reversal was not strong. It did not suggest that the more involved were *more* likely to defect in the off-year than in the presidential year. Overall, the amount of defection was notably reduced relative to the presidential year voting. This fact, as well as the reversal of gradients, is embraced by simple recognition of the weaker information flow.

Second, we have thrown new light on the indifferent empirical confirmation that the floating voter hypothesis has tended to receive. In this regard we may point out that the number of people involved in our "no-media" data points was few (for the 1952 test, an N of 22 in the two-by-two case, 92 in the three-by-three case). Normally in crude divisions of a sample by involvement the investigator would lose such no-media cases from sight in the larger number of uninvolved who are represented on the media scale as having received some little information. This adulteration of the highly unstable slight-information people with a set of perfectly stable no-information people would inevitably cloud the relationship, although not sufficiently either to obscure it completely or to betray the underlying curvilinearity.

Discussion

A question frequently posed is: How large is the floating vote? From our point of view, the question is unanswerable in this form, presuming as it does an unrealistic division of the electorate into two camps, floaters and nonfloaters. As we have observed, the matter is one of differential susceptibility to partisan change, and hence we must think in terms of gradients rather than a sharp dichotomy. Even in these terms, however, an analogous question may be posed concerning the susceptibility of a mass public to swings in partisan voting patterns of greater or lesser magnitude in response to varying short-term forces.

In the course of this presentation we have taken for granted one factor that is, in the larger view, itself a variable—the aggregate development of partisan loyalties in an electorate. We have explored elsewhere the implications of the fact that partisan loyalties are less strongly developed in some segments of a society than in others, with young voters and rural populations as cases in point.[15] There are, furthermore, interesting cross-national variations in the development of such loyalties,[16] and it seems clear if fairly obvious that the mere passage of time is an important factor in the jelling of deep partisan identifications in large portions of a mass population. When democratic systems are newly launched or when their traditional party structures have been shattered by war, some time must elapse before stabilizing loyalties are developed or redeveloped.

In a system where partisan loyalties are fully developed, however, the volume of information flow can be seen as an important governor upon the magnitude of oscillations in party fortunes. In the United

[15] Campbell et al., *op. cit.*, pp. 402–440, 497–498.
[16] These will be explored in Chapters 13 and 14.

States of the 1960's, our modification of the floating voter hypothesis may appear to be of limited significance, simply because of the meager proportion of voters who fall in the "no media" cell where presidential campaigns are concerned. In 1952 less than 2 per cent of the voters, or 6 per cent of the potential electorate, were so classified. On the other hand, it can be argued that in times past (as well as for off-year elections currently) this proportion must have been very much larger, given what we know of changes in conditions of information flow in the past century. In a historical perspective, then, not to mention one which looks toward less developed nations, the refinement is by no means trivial.

The dramatic changes in information propagation are too familiar to require much elaboration. In brief, two broad trends have converged: (1) rising levels of education have given increased proportions of the adult population access to the printed media; and (2) the development of the spoken media has provided channels of information accessible even to those not motivated to read. The cumulative change has been of awesome proportions. Historical trends hinging on shifts of 5 or 10 per cent in relevant societal rates often draw comment; here, conditions of information propagation have shifted in ways that affect a vast majority of the population.

Of these two changes, it can be argued that the advent of the spoken media has been even more crucial than the upgrading of education, where mass political behavior is concerned. In the first place, of course, a number of states even outside the South have had literacy requirements for the franchise, thereby "neutralizing" any effects on the electorate of variations in literacy rates. The spoken media loom even more important, however, as we come to realize that the critical phenomenon is less illiteracy in the strict sense than what is sometimes called functional illiteracy. Even currently, after more than a century of expansion in education, the proportion of adults who eschew any serious reading that is not imperative (and most printed information on politics is of this sort) is often estimated to be as high as 60 per cent.

In modern data we typically find that 70 to 80 per cent of the electorate reports having read "something" about the presidential campaign in one of the printed media. This figure is quite high, and eighty years ago it must have been substantially lower. Nonetheless, it leaves a fair residual population that received its *only* current information from the spoken media. If we can imagine that prior to 1920 such a residuum simply went without information, then the ranks of our "no media" people would be increased by a factor of three, and the proportion of "no media" voters by a factor of six. We would then be talking of a significant fraction of the voting public, enough to create noticeable differences in the cast of election returns.

Furthermore, we must bear in mind that this 70 to 80 per cent that learns "something" from a printed medium passes only the weakest of tests: merely discovering from a headline the names of the candidates would qualify. Indeed the slight amount of information gleaned from the printed media by many of these readers is betrayed by another datum: less than one-third of the current population when asked the medium from which it draws most political information mentions a printed medium. In other words, a majority of those who do notice some political news in the printed media nonetheless feel that they learned more about what is going on politically from the spoken media. Given the sketchy coverage of politics in the spoken media by contrast with the written, this is quite a commentary on the relative "reach" and impact of the newer spoken media.

All this being so, we find that we have traversed a rather strange circle. We began by remarking upon the extremely low levels of political information in the current period. Now we adduce evidence in some depth that the effective reach of the communication system has advanced enormously, and that the citizen himself recognizes a greater information intake than he would have had short of the newer media. Naturally this juxtaposition of findings underscores among other things a fundamental motivation problem. At one time it might have been argued that electorates were uninformed for lack of realistic access to information. Now a fair flow of information is *accessible* to almost everybody in the society; the fact that little attention is paid to it even though it is almost hard to avoid is a fair measure of lack of public interest. But all these facts do no more than stir our curiosity; if levels of public information are extremely low now, when access to rudimentary information is not a primary problem, what must this level have been a century ago?

There is, of course, a considerable literature that makes of nineteenth-century America a Golden Age of democratic politics. In effect, it is argued that the conditions of life entailed by modern industrialized society have destroyed the free give and take of political discussion that once characterized the small towns and rural hamlets of the relatively agrarian nation. The public is less capable now than it once was of approximating the assumptions of normative democratic theory. Among recent versions of this panorama, perhaps that by C. Wright Mills in *The Power Elite* is as imaginative as any.[17] Since

[17] C. Wright Mills, *The Power Elite*, New York: Oxford, 1956, Chap. 13.

this view is diametrically opposed to any reconstruction we can suggest, it is worth a moment to consider points of divergence.

Mills's account is somewhat difficult to address because of the range of disparate phenomena that flow into and out of the argument. If, for example, the point is to compare a restricted elite of functionally literate voters with modern universal suffrage, then one would grant out of hand that a major change has occurred. In context, however, this is hardly the point Mills wished to press. Or if the point is to compare the informed character of a debate between villagers as to the laying of a local drainpipe and the information the same villagers can bring to the debates of national politics (often equally crucial to their lives), then once again there can be little argument, and the difference is of profound importance. Or, finally, if the point is that the modern mass media leave a good deal to be desired in terms of breadth of alternatives presented or general level of discussion, the contention is as readily granted.[18]

Despite fleeting attention to all of these points, the true burden of Mills's argument seems to be that the modern mass media stifle what once was free discussion. Most concretely it is argued that the modern media have decreased the number of "opinion givers" relative to the number of "opinion receivers." "More than anything else," Mills observes, "it is the shift in this ratio which is central to the problems of the public and public opinion in latter-day phases of democracy." Here our arguments collide most directly, for it seems patent that opinion giving presupposes opinion formation, and opinion formation presupposes information that there is something to form a political opinion about.[19] We have suggested that opinion-stimulating informa-

[18] Although we should not lose sight of the apparent fact that one reason people who both read and listen feel they get more information from the spoken media is precisely this lower level of presentation. The printed media are less palatable in part because their somewhat more elevated discussions presuppose more information.

[19] One might distinguish two classes of events here, both of which require information before political opinions are stimulated. The first includes events that have no discernible effect on the life of the individual, at least as he comprehends his existence. Here the outside information is required even to know there is a debatable problem. There is a second class of events that *do* bear directly upon him (e.g., the loss of a job as part of a general economic contraction in his community), which he cannot fail to cognize as events. Even here, however, further information is important: that politics is relevant to such an event is hardly a "given," an innate idea. Perception of a potential link requires other information. Even now, this "other" information cannot be presupposed for all American voters. Since a century ago a potential link between such an event and national politics was not invariably perceived by well-educated people who left written traces, one would certainly hesitate to presuppose it for most mass voters.

tion about national politics must have been a much rarer commodity in the mass public a century ago.

Despite the evidence we have already presented, there remain ways in which we might try retrospectively to bootleg increased amounts of information to the nineteenth-century voter. It might be argued, for example, that nowadays people read *less* political material than in the past simply because they now can fill their needs with less effort through the spoken media. In other words, there are some fixed needs for political information, and in an era when such information was less accessible, more energy would have been expended in compensation to secure it. Direct evaluation of such a hypothesis would require data that do not and will not exist, since turning back the clock empirically is impossible. However, none of the indirect ways in which we may turn back the clock lend any credence to this possibility.

There are, for example, pockets of modern American society—remote rural areas—that tend toward a rough representation of the older conditions of communication, in that they have newspaper distribution but up until recently have had inadequate service by electronic media. In such areas, of course, it may be demonstrated to any reasonable degree of satisfaction that the intake of political information is less in an absolute sense, political interest is lower, and the incidence of opinion giving is lower as well, relative to more urban areas. Or again, we may turn back the clock by considering data from societies somewhat behind us in industrial evolution. France, with less popular access to the spoken media and an educational distribution that roughly resembles that of the United States several decades ago, shows no heavier public consumption of political news through the printed media. Instead rates of information intake via newspapers and magazines seem very much like those in the United States for comparable levels of education; since the education level is lower in France, so is the intake of information from printed media.[20]

The fact of the matter is that in the current period the tendencies to monitor different media for political information follow Guttman scalar patterns very closely, with magazines the "hardest" item, and the

[20] See Chapter 14. The French example is of added interest because another claim is frequently made that the state of public information about politics in America reflects a political indifference that has grown up recently as a result of the absence of "real" policy alternatives offered by the two major parties. Few voters are provided with the wealth of clear-cut policy alternatives available to French voters, yet, if anything, mass political interest in France over recent years has been slightly less than that in the United States.

spoken media the easiest.[21] Such a scale is, of course, highly correlated with education: 74 per cent of college graduates fall in the top category, as opposed to 17 per cent of the grade-school educated; 6 per cent of college graduates monitor only a spoken medium or none at all, as opposed to 40 per cent of the grade school people. In other words, the stratum most vitally affected by the new currents of information is that which would have had least option in times past of compensating for an absence of these media with newspapers or magazines.

A rather different means of bootlegging information to the nineteenth-century voter is to shift weight to informal social communication for the transmission of political information. Before the mass media corrupted the majority of voters with "direct information," it can be claimed that the nets of informal communication buzzed with all the political information inaccessible through other channels. This is a particularly interesting argument, since it hews very closely to the spirit of the Mills contentions about free and fervent informal political discussion.

We are less interested here in the "power to persuade" of informal communications as opposed to the mass media than we are in (1) the characteristics of informal communication as a source of information supply, and (2) the motivation to sustain transmission of political information along the chain. With regard to the nature of the information transmitted, our interviews frequently represent the respondent's transmission of things he has recently seen, heard, or read in the media. This is information at only a first remove, yet the "sea change" in content emphasis and accuracy is quite striking. It is not at all unusual that a voter who exposes himself to an information presentation that is 95 per cent current issues and 5 per cent personal background of a political personality comes away with the personal oddments burning in the memory and the rest lost. Although political content in the spoken media may strike an academic observer as somewhat light, its devaluation at one remove is hardly calculated to raise regard for informal transmission involving multiple steps. Our point is not that people are more capable today of absorbing critical information than they were a century ago, but rather that if information depends on informal communication, any potential receiver who might have

[21] That is, people who report having drawn political information from magazines are very likely to report having monitored newspapers and a spoken medium as well. People who report the monitoring of newspapers do not in large measure read magazines, but are very likely to have monitored radio or television. Among people who have monitored one of the spoken media, there are a disproportionate number who have monitored nothing else.

stronger policy interests is at the mercy of the weakest link in the informal communication chain prior to him. Since currently the flow of information is directly accessible to him, he at least may select the information that strikes him as important, for better or for worse. A person at third or fourth remove in a chain during the Golden Age would have had a much greater probability of hearing something about Cleveland's love life than he would of hearing that labor problems, tariffs, or free silver were subjects for debate.

And even this devaluation process supposes that there is some motivation to communicate about politics, or the chain is broken. Indeed, Mills assumes quite directly that prior to the incursions of the mass media, people were *more* motivated to communicate informally about politics. Current data make this position hard to accept. Studies of the 1960 television debates, for example, suggest that these performances were responsible in the most direct way for lively spates of informal political discussion which undoubtedly would not otherwise have taken place.[22]

We have more direct data on opinion giving that tell exactly the same story. For several elections we have asked respondents, "Did you talk to any people and try to show them why they should vote for one of the parties or candidates?" The probability of opinion giving thus defined is tied in the most extreme fashion to information intake. In 1960, for example, 52 per cent of the people who drew information from four media were opinion givers; for three media, the figure was 44 per cent; for two, 23 per cent; for one, 15 per cent. Among the no-media people, who are currently few in number but who we contend bulked larger a century ago, 0 per cent reported opinion giving (N of 82).[23]

[22] E. Katz and J. Feldman, "The Debates in the Light of Research and Vice Versa," in Sidney Kraus, editor, *The Great Debates,* Bloomington: Indiana University Press, 1962. No judgment is implied here that the quality of such discussions was high—it is almost axiomatic that over the electorate as a whole they must have been something below the quality of the debates themselves. The critical matter is that the alternatives were not good discussion or poor discussion but rather some discussion or no discussion at all.

[23] These are familiar data of the opinion-leader type. It is unfortunate that we lack comparable materials on "opinion receiving" from informal sources. Within any given milieu, the "two-step flow of communication" helps to spread opinions, along with the information they presuppose, beyond the immediate receivers. However, the effects of such communications upon our argument fall far short of what one would expect were the who-to-whom matrices of communication random. Thus, for example, the most prevalent special case of the two-step flow where politics is concerned runs between the husband who is somewhat attentive to political information

None of these data establishes any causal link between the stimulation of information reception and the motivation to communicate informally about politics. That is, prior political involvement clearly predisposes both to a more vigorous information search *and* to an increased tendency to form and give opinions. But the data do make it extremely difficult to argue that somehow a weaker information flow from the mass media generates a vacuum that people attempt to fill by increasing informal communication about politics. With regard to the Mills argument, then, it seems much simpler to conclude that the historical alternative to the strong information flow of the mass media was not more and better opinions but rather no opinion formation at all.

Attempts to reconstruct historical conditions that affected large populations are often unsatisfying because direct proof is impossible. Historians have become painfully aware of the optical illusion created by history where trends in ideas are concerned, since the populations that have left ideational traces of their days and ways become increasingly narrow (and elite) as we probe more deeply into the past. Whether we are studying trends in wit, conformity, or political acumen, to lay an implicit eighteenth-century population of Voltaires, Diderots, and Ben Franklins against the current Everyman, as revealed by all the mass feedback techniques of modern research, is to assure terrifying conclusions about man's evolution. It is ironic that in the voting case, however, we do have one of the few bodies of systematic records—mass voting statistics—struck off by the hand of Everyman himself.

Although we are only on the brink of extracting more sophisticated information from these records, one comment is worth venturing. If

and the wife who is content to receive it secondhand. This pattern occurs within all milieux. However, the lower-class wife, who is less likely than anyone else in the society to receive information from the media, at the same time has a husband who is less likely than any other male in the society to receive such information, or to bother transmitting it in the instances when he does receive something. In point of fact, our no-media people who reported no opinion giving departed from the question sequence in marked numbers to note as well that they had simply not conversed about politics with *anyone*. In sum, then, were these informal political communications to be aggregated over the society as a whole, there is every reason to believe that opinion receiving would show a high positive correlation with opinion giving, and not the negative correlation required for an efficient diffusion of information through the system. These facts have been recognized quite explicitly by theorists developing the two-step flow hypothesis. See E. Katz, "The Two-Step Flow of Communication: An Up-to-Date Report on an Hypothesis," *Public Opinion Quarterly*, 21, especially 76–77 (1957).

our model has merit, and if it is true that for any given election the cell comprised of no-current-information voters must once have bulked much larger than it does today, then it would follow that the amplitude of the oscillations in voting for political objects at a national level must have been materially less in an earlier period, for precisely the same reason of weakened information flow that limits swings of the congressional vote in the current period. And, conversely, there should be an increasing amplitude of these swings as the information flow has increased during the current century.

In a cursory inspection of the vote trends, at least, this is precisely what we *do* find. The general cast of the American historical statistics suggests three rough periods. In the first, terminated abruptly by the Civil War, the parties were undergoing frequent splits and shifts in manifest identity. In this period, relatively large voting oscillations were quite common, and it is likely that party loyalties in the broad public had not as yet had a chance to develop in any wide degree. The abrupt "settling down" after the Civil War creates the impression that conditions surrounding the war filled the mass of voters with deep-seated party feeling.[24] For several decades after the Civil War, vote oscillations were extremely muffled, producing the sort of record we would associate today with prevalence of partisan attachment accompanied by extremely weak information flow. (Just as the Nebraska woman cited above has continued to vote Prohibition for thirty years, so there must have been a much larger pool of poorly informed and *potentially* mobile voters in the late nineteenth century who for decades voted the Civil War not only because of the impress of that tragic episode but in part as well because of an absence of information as to what political elites were currently competing about or, for that matter, who the current political elites were.) As such information has become more accessible, this cell of perfectly stable voters has dwindled and the oscillations of the vote have regained amplitude.

Such historical reconstruction is of necessity loose and crude. Prob-

---

[24] Outside of the ravaged South, this galvanizing process did not penetrate the more remote rural areas, which continued to show great voting lability on into the early twentieth century and which even now manifest weaker levels of partisan identication. Such urban-rural discrepancies in partisan stability are very frequent evolutionary phenomena, with one of the most noteworthy cases being that of the Weimar Republic. Nazi party workers stumbled to their surprise upon the fact that although the movement was essentially urban and recruited its activists from the cities, the harvest of mass votes that could not be dislodged in the distressed cities because of prior development of party loyalties could be had for the asking in distressed rural areas. See Campbell et al., *op. cit.*, Chap. 15.

ably our extrapolations from current data are in the final analysis more solidly anchored. But the fact remains that there is historical evidence that seems of a piece with our theoretical understanding of more thorough modern data, and this is encouraging. Since changes in the information-propagating capacities of a society occur at a fairly slow rate, it is in such historical perspective that a link between the volume of information flow and the partisan stability of an electoral system has its most interesting implications.

II

Voting and the Party System

No branch of political studies has grown more rapidly in the last thirty years than research on political parties. It was not always so. Largely for normative reasons, parties remained a stepchild of political inquiry long after they had assumed immense importance in the politics of modern nations. Today, however, their importance is fully recognized, and the literature of parties and party systems has grown apace.

Like all normative or descriptive theories, those treating of parties have important empirical elements. It is therefore exceedingly likely that any significant extension of political data will have an impact on the theory of parties and party systems. Such a modification of theory is explicitly sought by this section's opening chapter, Chapter 9. It considers several empirical assumptions of spatial theories of party choice in the light of survey evidence from mass publics.

Chapter 10 in some ways stands the role of survey evidence on its head. Instead of testing an existing theory with survey data, this article begins with an explanation of America's two-party competition which was developed from survey analysis and searches the evidence of American electoral history to see whether the phenomenon being explained is a real one, in the sense of being more than a chance occurrence. This sort of commerce between survey and historical analysis is likely to be increasingly common. Confronted with the limited configurations of the present, the survey analyst will more and more be tempted to search for similar phenomena in the nearer and farther past. Far from being necessarily antihistorical, as they are sometimes supposed to be, survey studies can provide a fresh stimulus to historical analysis.

The most influential normative theory of parties is the conception of government by disciplined parties which competitively seek the electorate's support. Although the doctrine of responsible party government was adumbrated largely from British experience, it has strongly influenced American thought and is still the favorite model of liberally inclined reformers of our national government. The model's uses, however, are not solely normative. As the reformer's case suggests, American practice departs a good deal from the canons of party government; why this is so becomes therefore an interesting problem for causal analysis. Chapter 11 offers a partial answer. From the evidence about the electoral support of American Congressmen this chapter suggests several reasons why our national politics should be so unlike the model of disciplined party government.

One reason for the departure of American practice from the party government model is the historical importance of regional party alignments, especially the Democratic Party's traditional southern hegemony. The closing chapter of this section, Chapter 12, examines the prospects of major realignment in the South. This examination depends partly on the accumulated survey evidence about the political attitudes and identifications of Southerners. But it also depends on an estimate of what is likely to happen in the leadership cadres of the national parties. In other words, whether there will be more than incremental change in the South is a question about the future interaction of mass and elite; it is a problem involving the party system and not simply the future behavior of individual voters.

CHAPTER 9

Spatial Models of Party Competition

Donald E. Stokes

The use of spatial ideas to interpret party competition is a universal phenomenon of modern politics. Such ideas are the common coin of political journalists and have extraordinary influence in the thought of political activists. Especially widespread is the conception of a liberal-conservative dimension on which parties maneuver for the support of a public that is itself distributed from left to right. This conception goes back at least to the French Revolution and has recently gained new interest for an academic audience through its ingenious formalization by Downs and others.[1] However, most spatial interpretations of party competition have a very poor fit with the evidence about how large-scale electorates and political leaders actually respond to politics. Indeed the findings on this point are clear enough so that spatial ideas about party competition ought to be modified by empirical observation. This chapter will review evidence that the "space" in which American parties contend for electoral support is very unlike a

[1] For expositions of Downs's model see Anthony Downs, *An Economic Theory of Democracy*, Harper and Brothers: New York, 1957, pp. 114–141, and "An Economic Theory of Political Action in a Democracy," *Journal of Political Economy*, 65, 135–150 (1957). For a similar model developed independently see Duncan MacRae, Jr., *Dimensions of Congressional Voting: a Statistical Study of the House of Representatives in the Eighty-First Congress*, Berkeley and Los Angeles: University of California Press, 1958, pp. 354–382.

This chapter appeared originally in the *American Political Science Review*, 57 (June 1963).

single ideological dimension and will offer some suggestions toward revision of the prevailing spatial model.

The Hotelling-Downs Model

Because spatial ideas have been woven into popular and scholarly commentaries on politics with remarkable frequency, the observations offered here will reach well beyond recent efforts to formalize the spatial model of party competition. However, the work of Downs gives this conception admirable clarity without removing it too far from familiar usage, and we may begin with a brief review of his system. The root idea of Downs's model is that the alternatives of government action on which political controversy is focused can be located in a one-dimensional space, along a left-right scale. At least for illustration, Downs interprets this dimension as the degree of government intervention in the economy. At the extreme left is complete government control and at the extreme right no government intervention beyond the most limited state operations. Each voter can be located on the scale according to how much government control he wants and each party according to how much government control it advocates.[2]

As Downs is careful to make clear, this model extends a line of thought tracing back to the work of Harold Hotelling.[3] Thirty years ago Hotelling had sought to answer the question of why two competing firms are so often found in adjacent positions near the middle of a spatial market (Kresge's and Woolworth's are not at opposite ends of Main Street; they are right next door). Assuming (1) that the buying public is evenly distributed along a linear market (a transcontinental railroad, say), and (2) that demand is inelastic (that is, consumers at a given point of the market will buy a fixed amount of goods from whichever of two producers is closer and, hence, can offer the lower transportation costs to consumers located at that point), Hotelling

---

[2] Downs's model is a little more complicated than this. Each voter has not only a most-preferred degree of government intervention (let us say his "point" on the scale); he has some amount of preference for every other degree of government intervention (the other points on the scale), the amount decreasing monotonically the farther the point is from his optimum. Hence, the preference of the electorate as a whole for a given degree of government intervention is the sum of the preferences of individual voters for that degree of intervention. Moreover, a party's position on the scale may be thought of as the sum or average of the positions it takes on a variety of particular issues.

[3] Harold Hotelling, "Stability in Competition," *Economic Journal,* 39, 41–57 (1929).

was able to show that two competing firms would converge toward adjacent positions at the middle of the market. If one firm is farther from the middle than its competitor, it can increase its share of the market by moving toward the middle; and so on, until equilibrium is reached. Substituting voters for consumers, parties for firms, and the "costs" of ideological distance for transportation costs, Hotelling felt that his model could explain why the Democratic and Republican parties are so often found close to the center of a liberal-conservative dimension.

Those who have extended Hotelling's ideas have done so by relaxing one or both of the assumptions given above. Arthur Smithies and several other economists dispensed with (2), the assumption of inelastic demand.[4] Smithies assumed instead that demand depends on price and that sales at any given point of the market will vary according to how much delivered prices are raised by transportation costs. For this reason two competing firms will be under pressure not only to move closer together to improve sales in their "competitive region"; they will also be under pressure to move farther apart to improve sales in their respective hinterlands. When these two opposite forces are in equilibrium the competing firms could well be some distance apart. Continuing the side discussion of politics, Smithies argued that electoral "demand" also is elastic, since a voter who feels that both parties are too far from his ideological position can simply stay away from the polls. With this assumption added, Smithies felt that the model could explain why the Republicans and Democrats (by the time of the New Deal era) were some distance apart, ideologically speaking.

Downs has retained Smithies's assumption of elastic demand and has further modified the Hotelling model by dispensing with (1), the assumption that the public is evenly distributed over a one-dimensional space. Indeed, in Downs's system, the way the public is distributed along the liberal-conservative scale is a *variable* of great importance, one that he uses to explain some very notable attributes of (constructed) political systems.[5] Under Downs's revision the model not only can explain the strategic choices of existing parties as they place themselves along the left-right scale, it can also explain the emergence of

[4] Arthur Smithies, "Optimum Location in Spatial Competition," *Journal of Political Economy*, 49, 423–429 (1941).

[5] Downs makes several other modifications of Hotelling's and Smithies's models in addition to treating the distribution of the public on the scale as a variable. Especially important is the assumption that one party will not "jump over" the position of another on the liberal-conservative dimension.

new parties and the disappearance of old ones. Downs's discussion can be read equally as a theory of voter choice, a theory of party positioning, and a theory of party number.

As any good theorist, Downs should be read in the original. However, the inferences he makes to the number and positions of competing parties from different distributions of the public on the left-right scale may be summarized as follows. *If the distribution has a single mode,* the party system will be in equilibrium when two parties have converged to positions that are fairly close together. Just how close depends on how elastic the turnout is and on how sharp the peak of the distribution is, as well as other factors.[6] *If the distribution has two modes,* the system will be in equilibrium when two parties are present, each having assumed a position somewhere near one of the modes. *If the distribution has more than two modes,* the system will be in equilibrium when a party occupies each of the several modal positions. In this sense, the presence of more than two modes of opinion encourages the development of a multiparty system.

Reviewing these ideas, one must first admire the ingenuity with which Downs has transformed Hotelling's brilliant analogy into a model of party systems. However, the model includes some cognitive postulates that need to be drastically qualified in view of what is known about the parties and electorates of actual political systems. Of course, it is in the nature of models not to represent the real world exactly. The more general and powerful a model is, the more severely it will cut away unnecessary aspects of reality, and any first-class formalization should be forgiven a host of empirical peccadilloes. However, what is wrong with the hidden postulates of Downs's model is more than a petty fault. These postulates are introduced when the argument shifts from economic competition in a spatial market to political competition in an ideological market. In Downs's (and Hotelling's) exposition this transition is rather too easily accomplished. The consequences of placing competitors and consumers in a linear space are developed persuasively for the economic problem, where the meaning of the space is clear, and transferred too easily to the political problem, where the meaning of the space can be far from clear. The ground over which the parties contend is *not* a space in the sense that Main Street or a transcontinental railroad is. Treating it as if it were

---

[6] The assumption that no party can move past another on the left-right scale makes the equilibrium positions of two competing parties less well defined than it is for the competing firms of the models of Hotelling and Smithies.

introduces assumptions about the unidimensionality of the space, the stability of its structure, the existence of ordered dimensions and the common frame of reference of parties and electorate that are only poorly supported by available evidence from real political systems.[7]

The Axiom of Unidimensionality

The most evident—and perhaps least fundamental—criticism to be made of the spatial model is that the conception of a single dimension of political conflict can hardly be sustained. Such an assumption clearly is false to the realities of two-party systems, including the American, on which intensive studies have been made. And there is evidence that it falsifies the realities of many multiparty systems, in which the appearance or continued existence of parties depends less on the electorate's distribution along a single dimension than on the presence of several dimensions of political conflict.

The unreality of a one-dimensional account of political attitudes in America is attested by several kinds of evidence from the electoral studies of the Survey Research Center. The relative independence of various attitude dimensions is a repeated finding of these studies. For example, over a period of years this research has measured public attitudes toward social and economic welfare action by government and toward American involvement in foreign affairs. The lore of popular journalism would make these two domains one, with the liberal internationalist position going hand in hand with the liberal social welfare position. However, the empirical support for this conception is weak indeed. Across a national sample of the electorate, there is *no* relation between attitudes toward social welfare policies and American involvement abroad.[8] These dimensions of attitude are independent in a statistical sense; knowing how "liberal" a person is on one gives no clue whatever as to how "liberal" he will be on the other.

[7] These remarks are directed solely to Downs's spatial model of party competition. *An Economic Theory of Democracy* (*op. cit.*) sets forth a whole collection of models, elaborated from a few central variables. All are worth detailed study. Paradoxically, the spatial model described here is likely to have great intuitive appeal for a wide audience, yet its postulates are almost certainly as radical as those of any model in Downs's collection.

[8] A. Campbell, P. E. Converse, W. E. Miller, and D. E. Stokes, *The American Voter*, New York: John Wiley and Sons, 1960, pp. 197–198.

If the voters' own positions on social welfare and foreign involvement prevent our treating these two dimensions as one, their reactions to the domestic and foreign policies of the parties can also be strongly discrepant. For example, in the presidential election of 1952 the Democratic Party was approved for its domestic economic record but strongly disapproved for its record in foreign affairs, particularly the unfinished conflict in Korea. With even-handed justice the public rewarded the party for prosperity and punished it for war without reducing the Democrats' performance to a summary position on some over-arching dimension of political controversy.

An intensive search for such a dimension has met little success. In the presidential elections of 1952, 1956, and 1960 the Center's interviews opened with an extended series of questions designed to elicit the ideas that are actually associated with the parties and their presidential candidates. When the answers, amounting on the average to a quarter hour of conversation, are examined closely for ideological content, only about a tenth of the electorate by the loosest definition is found to be using the liberal-conservative distinction or any other ideological concept. By a more reasonable count, the proportion is something like 3 per cent.[9] What is more, when our respondents are asked directly to describe the parties in terms of the liberal-conservative distinction, nearly half confess that the terms are unfamiliar. And the bizarre meanings given the terms by many of those who do attempt to use them suggest that we are eliciting artificial answers that have little to do with the public's everyday perceptions of the parties.

The axiom of unidimensionality is difficult to reconcile with the evidence from multiparty systems as well. The support for the parties of a multiparty system is often more easily explained by the presence of several dimensions of political conflict than it is by the distribution of the electorate along any single dimension. At least since Marx, the dimension we would choose to account for party support, if allowed only one, would be socio-economic or class-related. Yet the politics even of western nations exhibit many parties that owe their existence to religious or racial or ethnic identifications or to specialized social and economic interests (such as the agrarian) that do not fit readily into the stratification order. For example, the *Zentrum* of Weimar Germany and before, as the prototype confessional party, drew support from Catholics at all levels of German society. The party could scarcely have survived if its strength had depended entirely on public

9 Campbell et al., *op. cit.*, pp. 227–234.

response to its socio-economic policies.[10] We shall see in Chapter 14 that the party preferences of the mass French public are more highly associated with attitudes toward religious issues than with attitudes toward socio-economic issues, despite the immensely greater attention given the latter by government and elite circles. If the parties and electorate of contemporary France are to be located in spatial terms, the space must be one of at least two dimensions.

Even support for the occasional third party of American politics may be understood better if more than one dimension is considered. The Dixiecrat Party of 1948 is a good case in point. Downs himself describes the Dixiecrats as a "blackmail party" whose intent was to force the national Democratic Party farther to the right on the general liberal-conservative dimension.[11] But it is at least as plausible to say that their rebellion was directed at Truman's civil rights program, as the southern walkout over adoption of a civil rights plank by the national Democratic convention of 1948 would suggest. Undoubtedly for some Southerners civil rights were closely linked with issues of economic and social welfare policy. But for others these issue domains were quite distinct. American political beliefs are sufficiently multi-dimensional so that many Dixiecrat votes were cast by Southern economic liberals.

Although the assumption of unidimensionality is a familiar part of prevailing spatial conceptions of party competition, it might well be dispensed with. Hotelling's original argument can easily be generalized to two dimensions, as Hotelling himself observed (in most of the towns we know about, Kresge's and Woolworth's are still right together even though their customers live on a two-dimensional surface).[12] That the model has not been extended may be due in part to

[10] It is a curious and interesting fact that the agrarian party of modern Norway, like the Catholic party of pre-Hitler Germany, has chosen to call itself the "Center" Party, that is, to call itself by a name that refers to a dimension other than the one on which the party's main support is based. By selecting a title that is neutral in terms of a primary dimension of political conflict, the party invites potential supporters to ignore that dimension and rally to the party's special cause.

[11] Downs, op. cit., p. 128.

[12] A troublesome problem in applying a more general model to the real world is that of defining some kind of distance function over all pairs of points in the space. The need for such a function is less acute in the one-dimensional case, because an approximate ordering of distances between points can be derived from the strong ordering of points in the space. However, the points of a multidimensional space are no longer strongly ordered, and it may not be possible to compare the appeal of two or more parties for voters located at a given point by measuring how far from the point the parties are. Of course, if the space can be interpreted in physical terms, as Hotelling's could, this problem does not arise.

the fact that introducing more dimensions raises other questions about its fit with the real world that are not likely to be asked about the simple one-dimensional model. In particular, accommodating a greater number of dimensions draws attention to the assumption that the space of party competition, whether unidimensional or multidimensional, has a stable structure.

The Axiom of Fixed Structure

The mischief of too facile a shift from the economic to the political problem is plainly seen in connection with the assumption of stable structure. Since the space represented by a transcontinental railroad depends on physical distance, its structure is fixed, as the structure of Main Street is. The distribution of consumers within these spaces may vary; the space itself will not. Hotelling applied his economic model to some kinds of spaces whose structure was not derived from physical distance, for example, the degree of sweetness of cider. But these, too, were spaces of fixed structure.

By comparison, the space in which political parties compete can be of highly variable structure. Just as the parties may be perceived and evaluated on several dimensions, so the dimensions that are salient to the electorate may change widely over time. The fact of such change in American politics is one of the best-supported conclusions to be drawn from the Survey Research Center's studies of voting behavior over a decade and a half. For example, between the elections of 1948 and 1952 a far-reaching change took place in the terms in which the parties and candidates were judged by the electorate. Whereas the voter evaluations of 1948 were strongly rooted in the economic and social issues of the New Deal-Fair Deal era, the evaluations of 1952 were based substantially on foreign concerns. A dimension that had touched the motives of the electorate scarcely at all in the Truman election was of great importance in turning the Democratic administration out of power four years later. If the difference between these two elections is to be interpreted in spatial terms, we would have to say that the intrusion of a new issue dimension had changed the structure of the space in which the parties competed for electoral support.

However, this way of putting it implies that a dimension either *is* part of the structure of the space or it is *not,* whereas the presence of a given evaluative dimension is often a matter of degree. What is needed is language that would express the fact that different weights should be given different dimensions at different times. At some moments of political history class, religious, foreign, or regional dimensions are of greater cognitive and motivational significance to the electorate than they are at other times, quite apart from shifts in the positions of the competing parties and their consuming public. Drastic electoral changes can result from changes in the *coordinate system* of the space rather than changes in the distribution of parties and voters.

The evidence shows that party managers are very sensitive to changes in the grounds of electoral evaluation. Political fortunes are made and lost according to the ability of party leaders to sense what dimensions will be salient to the public as it appraises the candidates and party records. To be sure, this awareness is not universal, and some political leaders have imputed to the electorate a stereotyped cognitive map that is very close to the Downs model. But the skills of political leaders who must maneuver for public support in a democracy consist partly in knowing what issue dimensions are salient to the electorate or can be made salient by suitable propaganda. The deftness with which Republican leaders turned the changing concerns of the country to their advantage in 1952 provides an excellent modern example. Dewey and the other Eisenhower managers knew that victory lay in exploiting relatively new and transitory political attitudes, including the one they could inject into the campaign by nominating an immensely popular military figure who was seen in wholly nonideological terms. The brilliant slogan of the "three K's"—Korea, Corruption, Communism—with which the Republicans pressed the 1952 campaign was hardly the work of men who perceived the cognitions and motives of the electorate as tied primarily to the left-right distinction. The dominant Republican leadership showed a highly pragmatic understanding of the changing dimensions of political evaluation.

The case of 1952 leads to a further point of great importance. The new issues of that year are called "dimensions" above to keep them within the terms of this discussion. But one does not have to take a very searching look at these issues to feel that some at least are not dimensions in any ordinary sense. The issue of corruption, for example, was hardly one on which the Democratic Party took a position *for* the "mess in Washington" and the Republicans a position *against* it in appealing to an electorate that was itself distributed on a dimension extending from full probity in government to full laxity and disarray. A consideration of this point raises a third difficulty in applying the Downs model to actual party systems.

The Axiom of Ordered Dimensions

For the spatial model to be applied, the parties and voters of a political system must be able to place themselves on one or more common dimensions. That is, there must be at least one ordered set of alternatives of government action that the parties may advocate and the voters prefer. Degrees of government intervention in the economy is such a set, as Downs observed; so is the extent of American involvement in foreign affairs or the extent of federal action to protect the rights of Negroes. Obviously a good deal depends on how many elements the set has. A spatial language tends to suggest that the number is indefinitely large, like the number of points in Euclidean one-space or the real line of mathematics. The number of alternatives in a political dimension is clearly more limited, though it cannot be too limited if such ideas as modal position and relative distance are to have more than trivial meaning. However, to make the point as strong as possible, let us include within the notion of an ordered set one in which there are only *two* alternatives of government action that the parties may endorse and the voters prefer.

The empirical point that needs to be made is that many of the issues that agitate our politics do not involve even a shriveled set of two alternatives of government action. The corruption issue of 1952 did not find the Democrats taking one position and the Republicans another. And neither were some voters in favor of corruption while others were against it. If we are to speak of a dimension at all, both parties and all voters were located at a single point—the position of virtue in government. To be sure, enough evidence of malfeasance had turned up in the Democratic administration so that many voters felt the party had strayed from full virtue. But throwing the rascals out is very different from choosing between two or more parties on the basis of their advocacy of alternatives of government action. The machinery of the spatial model will not work if the voters are simply reacting to the association of the parties with some goal or state or symbol that is positively or negatively valued.

To emphasize the difference involved here let us call *"position issues"* those that involve advocacy of government actions from a set of alternatives over which a distribution of voter preferences is defined. And borrowing a term from Kurt Lewin let us call *"valence issues"* those that merely involve the linking of the parties with some condition that is positively or negatively valued by the electorate.[13] If the condition is past or present ("You never had it so good," "800 million people have gone behind the Iron Curtain"), the argument turns on where the credit or blame ought to be assigned. But if the condition is a future or potential one, the argument turns on which party, given possession of the government, is the more likely to bring it about.

It will not do simply to exclude valence-issues from the discussion of party competition. The people's choice too often depends upon them. At least in American presidential elections of the past generation it is remarkable how many valence-issues have held the center of the stage. The great themes of depression and recovery, which dominated electoral choice during the thirties and forties, were a good deal of this kind. What happened to Hoover and the Republicans was that they got bracketed with hard times, much as the Democrats later, although less clearly, were to be bracketed with war. Twenty years after the Hoover disaster the Republicans were returned to power in an election that was saturated with the valence-issues of the Korean War and corruption in Washington. And the question of American prestige abroad, to which Kennedy and Nixon gave so much attention in the campaign of 1960, was a pure specimen of valence-issue. Both parties and all voters, presumably, were for high prestige. The only issue was whether or not America had it under the existing Republican administration.

The failure to distinguish these types of issues, whatever they are called, is one reason why journalistic accounts of political trends so often go astray. Apparently the urge to give an ideological, position-issue interpretation of election results can be irresistible, despite the reams of copy that have been devoted to Madison Avenue technique and the art of image-building. One becomes aware of how often the impact of valence-issues is mistaken for ideological movements ("with the election of Kennedy America has again moved to the left") simply by reading what the newspapers have continued to say even after care-

---

[13] These terms may recall the distinction between "position issues" and "style issues" made by Bernard R. Berelson, Paul F. Lazarsfeld, and William N. McPhee, *Voting*, Chicago: University of Chicago Press, 1954, pp. 184–198. In their account, the difference between issues of position and style rests on a material-ideal distinction and hence tends to oppose class-related issues to all others. Their account of style issues sounds at places like the conception of valence-issues here. But many of the style issues they cite (e.g., prohibition, civil liberties) would be position-issues under the definitions given here.

ful studies of American voting behavior began to report their findings.

It is of course true that position-issues lurk behind many valence-issues. The problem of Korea, which benefited the Republicans so handsomely in 1952, is a good case. The successful Republican treatment of this issue was to link the unfinished Korean conflict with the fact of Democratic Presidents during two world wars to hang the "war party" label on the Democrats. However, it is not hard to find alternatives of government action that *might* have provided a focus to the debate. For example, the controversy might have centered on how aggressive a policy toward the Red Chinese forces America should adopt. Should the United States carry the war to Manchuria, using all weapons? prosecute the war more vigorously within Korea? negotiate a settlement on the basis of existing conditions, essentially the course the Eisenhower Administration took? or pull back to Japan? The point is that neither this ordered set of alternatives nor any other provided the terms of the debate. Both in Republican propaganda and popular understanding the issue was simply a matter of the Democrats having gotten the country into a war from which Eisenhower would extract us—whether by bombing Manchuria or evacuating South Korea was not made clear.

The question whether a given problem poses a position- or valence-issue is a matter to be settled empirically and not on a priori logical grounds. This point is illustrated by the issue of the country's economic health. At least since the panic of 1837 did Van Buren in, prosperity has been one of the most influential valence-issues of American politics. All parties and the whole electorate have wanted it. The argument has had to do only with which party is more likely to achieve it, a question on which the public changed its mind between McKinley's full dinner pail and Franklin Roosevelt's New Deal. However, to make the point as sharp as possible, let us imagine that part of the electorate wants something less than full prosperity—even that it wants economic distress, for the bracing effect that economic difficulties have on individual conduct and the moral fiber of society as a whole. If this unlikely condition came to pass and the parties maneuvered for support by advocating different degrees of prosperity or distress, the issue would have been transformed from a valence-issue into a position-issue. That it is *not* such an issue in our politics is due solely to the fact that there is overwhelming consensus as to the goal of government action.

Since the preferences of parties and voters must be distributed over an ordered set of policy alternatives for the spatial model to work, valence-issues plainly do not fit the spatial scheme. Unless the interaction of voters and parties is focused on position-dimensions the model cannot serve as a theory either of the motivation of voters or of the positioning of parties.[14] This is not to say that the interaction of parties and voters on valence-issues is uninteresting or incapable of being represented by a different model. It is only to say that the model would be different. When the parties maneuver for support on a position-dimension, they choose policies from an ordered set of alternatives belonging to the same problem or issue. But when the parties maneuver in terms of valence-issues, they choose one or more issues from a set of distinct issue domains. As the Republicans looked over the prospective issues for 1952, their problem was not whether to come out *for* or *against* Communist subversion or prosperity or corruption in Washington. It was rather to put together a collection of issues of real or potential public concern whose positive and negative valences would aid the Republicans and embarrass the Democrats.

To be sure, Downs makes allowance for valence-issues by granting that some voting is "irrational," that is, nonideological in his spatial sense. He asserts, in fact, that rational behavior by the parties of a two-party system tends to encourage irrational behavior by voters. As the parties converge to ideologically similar positions (assuming a unimodal distribution of voters) their relative position provides fewer grounds for choice, and the voters are driven to deciding between them on some irrational basis. This is an admirable defense—indeed Downs has come close to constructing a theory that cannot be disproved, since evidence of voter motivation and party propaganda outside the bounds of the theory can be cited as evidence that the model applies. For the defense to be convincing, however, we must be shown that the ideological dimension on which the parties are presumed to be close together has empirical validity.

But empirical validity for whom? The space of Downs's model is formed out of the perceptions held by the actors who play roles in the political system. However, the model includes at least two classes of actors—voters and party managers—and their perceptions of what the political fighting is all about can diverge markedly. Here again, the economic problem has left its imprint; Kresge's Main Street and the

---

[14] Because the public's evaluation of political actors is so often and so deeply influenced by valence-issues the Survey Research Center has used a model of individual electoral choice (and, by extension, of the national vote decision) that measures only the valence and intensity of the affect associated with the parties and candidates. The model is described in Donald E. Stokes, Angus Campbell, and Warren E. Miller, "Components of Electoral Decision," *American Political Science Review,* 52, 367–387 (June 1958).

customer's Main Street are the same, and the question of divergent spaces does not arise. Yet it can easily arise in the political context. It is quite possible that the voters see political conflict in terms that differ widely from those in which the parties see it, and this possibility draws attention to a fourth unstated assumption of the Downs model.

The Axiom of Common Reference

The versatility of the spatial scheme as an interactional model is enhanced a good deal by assuming that the public and those who seek its support impose a common frame of reference on the alternatives of government action. In particular, it is the assumption of a commonly perceived space of party competition that allows the model to serve at once as a theory of voter motivation and of party positioning. But with the space formed out of perceptions, there is no logically necessary reason why the space of voters and of parties should be identical, and there is good empirical reason to suppose that it often is not. Indeed in view of the emphasis on imperfect information elsewhere in his discussion, one might expect Downs to regard such an assumption with considerable skepticism. The postulate may be faithful to the realities of economic competition, and it serves the cause of theoretical parsimony, but its factual validity in the political context is doubtful, to say the least.

If the model's assumption of common reference is relaxed, its unified theory of voter behavior and party positioning breaks at least in two. The behavior of voters depends not on where or whether the parties are on an ideological dimension but only on the electorate's *perception* of these things. It would be possible, although highly improbable in view of what is known about large-scale publics, for the motivation of voters to be governed by a calculus of ideological distance, even though the parties were not competing for support in these terms at all. And it would be possible, and a good deal more probable, for the parties to seek electoral support by positioning themselves on an ideological dimension, even though the public evaluated their stands in wholly nonideological terms. Admittedly, it is extreme to think of the pieces into which the spatial model divides (without the assumption of common reference) as two *completely intrapsychic* theories, since the voters' perceptions of parties depend to some degree on what the parties are actually doing and vice versa. But it is equally extreme to assume away the possibility of divergence between the space that is real to voters and the space that is real to party leaders.

Relaxing the assumption of common reference necessarily opens Pandora's box. If we are willing to assume that Kresge's and the customer's Main Street are not the same, there is no reason why Woolworth's Main Street cannot be different too. We may, in fact, have as many perceived spaces as there are perceiving actors. Certainly the way public policy alternatives are perceived varies widely across the electorate. A few voters, as we have seen, impose a clear ideological structure on political conflict. But the vast majority rely on assorted nonideological ways of structuring the political world. And an appreciable stratum of voters can scarcely be said to have any cognitive structure at all as it tries to make sense out of that distant and confusing world.

Likewise, different political leaders may impose different frames of reference on the alternatives of government policy. And they may attribute very different cognitive structures to the public. In the intraparty struggle preceding the 1952 Republican convention's choice, Senator Taft and his lieutenants offered a diagnosis of the Republican situation that was remarkably faithful to the one-dimensional ideological model. According to Taft the country had been moving strongly to the right on the liberal-conservative dimension since the heyday of the New Deal, but millions of potential Republican voters had been kept from the polls by the party's liberal, "me-too" candidates (because demand is elastic, Willkie and Dewey were said to have lost more votes in the party's hinterland than they gained in its competitive region). Hence, victory lay in nominating an unmistakably conservative candidate. The Taft diagnosis and prescription had an appealing simplicity, but the convention was dominated by men whose view of popular thought was very different and far more realistic. Their struggle to control the nomination was fought at least in part on the issue of how the public looks at party competition.

The truth is that we do not yet have very careful evidence about what frames of reference party leaders use in their perceptions of the alternatives of government policy and little enough evidence about the cognitive structures the voters use. Various scaling studies of legislatures suggest that at least the political space of legislators has a fairly definite structure, although it is typically multidimensional.[15] In a variety of multiparty systems the simple factor of seating legislators

---

[15] See, among others, Duncan MacRae, Jr., "The Role of the State Legislator in Massachusetts," *American Sociological Review*, **19**, 185–194 (1954); Duncan MacRae, Jr., and Hugh D. Price, "Scale Positions and 'Power' in the Senate," *Behavioral Science*, **4**, 212–218 (1959); and George M. Belknap, "A Method for Analyzing Legislative Behavior," *Midwest Journal of Political Science*, **2**, 377–402 (1958).

from left to right helps give political conflict a dimensional character —and has done so as far back as the National Convention of revolutionary France.[16] It is likely that political leaders impute more structure to the perceptions formed by the public than actually exists; in some cases party activists see the electorate in thoroughly Downsian terms, as Senator Taft did. But the question of what cognitive structures are meaningful to political leaders remains an immensely important matter for future inquiry.

Toward Reformulation

The conclusion to be drawn from all this is not that the spatial model should be rejected root-and-branch, but rather that we should treat as explicit variables the cognitive phenomena that the prevailing model removes from the discussion by assumption. Bringing these variables into the model would lessen its elegance and parsimony in some respects but would vastly increase the scientific interest of the model as a theory of party systems. Without these variables the model is likely to remain a kind of instructive insight that seems plausible in some contexts, implausible in others, and only poorly suited to guide empirical observation of real political events.

One implication of treating these cognitive factors as variables is to acknowledge that they can assume a configuration of values in the real world that approximates the assumptions of the classical spatial model. Political conflict *can* be focused on a single, stable issue domain which presents an ordered-dimension that is perceived in common terms by leaders and followers. Let us call this the case of *strong ideological focus.* On the other hand, political controversy can be diffused over a number of changing issue concerns which rarely present position-dimensions and which are perceived in different ways by different political actors. Let us call this the case of *weak ideological focus,* a case that is well illustrated by the contemporary American scene.

Treating these cognitive phenomena as variables would lead naturally to a comparison of political systems in these terms. Certainly there

---

[16] In view of the ambiguity of party ideologies and the multidimensional grounds of party conflict, the necessity of agreeing upon a unidimensional seating order can itself lead to conflict in a legislative chamber that follows a left-right scheme. An interesting example of this is the attempt of the Finnish People's Party to move its seats to the left of the Agrarian Party in Finland's Eduskunta after the 1951 election.

are very significant differences in the values these variables assume in different party systems, just as there are very important differences in their values for the same system over time. Although the historical evidence is tantalizingly ambiguous, it is reasonable to conclude that the strength of ideological focus in the United States was greater during the Roosevelt New Deal than it is today. Then, more than now, the intervention of government in the domestic economy and related social problems provided a position-dimension that could organize the competition of parties and the motivation of electors.

However, the moment of American political history when political conflict was most intensely focused on a single ordered-dimension was undoubtedly the period just prior to the Civil War. As the prewar crisis deepened, political discussion became more and more absorbed in the overriding issue of slavery and its attendant controversies. The fact that the struggle over slavery had overtones of economic interest and constitutional theory and regional loyalty does not undermine the point; it is exactly the gathering of several facets of conflict into a single dimension that characterized the politics of the day. The focusing of controversy on this dimension became at last so strong that it provided a basis for the dissolution of long-standing party loyalties in much of the electorate, something that has not happened again to an equal degree in a hundred years. This historical case is the more interesting since the all-consuming dimension of conflict had so little to do with the class-related dimensions that we usually associate with the spatial model.

If a single position-dimension was of transcendant importance in the convulsions leading to civil war, the spatial model ought to predict the appearance of the new party of the prewar era. The period of the Republican Party's early success exhibited the strong ideological focus that would make the model applicable. Then the period ought also to exhibit the conditions from which we would predict the birth of a new party. There is persuasive evidence that it did. As the dimension of slavery became more and more salient, almost certainly there was an anti-slavery shift of opinion in the older states of the North, just as there was a shift to a more aggressively pro-slavery opinion in the South. And what is equally important, the Northern electorate was rapidly extended in the fifteen years prior to 1860 by the granting of statehood to five new states—Wisconsin, Iowa, Minnesota, California, and Oregon—all anti-slavery. These changes in the North presented the Republican Party with the chance to exploit a new "mode" of anti-slavery opinion to which the Democrats and Whigs, in seeking to keep the allegiance of old friends, were much less able to respond.

Yet if the slavery dimension had been only one of several influencing the electorate, the new party would hardly have succeeded. Only with the cognitive preconditions of the spatial model satisfied could the distribution of voters on the slavery question bring a revolutionary change in the structure of the party system.

Elaborating the model to take account of these cognitive variables is more than a matter of seeing that Downs' assumptions are met before plugging the model in. In particular, extending the model to the case of two or more stable, ordered dimensions will lead to results that do not have any analogues in the one-dimensional case. For example, the degree of orthogonality of several dimensions clearly has implications for electoral behavior, party positioning, and party number. And in the multidimensional case a good deal would rest on whether the electoral support of the parties is defined in terms of several dimensions at once; that is, on whether the parties' support is based on joint distributions or marginal distributions. At the very least the formation of coalitions will differ according to whether the parties' electoral strength is differentiated on common or distinct dimensions. The politics of Israel, for instance, will be quite different according to whether the parties are referred to *all* major dimensions of conflict—Zionism, secularism, socialism, attitude toward the West, and so forth—or tend to attract their support on the basis of one or a very few dimensions only.

The reaction to political models is likely to depend partly on taste for some time to come. So few formalizations have added to our knowledge of politics that their potential value can be a matter for honest debate. The Hotelling-Downs model makes a good case for model-building in political research. Certainly no one who compares the inferences this apparatus permits with the inferences that can be drawn from loose popular ideas of spatial competition will fail to gain new respect for a model of this sort. However, the usefulness of models depends absolutely on the interchange between theory-building and empirical observation. This interchange is essential to show the limits of a model's application and guide its future development. No theory is unconditionally true. Learning what the conditions are is an indispensable step toward giving the theory a more significant domain of application.

If anything, the exchange between theory-building and empirical observation is more important in social than in natural science, since the social scientist so rarely has it in his power to make the conditions of his theory come true, as the natural or physical scientist often can. One reason the physicist is untroubled by the fact that his law of gravity does not describe the behavior of many falling bodies (snowflakes, for example) is that he is able to control the disturbing factors whenever the need arises. But the social or political theorist cannot manipulate the conditions of party systems whose dynamics he would predict or explain. No engineering is available to produce the conditions of strong ideological focus so that the prevailing model of spatial competition will apply. If it is to be empirically successful, the theory itself must be extended to take account of the varying cognitive elements found in the competition of parties in the real world.

CHAPTER 10

On the Existence of Forces Restoring
Party Competition

Donald E. Stokes and Gudmund R. Iversen

Observers of American politics have proposed a variety of reasons why
the two-party division of the popular vote, having favored one party,
should in subsequent elections tend to restore the fortunes of the
other. Despite the uncertainty as to their period and amplitude, the
cycles of party strength over the hundred years since the Civil War are
thought to express a basic characteristic of our politics. Examples are
plentiful enough in human affairs of the competition of two organizations leading to the permanent ascendancy of one over the other. The
failure of this to happen in the competition of our parties is counted a
signal fact of the American political system.

The search for influences that could be said to restore the party
balance has covered a broad conceptual terrain. Restoring forces have
been seen in such diverse factors as the tendency of interest groups to
remember the favors an administration has dispensed less than the
favors it has not; the ability of the party out of power to make more
flexible and extravagant promises of future benefit whereas the party
in power is limited by what it can actually deliver; the greater motivational strength of the public's negative response to an administration's
mistakes than of its positive response to an administration's successes;
the liability of the party in power to disastrous splits as its majority
grows and its sense of electoral pressure lessens; movements of the

This chapter appeared originally in the *Public Opinion Quarterly,* 26 (Summer 1962).

business cycle, generating new support for the opposition party in periods of economic decline; the alternating moods of liberalism and conservatism that have marked our national temper; and a vigorous popular belief in rotation in office, which turns the peccadilloes of a party long in power into convincing evidence that the time for a change has arrived.[1]

All such explanations share the premise that there is something to be explained. Reviewing past variations of party strength, most observers have assumed that powerful equilibrium forces are present and have sought to discover the nature of these forces. To be sure, an occasional doubt is heard. V. O. Key wrote some years ago:

It may not be correct to assume that party cycles are a permanent feature of American politics. The behavior of the [two-party vote for President] in the period following the Civil War suggests that one may not be on completely solid ground in supposing that we will continue to have our party ups and downs, with the periods of dominance of each party of fairly regular duration.[2]

What is more, some of the properties often attributed to voting behavior in the United States would tend to make an electoral system *unstable* at or near an equal division of party strength. Any bandwagon effect, for example, would have this result.

Therefore, it has seemed to us appropriate to re-examine the modern period of American party competition to see whether the assumption that electoral movements have been unexpectedly generous to the party out of power can be sustained under hard examination. Our interest in this problem springs in part from an earlier effort to develop a social-psychological theory of restoring forces.[3] The attempt to re-interpret past electoral movements in terms of this theory left a strong

[1] Interpretations of the restoring forces in American politics are spread over an extensive scholarly and popular literature. For a discussion of the perfidy of interest groups, see Dayton D. McKean, *Party and Pressure Politics* (New York: Houghton Mifflin, 1949, pp. 405–406); of the dominance of negative over positive public attitude see A. Campbell, P. E. Converse, W. E. Miller, and D. E. Stokes, *The American Voter* (New York: John Wiley and Sons, 1960, pp. 554–556); of the importance of factional disputes in the majority party, see Samuel Lubell, *The Future of American Politics* (New York: Harper, 1952, p. 204); of the political effects of the business cycle, see Louis H. Bean, *How to Predict Elections* (New York: Alfred A. Knopf, 1948, p. 54); of liberal and conservative policy moods, see Arthur M. Schlesinger, "Tides of American Politics," *Yale Review*, 29, 220 (December 1939).

[2] V. O. Key, *Parties, Politics, and Pressure Groups*, 3rd ed., New York: Crowell, 1952, p. 210.

[3] See Campbell et al., *loc. cit.*

sense that the historical evidence of the existence of restoring forces had never been put to a careful test.

What judgment *can* be made as to the likelihood that the two-party vote actually observed in the United States since the Civil War could have been generated by historical processes in which restoring forces played a negligible part? A way of answering this question is to choose some aspect or property of the electoral past that seems to reflect the presence of equilibrium forces and then to decide whether this property might reasonably be found in movements of the party vote from which such forces are known to be absent. As will be seen below, confronting the historical evidence with a priori expectations in this manner will require the construction of a probability model of the party vote that is faithful to history in certain respects but is known to be free of the influence of restoring forces.

Boundaries of the Major Party Vote

Of all the properties that might be taken as evidence that the party vote is forced back toward an equal division as it moves away from this point, one of the most impressive is the fact that neither of our parties in a hundred years has won more than 65 per cent of the vote. As Figure 10-1 shows, the time series representing the two-party vote for President and the House of Representatives since the Civil War have moved in a very limited region around 50 per cent.[4] There has been substantial variation in the party division of the vote from election to election; indeed, the average difference between successive presidential elections is nearly 6 per cent. Yet over this entire period neither the Republican nor the Democratic Party has succeeded in winning more than 15 per cent beyond an equal share of the vote.[5]

[4] Despite the obvious importance of these electoral series, the national percentages for the congressional vote as far back as the Civil War have not to our knowledge appeared in print before. An account of original sources and the detailed decisions that have gone into these figures is available from the Survey Research Center of The University of Michigan.

[5] It should be noted that both the election in which the Democratic Party achieved its largest share of the two-party vote (1912) and the election in which the Republican Party achieved its largest share (1924) were contests in which a third party cut heavily into the normal support of the losing party. These elections excepted, the Republicans have not won more than 13.8 per cent beyond an equal share of the two-party vote, and the Democrats have not won more than 12.5 per cent beyond an equal division. Because the elections of 1912 and 1924 are not excluded from our test of the restoring-force hypothesis, the test is more severe than it otherwise would be.

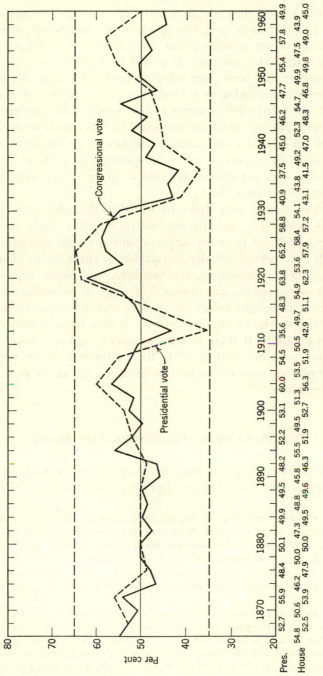

Figure 10-1. Republican percentage of major party vote for President and House since the Civil War.

| Pres. | 52.7 | 55.9 | 48.4 | 50.1 | 49.9 | 48.2 | 52.2 | 53.1 | 60.0 | 54.5 | 35.6 | 48.3 | 63.8 | 65.2 | 58.8 | 40.9 | 37.5 | 45.0 | 46.2 | 47.7 | 55.4 | 57.8 | 49.9 |
| House | 54.8 | 50.6 46.2 | 47.3 | 50.0 | 49.6 | 45.8 55.5 | 51.9 | 52.7 | 51.3 53.5 | 51.9 | 42.9 51.1 | 54.9 62.3 | 53.6 57.9 | 58.4 57.2 | 54.1 43.1 | 43.8 41.5 | 49.2 47.0 | 52.3 48.3 | 54.7 46.8 | 49.9 49.8 | 47.5 49.0 | 43.9 45.0 |

Using the limited bounds in which the vote has stayed as the historical property indicating the presence of equilibrium forces has the advantage of not assuming that these forces act with any mathematical or statistical regularity.[6] It would be a gratuitous addition to most hypotheses that have been offered about the nature of restoring forces to require a regular or periodic movement of the vote; indeed several of these hypotheses suggest that equilibrium tendencies in party competition are set off by historical factors that intrude on our politics in an irregular or random fashion. A desideratum of the narrowness of the region of party competition as a "test" property is that its use does not oblige the vote to move as any well-behaved mathematical function of time.

An analogy from a very different world of discourse may help to make this point. Changes in barometric pressure yield statistical time series which are in many respects similar to our electoral series and which have proved equally intractable to curve-fitting efforts. As in so many social phenomena, random influences loom very large in the march of meteorological events. Yet there is no doubt whatever that strong equilibrating forces are at work on the barometric pressure and that the weight of the atmosphere is free to vary only within fairly narrow limits. If these barometric series were as "short" as the electoral series we are dealing with, the narrowness of the region in which the pressure stays might well be used in a test of the presence of equilibrium forces.[7]

The Choice of an Equilibrium-Free Model

Is it reasonable to suppose that the two-party vote would have kept inside such narrow bounds over the years since the Civil War if it

[6] We use the term "restoring" or "equilibrium" force as a generalized name for factors tending to return the party division to 50 per cent in the long run. If our purposes were different, a very different terminology might be appropriate. In particular, if we were concerned with the short-run maintenance of the dominant strength of a majority party, some factors that we treat here as "restoring forces" might be regarded instead as "disturbing forces" tending to break up the majority coalition.

[7] Despite the need for restrictive assumptions of some kind, inspecting the form of the movements of the party vote yields some suggestive clues as to the presence of equilibrium tendencies. In particular, if the division of the vote at one presidential election is correlated with the *change* of the vote from that election to the next, a negative correlation of $-.55$ is obtained. In other words, the greater a party's share of the vote at one election, the greater is its share likely to be reduced at the next.

were governed by historical processes from which restoring forces were absent? The critical step in the test for such forces is finding an explicit way of deciding whether the historical boundaries of the party vote might have been the same even if equilibrium tendencies were missing. We have dealt with this problem by constructing models of party competition that reflect accurately the variability of the vote division from election to election yet are entirely free of equilibrium tendencies, using these models to reach firm expectations as to the chance of the vote remaining within so narrow an interval without the influence of restoring forces.

In the design of these models, meaning is given to the absence of equilibrium forces by requiring that, however much the division of the vote favors a majority party at one election, it is as likely to move in the direction of that party as of the other party at the next election. If the division of the vote is conceived as a random particle moving on a scale extending from 0 to 100 per cent Republican, the essential feature of these equilibrium-free models is that the probability laws governing the movement of this particle make it equally likely that the particle will move either way at each election trial. In the language of probability theory, these models conceive the movement of the party division as a *symmetric random walk* in one dimension.

With this requirement fulfilled, the probability laws that have been used in these models have been designed to reflect the historical record as faithfully as possible. For this purpose, we have calculated the absolute value of the percentage difference in the vote between each pair of elections since the Civil War and have used these differences as the basis of the probability distributions governing the variation of the vote in our models of party competition. This can be done in several ways. The simplest way is to calculate the mean absolute difference (5.7 per cent for the presidential vote) and treat the party division as if it moved at each election just this "expected" distance toward one party or the other. Conceived in this way the problem becomes an ordinary random walk in one dimension, with the electoral particle moving a single step toward the Republicans or the Democrats at each trial. Although our conclusions will not ultimately rest on this simplified model, its use helps clarify how the probability of the vote's staying in so limited a region over the life of our modern party system can be estimated from a model of this kind.[8]

---

[8] The reader who would prefer a more formal description of the models used to derive these probability estimates may turn directly to the appended note.

The Presidential Vote as a Random Walk

A model of party competition that treats the division of the vote as if it moves only one mean-difference step in either direction at each trial clearly transforms the original percentage scale to a scale whose units are 5.7 per cent. We may locate the historic bounds of the presidential vote between two and three steps away from the point of equal division in each direction on this transformed scale, since moving three mean-difference steps from the equal-division point in either direction will exceed the largest share of the vote captured by the parties, whereas moving two such steps will not. For this simplified model the absence of equilibrium forces is given definite meaning by requiring that at each trial the probability of the particle taking a step in one direction be equal to the probability of its taking a step in the other direction.

There have been twenty-four presidential elections from 1868 to 1960. Finding the probability that the party vote, starting at the point of equal division,[9] would stay within the actual bounds of presidential voting over twenty-three subsequent election trials requires a counting operation on the set of paths the electoral particle can follow. Although computational formulas are reserved for the Methodological Note, what this operation involves is easily shown by a simple figure, in which time (from Trial 0 to Trial 5) is shown along the horizontal dimension and the party division (on both the original percentage scale and mean-difference scale) is shown along the vertical dimension. The possible movements of the electoral particle over these early trials are described completely by the set of paths shown in Figure 10-2. Starting at the point of equal division, the particle will move at the first trial one step in either the Republican or Democratic direction. From either of these positions the particle will move at the second trial either back to the point of equal division or one more step in the partisan direction it took at the first trial. Hence, by the second trial there are four distinct paths, two of which return the particle to the point of equal division. As the paths increase over subsequent trials the number of distinct paths that can bring the particle to a given

[9] As Figure 10-1 indicates, the presidential vote did not start exactly at 50 per cent in the election of 1868, and neither did the congressional vote start exactly at 50 per cent in the election of 1870. These discrepancies have no effect whatever on the probabilities derived from the simplified model, and their effect on the more generalized model to be discussed below is negligible.

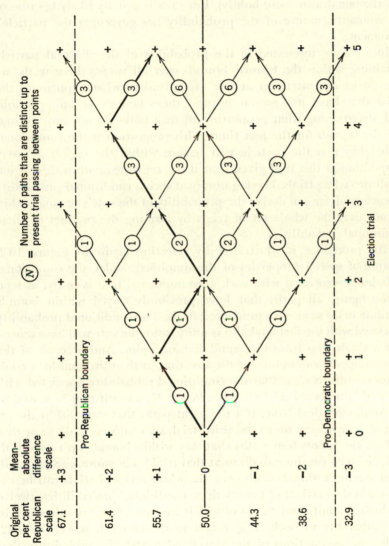

Figure 10-2. Paths of the presidential vote over the initial five trials of a random walk.

point at a given trial is shown by the number superimposed on the arrows leading *away* from that point. Only one path would actually be followed over these five trials (for illustration, let us suppose that it is the one drawn more boldly), but each is equally likely because of the symmetric nature of the probability law governing the particle's movement.

Since we are interested in the probability of the electoral particle remaining within the historic bounds over all twenty-three trials, we can restrict our attention at any given trial to what happens to the paths that have not gotten outside these bounds at any previous trial, determining what proportion of such paths do not now go outside the bounds for the first time. This proportion is the conditional probability that the particle will remain within the region of party competition at this trial given that it has remained within this region on all preceding trials. Having obtained such a conditional probability for each trial, we can derive the probability of the vote's staying within bounds over the whole set of trials by forming the product of these conditional probabilities.

This procedure is illustrated by referring again to Figure 10-2. Because of special properties of the simplified model, the conditional probability associated with each even-numbered trial is unity; as seen in the figure, all paths that have previously stayed within bounds continue to do so at even-numbered trials. The conditional probability associated with the first trial also is unity, since the vote will have moved only a single step from the equal-division point. And a count of the paths going out of bounds for the first time at the third and fifth trials makes intuitively clear that the conditional probability associated with every odd-numbered trial after the first is $3/4$, a result that is proved in the Methodological Note. (Of the eight paths that stay within the region of competition up to the third trial, six continue to do so at that trial; of the twenty-four paths that stay within bounds up to the fifth trial, eighteen continue to do so at that trial.) Therefore, the probability of staying within bounds over the whole series of trials can be expressed as the product of twenty-three conditional probabilities, twelve of which are unity and eleven of which are equal to $3/4$; in other words, the probability we seek is $3/4$ raised to the eleventh power, or .042. Under the assumptions of the simplified model, the probability that the division of the vote for President would have stayed within such a narrow region since the Civil War if it were totally free of equilibrium forces is less than five in a hundred.

Yet this simplified model is artificial in several respects. Particularly troublesome is the problem of locating the historic bounds of party competition on the scale of mean-difference units. Clearly these bounds fall between the second and third steps away from the equal-division point. But they are nearer the third position than they are the second, and requiring the electoral particle to stay in the interval from -2 to $+2$ falsifies somewhat the actual restriction of movements of the party vote for President. It is more natural to return to the original percentage scale and to allow the electoral particle to move one, two, or more percentage steps in either direction at each trial, according to a more complex probability law. Conceived in this way the problem becomes a *generalized* random walk in one dimension.

The Party Vote as a Generalized Random Walk

In large part, the adequacy of our test of restoring forces depends on how well a model reflects the real behavior of the major party vote—save only for the aspect of its motion that is taken as evidence of equilibrium tendencies. So that the behavior of the party division in our generalized model would be as true to the real world as possible we have derived a probability law for the electoral particle directly from the empirical distribution of absolute differences actually recorded between successive elections since the Civil War. In fact, this empirical distribution, adjusted to satisfy the requirements of a probability law, has simply been used as one-half of a theoretical probability distribution governing the vote, and its mirror image used as the other half. So constructed, the model permits the party division at a given trial to move in either direction any percentage distance that it has actually moved in the real world and with a probability proportional to the number of times that it has moved each such distance in the elections of the past century. The model is free of restoring forces since the probability law is symmetric about the present division of the vote; at each trial the sum of the probabilities of moving one way is equal to the sum of the probabilities of moving the other way.

Representing party competition as a generalized random walk complicates the counting operation required to gauge the probable movements of the vote, but does not change the operation's basic character. Instead of doubling at each trial, the number of paths the vote can take now increases more than fortyfold. However, by suitable computer routines we are able to determine at each trial the number of paths that have not exceeded the bounds of party competition at any preceding trial. And we are able to determine the number of such paths that do not go out of bounds at this trial. The second figure, expressed as a proportion of the first, gives the conditional probability that the electoral particle will stay within the region of party competition at this trial given that it has stayed within this region at all preceding trials. The probability that the party vote will stay within bounds over the full series of trials is again obtained by forming the product of the conditional probabilities associated with the several trials. The value of this probability figure for the presidential vote is .031; under the assumptions of this generalized model, the chances that the party division could have stayed within the historic boundaries of the vote for President without the influence of equilibrium forces is less than four in a hundred.

Adapting this generalized model to the congressional case requires only the substitution of a new theoretical probability distribution, derived from the historical record in the same way as the distribution used to govern the presidential vote; a redefinition of the actual region of party competition; [10] and an increase in the number of trials from twenty-four (including the starting election) to forty-six, the number of elections for the House from 1870 to 1960. When these changes are made, the probability of the party division's remaining within the observed bounds for the congressional vote is .028; under the assumptions of the model, the chances that the electoral particle, free of restoring forces, could have stayed within the historic region of the vote for Congress is less than three in a hundred.

Conclusion

These probabilities strongly bear out the view that our electoral history has dealt more kindly with the minority party than we would expect of a system in which equilibrium tendencies played a negligible role. If a judgment is given on the restoring-force hypothesis according to the probability requirements that have become conventional in social science, the presence of such forces is accepted; the notion that the strength of the parties has fluctuated as a symmetric random walk is not credible.

A word should be added about the time encompassed in this test.

[10] The Republicans never have won more than 62.3 per cent of the two-party vote for Congress, the Democrats never more than 58.5 per cent. To keep the region of party competition symmetric about 50 per cent in the model, the bounds used were 37 per cent and 63 per cent Republican. Moving the pro-Democratic boundary more than 4 per cent farther out from an equal division makes the test of the restoring-force hypothesis more severe than it would otherwise be.

Our model has been applied to the whole life of the modern party system, yet an inspection of the electoral series shown in Figure 10-1 suggests that the behavior of the party division in the seventies and eighties of the last century was quite unlike its later movement, as V. O. Key has observed. Although the national series for this period conceals some compensating movements at state and lower levels, it is persuasive evidence that partisan attachments were more tightly fixed in the first decades after the Civil War than they ever again have been. Perhaps a full generation's time was needed for the tremendous passions of war and reconstruction to loosen their grip on an electorate whose memories gradually faded and whose older members gave way to the new.

It is the present century that furnishes the clearest evidence of the influence of equilibrium forces in the competition of our parties. Indeed, if we truncate our electoral series and perform an identical test for the period from 1892 to 1960, the result is not essentially different from that obtained for the whole period. In the election of 1892 the Republican share of the vote for President stood less than 2 per cent below half. In 1960, having fluctuated more than 120 percentage points over the intervening years, the Republican share of the presidential vote was again just below half. That this remarkable performance of the party system could result from historical causes in which restoring forces played no part can be discounted at a high level of confidence.

METHODOLOGICAL NOTE

We have conceived the party division of the vote for President and the House as symmetric random walks in one dimension and have tested the restoring-force hypothesis by determining the probability that these random walks, beginning at a specified point, would not reach certain absorbing barriers over a given number of trials. In the simplified version (Model I) the random walk is a series of Bernoulli trials with $p = q = 1/2$. In the generalized version (Model II) the random walk is governed by an arbitrary distribution for which $\Sigma p = \Sigma q = 1/2$. The variances of these theoretical distributions in all cases have been made identical with the empirical variances of the observed distributions of differences of the vote since the Civil War. Historical fact has also been allowed to determine the width of the intervals about 50 per cent in which the party division of the vote can move without reaching an absorbing barrier, as explained in the text.

For both models the problem of determining the probability of the random walk not reaching an absorbing barrier over a given number of trials can be stated as follows. Let $P(A_k)$ be the probability of the particle not reaching an absorbing barrier at the kth trial. We require the joint probability $P(A_1 A_2 \cdots A_n)$, with $n = 23$ for the presidential case and $n = 45$ for the congressional case. This probability may be obtained by direct means or it can be expressed as a product of conditional probabilities:

$$P(A_1 A_2 \cdots A_n) = P(A_1) \cdot P(A_2 | A_1) \cdot P(A_3 | A_1 A_2) \cdots P(A_n | A_1 A_2 \cdots A_{n-1}) \quad (1)$$

Hence the joint probability may be calculated by obtaining for each trial the conditional probability of the particle's not reaching an absorbing barrier given that it has not reached an absorbing barrier at any preceding trial.

For Model I these conditional probabilities may be found by means of simple recursive formulas. From Figure 10-2 it is clear that in the presidential case the particle can reach an absorbing barrier only at odd-numbered trials. For the $(2i + 1)$th trial let us denote the number of paths reaching the upper absorbing barrier at $+3$ by $N_1^{(i)}$, the number of paths passing through the points $+1$ and -1 by $N_2^{(i)}$ and $N_3^{(i)}$, and the number of paths reaching the lower absorbing barrier at -3 by $N_4^{(i)}$. We then have:

$$P(A_{2i+1} | A_1 A_2 \cdots A_{2i}) = \frac{N_2^{(i)} + N_3^{(i)}}{N_1^{(i)} + N_2^{(i)} + N_3^{(i)} + N_4^{(i)}} \quad (2)$$

It is also clear from Figure 10-2 that all these paths are generated by paths passing through the points $+1$ and -1 at the $(2i - 1)$th trial. For uniform notation, let us denote the number of paths passing through these points at the earlier trial by $N_2^{(i-1)}$ and $N_3^{(i-1)}$, respectively.

Because of the way distinct paths are generated in the model, the following relations hold between the numbers of paths at successive odd-numbered trials:

$$\begin{aligned}
N_1^{(i)} &= N_2^{(i-1)} \\
N_2^{(i)} &= 2N_2^{(i-1)} + N_3^{(i-1)} \\
N_3^{(i)} &= N_2^{(i-1)} + 2N_3^{(i-1)} \\
N_4^{(i)} &= N_3^{(i-1)}
\end{aligned} \quad (3)$$

Since the model is symmetric about the point of equal division, $N_2^{(i-1)} = N_3^{(i-1)}$ for all i; (3) can be rewritten:

$$\begin{aligned}
N_1^{(i)} &= N_2^{(i-1)} \\
N_2^{(i)} &= 3N_2^{(i-1)} \\
N_3^{(i)} &= 3N_2^{(i-1)} \\
N_4^{(i)} &= N_2^{(i-1)}
\end{aligned} \quad (4)$$

Substituting (4) in (2) gives:

$$P(A_{2i+1} | A_1 A_2 \cdots A_{2i}) = \frac{3N_2^{(i-1)} + 3N_2^{(i-1)}}{N_2^{(i-1)} + 3N_2^{(i-1)} + 3N_2^{(i-1)} + N_2^{(i-1)}} = \frac{3}{4} \quad (5)$$

Hence, for the presidential case the conditional probability associated with each odd-numbered trial after the first is the constant $\frac{3}{4}$. When Model I is applied to the congressional case, the location of the barriers has to be changed. Similar procedures as shown above will lead to a recursive formula for the conditional probability.

Finding the necessary conditional probabilities in Model II also involves a counting of paths. In this model each distinct path is not equally likely, since at each trial the particle moves a given distance with probability proportional to the number of times the party division has moved each such distance in the elections of the past century. However, the equally-likely property may be restored by introducing multiple identical paths. Each path reaching a given point at a given trial may be regarded as generating not just a single path to each of the points to which the particle can move at the next trial: it may be regarded as generating as many paths to each of these points as the party division has moved each such distance between successive elections since the Civil War. With this modification the task of obtaining the conditional probability $P(A_j|A_1A_2\cdots A_{j-1})$ is again a matter of expressing the number of paths not reaching an absorbing barrier at the jth trial as a proportion of the total number of paths generated up to the jth trial that have not reached an absorbing barrier at any preceding trial.

CHAPTER 11

Party Government and the Saliency
of Congress

Donald E. Stokes and Warren E. Miller

Any mid-term congressional election raises pointed questions about
party government in America. With the personality of the President
removed from the ballot by at least a coattail, the public is free to
pass judgment on the legislative record of the parties. So the civics
texts would have us believe. In fact, however, an off-year election can
be regarded as an assessment of the parties' records in Congress only
if the electorate possesses certain minimal information about what
that record is. The fact of possession needs to be demonstrated, not
assumed, and the low visibility of congressional affairs to many citizens
suggests that the electorate's actual information should be examined
with care.

How much the people know is an important, if somewhat hidden,
problem of the normative theory of representation. Implicitly at least,
the information the public is thought to have is one of the points on
which various classical conceptions of representation divide. Edmund
Burke and the liberal philosophers, for example—to say nothing of
Hamilton and Jefferson—had very different views about the information the public could get or use in assessing its government. And the
periods of flood tide in American democracy, especially the Jacksonian
and Progressive eras, have been marked by the most optimistic assumptions as to what the people could or did know about their government.

This chapter appeared originally in the *Public Opinion Quarterly*, 26 (Winter 1962).

To put the matter another way: any set of representative institutions will work very differently according to the amount and quality of information the electorate has. This is certainly true of the institutional forms we associate with government by responsible parties. A necessary condition of party responsibility to the people is that the public have basic information about the parties and their legislative record. Without it, no institutional devices can make responsibility a fact.

To explore the information possessed by those who play the legislative and constituent roles in American government, the Survey Research Center undertook an interview study of Congressmen and their districts during the mid-term election of Eisenhower's second term. Immediately after the 1958 campaign the Center interviewed a nationwide sample of the electorate, clustered in 116 congressional districts, as well as the incumbent Congressmen and other major-party candidates for the House from the same collection of districts.[1] Through these direct interviews with the persons playing the reciprocal roles of representative government, this research has sought careful evidence about the perceptual ties that bind, or fail to bind, the Congressman to his party and district. We will review some of this evidence here for the light that it throws on the problem of party cohesion and responsibility in Congress.

The Responsible-Party Model and the American Case

What the conception of government by responsible parties requires of the general public has received much less attention than what it requires of the legislative and electoral parties.[2] The notion of respon-

---

[1] The 116 districts are a probability sample of all constituencies, although the fact that the study was piggy-backed onto a four-year panel study of the electorate extending over the elections of 1956, 1958, and 1960 made the design of the 1958 representation sample unusually complex. In particular, since metropolitan areas and nonmetropolitan counties or groups of counties, rather than congressional districts, were used as primary sampling units when the panel sample was originated in 1956, the districts represented in our 1958 sample did not have equal probability of selection, and the efficiency of the sample of districts was somewhat less than that of a simple random sample of equal size.

[2] For example, the 1950 report of the American Political Science Association's Committee on Political Parties, the closest approach to an official statement of the responsible-party view as applied to American politics, concentrates on the organization of Congress and the national parties and deals only very obliquely with the

sibility generally is understood to mean that the parties play a mediating role between the public and its government, making popular control effective by developing rival programs of government action that are presented to the electorate for its choice. The party whose program gains the greater support takes possession of the government and is held accountable to the public in later elections for its success in giving its program effect.

Two assumptions about the role of the public can be extracted from these ideas. First, in a system of party government the electorate's attitude toward the parties is based on what the party programs are and how well the parties have delivered on them. The public, in a word, gives the parties *programmatic* support. And, in view of the importance that legislative action is likely to have in any party program, such support is formed largely out of public reaction to the legislative performance of the parties, especially the party in power.

Second, under a system of party government the voters' responses to the local legislative candidates are based on the candidates' identification with party programs. These programs are the substance of their appeals to the constituency, which will act on the basis of its information about the proposals and legislative records of the parties. Since the party programs are of dominant importance, the candidates are deprived of any independent basis of support. They will not be able to build in their home districts an electoral redoubt from which to challenge the leadership of their parties.[3]

---

role of the public. See *Toward a More Responsible Two-Party System* (New York: Rinehart, 1950). In general, theoretical and empirical treatments of party government have focused more on the nature of party *appeals*—especially the question of whether the parties present a real "choice"—than on the cognitive and motivational elements that should be found in the *response* of an electorate that is playing its correct role in a system of responsible-party government. For example, see the excellent discussion in A. Ranney and W. Kendall, *Democracy and the American Party System* (New York: Harcourt, Brace, 1956, pp. 151–152, 384–385, 525–527).

It should be clear that the data of this report are taken from a particular election of a particular electoral era. We would expect our principal findings to apply to most recent off-year elections, but they are of course subject to modification for earlier or later periods.

[3] This assumption does not imply that pressures toward party cohesion come *only* from the mass public. Other sanctions against party irregularity are of equal or greater importance, especially those available in the nominating process and within the legislative parties themselves. To cite the most celebrated empirical case, the cohesiveness of the British parliamentary parties is not enforced primarily, if at all, by the British electorate. Nevertheless, the public ought not to give aid and comfort to the legislative party irregular; the idea of the candidate building a local bastion of strength from which he can challenge the party leadership is clearly contradictory to the party-government model.

How well do these assumptions fit the behavior of the American public as it reaches a choice in the off-year congressional elections? A first glance at the relation of partisan identifications to the vote might give the impression that the mid-term election is a triumph of party government. As we have remarked at numerous points in this book, popular allegiance to the parties is of immense importance in all our national elections, including those in which a President is chosen, but its potency in the mid-term congressional election is especially pronounced. This fact is plain—even stark—in the entries of Table 11-1, which break down the vote for Congress in 1958 into its component party elements. The table makes clear, first of all, how astonishingly small a proportion of the mid-term vote is cast by political Independents. We have seen in Figure 2-1 that approximately 1 American in 10 thinks of himself as altogether independent of the two parties. But in the off-year race for Congress only about a twentieth part of the vote is cast by Independents, owing to their greater drop-out rate when the drama and stakes of the presidential contest are missing.

Table 11-1 also makes clear how little deviation from party there is among Republicans and Democrats voting in a mid-term year. The role of party identification in the congressional election might still be slight, whatever the size of the party followings, if partisan allegiance sat more lightly on the voting act. But almost 9 out of every 10 partisans

TABLE 11-1

1958 Vote for House Candidates, by Party Identification
(in per cent)

	Party Identification *			
	Democratic	Independent	Republican	Total
Voted Democratic	53 †	2	6	61
Voted Republican	5	3	31	39
Total	58	5	37	100

* The Democratic and Republican Party identification groups include all persons who classify themselves as having some degree of party loyalty.

† Each entry of the table gives the per cent of the total sample of voters having the specified combination of party identification and vote for the House in 1958.

voting in the off-year race support their parties. Indeed, something like 84 per cent of *all* the votes for the House in 1958 were cast by party identifiers supporting their parties. The remaining 16 per cent is not a trivial fraction of the whole—standing, as it did in this case, for 8 million people, quite enough to make and unmake a good many legislative careers. Nevertheless, the low frequency of deviation from party, together with the low frequency of independent voting, indicates that the meaning of the mid-term vote depends in large part on the nature of party voting.

The Saliency of the Parties' Legislative Records

If American party voting were to fit the responsible-party model it would be *programmatic* voting, that is, the giving of electoral support according to the parties' past or prospective action on programs that consist (mainly) of legislative measures. There is little question that partisan voting is one of the very few things at the bottom of our two-party system; every serious third-party movement in a hundred years has foundered on the reef of traditional Republican and Democratic loyalties. But there is also little question that this voting is largely nonprogrammatic in nature. A growing body of evidence indicates that party loyalties are typically learned early in life, free of ideological or issue content, with the family as the main socializing agency. Certainly our findings have shown that such loyalties are extremely long-lived and, summed across the population, give rise to extraordinarily stable distributions. The very persistence of party identification raises suspicion as to whether the country is responding to the parties' current legislative actions when it votes its party loyalties.

That this suspicion is fully warranted in the mid-term election is indicated by several kinds of evidence from this research. To begin with, the electorate's perceptions of the parties betray very little information about current policy issues. For the past ten years the Survey Research Center has opened its electoral interviews with a series of free-answer questions designed to gather in the positive and negative ideas that the public has about the parties. The answers, requiring on the average nearly ten minutes of conversation, are only very secondarily couched in terms of policy issues. In 1958, for example, more than six thousand distinct positive or negative comments about the parties were made by a sample of 1,700 persons. Of these, less than 12 per cent by the most generous count had to do with contemporary legislative issues. As this sample of Americans pictured the reasons it liked and disliked the parties, the modern battlefields of the legislative wars—aid-to-education, farm policy, foreign aid, housing, aid to the unemployed, tariff and trade policy, social security, medical care, labor laws, civil rights, and other issues—rarely came to mind. The main themes in the public's image of the parties are not totally cut off from current legislative events; the political activist could take the group-benefit and prosperity-depression ideas that saturate the party images and connect them fairly easily with issues before Congress. The point is that the public itself rarely does so.

How little awareness of current issues is embodied in the congressional vote also is attested by the reasons people give for voting Republican or Democratic for the House. In view of the capacity of survey respondents to rationalize their acts, direct explanations of behavior should be treated with some reserve. However, rationalization is likely to increase, rather than decrease, the policy content of reasons for voting. It is therefore especially noteworthy how few of the reasons our respondents gave for their House votes in 1958 had any discernible issue content. The proportion that had—about 7 per cent—was less even than the proportion of party-image references touching current issues.

Perhaps the most compelling demonstration of how hazardous it is to interpret party voting as a judgment of the parties' legislative records is furnished by the evidence about the public's knowledge of party control of Congress. When our 1958 sample was asked whether the Democrats or the Republicans had had more Congressmen in Washington during the two preceding years, a third confessed they had no idea, and an additional fifth gave control of the Eighty-fifth Congress to the Republicans. Only 47 per cent correctly attributed control to the Democrats. These figures improve somewhat when nonvoters are excluded. Of those who voted in 1958, a fifth did not know which party had controlled Congress, another fifth thought the Republicans had, and the remainder (61 per cent) correctly gave control to the Democrats. However, when a discount is made for guessing, the proportion of voters who really *knew* which party had controlled the Eighty-fifth Congress probably is still not more than half.[4]

---

[4] Plainly, some deduction has to be made for guessing. One model of the situation would be to think of the sample as composed of three types of people: those who knew, those who didn't know and said so, and those who didn't know but guessed. Assuming that for those who guessed $p = q = \frac{1}{2}$, where p is the probability of guess-

It would be difficult to overstate the significance of these figures for the problem of party government. The information at issue here is not a sophisticated judgment as to what sort of coalition had *effective* control of Congress. It is simply the question of whether the country had a Democratic or a Republican Congress from 1956 to 1958. This elementary fact of political life, which any pundit would take completely for granted as he interpreted the popular vote in terms of party accountability, was unknown to something like half the people who went to the polls in 1958.

It is of equal significance to note that the parties' legislative records were no more salient to those who *deviated* from party than they were to those who voted their traditional party loyalty. It might be plausible to suppose that a floating portion of the electorate gives the parties programmatic support, even though most voters follow their traditional allegiances. If true, this difference would give the responsible-party model some factual basis, whether or not the greater part of the electorate lived in darkness. But such a theory finds very little support in these data. In 1958 neither the issue reasons given for the congressional vote nor the awareness of party control of the Eighty-fifth Congress was any higher among those who voted *against* their party identification than it was among those who voted *for* their party, as the entries of Table 11-2 demonstrate. If anything, correcting perceived party control for guessing suggests that voters who deviated from their party in 1958 had poorer information about the course of political events over the preceding two years.

Nor do the perceptions of party control of Congress that *are* found supply a key to understanding the congressional vote. Whatever awareness of control the electorate had in 1958 was remarkably unrelated to its support of candidates for the House. To make this point, Table 11-3 analyzes deviations from party according to three perceptions held by party identifiers voting in 1958: first, whether they thought the country's recent domestic affairs had gone well or badly; second (to

---

ing Republican, we would deduct from the Democratic answers a percentage equal to the 18 per cent who guessed Republican incorrectly, hence reducing the proportion of voters who really knew which party controlled Congress to 43 per cent. This model may be too severe, however, in view of the presence of the Republican President. It may be more reasonable to admit a fourth type of person, those who did not guess but were misled by Republican control of the White House. Or we might think of the guessers as following a probability law in which $p > \frac{1}{2} > q$. In either of these cases something less than 18 per cent would be deducted from the Democratic answers; hence, the proportion of voters who *knew* which party controlled Congress would lie somewhere between 43 and 61 per cent.

TABLE 11-2

Issue Responses and Awareness of Which Party Controlled 85th Congress among Party Supporters and Voters Who Deviated from Party

	Of Party Identifiers Who	
	Voted for Own Party	Voted for Other Party
Per cent aware of party control		
Uncorrected	61	60
Corrected for guessing *	44	35
Per cent giving issue reasons for House vote	6	7

* This correction deducts from the proportion attributing control to the Democrats a percentage equal to the proportion attributing control to the Republicans. See footnote 4.

TABLE 11-3

Percentage of Party Identifiers Voting against Party in 1958, by Perception of Party Control of Government and Course of Domestic Affairs

Thought That Domestic Affairs	Thought That More Effective Branch of Government Was Controlled by	
	Own Party	Other Party
	I	II
Had gone well	16	22
	(N = 43)	(N = 46)
	III	IV
Had gone badly	14	13
	(N = 152)	(N = 122)

allow for the complication of divided government), whether they thought Congress or President had the greater influence over what the government did; and third, whether they thought the Democrats or Republicans had controlled Congress. To recreate the basis on which the voter might assign credit or blame to the parties, the second and third of these perceptions may be combined; that is, partisans may be classified according to whether they thought their own party or the opposite party had controlled the more effective branch of government. Crossing this classification with perceptions of whether domestic affairs had gone well yields four groups for analysis, two of which (I and IV) might be expected to show little deviation from party, the other two (II and III) substantially more. In fact, however, the differences between these groups are almost trifling. According to the familiar lore, the groups that thought affairs had gone badly (III and IV) are the ones that should provide the clearest test of whether perceptions of party control are relevant to voting for the House. Moreover, with a recession in the immediate background, most people who could be classified into this table in 1958 fell into one of these two groups, as the frequencies indicate. But when the two groups that felt there had been domestic difficulties are compared, it seems not to make a particle of difference whether the Democrats or Republicans were thought to have controlled the actions of government. And when the two groups (I and II) that felt things had gone well are compared, only a slight (and statistically insignificant) difference appears. Interestingly, even this small rise in the rate of deviation from party (in cell II) is contributed mainly by Democratic identifiers who wrongly supposed that the Congress had been in Republican hands.

The conclusion to be drawn from all this certainly is not that national political forces are without *any* influence on deviations from party in the mid-term year. Clearly these forces do have an influence. Although the fluctuations of the mid-term party vote, charted over half a century or more, are very much smaller than fluctuations in the presidential vote or of the congressional vote in presidential years, there is *some* variation, and these moderate swings must be attributed to forces that have their focus at the national level.[5] Even in 1958 one party received a larger share of deviating votes than the other. Our

---

[5] A simple but persuasive comparison is this: from 1892 to 1960 the standard deviation of the two-party division of the mid-term congressional vote was 3.9 per cent; of the presidential-year congressional vote, 5.5 per cent; of the presidential vote, 8.2 per cent. Moreover, if the realignment of party loyalties that occurred in the early 1930's is taken into account by computing deviations from pre- and post-1932 means, rather than from a grand mean for the whole period, the standard deviation of the mid-term congressional vote is found to have been 2.4 per cent, compared with a standard deviation of 7.5 per cent for the presidential vote. Some of the remaining variability of the mid-term vote may be due to fluctuations of turnout that do not involve deviations from party. Yet, even ignoring this possibility, the bounds within which national political forces can have influenced the off-year vote by inducing deviations from party appear narrow indeed.

main point is rather that the deviations that *do* result from national forces are not in the main produced by the parties' legislative records and that, in any case, the proportion of deviating votes that can be attributed to national politics is likely to be a small part of the total votes cast by persons deviating from party in a mid-term year. This was specifically true in 1958.

If the motives for deviations from party are not to be found primarily at the national level, the search moves naturally to the local congressional campaign. A third possibility—that deviations are by-products of statewide races—can be discounted with some confidence. Despite the popular lore on the subject, evidence both from interview studies and from aggregate election statistics can be used to show that the influence of contests for Governor and Senator on the outcome of House races is slight in mid-term elections, although these contests can have an immense influence on turnout for the House.[6] In our 1958 sample, a majority of those who deviated from party in voting for the House *failed* to deviate also at the state level; more often than not, what had moved them into the other party's column at the House level was dissociated from the contests for Governor or Senator in which they voted. Moreover, the fact that an elector deviates from his party in voting both for the House and some office contested on a statewide basis is not conclusive evidence that the state race has influenced his choice for the House, rather than the other way round. When the possibility of *reverse* coattail effects is allowed for, the reasons for believing that the statewide race is a potent force on the House vote seem faint indeed.[7] As we search for the motives for

---

[6] A remarkable fact is that although the total vote for the House increased by 3 million between 1954 and 1958, more than 2 million of this increase was contributed by New York, where Rockefeller sought the governorship; by Ohio, where a fierce referendum battle was fought over the issue of "right-to-work"; and by California, where the fantastic Knight-Knowland-Brown free-for-all was held.

[7] This conclusion is fully supported by an analysis of the variance of turnout and party vote in the mid-term congressional elections of the 1950's. If statewide races have a major influence on local House races, the election results for the several congressional districts of a state should vary together; similar changes of turnout and party division should be seen in the districts that are influenced by the same statewide contests. An analysis of the variance of the differences between the 1954 and 1958 turnout level and partisan division for all congressional districts in states having at least two districts indicates that state races have a large effect on turnout; the intraclass correlation expressing the ratio of the between-state variance to the total variance of turnout was more than .45. But this analysis shows, too, that statewide races have almost no effect whatever on the party division of the House vote; the intraclass correlation expressing the ratio of the between-state variance to the total variance of the party division was not more than .02.

deviation from party, analysis of the local congressional race pays greater dividends.

The Saliency of Congressional Candidates

By the standards of the civics text, what the public knows about the candidates for Congress is as meager as what it knows about the parties' legislative records. Of the people who lived in districts where the House seat was contested in 1958, 59 per cent—well over half— said that they had neither read nor heard anything about either candidate for Congress, and less than 1 in 5 felt that they knew something about both candidates. What is more, these remarkable proportions are only marginally improved by excluding nonvoters from the calculations. Of people who went to the polls and cast a vote between rival House candidates in 1958, fully 46 per cent conceded that they did so without having read or heard anything about either man. What the other half *had* read or heard is illuminating; we will deal with its policy content presently. Many of our respondents said they knew something about the people contesting the House seat on the basis of very slender information indeed.

The incumbent candidate is by far the better known. In districts where an incumbent was opposed for re-election in 1958, 39 per cent of our respondents knew something about the Congressman, whereas only 20 per cent said they knew anything at all about his nonincumbent opponent. The incumbent's advantage of repeated exposure to the electorate is plain enough. In fact, owing to the greater seniority and longer exposure of Congressmen from safe districts, the public's awareness of incumbents who were unopposed for re-election in 1958 was as great as its awareness of incumbents who had had to conduct an election campaign that year.

The saliency of a candidate is of critical importance if he is to attract support from the opposite party. However little the public may know of those seeking office, any information at all about the rival party's candidate creates the possibility of a choice deviating from party. That such a choice occurs with some frequency is shown by the entries of Table 11-4, whose columns separate party identifiers in contested districts in 1958 according to whether they were aware of both candidates, the candidate of their own party or the other party only, or neither candidate. The condition of no information leads to fairly unrelieved party-line voting, and so to an even greater degree does the condition of information only about the candidate of

TABLE 11-4

Percentage Voting for Own Party Candidate and Other Party Candidate for House in 1958, by Saliency of Candidates in Contested Districts

Voted for Candidate	Voter Was Aware of			
	Both Candidates ($N = 196$)	Own Party Candidate Only ($N = 166$)	Other Party Candidate Only ($N = 68$)	Neither Candidate ($N = 368$)
Of own party	83	98	60	92
Of other party	17	2	40	8
Total	100	100	100	100

the voter's own party. But if partisan voters know something about the opposition's man, substantial deviations from party appear. In fact, if such voters know *only* the opposition candidate, almost half can be induced to cast a vote contrary to their party identification. In the main, recognition carries a positive valence; to be perceived at all is to be perceived favorably. However, some *negative* perceptions are found in our interviews, and when these are taken into account the explanation of deviation from party becomes surer still. For example, if we return to Table 11-4 and select from the third column only the voters who perceived the candidate of the other party *favorably,* a clear majority is found to have deviated from party allegiance in casting their votes. And if we select from the first column only the handful of voters who perceived the candidate of their own party *negatively* and of the opposite party *positively,* almost three-quarters are found to have deviated from their party loyalty in voting for the House.

What our constituent interviews show about the increment of support that accrues to the salient candidate is closely aligned to what the candidates themselves see as the roots of their electoral strength. Our interviews with incumbent and nonincumbent candidates seeking election to the House explored at length their understanding of factors aiding—or damaging—their electoral appeal. In particular, these interviews probed the candidates' assessment of four possible influences on the result: traditional party loyalties, national issues, state and local contests, and the candidates' own records and personal standing in the district. Caution is in order in dealing with answers to questions that touch the respondent's self-image as closely as these. Specifically, we may expect some overstatement of the candidate's own importance, particularly from the victors, and we may expect, too, that too large a discount will be applied to party allegiance, since this "inert" factor, having little to do with increments of strength, is so easily taken for granted.

After these allowances are made, it is still impressive how heavy a weight the incumbent assigns his personal record and standing. The Congressman's ranking of this and the other factors in the election is shown in Table 11-5. As the entries of the table indicate, more than four-fifths of the incumbents re-elected in 1958 felt that the niche they had carved out in the awareness of their constituents had substantial impact on the race, a proportion that exceeds by half the percentage who gave as much weight to any of the three other factors. This difference is more than sheer puffing in the interview situation, and the perceptual facts it reveals deserve close attention. Among the forces the Representative feels may enhance his strength at the polls, he gives his personal standing with the district front rank.

In view of the way the saliency of candidates can move the electorate across party lines, great stress should be laid on the fact that the public sees individual candidates for Congress in terms of party programs scarcely at all. Our constituent interviews indicate that the popular image of the Congressman is almost barren of policy content.

TABLE 11-5

Relative Importance of Factors in Re-election as Seen by Incumbent Candidates in 1958
(in per cent)

Perceived As	Personal Record and Standing	National Issues	Traditional Party Loyalties	State and Local Races
Very important	57	26	25	14
Quite important	28	20	21	19
Somewhat important	9	20	24	27
Not very important	3	27	18	19
Not important at all	3	7	12	21
Total	100	100	100	100

A long series of open-ended questions asked of those who said they had any information about the Representative produced mainly a collection of diffuse evaluative judgments: he is a good man, he is experienced, he knows the problems, he has done a good job, and the like. Beyond this, the Congressman's image consisted of a mixed bag of impressions, some of them wildly improbable, about ethnicity, the attractiveness of family, specific services to the district, and other facts in the candidate's background. By the most reasonable count, references to current legislative issues comprised not more than a thirtieth part of what the constituents had to say about their Congressmen.

The irrelevance of legislative issues to the public's knowledge of Representatives is underscored by the nature of some primary *determinants* of saliency. A full analysis of the causes of constituent awareness of candidates goes beyond the scope of this paper. Although our investigation has given a good deal of attention to communication factors and to characteristics of Congressmen and constituents themselves that determine the probability a given Congressman will be known to a given constituent, this interplay of causes cannot be explored very deeply here. However, it *is* noteworthy in the present discussion that many factors increasing the saliency of candidates are unlikely to enhance what the public knows about their stands on issues. An excellent example is sex. Both for incumbents and non-incumbents, a candidate property that is related to saliency is gender; one of the best ways for a Representative to be known is to be a Congress*woman*. How irrelevant to policy issues this property is depends on what we make of the causal relation between sex and salience. The fact of being a woman may make a candidate more visible, but a woman may have to be unusually visible (as a Congressman's widow, say) before she can be elected to the House, or even become a serious candidate. If the first of these inferences is even partially right, the salience of the candidate is not likely to be in terms of positions taken on legislative issues.

Given the number of women who run for Congress, the role of sex may seem a trivial example to demonstrate the irrelevance of issue stands to saliency. However, the same point can be made for a much wider set of districts by the greater saliency of candidates who live in the constituent's home community. Just as there is enormous variety in the communities that make up the American nation, so there is the widest possible variation in how well a congressional district coincides with a natural community, and the goodness of this fit is a fundamental way of typing districts. At one extreme is the constituency whose area is lost within one of the country's great metropolitan centers, comprising at best a small fraction of the whole community. At the middle of the range is the district that is itself a natural community, consisting of a single medium-sized city and its environs. At the other extreme is the district whose territory includes a great number of small communities, as well as surrounding open country that goes on, in some cases, for hundreds of miles. In all but the metropolitan districts the salience of the candidate for the voter differs markedly according to whether candidate and voter live in the same community. The fact of common residence—of being "friends and neighbors"— stands for important facts of communication and community identification. Candidates will be joined by formal and informal communication networks to many of the voters living in the same community, and they may also be objects of considerable community pride.

The reality of this local effect is demonstrated by Table 11-6. As the entries of the table show, dividing a nationwide sample of constituents according to whether they live in the same community as their Congressman or his opponent produces marked differences of saliency. The "friends and neighbors" effect made familiar by studies of primary voting in one-party areas has a counterpart in voting for

TABLE 11-6

Influence of "Friends and Neighbors" Factor on Saliency of Candidates for Voters *
(in per cent)

	Incumbent Candidate Lives in		Nonincumbent Candidate Lives in	
Voter Is	Same Community as Voter (N = 269)	Other Community than Voter (N = 414)	Same Community as Voter (N = 304)	Other Community than Voter (N = 447)
Aware of candidate	67	45	47	22
Not aware of candidate	33	55	53	78
Total	100	100	100	100

* Metropolitan and large urban districts, for which the notion of the candidate living outside the voter's community has no clear meaning, are excluded from the analysis.

Representatives throughout the country, apart from the large metropolitan areas.[8] And despite the fact that localism is found here in the context of as tightly party-determined an election as any in American politics, the irrelevance of local appeal to legislative issues is probably as great as it is in the wide-open, one-party primary.

Conclusion

What the public knows about the legislative records of the parties and of individual congressional candidates is a principal reason for the departure of American practice from an idealized conception of party government. On the surface the legislative elections occurring in the middle of the President's term appear to be dominated by two national parties asking public support for their alternative programs. Certainly the electorate whose votes they seek responds to individual legislative candidates overwhelmingly on the basis of their party labels. Despite our kaleidoscopic electoral laws, the candidate's party is the one piece of information every voter is guaranteed. For many, it is the only information they ever get.

However, the legislative events that follow these elections diverge widely from the responsible-party model. The candidates who have presented themselves to the country under two party symbols immediately break ranks. The legislative parties speak not as two voices but as a cacophony of blocs and individuals fulfilling their own definitions of the public good. Party cohesion by no means vanishes, but it is deeply eroded by the pressures external to party to which the Congressman is subject.

The public's information about the legislative record of the parties and of members of Congress goes far toward reconciling these seemingly contradictory facts. In the congressional election, to be sure, the country votes overwhelmingly for party symbols, but the symbols have limited meaning in terms of legislative policy. The eddies and crosscurrents in Congress do not interrupt a flow of legislation that the public expects but fails to see. The electorate sees very little altogether of what goes on in the national legislature. Few judgments

[8] See V. O. Key, Jr., *Southern Politics* (New York: Alfred A. Knopf, 1949, pp. 37 ff.). We have demonstrated the "friends and neighbors" effect in terms of candidate salience because of our interest in the policy content of candidate perceptions. However, owing to the impact of salience on the vote, living in the same community with the candidate has a clear effect on voting as well.

of legislative performance are associated with the parties, and much of the public is unaware even of which party has control of Congress. As a result, the absence of party discipline or legislative results is unlikely to bring down electoral sanctions on the ineffective party or the errant Congressman.

What the public's response to the parties lacks in programmatic support is not made up by its response to local congressional candidates. Although perceptions of individual candidates account for most of the votes cast by partisans against their parties, these perceptions are almost untouched by information about the policy stands of the men contesting the House seat. The increment of strength that some candidates, especially incumbents, acquire by being known to their constituents is almost entirely free of policy content. Were such content present, the Congressman's solidarity with his legislative party would by no means be assured. If the local constituency possessed far greater resources of information than it has, it might use the ballot to pry the Congressman away from his party quite as well as to unite him with it. Yet the fact is that, by plying his campaigning and servicing arts over the years, the Congressman is able to develop electoral strength that is almost totally dissociated from what his party wants in Congress and what he himself has done about it. The relevance of all this to the problem of cohesion and responsibility in the legislative party can scarcely be doubted.

The description of party irresponsibility in America should not be overdrawn. The American system *has* elements of party accountability to the public, although the issues on which an accounting is given are relatively few and the accounting is more often rendered by those who hold or seek the Presidency than by the parties' congressional delegations. Especially on the broad problem of government action to secure social and economic welfare it can be argued that the parties have real differences and that these have penetrated the party images to which the electorate responds at the polls.

Nevertheless, American practice does diverge widely from the model of party government, and the factors underlying the departure deserve close analysis. An implication of the analysis reported here is that the public's contribution to party irregularity in Congress is not so much a matter of encouraging or requiring its Representatives to deviate from their parties as it is of the public having so little information that the irregularity of Congressmen and the ineffectiveness of the congressional parties have scant impact at the polls. Many of those who have commented on the lack of party discipline in Congress have assumed that the Congressman votes against his party because he is forced to by the demands of one of several hundred constituencies of a superlatively heterogeneous nation. In some cases, the Representative may subvert the proposals of his party because his constituency demands it. But a more reasonable interpretation over a broader range of issues is that the Congressman fails to see these proposals as part of a program on which the party—and he himself—will be judged at the polls, because he knows the constituency isn't looking.

CHAPTER 12

On the Possibility of Major Political Realignment in the South

Philip E. Converse

In the several decades since Warren G. Harding first cracked the Solid South, observers have awaited a collapse of the Democratic grip on the region with notable impatience. For some time the collapse has seemed "just around the corner." Although the signs of impending change persist, the South has yet to see anything like the major partisan realignment which appeared so imminent fifteen years ago.

No one would quarrel with the proposition that the South is undergoing a real and rapid change on many important fronts. Fundamental shifts in the technological and economic base of the region have begun to have at least scattered repercussions in legal and political institutions. Nevertheless, the fact of change itself—even change as fundamental as this—does not guarantee that changes will follow in all other sectors of southern life. Quite to the contrary, it seems reasonable to suppose at this point that members of human societies are rather adept at muffling and hedging in such change as cannot be avoided. Man seems to respond to change as slowly and narrowly as the situation permits, and what the situation permits is often surprising.

Our interest here is limited not only to political change, but to a particular type of political change involving the basic party loyalties

A version of this chapter appeared originally in *Change in the Contemporary South*, Allan P. Sindler, editor, Durham, N.C.: Duke University Press, 1963, pp. 195–222.

of the mass southern electorate. It is our purpose to take survey of those signs of change which have been visible over the past decade, and to see what meaning these signs may reasonably hold for the partisan future of the South. Even where a matter as simple as mass partisanship is concerned, there are a number of distinctive outcomes —including that of no change—which are logically possible for the South. Since our view of the future may vary a good deal according to which of these outcomes we have in mind, it is worth taking stock of the major possibilities.

The most dramatic outcome, of course, would be a rapid shift of the South from a relatively one-party Democratic status to a one-party Republican one. Following the vocabulary we have used elsewhere, we shall call this the *realignment* outcome. It has long been obvious against the backdrop of national politics that the historical link between the South and the Democratic Party has become quite implausible from an ideological point of view. The facts are commonplace. The nominal coalition between northern and southern wings of the Democratic Party has lost much of the rationale it once had and has ceased to function in Congress at all on a fair range of major issues. The marriage has remained tolerable to each partner only on rather expedient grounds, such as easy presidential votes for the northern wing and congressional seniority for the southern. On most other counts, however, the grounds for divorce have become overwhelming. Hence it has not been unreasonable to look for the development of a South as solidly Republican as it once was Democratic, thereby joining the rural and small-town conservatism of the South to that so clearly represented by Republicanism in much of the rest of the nation.

Yet the most salient features of current southern change might suggest a much milder outcome. Growing industrialization and urbanization with all of their attendant characteristics are wearing away at the regional distinctiveness of the South. Regionalism elsewhere in the United States has been waning for decades, and the South is its last prime bastion. Politically these changes might suggest less a realignment outcome than a *convergence* outcome, whereby the South might slip more directly into the mainstream of American political life. Such an outcome would not require that the South become Republican or even, for that matter, lose its Democratic majority. But it would mean several important political changes at the mass level: some growth in Republicanism, sufficient to maintain a more vigorous party competition; voting trends in national elections which parallel more clearly those elsewhere in the country; the development of political divisions of the vote based more on social class and urban-rural distinctions than on the older regional questions and the like.

A third broad outcome, the development of a more permanent third party in the South, could stem from southern disaffection with both national parties on the race question. Such a development, contrary to the convergence outcome, would be a step in the direction of greater rather than less regionalism.

There are, of course, other possible outcomes involving combinations of these three basic types of change. For example, one of these changes might arise at one level of office—the presidential, perhaps—without comparable change at other levels. In this discussion, however, we choose to focus on the outcomes which involve at least some development of Republican allegiances among voters in the South, which means either the convergence or the realignment outcomes. We have two reasons for such a choice.

First, as a matter of practical politics these two outcomes seem to be the primary *stable* outcomes, representing something more than halfway houses to some other state of affairs. Thus while there may be spates of Dixiecrat protest, there seems to be little stomach among southern politicians for developing a truly independent third party, and there are many forces which are operative in American politics to counter such a development in the long term. Combined outcomes, such as presidential Republicanism but maintenance of Democratic supremacy at other levels of office, seem intrinsically unstable as well.

Second, we shall focus on the growth of some stable Republicanism, because we are much better equipped conceptually and empirically to handle such change. For many years now we have studied the characteristics of basic party loyalties where the choice lies between the two major parties. However, we have had little experience with the dynamics of voting when a third-party alternative is offered, especially when that alternative is only poorly dissociated from that presented by one of the existing parties, as tends to be true of Dixiecrat movements.[1]

In sum, then, we address ourselves specifically here to an assessment of the likelihood that the number of Republican loyalists in the

---

[1] By this we mean simply that a fervent Democrat in the South can vote for a candidate who has always been known as a Democrat, running under a label such as "States' Rights Democrat," with greater comfort than he could vote for some entirely new party, and with much greater comfort than he could vote for a Republican candidate. From this point of view, the size of the vote garnered by Thurmond in 1948 was not surprising, any more than was the return of much of this vote to normal Democratic channels when the alternative was no longer offered.

South will grow sufficiently either to bring southern voting patterns more in line with those elsewhere in the nation or to create a truly Republican South.

Long-Term Party Loyalty versus Short-Term Voting Choice

We find it useful, however, to re-emphasize one other distinction before we undertake this assessment. We have noted that a common phenomenon in current American voting behavior is that of the momentary party defection, either in a particular election or, more narrowly still, in casting one vote for a specific office in a given election. It is not entirely rare that a Democrat or a Republican will decide to throw a vote across party lines. The defection is momentary in a sense that can be clearly defined: the voter himself does not consider that he has changed his party loyalty in any way as a result of the defection, and he is no more likely to defect again in an ensuing election marked by a new configuration of forces than is someone else of the same party who had not defected.

The distinction between the short-term defection and what we call party identification seems to be a crucial one, for at times these defections become large and systematic in a particular vote. Thus, as we saw in Chapter 4, the Eisenhower victories in 1952 and 1956, handsome though they were, did not turn out to be the harbingers of basic partisan realignment which most observers took them to be at the time. Rather they involved momentary though massive defections on the part of people who continued to consider themselves Democrats, who voted Democratic in the off-year elections of 1954 and 1958, and who even voted Democratic at other levels of office in the Eisenhower elections themselves. Similarly, remarkable new voting patterns appeared in the South in 1960, with some of the traditional "Bible-belt" strongholds of the Democratic Party shifting markedly in a Republican direction. We have reviewed in Chapter 5 our reasons for believing that these changes represented once again momentary defection among devout and relatively narrow Protestants in the South, touched off by the religious question surrounding the 1960 Democratic candidate, rather than change in basic party loyalty in these areas.

Short-term phenomena of this sort, although interesting in themselves, have little to do with our central question regarding the development of stable Republican loyalties in the South. The ever-present possibility of defection means simply that one cannot be sure, in any given election, that the party enjoying the underlying majority of loyalties will win. But rather special circumstances are required to prevent it from winning, and it has every right to expect to capture the majority of any lengthy sequence of elections. It is in these terms that knowledge of the distribution of underlying party identifications is critical.

Hence we shall not rest our analysis on any recent vote in the South, but rather on trends in the expression of party loyalties given us by the southern portions of our national samples in the past decade.[2] Such a strategy requires some explanation, however, because it presumes implicitly that expressions of identification with the Democratic Party in the South have the same meaning and the same predictive value as do such expressions for the two parties outside the South. We frequently receive the complaint that this is not the case. A self-styled strong Democrat from Mississippi, it is said, does not respond to the national parties in the same way as a strong Democrat from Illinois. More specifically, it is often contended that there is in the South a substantial contingent of voters who see themselves as Democrats because of state and local party offerings yet who, at a national level in presidential races, are addicted to voting Republican.

This argument is so credible that we have invested a good deal of time evaluating it. However, we have thus far been unable to find any support for it. This is not to say that there are no self-styled Democrats in the South who have preferred to vote Republican at a presidential level over quite a sequence of elections. But it is to say that such people are so extremely rare in the total southern electorate that they cannot be identified as a meaningful proportion through a sample survey and hence can contribute little to the general flavor of southern voting.

Although the evidence against the hypothesis is varied, we shall present here two of the most definitive proofs as justification for our analysis strategy. First, for a decade we have asked our respondents the question "[In the elections since you have been old enough to vote] have you always voted for the same party or have you voted for different parties for President? [If 'same'] Which party was that?" Coded answers include "always" having voted for the same party, "mostly" having voted for the same party, and having voted for "different parties." If responses to our standard party identification

[2] In view of the sampling base on which our studies are constituted, we define the South somewhat broadly. Sixteen states are included with Delaware, Maryland, West Virginia, Kentucky, and Oklahoma added to the eleven states of the Confederacy.

question had a different meaning South and non-South, one would certainly expect that the differences could be demonstrated with such a question. That is, the hypothesis would suggest that we should find a lower proportion of strong Democrats in the South who have always voted for the same party for President than among strong Democrats elsewhere. Similarly, one would expect a visibly higher proportion of strong Democrats in the South who indicate that they have voted "mostly" Republican at the presidential level. Although one finds less party fidelity among weaker partisans everywhere in the nation, we should still expect parallel discrepancies to arise between North and South for weak Democrats, if these responses have different regional meaning for partisan behavior.

Table 12-1 gives little support to such expectations. The table is somewhat awkward from an analytic point of view, as it combines data from three quadrennial samples during which the general cast of responses showed some secular shift, and two of the component samples have a large overlap in personnel interviewed. However, the combination was made to permit sufficient cases outside of the two Democratic categories in the South for at least loose examination. The secular trend in party fidelity responses which the table masks follows in the most natural way from political realities of the period. That is to say, the first major "deviating" election since the realignment of party loyalties due to the Great Depression occurred in 1952 and was rapidly followed by another massive defection to Eisenhower in 1956. The election of 1960 brought a new and relatively independent wave of defections on the religious question. Hence reports of past party fidelity (particularly among Democrats) were weaker in 1960 than they had been in 1956, and weaker in 1956 than in 1952. Similarly, Southern Democrats who had reported slightly greater party fidelity in 1952 and 1956 than comparable non-Southern Democrats slightly surpassed the non-Southern Democrats in reports of infidelity in 1960. However, this 1960 difference is a direct consequence of the far more numerous Protestant Democrats who avoided a Kennedy vote on religious grounds in the South; equally fervent Protestant Democrats *outside* the South show the same decline in reports of fidelity. All of these regional differences are rather weak at best, and the largest summation possible (Table 12-1) shows but slight and irregular differences overall.[3]

[3] The regional differences which are largest in an absolute sense lie outside the two critical Democratic columns on the left, where most of the southern cases fall. It must be remembered that where southern cases are fewest in the central columns, sampling error is largest. The only striking differences here cast a rather mixed light on the hypothesis.

TABLE 12-1

Reports of Past Party Fidelity in Presidential Voting by Party Identification Category, South and Non-South *

Report of Past Presidential Voting Choices	Party Identification						
	Strong Dem.	Weak Dem.	Ind. Dem.	Ind. Ind.	Ind. Rep.	Weak Rep.	Strong Rep.
Non-South:							
Always Dem.	81%	56%	29%	6%	4%	3%	1%
Mostly Dem.	3	5	3	1	1	1	†
Different	15	37	65	87	65	42	21
Mostly Rep.	0	†	0	0	0	3	6
Always Rep.	1	2	3	6	30	51	72
	100%	100%	100%	100%	100%	100%	100%
Number of cases *	557	628	234	246	259	530	586
South:							
Always Dem.	83%	55%	26%	5%	14%	2%	1%
Mostly Dem.	6	5	14	2	0	1	1
Different	10	38	50	75	57	33	21
Mostly Rep.	0	0	0	0	0	1	9
Always Rep.	1	2	10	18	29	63	68
	100%	100%	100%	100%	100%	100%	100%
Number of cases *	324	349	42	56	35	96	101

* The table includes only white respondents in the two regions who had voted sufficiently to respond to the question, and is based on a combination of samples from 1952, 1956, and 1960. Since a large number of the same respondents were reinterviewed in 1956 and 1960, the numbers of cases indicated cannot be taken as totally independent observations, although the question was posed anew in 1960 and reports were shifted to take account of more recent voting behavior.

† Indicates less than half of one per cent.

A second test is equally convincing. In 1958, out of continued concern with the southern problem, we asked respondents who had just given us their direction and degree of party identification in the normal way whether in making the response they had been thinking primarily of the national level or of the state or local level of political competition. Here again, the hypothesis of presidential Republicans in the South would lead one to anticipate an unusual proportion of Southerners who would confess after the fact that their stated Democratic allegiance had been given assuming a state and local context only.

We were surprised to discover that very few people in either North or South discriminated between national and state party allegiances. In the nation as a whole about 94 per cent of the respondents indicated that they would enter the same report of party identification indiscriminately for either level. Furthermore, of the 6 per cent who wanted to indicate some discrimination between levels, less than one-fifth (1 per cent of the total population) felt that they had different party loyalties at the two levels; the vast majority of discriminators simply felt that they were independent at one level and partisan at the other. There were slight regional differences in these figures which are nearly significant in a statistical sense: 95 per cent of non-Southerners failed to discriminate between levels whereas the corresponding figure for the South was 91 per cent.

However, the item which is important for our purposes is not the fact of discrimination itself, but rather what statement of party identification had naturally been given in response to the party identification question before the novel probing. Here again the answer from the data is very clear. None of the respondents either North or South who had discriminated between levels had given his more local response to our general question. In other words, all of the few (N of 6, out of 441 cases) southern respondents who considered themselves Democrats in state politics but Republicans nationally had spontaneously labeled themselves "Republicans" in first indicating their party identification.

In short, there is little reason to believe that our measure of basic party loyalty has any notably different meaning in the South. Hence we may turn directly to our central problem, using for a key criterion not the result of any specific vote but rather expressions of basic party identification. We want to know quite simply whether there are signs of any change in the South which would token a partisan realignment of the region or a convergence with political behavior in the rest of the nation.

Convergence in Voting Behavior, South and Non-South

There are indeed several signs pointing to some slow convergence between critical facets of mass electoral behavior as they appear in the South and elsewhere in the nation. As perhaps the most important example, there is some evidence that the great gulf between the strongly Democratic mass loyalties in the South and the more balanced but slightly Republican loyalties typical outside the South is in the process of narrowing. Figure 12-1 presents a portrait of this convergence from data collected between 1952 and 1964. For the purposes of this figure we have used a technique which permits a distribution of party identification to be reduced to a single proportion or an "expected" vote division, following norms established over the years for identifiers of different types. The figure presents the trend in the difference between these proportions for South and non-South. Thus the declining slope reflects a decreasing difference in partisanship between South and non-South.[4]

We have taken the liberty to add a straight line to Figure 12-1 to show the linear trend which best fits the data.[5] This line, if extended, would arrive at the point of convergence (the baseline of zero difference) in the month of June 1983. We cite such a precise figure facetiously, of course, since we know enough about the dynamics underlying the trend to be assured that the change could hardly be linear in any long term. Hence our point is figurative, not a literal prediction. But this extrapolation does serve to give us a concrete sense of the current rate of change. The change which is occurring is proceeding at a snail's pace. It smacks more of a slow erosion of regional differences than of any dramatic partisan realignment, even in its early stages.

This fact is further underscored where the South itself is concerned, for the North is contributing more to the convergence than is the South. The relevant data are presented in the box inserted in the lower left corner of Figure 12-1, where the slope changes which combine in the overall convergence are isolated. The South in this period has been losing Democratic strength (at an average rate represented by the slope of −0.25 per cent per year), but Democratic strength outside

[4] The actual observations in Figure 12-1 are somewhat irregular, with the short-term reversals of the trend. It should be kept in mind that each observation contains some sampling error. Nonetheless, there seems to be little question but that overall, a convergence is underway.

[5] The linear function is estimated by the method of least squares.

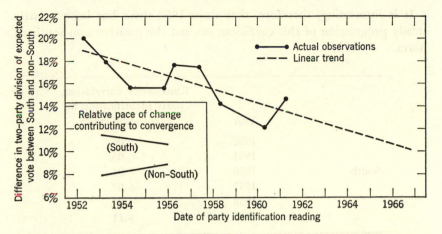

Figure 12-1. Declining differences in partisan loyalties, South and non-South.

the South has been increasing slightly more rapidly than this (slope of +0.35 per year). Perhaps if there had not been a mild motion toward the Democrats in the nation as a whole, the southern shift toward the Republicans would have registered in an absolute sense as more rapid. However this may be, it is clear that partisan change within the South has been sufficiently feeble in the past decade as to render analyses of that change rather difficult. Nonetheless, Figure 12-1 will serve as a primary point of departure, for it sums up change in a rather vital statistic.

Convergence in class voting patterns. There are other indicators of slow convergence that are worth at least brief mention. One is the development of a class flavor to voting patterns in the South which is more akin to those patterns familiar elsewhere. Until very recently, it seems, the Democratic Party in the South had been quite generally the symbol of small-town, middle-class respectability, much as the Republican Party has maintained this image in the small towns outside the South. Indeed, in our earliest studies it appeared that middle-class voters in the South were if anything more solidly committed to the Democratic Party than were blue-collar workers. This arrangement, anomalous from the point of view of national politics, may be expressed usefully as a *negative* coefficient of status polarization, in the terms we have employed elsewhere.[6]

6 This measure represents roughly the difference in proportions of partisans between status levels. See P. E. Converse, "The Shifting Role of Class in Political Attitudes and Behavior," *Readings in Social Psychology*, Maccoby, Newcomb and

It is interesting, therefore, that since 1952 there has been a fairly steady progression of this coefficient toward the positive non-Southern norm.

	Year	Rank-order correlation, party identification by occupation status
	1952	−.06
	1954	−.05
South	1956	−.04
	1957	+.02
	1958	−.02
	1960	+.11

Two facts seem rather evident again. First, one can hardly doubt that this "normalization" of the class-party correlation in the South is a product of growing industrialization. Indeed, it can be shown that the new polarization is focused in areas of the South that have become most industrialized, and that the old negative correlation persists in more rural or economically stagnant counties of the South.[7]

	Southern Counties *		
	Rural	Intermediate	Industrialized
1960 status polarization, occupation by party identification	−.11	−.05	+.16
Number of cases	62	158	168

* Counties are subdivided according to the relative proportions of agricultural and manufacturing workers.

Hartley, editors, Third Edition (New York: Henry Holt, 1958, pp. 388–399). The conceptual character of the coefficient depends to some degree on the type of measure of partisanship employed. Thus the association of status and vote tells something of the short-term disposition of class political alignments, in the degree that it departs from the association between status and underlying party identification, which represents more closely a long-term description. See the distinction drawn in A. Campbell, P. E. Converse, W. E. Miller, and D. E. Stokes, *The American Voter* (New York: John Wiley and Sons, 1960, pp. 365–368). Here our interest lies in the long-term loyalty component.

[7] Donald S. Strong has provided a number of careful analyses documenting Re-

Second, the evidence seems to suggest once again a slow erosion of distinctive regional patterns and a drift toward the type of voting norms more characteristic of the rest of the country.

Increased voting turnout. It seems likely that convergence is going on as well in matters of voting turnout. That is, the one characteristic which has long distinguished the South as clearly as any—low rates of voting turnout in presidential elections—appears to be on the wane. Such an assessment is a difficult one to make, for middle-term fluctuations in voting turnout are notoriously confusing. However, Strong has worked with aggregate data for a much longer term than those spanned by our studies, and feels there is evidence of genuine secular rise in southern turnout.[8]

Later analyses of this turnout trend may illuminate an important facet of the decline of regionalism, because low southern turnout, like many other regional peculiarities, may be seen partly as regional in a direct sense and partly as regional only in a very indirect way. That is, two of the more distinctive southern characteristics even in the current period are its low level of education and its relatively rural economy. Both of these factors are quite strongly associated with low voting turnout, not simply in the South but in other parts of the United States as well. This may be seen as an indirect regional influence on turnout. Turnout will increase "automatically" as southern education is increased but cannot be expected to converge fully on figures typical of other areas until education levels have come to match those elsewhere. On the other hand, even when all of the factors known to be important in determining turnout (and here we include the problem of Negro franchise, to be sure) are held constant, the Southerner still typically votes less regularly in presidential elections than does his non-Southern counterpart. Until clearer causes may be located, this residual difference can be considered the result of a more direct regional influence. It would be interesting to know how much of the current upgrading of turnout in the South could be traced to changes in some of the indirect terms (rising education and urbanization) and how much would represent a decline in direct regional influences.

However this may be, changes in turnout in the current South

---

publican trends in relatively well-to-do sections of the larger southern urban areas. These trends represent the leading edge of the change in southern class voting patterns being discussed here. See D. S. Strong, *Urban Republicanism in the South* (University of Alabama, Bureau of Public Administration, 1960).

[8] Personal communication, July 1961.

probably deserve a place among convergence symptoms. Other trends might be mentioned as well, but these are some of the more notable signs of political change in the South where mass voting patterns are concerned. Although they are a rather varied collection of symptoms, they all seem to hint in common at (1) change which is rather slow, and (2) change which is edging the South toward convergence with the mainstream of American political life, rather than toward a more dramatic political realignment.

Mechanisms Underlying Southern Political Change

Whenever change is at stake, as it seems to be in some measure in the South, we can make a better projection of the future if we can understand the mechanisms that are producing the change. Although we often make the simple assumption that change in the distribution of an attitude in a population means that people are changing their minds, this is not necessarily the case. It we take the drift away from purely Democratic allegiances in the South as an example, it is true that such change could be produced through re-evaluations of the major parties by the existing Southern population. Such change we shall call individual partisan *conversion*. Nevertheless, the partisan drift in the South could also be produced by a change in the composition of the population, without any individual conversion whatever. A change in population composition can come about either through *replacement* of a dying generation by one with different partisan preferences, or through population exchanges with other regions (migration). With the aid of data from our 1956–1960 panel studies, we can arrive at a rough estimate of the contribution of each of these three sources of change (conversion, population replacement, migration) to the slight drift observed toward Republicanism. We must stress the crudity of such an estimate, for the observed drift is so slight that the change wrought over even a four-year period lies within our sampling error. Nonetheless, the relevant data have some general interest.

Partisan conversion of white Southerners.[9] It is undoubtedly true that individual conversion is the most exciting type of change. Certainly conversion must be involved in any rapid and dramatic partisan realignment, for population turnover mechanisms can account for

---

[9] Since we are dealing here with rather dynamic factors, it will be useful from this point on to keep our southern population subdivided by race, considering whites and Negroes separately.

nothing more than slow change. Conversion is probably the type of change most pregnant with political meaning as well, since change stemming only from something as politically neutral as population turnover is likely to strike us as change by default.

Yet if individual partisan conversion is occurring in a manner which systematically favors one party over the other in the South, the phenomenon is so weak that it very nearly eludes any sample analysis for the 1956–1960 period. The portion of Table 12-2 dealing with the

TABLE 12-2

1956–1960 Change in Party Identification among Whites, South and Non-South
(in per cent)

	Party Identification Pre-Election, 1960			
	Democrat	Independent	Republican	1956 Overall
Southern White *				
Party Ident., 1956:				
Democrat	62 †	3	2	67
Independent	3	11	2	15
Republican	2	2	14	18
1960 overall	67	16	17	100
				(N = 318)
Non-Southern White *				
Party Ident., 1956:				
Democrat	31	5	‡	36
Independent	9	16	5	30
Republican	2	5	27	34
1960 overall	42	25	33	100
				(N = 901)

* Excluded from the table are those respondents who moved into or out of the South between the 1956 and 1960 interviews.

† The box of nine (three-by-three) percentages adds to 100%, as do the summary rows and columns, which give the "marginal" distributions for each year. Due to differences in rounding, occasional rows or columns forming the internal box fail to sum precisely to the marginal entry.

‡ Indicates less than half of 1 per cent.

South shows a modest amount of *gross* change in partisanship in the interior of the table. However, most of this change is self-compensating; the marginals show almost no *net* change. If we reduce the 1956 and 1960 marginals from the South to precise "expected" votes, we do find that the 1960 distribution would generate a vote about one-half of 1 per cent more Republican than the 1956 distribution.

Nevertheless, the southern half of the table stands in rather sharp contrast to the non-southern portion, where there seems to be greater gross change and a very unmistakable net change favoring the Democrats. It is not our purpose here to explore this non-southern change. However, this shift is, of course, the non-southern contribution to the convergence phenomenon noted above, and it is interesting that outside the South we capture this change quite clearly as individual conversion. The amount of change to be expected in the South is sufficiently slight and our sampling error sufficiently large, that it would be impossible to claim that individual conversion toward the Republicans could not account for all of the observed Republican drift. Nonetheless, the evidence that such is the case is weak indeed, and it behooves us to consider the other mechanisms in their turn as possible sources of the drift.

Population replacement: the younger generation of southern whites. Since the younger generation often serves as the leading edge of change, we look with particular interest at recent trends in expressions of partisanship by younger whites in their twenties in the South.

A survey of these newer voters as they have been interviewed in our samples during the 1950's shows little of interest, however, with respect to long-range change. We know from much experience that the incoming generation of voters has somewhat less stable party loyalties and, hence, shows some slight tendency to "float" with the momentary national tide in reports of party identification. This familiar phenomenon is visible if one compares the cohort of southern voters in their twenties with their elders, and particularly the oldest generation, which the new is replacing. That is, in 1956 when the Republican tide nationally was at its peak for the series, these young southern white voters were slightly more Republican than their elders, and in 1958 when the Democratic tide was at its peak, they were slightly more Democratic. But these differences have been weak at best, and the total pattern is relatively meaningless. Over the years the younger southern white generation seems no more and no less Democratic than older generations. The inevitable population replacement seems to be contributing nothing toward long-range partisan change among whites in the South.

Migration. If persons moving from one area of the country to another adopted the partisan norms of their new habitat with fair speed, the regional redistribution of the mobile American population would do very little toward erasing the partisan distinctiveness of regions; however, this does not appear to be the case. It now seems that once an adult has developed relatively firm partisan loyalties—usually by the time he is 30 or 35—migration has little effect in inducing partisan change. A Republican moving from a Republican area, for example, is little or no more likely to change his party identification over ensuing periods than is the Republican who remains.[10] Under such circumstances, migration can serve to reduce regional differences in partisanship in a notable way.

One can conclude with unusual certainty that migration has been playing a considerable role in some of the convergence phenomena noted between South and non-South. The effect has been particularly marked in the past ten years due to certain new characteristics of the interregional exchange in this period. The U.S. Census Bureau materials on this exchange are not too definitive; however, we can use our sample data to aid in a rough description of recent trends.

First, the relative size of the North-to-South and the South-to-North streams has been rather uneven over time. For several decades, the South has exported substantial numbers of both white and Negro migrants seeking urban industrial jobs elsewhere. However, this stream reached a peak in the 1940's during the Second World War, and seems to have been tapering to a weaker flow during the 1950's. At the same time, the 1950's have seen a very rapid increase in movement to the South. Thus, for example, sample estimates in 1952 showed that over three-quarters (77 per cent) of the whites who were currently residing in a region other than that in which they had grown up were of the South-to-North, rather than the North-to-South, stream. By 1956 this figure had been cut to 61 per cent. The result is well summed up by Table 12-3, which shows the distribution of periods reported for entry into the state of current residence as of 1960 on the part of people who had migrated from one region to the other since the period in which they grew up.[11]

10 Campbell et al., *op. cit.*, Chap. 16.

11 It should be noted that the periods entered in Table 12-3 do not refer specifically to the dates at which the migrant changed region. Instead, they refer to the time at which the migrant reported that he had established residence in the state where he currently lives. There is thus some margin for error in deductions from the table, although by and large the times of entry into the state are likely to coincide with the times of movement from one region to the other.

TABLE 12-3

Period of Entry into State of Current Residence, for White and Negro Interregional Migrants

Grew Up: Currently:	White				Negro	
	Non-South South		South Non-South		South Non-South	
Period of entry into state of current residence:						
1956–1960	41%	45%	10%	15%	10%	10%
1952–1955	23	25	15	22	19	21
1948–1951	14	16	10	15	17	18
1940–1947	13	14	31	48	47	51
		100%		100%		100%
Prior to 1940	9		34		7	
	100%		100%		100%	
Number of cases	56	51	60	40	42	39

Prior to 1950 the steady exodus of Southerners (at first primarily white, but joined in increasing numbers by Negroes in the 1940's) contributed something to a regional convergence in partisanship, since the migrants were much more Democratic than the populations they joined outside the South. They have tended to remain so and have thereby increased the Democratic partisanship of non-Southern areas into which they have moved. But the partisan effects of this migration were felt only outside the South. In general, the departing Southerners have had much the same partisan coloration as the non-migrants whom they have left behind; their departure has done little to change the overall partisanship of the region.

The population redistribution since 1950, however, has had a much different influence on the South. For the first time the South is not only losing Democrats but is receiving a significant non-Southern population, more Republican than the native Southerner. Furthermore, unlike the South-to-North migration, the new North-to-South stream is selective along partisan lines. It turns out that the non-Southerner moving into the South is actually *more* Republican than the non-Southerners he leaves behind. This fact means that inter-regional convergence in partisanship is corrrespondingly speeded, for the departure of these Republicans leaves the non-South more Democratic than it would otherwise be at the same time as the South becomes the more Republican.

The selectivity along partisan lines which operates in the North-to-South migration is an accident of the types of persons who are moving South. In the first place, the migration is a high-status migra-tion, in marked contrast to the traditional South-to-North movement. As of 1956, for example, only about one-quarter of North-to-South white migrants were blue-collar workers, whereas almost two-thirds of South-to-North white migrants (and well over four-fifths of Negro mi-grants) were engaged in blue-collar occupations. Since higher-status persons have for a long period been more Republican than low-status persons outside the South, much of the explanation of the partisan selectivity lies in the status characteristics of the migrants. However, there are two social types particularly prominent in the North-to-South movement, and these two types are notably Republican even among higher-status non-Southerners: the young white-collar person whose move to the South is more or less directly associated with the growth of industry in the region (e.g., the junior executive transferred to a southern subsidiary), and the retired non-Southerner of sufficient means to establish new residence for the remainder of his days in the sunnier southern climate.

In short, then, peculiarities of migration to the South in the 1950's have been such as to maximize its impact both on partisan change in the South and on the more general phenomenon of partisan con-vergence between regions. At the same time, the fact that this mi-gration has been biased rather sharply from a partisan point of view should not obscure the attendant truth that migration is normally a very limited mechanism of change, in the sense that relatively small proportions of the parent populations are involved. Nonetheless, it does not seem likely that the number of non-Southerners who have taken up residence in the South in any given year in the 1950's could much exceed 1 per cent of the region's prior population. At such a rate of transfer, even a migration pattern strongly biased toward par-tisan change will only produce small shifts in any limited period, such as the four-year span between presidential elections.

Still, we must return to the fact that the amount of partisan change to be explained in the South in the 1950's is relatively small as well.

Indeed, making a set of somewhat conservative assumptions on the basis of sample data, we can calculate roughly the partisan change which migration phenomena could be expected to have induced in the South in this period, and we find that the effects would easily account for the observed Republican drift.[12]

From a southern point of view, however, the effects of migration may appear more impressive on a number of counts. First, the emigration and immigration are geographically concentrated in ways which give them maximum visibility and which, in the long range, may have maximal political implications. That is, the exodus from the South has been heaviest in the poor and backward interior uplands, and the new carpet-baggers of the 1950's have not, of course, been settling in these areas. Rather they have moved either to the littoral or to burgeoning urban-industrial areas. Among southern states, probably Florida is most clearly receiving both streams of non-Southerners at once—the retired and the young white-collar personnel. The population of Florida increased at a more rapid rate between 1950 and 1960 than did the population of California. Census figures show that of 1960 Floridians, 26 per cent had not been residing in Florida in 1955. Although one could hardly consider all of this 26 per cent to have entered from outside the South, the figure remains a rather astonishing one. It is in such areas that the effects of migration patterns will be most clearly felt.

Second, the immigrants bring with them not only a more Republican coloration, but also voting habits which are quite unlike those of their Southern counterparts. Hence they contribute to the rising turnout in the South and also have a somewhat higher partisan impact on voting patterns than could be expected if native Southerners were turning out at equal rates.

In the third place, the immigrants to the South are contributing in a clear fashion to the increase in status polarization of the southern

---

12 We ignore the replacement of the southern population by a new generation. We assume that slightly more than 1 per cent of the southern adult population departs from the region per year, and that this exodus is made up of Democrats in normal southern proportions. We assume further that non-Southerners enter the South in numbers slightly less than 1 per cent of the southern population, and that these non-Southerners are between 40 and 45 per cent Democratic, rather than the 50 per cent Democratic proportion characteristic of the non-South in the middle of this period. Under such circumstances, the proportion Democratic of the expected southern vote would be declining by about 1 per cent every four years, or the observed rate of change in the period. If these estimates are in error, it is likely that they overrepresent the rate of transfer.

vote. They are of remarkably high status, and are much more Republican than their southern high-status counterparts. The effects are obvious, and the clear localization of status polarization in urban and industrialized counties is in part a reflection of the areas which attract these migrants.

On the other hand, the increase in status polarization of partisanship in the South since 1952 cannot be entirely explained by immigration, for the change has been quite marked. It involves many more people than the slight net drift toward Republican loyalties, and the number of high-status immigrants would simply be insufficient to account for all of the change. Hence we may return to see if some of the gross partisan conversions represented for the South between 1956 and 1960 (Table 12-2) conceal any differential change by social class. Table 12-4 shows this division, and it is clear that the two class groups among Southerners [13] are evolving in differential, though largely self-compensating, partisan directions.

Although these instances of "real" partisan conversion are few in terms of numbers of interviews,[14] it has been instructive to read the interviews, spaced as they are over a four-year period, to get some flavor of the partisan perceptions which underlie the changes in loyalties. At an entirely clinical level, the interviews which create the increase in polarization fall roughly into three classes of changers. The first group, made up of higher-status respondents, has shifted from Democratic to Republican in party identification between 1956 and 1960 out of indignation at the Democratic Party for having nominated a Catholic. This is not to say that lower-status Southerners were not upset as well, but the few instances in which party identification as well as 1960 vote was shifted on such grounds turn out to have come from devout middle-class Protestants. From our experience in these matters we would highly suspect that these changes are transient. However, these interviews contribute to the rather sudden leap which the polarization coefficient takes between 1958 and 1960. We suspect that the underlying evolution is more regular than this leap would suggest.

The second group of interviews are those from lower-status Southerners who defend their shifting allegiance on the ground that the Democratic Party is "the party of the common man," the archetype of

[13] Exceptionally, Table 12-4 includes both Negroes and whites, although the polarization shown is not primarily a Negro phenomenon.

[14] And we cannot stress too much how slight such change appears to be. The fact that our subject is "change," or better, "such change as exists," should not hide the fact that change at the level of these basic loyalties is rare.

TABLE 12-4

1956–1960 Change in Party Identification among Southerners, by Class

	Party Identification Pre-Election, 1960			
	Democrat	Independent	Republican	1956 Overall
South, Blue-Collar *				
Party Ident., 1956:				
Democrat	65% †	3%	0%	68%
Independent	2%	10%	2%	14%
Republican	2%	4%	12%	18%
1960 overall	69%	17%	14%	100%
				(N = 107)
South, White-Collar *				
Party Ident., 1956:				
Democrat	57%	7%	5%	68%
Independent	3%	11%	1%	15%
Republican	3%	1%	12%	17%
1960 overall	63%	18½%	18½%	100%
				(N = 103)

* Excluded from the table are those respondents who moved into or out of the South between the 1956 and 1960 interviews.

† The box of nine (three-by-three) percentages adds to 100 per cent, as do the summary rows and columns, which give the "marginal" distributions for each year. Due to differences in rounding, occasional rows or columns forming the internal box fail to sum precisely to the marginal entry.

the working class reaction. The third group is made up of higher-status Southerners who are concerned about the economic liberalism of the Democratic Party at a national level. These people talk in typically conservative fiscal terms and mourn the lack of national power of the southern conservative Democrats. Their shifts are equally class shifts and are indicative of increasing weight placed on politics at the national level.

Most surprising among the white contributors to the second and third groups of interviews, however, is the integral role which partisan perceptions concerning desegregation and the Negro problem play in the accounts of change. By and large, the Negro question seems *as* salient if not *more* salient in the partisan shift than do the socio-economic perceptions. The fact that the question is salient is not surprising, as this is true of many southern interviews. But the interesting fact is that lower-status Southerners who have been Republican blame the Republicans for desegregation pressure and thereby help to justify a shift to the Democrats, whereas the higher-status changers justify their shift by precisely the inverse perceptions. It is not at all clear whether this perceptual difference is merely a rationalization after socio-economic pressures have led to the shift, or whether it springs from more genuine differences in attention to national events. Where the latter hypothesis is concerned, the flavor of some interviews suggests that possibly the flamboyant events at Little Rock, associated with Eisenhower and hence the Republicans, had greater weight in the minds of the relatively uninformed lower-status Southerners, while the higher-status Southerners were seeing the forest and not the trees, perceiving the national Democratic Party as a more radical long-term threat on the race question. One crucial fact is clear, however: the competition of both national parties to become associated with a strong stand on civil rights creates an ambiguous situation which southern voters can interpret to justify partisan shifts in either direction.

The southern Negro and partisan change. We have left the southern Negro apart from most of our analyses up to this point The subject is a difficult one to treat, in part because there is such a considerable discrepancy between the total number of southern Negroes in our sample and the number who are actually in a position to vote. The latter cases are too few for much direct analysis.

The subject is difficult as well because our panel materials make clear that in the current period, the reports of party identification on the part of southern Negroes as a total group are extremely labile, showing much gross change from one interview to the next. This lability is rather typical of very poorly educated and relatively apolitical populations, and hence encountering it among southern Negroes is scarcely surprising. However, it makes any reasonable prognosis almost impossible. Change among southern Negroes at the time of the 1960 election serves as an excellent case in point. The matrix showing changes in party identification between 1956 and the pre-election report in 1960 seems to show a marked swing toward the Republicans among southern Negroes as a whole, and when seeing this table alone,

one would rapidly conclude that the Negro was making a visible contribution to the net Republican drift in southern partisanship. (See top portion of Table 12-5.) However, the second report in 1960, taken after the election, not only fails to reproduce this 1956–1960 swing but actually shows a swing toward the Democrats! (See bottom portion of Table 12-5.) [15] Uninformed and labile citizens are particularly susceptible to bandwagon effects, and it is likely that this singular performance represents a reaction to Kennedy's election victory.

A scanning of the southern Negro interviews over time suggests that we should distinguish two types of changeability in party loyalties. The first is lability properly speaking and could be applied to the great majority of the Negro interviews. Most of these respondents are extremely ignorant, disoriented, and in the most utter confusion about politics. However, there are a handful of interviews which are politically quite articulate. They come without fail from relatively young Negroes who have been exposed to a fair amount of education: a schoolteacher in Louisiana, a young man in Alabama trying to finish high school at night, and the like. These latter Negroes figure prominently among those whose party identifications have changed over the course of our interviewing. However, this change is not the lability of ignorance; rather, the respondents are attempting to adjust their party choice to a civil rights calculus, and the assessment is difficult enough that choices shift rather readily over time. Whereas the older and more ignorant southern Negroes change parties without any apparent coherence or rationale, indicating in one interview that they are "strong Democrats" and a few weeks later that they are "strong Republicans," the interviews from these younger Negroes tend to show a coherent evolution of party perceptions and party loyalties over time, passing from one party through periods of doubt to the opposing party, etc. What is striking here, exactly as in the case of the southern white changers, is that one set of these coherent Negro respondents moves from Republican identification in 1956 to Democratic identification in 1960, justified on civil rights grounds, whereas the other set, attempting the same calculus for the same reasons and with the same information in the form of broad national political events, moves from Democratic identification in 1956 to Republican identification in 1960. Once again, the ambiguity of the major party positions in

[15] This second table is particularly curious since, of 42 Negroes who gave some party identification at both of the readings, only one considered himself a Republican both times.

TABLE 12-5

1956–1960 Change in Party Identification among Southern Negroes

| | Party Identification Pre-Election, 1960 | | | |
	Democrat	Independent	Republican	1956 Overall
Southern Negro *				
Party Ident., 1956:				
Democrat	52% †	0%	18%	70%
Independent	4%	9%	0%	13%
Republican	4%	2%	11%	17%
1960 overall	61%	11%	28%	100% (N = 46)

| | Party Identification Post-Election, 1960 | | | |
	Democrat	Independent	Republican	1956 Overall
Southern Negro *				
Party Ident., 1956:				
Democrat	56%	2%	10%	69%
Independent	10%	0%	5%	14%
Republican	10%	5%	2%	17%
1960 overall	76%	7%	17%	100% (N = 42)

* Excluded from the table are those respondents who moved into or out of the South between the 1956 and 1960 interviews. Excluded from the table also are numerous Negroes who gave "apolitical" responses on one or the other of the readings.

† The box of nine (three-by-three) percentages adds to 100 per cent, as do the summary rows and columns, which give the "marginal" distributions for each year. Due to differences in rounding, occasional rows or columns forming the internal box fail to sum precisely to the marginal entry.

the civil rights debate leads to the same aggregate diffusion of voting strength, as is apparent among southern whites concerned with the problem.

The Long-Term Perspective on Partisan Change in the South

Shortly after the Second World War, the support given "civil rights" by President Truman, as well as the bitter fight on the issue within the 1948 Democratic National Convention, was expected in many quarters to touch off a rapid political realignment removing the South from the Democrats as a basis for electoral support. The relative success of the Dixiecrat movement in the 1948 election seemed to be the halfway house toward immediate confirmation of these predictions. Although Eisenhower failed to capture a majority of the popular vote in the South in 1952, he did indeed make handsome inroads relative to earlier Republican presidential candidates, gaining about a 16 per cent greater portion of the southern two-party vote than had Dewey in the next preceding two-party presidential election (1944). Perhaps this was indeed another step in the predicted realignment, although on a somewhat slower timetable than had been expected in the excitement of 1948.

However, a dozen and more years after 1948 and despite a persistent growth of Republican Party organization over this period, the South was continuing to send overwhelmingly Democratic congressional delegations to Washington, and the most that could be said at the presidential level was that the Democrats were now obliged to engage in serious competition with the Republicans even to take a majority of electoral votes from the region. In short, then, although a slow but steady drift away from near-total Democratic fealty in the South was changing it toward a two-party region throughout these years, the pace of change which had attracted attention in 1948 and 1952 turned out to have been in one important sense an illusion.

The portion of the 1944–1952 change that was illusory, if interpreted as any fundamental realignment of mass partisan loyalties having to do with civil rights or any other sources of disaffection with the Democrats peculiar to the South as a region, was fairly well indicated by the fact that although the South had indeed moved massively away from the Democrats at the presidential level in 1952, the rest of the nation as well had gone a fair distance in this direction, and certainly not on "Southern" grounds associated with civil rights. Furthermore, although the significance of this shift was widely misinterpreted at the time as a permanent realignment of the country generally, there were many signs from sample survey data that much if not all of the movement was no more than a temporary deviation favoring the Republicans. Moreover, the magnitude of this temporary deviation was artificially heightened by the backdrop represented by the Roosevelt era, during which a similar temporary deviation had favored the Democrats instead.

Hence where any developments peculiar to the South were concerned, the 1948–1952 changes were less part of a sudden realignment than part of a slow trend, momentarily exaggerated by the fact that they fell into phase with other but conceptually independent national tides. Indeed, it is likely that this trend has been alternately exaggerated and muffled by voting returns at various times in the past, and that the underlying drift is one which was underway not too long after the turn of the century, and one which may well continue its evolution to the turn of the next, barring dramatic and unforeseen interventions.

The rough sketches in Figure 12-2 may be helpful in presenting our view. The broken line, representing the presidential voting for the nation as a whole and 13 southern states (the ordinate is slightly compressed in the latter case), is a matter of public record (due to occasional incursions of third parties in one region or another, some portions of the curve must represent reasonable estimation). The more stable heavy line is intended to represent the basic division of party loyalties. For the period since 1952, this heavy line is faithful to existing data; prior to that time it is entirely putative, for no comparable measures exist. The most controversial assumption that has been made is the following: since the relationship of party loyalties to actual vote has been very similar in the South to those for the nation as a whole, 1952–1960, they probably were similar before this period as well, within such confines as the slightly different "pitch" which the voting curves suggest.

In view of the presumptive nature of part of the data, the reader should not put too much emphasis on early portions of the figure. In particular, the timing of the sharp and rapid realignment of basic loyalties connected with the Great Depression is quite imaginary, although there is a great deal of consensus that such occurred roughly in this time period. What the figure is primarily intended to portray is the likelihood that Republican candidates in the 1920's were receiving slightly more than their "fair share" of votes (as defined by party loyalties); that Roosevelt started the 1930's by receiving greatly more than a Democrat's "fair share" of votes; that in the 1950's Eisenhower received greatly more than a Republican's "fair share" of the votes, and Nixon slightly more in 1960, although among Protestants this

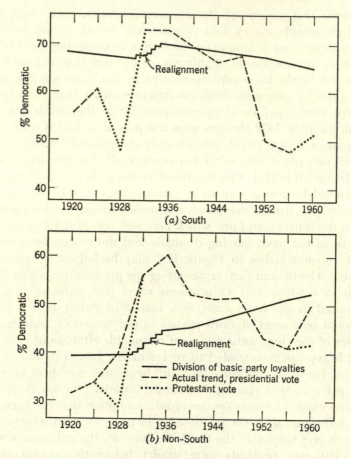

Figure 12-2. Presidential elections. Trends in voting and party loyalties, 1920–1960.

pro-Republican increment remained large. All of these facts were common to both South and North as the voting curves show and hence are not likely to be explained by factors unique to the South. These departures of the actual vote from the baseline set by party loyalties are attributable to what we have called short-term forces associated with transient political objects like Roosevelt, Eisenhower, and the religious question in 1928 and 1960.

Our view of the recent history of the "solid South" (as measured by electoral votes) is therefore as follows. From 1880 through 1916 the South was perfectly solid, save for McKinley's capture of the border state of Kentucky in one of the stronger pro-Republican swings of the period. We presume that considerably prior to 1920, however, some gradual convergence phenomenon had begun. In 1904, the last strong pro-Republican swing from the baseline prior to 1920, the South was still behaving quite like a region apart, even where short-term forces were concerned, and certainly was distinctive in the division of its underlying party loyalties. In 1912 voting patterns were confused by the Bull Moose Party, and 1916 brought a pro-Democratic swing. By 1920, however, convergence was far enough along that a strong pro-Republican swing nationwide was able to snare for Harding two of the more marginally Democratic states of the region. This Republican surge subsided somewhat in 1924, but Coolidge still captured Kentucky. Then came 1928, with its strong pro-Republican forces on devout Protestants, and the South actually gave Hoover the bulk of its electoral vote.

In the Roosevelt years it appeared that the South was as solid as ever. One can presume that the South did share in some measure in the genuine realignments of the period. However, it seems clear that most of the "re-solidifying" of the South was attributable to short-term forces associated with Roosevelt. Had a sharp pro-Republican swing occurred at a national level in this period, a Republican candidate could have won some southern electoral votes, for the "center of gravity" of southern partisanship was very nearly as much within reach as it had been in the 1920's. Once beyond the Roosevelt years, national trends moving back toward the central ground and, with Eisenhower, deep on the Republican side, exaggerated the apparent speed of partisan change in the South.

There is no doubt that southern partisanship is in the process of change. As various southern constituencies drift more nearly within reach of the opposition, Republican politicians begin to run candidates where interparty contests have been rare in the past. In the deeper Confederate South, for example, the number of national House seats contested in 1962 was almost three times as great as the number contested in 1958, and of course with this increase in the possibility for Republican minorities to vote Republican, the proportion of the Republican vote in this period nearly doubled. Nonetheless, even in 1962 the vote division at this level was more Democratic than the "expected" vote for the area and will remain so until all or most of the remaining seats are contested. Below the presidential level on the ballot, then, the Republican Party will be able by increasing its numbers of candidates to strike a new high-water mark in the popular vote every other election (or two elections out of every three) for some time to come, as has been true in the recent past. However, its successes are likely to be most impressive in narrower locales where there is a wave of discontent and with Republican candidates who make as little as possible of their party affiliation, for the Southern Democrat is still far from ready to receive Republicans with open arms. Finally, as Figure 12-2 suggests, voting at the presidential level is not likely to show any further Republican trend in the next few elections. Indeed, once the religious issue fades, the presidential vote division in the South is likely to move back to a more Democratic position.

It is in this sense that it does not seem reasonable to suppose that the South is about to become a reliably Republican region even in its presidential voting, as might be suggested were we to extend the general 1936–1960 voting trend of the South in the same direction (Figure 12-2) for as little as two more elections. This is not to question the tremendous importance of the racial question in the South. Indeed, of current issues on the American scene, the Negro problem comes closest (in the South, but not elsewhere) to showing those characteristics necessary if a political issue is to form the springboard for large-scale partisan realignment. That is, unlike the stuff of many great historical debates on tariffs, fiscal standards, foreign policy, the scope of government, or domestic Communism, the culture patterns at stake in the racial issue involve the immediate daily experience of the quasi-totality of the southern electorate. History suggests that this kind of immediacy is the first critical ingredient for large partisan realignments.

Yet such realignment requires something more as well. It requires that the alternatives offered by the parties be clear-cut in the public eye. Each of the antagonistic elements must be left in no doubt as to which party is the champion and which the enemy of its interests. This condition is clearly not fulfilled at present, either from voter interviews or from a cursory examination of party positions. The southern wing of the Democratic Party has, in forty years, been obliged to temper slightly its rabid antagonism to the uplifting of the Negro. The national Democratic Party, in the same period, has moved from a position of occasional flashes of embarrassment about Southern Democrats to a position of increasing intransigence. What has not happened, of course, is that the Republicans have come forth to champion the Southern white. Instead, their gestures toward the Southern Negro have come close to matching those of the Northern Democrats. If we doubt that partisan realignment is likely to occur, it is to say that we expect no dramatic change in this state of affairs.[16]

---

[16] A short two years after this was written, our confident expectation was overturned rather rudely, although perhaps temporarily. The capture of the Repub-

On the other hand, the slow partisan drift which marks the convergence outcome seems very nearly as inevitable as the realignment outcome is dubious. Convergence is underway, and there is nothing in the underlying mechanisms which would tempt us to predict that it will stop in the immediate future. Certainly in recent years migration from the North has contributed something to the phenomenon, and there is no reason to expect such migration to wither away.

There are, however, reasons to expect that the change will slow

---

lican Party by the Goldwater faction led to a 1964 campaign strategy attempting to make a Republican bastion of the South, largely by appealing to southern whites on the civil rights issue. This strategy, more colorfully described by Goldwater as "hunting in the pond where the ducks are," gave the 1964 Republican ticket a position on civil rights which for the first time was clearly differentiable from the position of the national Democratic Party, much to the surprise and alarm of the "mainstream" Republican strategists. In the wake of the Republican catastrophe at the polls and the likely return to power of the more familiar Republican Party leadership, it seems reasonable to expect that the Goldwater strategy will be reversed as hastily as possible. Nevertheless, this episode provides some loose test of our prognoses above both as to the potential power of the civil rights issue in the South, as well as to the less obvious countervailing force represented by the long-standing party attachments stressed in this chapter. With respect to the first, a rapid inspection as we go to press of the interview materials collected in the South during the 1964 campaign leaves no doubt that Goldwater was perceived by southern whites as a defender of segregation, even to a point well beyond any which the Senator actually took. The power of this appeal is documented handsomely by the fact that for the first time since Reconstruction, the South cast a vote less Democratic than that of any other region in the country. And in those areas of the deepest South where the segregation position is most extreme, he actually won his only electoral votes outside of his home state. In this sense, then, the civil rights question had the power which we expected in the case where it was unleashed by clear party differentiation. At the same time, the Goldwater strategy was fully as much a failure as it was a success, even within the South, for one has to return to 1948 to find an election in which a Republican presidential candidate has taken a smaller proportion of the popular vote and fewer electoral votes out of the South. This is true in spite of the fact that continuation of the Republican drift over the 16 years since 1948 has now begun to cumulate to a noteworthy number of new Republican voters (close to two million) in that region. The reason for the failure is perhaps best expressed as a paraphrase of the interview remarks made by the modal southern white voter in 1964: "Goldwater is right on the most important question—the Negro problem—but the Democratic Party holds all the rest of the cards." In sum, then, 1964 provided a supreme test of the capacity of the civil rights issue to touch off fundamental and rapid partisan realignment in the South, in contrast to the slow and long-term drift described above. Goldwater may have succeeded in converting to Republicanism on more than a transient basis some fraction of the southern electorate located primarily in the deepest areas of the Black-Belt South. Yet this fraction of the total southern electorate is too small to do more than speed slightly the rate of partisan change in the South.

down before anything like full convergence is achieved. That is, the convergence process will lead to a more vital Republican Party in larger urban areas, and a reshaping of the southern political map quite generally, with a new kind of political differentiation setting city apart from exclusive suburb, and both apart from rural counties 50 miles distant, in the manner which has become familiar in the North. We would, however, hazard a guess that it will *not* lead to widespread party competition in portions of the South which remain rural. For the foreseeable future, we would anticipate that the rural southern hinterland will remain largely a fief of the Democratic Party, just as more rural areas in New England and the Midwest have remained Republican fiefs. There are precedents for such arrangements in Europe, where through historical accident one rural region has crystallized as leftist and another as rightist, even though to the observer the demands of the two areas upon the polity seem entirely similar.

Nonetheless, increased convergence will have the important consequence of reducing the probability of any partisan realignment of the region as region. Although we have not labored the point in the course of this discussion, in many senses the convergence outcome and the partisan realignment outcome are intrinsically incompatible. The South will inevitably participate in future partisan realignments, but it will do so as part of the nation, demonstrating internal patterns akin to those shown elsewhere rather than moving en bloc by itself as a distinctive region. A decade or two ago the Democratic alignment of the small-town and agrarian South was highly anomalous next to the Republican alignment of non-southern small towns and rural areas. As urbanization and industrialization have progressed in the South, the two parties have been developing southern clienteles which are more appropriate to their national policy positions. From this point of view, the likelihood that the South as a region will undergo any distinctive and sudden party realignment is probably less today than it was in 1948 and is continuing to decline.

III

Comparative Political Analysis

The rewards of applying the insights gained from our contemporary inquiries to the illumination of our national political history lead us to a still more ambitious task: the study of contrasts in successions of collective events from nation to nation. The vistas suggested by the development of systematic cross-national comparisons are at the current time both challenging and frightening. Challenging because as we have observed, variation is the indispensable grist of science, and the nations of the world provide a handsome amount of variation in institutions and historical configurations. The prospect is frightening only because we may be faced with a surfeit of riches in this regard: the orderly explanation of variation in a particular parameter requires the isolation of meaningful covariation between this parameter and another, which means in turn holding many further confounding sources of variation constant. The restriction of empirical studies to a single nation does at least claim the advantage of holding more or less constant a confusing host of cultural and institutional factors. Yet most of the "grand" questions debated in traditional social and political theory have to do in the most direct way with the human political significance of these grossest variations in institutions and culture. It is only by comparable empirical work across national boundaries that research can begin to address these problems.

In the last decade work of this kind has begun at a number of levels. At the macrocosmic, or most highly aggregated level, investigators have begun to array large samples of nation-states in locations on various dimensions—gross national product, proportion illiterate, etc.— with each nation summarized as a single number.[1] Then analyses are

[1] For examples, see K. W. Deutsch, "Social Mobilization and Political Development," *American Political Science Review*, 55, 493–514 (1961) or A. S. Banks and R. B. Textor, *A Cross-Polity Survey*. Cambridge, Mass.: The M.I.T. Press, 1963.

made of the interrelations of these indexes. Although work in this mode automatically escapes the most glaring traditional pitfalls of selective evidence (i.e., citing cases of nations that fit a theory and ignoring those that contradict it), it still suffers from all of the familiar ambiguities that inhere in very limited numbers of quite indirect "surface" indicators. At the microcosmic end, meanwhile, an increasing amount of cross-national work is being done by psycholinguists in an effort to determine the ways in which peculiarities of language may affect basic meaning.[2]

Cross-national survey research studies fall between these two kinds of effort. They can profit from microcosmic work to develop increasingly sound and comparable verbal instruments of measurement across linguistic boundaries. At the same time the spread of such studies should yield an enormous increase in the number, relevance, and sophistication of aggregate indexes available for cross-national work, as well as an increasing depth of understanding of their underlying meanings. Naturally, at the moment we speak more of promise than of fulfillment. Current efforts at cross-national studies,[3] illustrations of which are presented in the following chapters, stand in much the same relation to the ultimate potential of these enterprises as do the limited empirical studies of the late 1930's and early 1940's to the current contributions of survey research within single nations. Yet as time passes and cross-national data accumulate in temporal depth and international scope, there would seem to be almost inevitable dividends from understanding contrasts between collective events from nation to nation and, ultimately, from more definitive theoretical treatment of variation in national histories.

[2] Charles E. Osgood, "Studies on the Generality of Affective Meaning Systems," *American Psychologist*, 17, 10–28 (1962).

[3] See, for example, S. Rokkan, "Party Preferences and Opinion Patterns in Western Europe: A Comparative Analysis," *International Social Science Bulletin*, 7 (1955); Daniel Lerner, *The Passing of Traditional Society*, Glencoe, Ill.: The Free Press, 1958; and G. Almond and S. Verba, *The Civic Culture*.

CHAPTER 13

Party Identification in Norway and the United States

Angus Campbell and Henry Valen

The importance of the identification of the citizen of a democratic state with the political party of his choice has been recognized for many years. David Hume wrote of party "affections," Washington and Madison of the "spirit of Party," and Calhoun of "party attachments." Generally regarded as deplorable by these early writers, party spirit was recognized as a natural accompaniment of the development of mass parties within the electorate.

As the reader has observed, we have relied heavily on the concept of party identification in the program of research which is reported in this volume. We have demonstrated in our earlier publications the significance of these standing commitments to party as an intervening variable lying causally prior to the individual's perceptions of his immediate political world.[1] We have been concerned in the preceding chapters with the role of these basic predispositions as a stabilizing element in the flow of the vote in the American elections.

As the result of certain fortunate circumstances, we now have an opportunity to compare the characteristics of party identification in two countries which resemble each other closely in their basic commitment to the principles of democratic government but differ sharply

---

[1] A. Campbell, P. E. Converse, W. E. Miller, and D. E. Stokes, *The American Voter*, New York: John Wiley and Sons, 1960.

This chapter appeared originally in the *Public Opinion Quarterly*, **25**, Winter 1961.

in their system of political parties. The availability of comparable data from Norway and the United States makes it possible to examine a number of hypotheses regarding the interaction of party systems and party identifications which could not be tested within a single country.

In the following pages we will first review the major similarities and differences between the political systems of Norway and the United States, with particular reference to the characteristics of the political parties in the two countries. We will then present survey data intended to show common characteristics in the phenomenon of party identification in the two countries. Finally we will propose certain hypotheses as to differences which we expect to find in Norway and the United States resulting from the different character of their political parties, and relate data from surveys in the two countries to them.

The Political Systems of Norway and the United States

The institutional arrangements within which the party systems of Norway and the United States function differ substantially. Most important is the fact that Norway has a parliamentary government whereas the United States has a presidential system. Norway is a unitary state while the United States is a federation of states. In Norway representatives to the Storting are elected by a system of proportional representation; representatives in the American Congress are elected by a plurality in single-member constituencies.

The party systems which have developed within these contrasting constitutional structures differ in a number of respects which have important implications for the character of party identification in the two countries.

(1) Whereas in the United States Democrats and Republicans are the only parties of any significance, Norway has a multiple system with six main parties: the Communists, the Labor Party, the Liberals, the Christian People's Party, the Agrarians, and the Conservatives.[2] The Labor Party holds a dominating position, and in the most recent elections it has obtained nearly half the votes. The Labor Party ran the government from 1935 to 1965.[3] The four nonsocialist opposition

---

[2] The Agrarian Party has changed its name to the Center Party since this study was completed.

[3] In the fall of 1963 the Labor Party was briefly displaced by a coalition government but immediately returned to power.

parties carry almost all the other half of the vote. The Communists play a rather insignificant role in Norwegian politics (in 1957 they obtained only 3 per cent of the vote). The difference in number of parties is obviously a basic difference between the two systems, and most other differences which may be recorded are related to this fact.

In the American system the goal of both parties at elections is to obtain a majority of the votes and thus gain control of the government. Each party has to rely upon support from all sections of the population, and both parties attempt to appeal to most social groups and interests. This tends to reduce the differences between the policies of the two parties, since they both have to avoid being too specific in their group appeals.

The Norwegian parties tend to appeal to distinctive clienteles. This is especially true of the three newer parties, the Agrarians, the Christians, and the Communists. The older parties, the Conservatives, the Liberals, and Labor, despite their historic connections with specific segments of Norwegian society, have tended in recent years to broaden the character of their appeal and to seek support from a wide range of groups within the electorate. They are still considerably more specific in their group appeals than the American parties, however.

(2) At elections Norwegian parties tend to commit themselves more clearly to specific policies than do American parties. Party platforms in Norway are rather detailed and specific compared with those in the United States. Furthermore, candidates running for election in Norway are strongly committed to the party platform. Therefore, in Norway, it is almost exclusively the parties which are made responsible for the policies, whereas in the United States a campaign is not only a contest between opposing parties, it also focuses heavily upon individual candidates.

(3) Norwegian parties possess better organizational facilities than American parties for communicating to the rank and file in regard to party policies and ideologies: (a) In contrast to the American system, Norwegian parties have a regular dues-paying membership. This difference implies that there is more party activity on the local level and more frequent interaction between party militants in Norwegian parties than in American parties. (b) Norwegian parties are more centralized than American parties, that is, central leadership is more influential in formulating party policies and decisions on organizational matters. In American parties centralization seems to be weakened by the federal system. (c) Contrary to the practices of the Republican and the Democratic Parties, the Norwegian parties make great efforts toward organizing educational activities for their mem-

bers and leaders. Through conferences, courses, and various types of group activities, the militants are trained and indoctrinated in political and organizational matters.

(4) The American press is less politicized than the Norwegian press. All American papers are financially independent of the two parties. Many papers take a stand for one of the two parties during the campaign, but in the periods between campaigns they tend to be politically neutral. In Norway almost all papers are strongly committed to some party or group of parties which they continuously defend. For a great number of papers, partisan attitudes are determined by the fact that they are owned or financially supported by the parties. The Labor Party, which has the most politicized press, runs (together with trade unions) altogether forty-one papers throughout the country. In order to provide the newspapers with partisan news and viewpoints, all Norwegian parties are equipped with a press bureau which is connected to the party headquarters. Thus the Norwegian daily press contributes much more than the American press to articulating differences between the parties.[4]

From these observations on the functioning of the party systems in the two countries, it seems justified to conclude that (1) differences between parties in stands on issues are both greater and clearer in Norway than in the United States; (2) Norwegian parties are more specific than American parties in appealing to various groups and sections of the electorate; (3) differences on policies between the parties are more effectively brought to the attention of the public in Norway than in the United States.

The Distribution of Party Identification in Norway and the United States

Although the party systems in Norway and the United States differ in important respects, the basic quality of the parties as social entities to which individual citizens may feel a greater or smaller degree of personal attachment is essentially the same. In both countries the parties have their group symbols, their prominent leaders, their historical accomplishments. As the groups most relevant to political affairs,

---

[4] Details on the relationships between the press, the parties, and the voters are presented in an article by Stein Rokkan and P. Torsvik, "Der Wähler, der Leser und die partei Presse," *Kölner Zs. f. Soziol.* ["The Voter, the Reader and the Party Press," *Cologne Journal of Sociology*], **12**, 278–301 (1960).

they offer the citizen a point of reference for guidance in the confusing world of politics.

The problem of obtaining comparable measures of the degree to which people identify themselves with the political parties in the two countries is not easily solved. Differences in language make it impossible to use precisely the same wording in the questions employed to record party identification, and make it difficult to compare in an absolute sense the values obtained in the categories of the scales used in the two countries. Thus we will not be able to say that more or fewer people in Norway are strongly party-identified than in the United States, but we can contrast the characteristics of strong and weak identifiers in Norway with strong and weak identifiers in the United States.

The data to be presented from Norway were gathered as part of a comprehensive study of the 1957 elections to the Norwegian Storting.[5] A nationwide sample of 1,546 persons, selected randomly from the Norwegian register of electors, was interviewed during October and November of 1957. An additional special sample of 1,017 persons was selected and interviewed in the province of Rogaland. Rogaland is located on the southwestern coast of Norway; Stavanger, an important harbor and industrial center, is its largest city. The Rogaland sample was asked a series of questions which make it possible to classify each respondent as strongly or weakly identified with a political party. The nationwide sample was not asked these questions, although each respondent was classified as a member or nonmember of a political party. Most of the Norwegian data presented in this article are based on the Rogaland sample, although they are supplemented at one point (Table 13-1) by data from the nationwide sample. It cannot be said that Rogaland is typical of the whole of Norway, but there is no obvious reason to believe that information regarding party identification in this area would differ substantially from information from the country as a whole.

The respondents in the Norwegian (Rogaland) sample were asked the following three questions during the course of their interview: "Are you now or have you been a member of a political party or an associated group (e.g., a political youth group or a political women's group)?" For those who were not party members: "Apart from formal party membership, would you say that you wholeheartedly support

[5] The Norwegian election study was carried out by the joint efforts of the Institute for Social Research in Oslo and the Chr. Michelsen Institute in Bergen, under the direction of Stein Rokkan. It was financially supported by the Rockefeller Foundation and by the Norwegian Social Science Research Council.

one special party; in other words, do you consider yourself a Liberal, a Conservative, a Laborite or what?" If "Yes" to either of these questions: "Suppose that your party for one reason or another was prevented from presenting a ballot at the Storting election in the Province of Rogaland, would that mean a great deal to you or would you not care at all?" If the respondent said that he was a member of a party or that he "considered himself" a Liberal or whatever, he was classified as a party identifier. If he rejected both these questions, he was classified as Independent. Those respondents who did identify themselves with a party were classified as strong or weak identifiers on the basis of the third question, in answer to which they expressed the strength of their feeling about the possibility that their party might be left off the ballot.

The data from the United States are taken from the national survey of the electorate conducted in the fall of 1956 by the Survey Research Center. The sample of 1,772 respondents was drawn by methods of probability sampling from the universe of persons living in private households in the United States. These people were given our standard scale for the measurement of party identification.

We find at the outset that the concept of personal affiliation with a political party is readily comprehended by virtually the entire electorate in both Norway and the United States. Only a minor fraction of the people interviewed in the two studies (4 per cent in the United States and 9 per cent in Norway) seemed unable to relate themselves to the alternatives offered in the survey questions.[6] The rest appeared to recognize the dimension implied by the questions and to place themselves in relation to it with little difficulty. The distributions of their self-identifications are given in Table 13-1.

When we examine the demographic and social characteristics of those people in the two countries who identify or do not identify with the political parties, we find very striking similarities. Considering first men and women in the two electorates, we find no consistent tendency in either country for party identifiers and Independents to differ in sex composition. In Norway strong identifiers are somewhat more likely to be men than are weak identifiers, but in neither country are women notably less likely to identify themselves with a party label.

In both countries strength of party identification tends to increase with age, and this is true among both men and women. In the absence

---

[6] The Norwegian figure includes a number of people of whom the questions on party identification were not asked.

TABLE 13-1

Extent of Party Identification in Norway and the United States
(in per cent)

	Norway	United States
Strong identifiers (consider themselves strong supporters of a party)	25	36
Weak identifiers (consider themselves supporters of a party but not very strong)	34	37
Identifiers whose intensity was not ascertained	7	0
Independents (reject party identification)	25	23
Unpolitical (do not understand concept or do not relate themselves to it)	9	4
Total	100	100

of life-cycle data which would reveal the course of development of individual attitudes toward political parties, we may speculate as to the source of this tendency toward strong political identification among the older levels of the electorate in the two countries. Since there is nothing to indicate that the Norwegian and American parties have gained or lost in significance during the lifetime of our respondents, we incline to the belief that partisanship tends to become more important for the average member of the electorate as he grows older. Concerned with interests of a more personal character during his early years, he may become involved with political affairs as he becomes more fully a member of society as a parent, a worker, a neighbor, a taxpayer. Once drawn into peripheral association with a party, the strength of his attachment to the party is likely to increase as his length of membership increases. Our data from Norway and the United States appear to conform to other observations regarding the relationship between frequency and strength of group interactions.[7]

People at the different levels of party identification do not differ greatly in the number of years of formal education they have completed. Among men, strong identification tends to be associated with lower educational attainment, independence with higher. The relationship is not high and it has some irregularities, but the pattern is

[7] For example, see George Homans, *The Human Group* (London: Routledge, 1951, Chap. 6).

very similar in the two countries. Among the women there is no consistent association with education in either country.

Serious difficulties are encountered when one attempts to compare occupational groups in different societies, even when the societies are as similar as those of Norway and the United States. For the purposes of the present analysis, we have had to be satisfied with a very rough system of classification by which we have divided our samples into white-collar workers, blue-collar workers, and farmers. When the members of the three identification groups are divided into these occupation categories, we find a pattern very similar to that which appeared when we considered educational level. Among men in both countries there is some tendency, although not a strong one, for the Independents to draw disproportionately from the white-collar workers at the expense of the farmers, with a converse tendency among the strong identifiers. This relationship is less clear among the women.[8]

A final comparison of the characteristics of party identifiers in Norway and the United States may be obtained by comparing the extent of participation in the electoral process shown by identifiers and Independents in the two countries. Similar questions were asked of the two samples intended to record the number of elections in which the respondent had voted "since you have been old enough to vote." As one might expect, the reported level of voting was higher in Norway than in the United States, and the strong identifiers were the most faithful in their voting in both countries. In Norway the weak identifiers reported a somewhat less impressive record than the strong identifiers, and the Independents were considerably less likely than the other groups to have voted in all the elections. In the United States the weak identifiers and Independents did not differ in their previous voting record.

We conclude from these findings that the phenomenon of party identification has similar qualities in the two countries. It is a group attachment very widely held in the population, it does not differentiate men and women, and it is only moderately related to measures of social and occupational status. The strength of this sense of attachment increases in the later decades of life, presumably as the result of long-continued association with the party. The stronger the attachment is, the more likely the individual is to be consistently active politically.

[8] In the United States there is a sharp difference between farmers in the North and South, with southern farmers tending toward strong party identification and northern farmers toward political independence. See Campbell et al., *op. cit.*, Chap. 15.

These common attributes give us confidence that we are indeed measuring the same phenomenon in the two countries and that the differences which are noted in the succeeding pages derive from actual differences in the party systems in the two countries and not from ambiguities in our measures of party identification.

Party Systems and Party Followers

The comparative study of nations differing in party structure provides an opportunity to examine the relationship between the nature of political parties and the character of the popular following these parties attract. Although we assume that party identification represents the same kind of psychological attachment in both Norway and the United States, we expect to find differences in the characteristics of partisans of the different parties in the two countries deriving from the differences in their party systems.

As we have seen, the Norwegian parties are considerably more ideological and class related in their appeals to the electorate than are the American parties. In such a party system it is to be expected that the adherents of the several parties will be more homogeneous than they would be in a system where the parties have no special class character and attempt to attract followers from all levels of the electorate. Because of the distinctive quality of their appeal, the Norwegian parties are likely to recruit from a narrower range within the electorate and to exert a stronger influence on the political attitudes and behavior of their members than do the American parties. We expect then to find the following differences between party identifiers in the two countries:

1. Identifiers of the different Norwegian parties will be more distinctive in socio-economic characteristics than identifiers of the two American parties.

2. Identifiers of the Norwegian parties will perceive greater policy differences between the parties than will identifiers of the American parties.

3. In stands on issues, identifiers of the Norwegian parties will be more distinctive than identifiers of the American parties.

4. Identifiers of the Norwegian parties will be more likely to vote in accordance with their identification than will identifiers of the American parties.

5. For all of the above hypotheses we not only expect to find dif-

ferences between identifiers of the different parties in the two countries, but within each country we expect party distinctiveness to be greater among those party adherents who are most strongly identified.

1. *Identifiers of the different Norwegian parties will be more distinctive in socio-economic characteristics than identifiers of the two American parties.* In testing this hypothesis we shall compare identifiers of the different parties in the two countries with regard to the following socio-economic characteristics: education, occupation, and class identification. Relationships between party identification and the demographic variables, age and sex, will also be explored, although possible differences between parties with regard to these characteristics do not necessarily reflect differences in the way in which parties are related to socio-economic groups.

Age. In both countries the parties differ with regard to age composition. In the United States, Democratic identifiers tend to be younger than Republican identifiers. In Norway the Labor Party has the relatively youngest identifiers. The discrepancies between parties are not as large in the United States as they are in Norway. In the American sample, 43 per cent of the Democrats are forty-five years or more in age whereas 53 per cent of the Republicans have reached this age. In Norway one finds an increasing number of older persons (over forty-five years) as one moves from the Labor Party (37 per cent), to the Liberal Party (48 per cent), to the Agrarian Party (51 per cent), to the Conservative Party (55 per cent), to the Christian People's Party (56 per cent). In both countries, the strong identifiers of each party are somewhat older than the less strongly identified, with the exception of the Christian People's Party, which had been active in Norwegian politics for only twelve years at the time of this study. This undoubtedly reflects the tendency we have noted earlier for group association to increase in strength as tenure of association is extended.

Sex. There is a marked difference between the two countries with regard to sex composition of party identifiers. In the United States there is a small but reliable difference between the proportions of men and women in the two parties: 47 per cent of the Democratic Party identifiers are men, 43 per cent of the Republican partisans. In Norway the differences between parties are much larger. The proportions of men in Norwegian parties range from 62 per cent of the Agrarian Party to 32 per cent of the partisans of the Christian People's Party. In the United States the sex composition of the strong and weak identifiers of the two parties does not differ significantly. In Norway there is a consistent tendency in all parties for the strong identifiers to have higher proportions of men than do the weak identifiers.

Education. In both the United States and Norway the level of education reported by party identifiers differs from one party to the other. Republican identifiers are more likely to report a high educational level than Democrats; 37 per cent of the Republicans have completed high school, 26 per cent of the Democrats. In Norway the Conservatives and Liberals report relatively high educational achievement; the Agrarians, Christians, and Laborites are substantially lower. Taking attendance at the "real skole" or beyond as a mark of a high educational achievement, we find 45 per cent of the Conservatives at this level, 23 per cent of the Liberals, 7 per cent of the Agrarians, 5 per cent of the Christians, and 7 per cent of the Labor Party. The Norwegian parties are clearly more variable in this respect than the American parties.

We have seen earlier that there is relatively little relationship between educational level and strength of party identification in the two countries. Within the respective parties there are various degrees of difference between the strong and weak adherents. In the United States, the educational differences between strong and weak Democrats are insignificant; among Republicans, the strong identifiers have a slightly higher educational level than the weak. In Norway the strong partisans of the Conservatives, Liberals, and Agrarians are markedly higher in education than the weak partisans. In the Labor and Christian Parties the strong and weak identifiers do not differ in formal education. In other words, such differences as we find in education between strong and weak identifiers occur in those parties where the educational level of identifiers is generally high.

Occupation. In both countries the occupational distribution of identifiers differs among the parties. In the United States, the differences are rather small. The Democratic Party draws 30 per cent of its adherents from the white-collar occupations, 46 per cent from the blue-collar. The Republicans come 36 per cent from the white-collar occupations and 39 per cent from the blue-collar. The occupational differences are very much greater among the various Norwegian parties. Of the Labor Party identifiers 79 per cent are blue-collar workers, 17 per cent are white-collar; among the Conservatives the proportions are 19 per cent and 76 per cent. The two center parties, Liberals and Christians, whose ideologies are not primarily economic, are somewhat less extreme, but even they are clearly more distinctive in their proportions of blue-collar and white-collar workers than are the American parties.

When we compare the parties in the proportion of their adherents who are farmers, we find no difference in the United States (Democrats 10 per cent and Republicans 9 per cent) and no great difference among the Norwegian parties except for the Agrarian Party. The distinctive appeal of this party to Norwegian farmers is shown by the 77 per cent of Agrarian identifiers who are classified as farmers. None of the other parties has a proportion of farmers higher than 14 per cent.

These occupational differentials between the Norwegian parties become even more pronounced when we divide each party's followers into strong and weak identifiers. In the Conservative, Liberal, and Christian People's Parties there are relatively more white-collar workers among strong identifiers than among weak whereas the proportions of blue-collar workers are higher among strong than among weak identifiers in the Labor Party. Similarly, farmers are most numerous among the strong Agrarians. In the United States the occupational levels of the strong and weak adherents of the two parties are very similar. There are minor tendencies in both parties in the expected direction but they are not significant.

Class Identification. The distribution of class identification follows the same pattern as occupational distribution in the two countries. The Democrats have a majority of working-class identifiers (66 per cent) whereas the Republicans divide themselves about equally between middle-class and working-class. In Norway some 80 per cent of Labor identifiers say they belong to the working-class whereas all the nonsocialist parties are dominated by middle-class identifiers, with majorities rising as high as 86 per cent in the case of the Conservative Party.

Strong identifiers in both countries tend to be more distinctive in their class position than weak identifiers. In the Norwegian nonsocialist parties and in the Republican Party, strong identifiers more often see themselves as middle-class than weak identifiers. In the Democratic Party there is a tendency for strong identifiers to be more working-class than weak identifiers but it is very slight. The Norwegian Labor Party forms an exception to this general pattern in that strong and weak identifiers are equally distributed in social-class position.

We see from these various comparisons that the constituencies of the Norwegian parties are considerably more distinctive in socio-economic background than are those of the American parties. The Democratic Party has a somewhat stronger working-class quality than the Republican Party, but neither party could be said to have a homogeneous membership; both draw significant numbers of followers from all the important segments of the electorate. The Labor Party and the Conservative Party, standing at the extremes of the political spectrum in Norway (excluding the Communists), do on the other hand draw their constituents from a different social-class base. The Agrarian Party also has a distinctive appeal to a particular segment of Norwegian society and is composed very largely of people from this segment. The Liberal and Christian Parties have a more heterogeneous membership, although middle-class identifiers dominate in number. In general, the Norwegian multiparty system may be said to be characterized by a relatively strong association between social class and political party, an association which is only weakly present in the American two-party system.

Our expectation that strong identifiers in the two countries would be more distinctive in social characteristics than weak identifiers (point 5 above) is only partially supported. In Norway this tendency is quite apparent for the nonsocialist parties but is hardly discernible for the Labor Party. In the United States, consistent with the smaller overall differences between party followers, there are smaller differences between strong and weak identifiers of each party than we find in Norway. But the difference between strong and weak identifiers tends to be greater in the Republican Party than among the Democrats.[9]

2. *Identifiers of the Norwegian parties will perceive greater policy differences between the parties than will identifiers of the American parties.* Our description of the organization and activities of the parties in the two countries makes it apparent that, unless there is a general failure of communication by the parties to the electorate, the Norwegian parties must be perceived by the Norwegian public as being more distinctive in their policy positions than the American parties are in the United States. It is not possible to make a precise estimate

[9] An analysis of the recruitment of party activists in Norway and the United States shows a corresponding difference between the middle-class and working-class parties of the two countries. Middle-class voters for the Republican Party and the nonsocialist parties of Norway were considerably more likely to be politically active than were working-class voters for these parties. This tendency was also found in much weaker degree among middle-class and working-class voters for the Democratic Party, but it was reversed among the supporters of the Labor Party in Norway. Perception of conflict or congruence between one's own class position and the class character of the party with which one identifies appears to discourage or support active participation in that party's activities. See S. Rokkan and A. Campbell, "Citizen Participation in Political Life: Norway and the United States of America," *International Social Science Journal*, 12, No. 1 (1960).

of the difference between the two countries in this regard, but the evidence available suggests strongly that our supposition is correct. The Norwegian sample was asked the following question: "Many people think there is so much agreement between the parties on important matters that it does not matter for which party one is voting this time. Are you of this opinion?" The American sample was asked: "Do you think there are any important differences between what the Democratic and Republican Parties stand for, or do you think they are about the same?" Of the Norwegian sample, 11 per cent felt that there were no differences between the parties; an additional 8 per cent did not know whether there were differences or not. Of the American sample, 40 per cent thought the two parties were about the same, and an additional 8 per cent didn't know whether they differed or not. Granting the variation in the wording of the questions, these differences are obviously sizable and in the direction of our expectation.

When we subdivide these data into the party groups, we find little difference between the parties in each country (Table 13-2). But in every case the strong identifiers of the party are more likely to feel that there are important differences between the parties than are the weak identifiers.

3. *In stands on issues, identifiers of the Norwegian parties will be more distinctive than identifiers of the American parties.* Both the Norwegian and American surveys contained questions intended to elicit the respondents' attitudes toward questions of national policy thought to be important in each of the two countries at the time. In Norway two questions were asked of the Rogaland sample, one dealing with the level of national taxation and the other with the level of expenditures for defense. In the nationwide sample, four additional questions were asked: one concerned with governmental activity in housing construction, one with governmental regulation of private enterprise, the third with governmental control of inflation, and the fourth with governmental promotion of religious values. In the American survey, sixteen questions were asked dealing with welfare legislation, foreign policy, governmental control of big business and labor unions, governmental production of power and housing, civil rights, and taxation. In both studies the issue questions were presented in such a way that the respondents answered in terms of whether they thought the government had not done enough, had gone too far, or had done about right in regard to the particular policy.

We obviously cannot make direct comparisons of distributions of attitudes in the two countries. We can, however, compare the different

TABLE 13-2

Relation of Party Identification to Perception of Policy Differences between the Parties
(in per cent)

Perception of Differences	Norwegian Party Identification									
	Labor		Liberal		Christian		Agrarian		Conservative	
	Strong	Weak	Strong	Weak	Strong	Weak	Strong	Weak	Strong	Weak
No differences	2	17	4	12	6	17		2	4	15
Communists differ from other parties	2	6	8	16	6		3	6		4
Labor and Communists differ from other parties	4	5		16		4	15	16	14	11
Big differences	88	63	85	45	80	66	82	68	79	66
Don't know	3	7	3	8	6	4		4	3	
Not ascertained	1	2		3	2	9		4		4
Total	100	100	100	100	100	100	100	100	100	100
(N)	(123)	(144)	(27)	(75)	(36)	(23)	(34)	(50)	(28)	(47)

Perception of Differences	United States Party Identification			
	Democratic		Republican	
	Strong	Weak	Strong	Weak
No differences	31	46	33	49
Minor differences	10	10	8	12
Some differences	36	24	34	23
Important differences	15	8	17	6
Don't know	6	10	5	9
Not ascertained	2	2	3	1
Total	100	100	100	100
(N)	(392)	(449)	(241)	(246)

parties within each country in order to determine the degree of inter-party difference. The extensive array of data presented in Table 13-3 can be summarized in the following statements:

(a) In Norway the adherents of the different parties differ substantially in their views on five of the six issues to which they were asked to respond, and their positions conform to the ideological positions of their party leadership. On the issue of national defense there

TABLE 13-3

Issue Positions of Party Identifiers in Norway and the United States *
(in per cent)

Issue †	Party Identification	Norway				
		Labor	Liberal ‡	Christian	Agrarian	Conservative
Government has raised taxes too high	Strong	27	44	37	47	74
	Weak	23	45	29	54	56
Government should reduce defense budget	Strong	51	29	51	29	25
	Weak	48	52	38	52	29
Government has gone too far in slowing down building of houses	Members	26		40	50	70
	Nonmembers	27	58	45	55	68
Government has interfered too much in economic life	Members	8		50	71	84
	Nonmembers	9	61	50	47	74
Government has not done enough to stop inflation	Members	12		44	64	75
	Nonmembers	15	54	45	58	62
Government has done too little to promote Christian morals and Christian faith	Members	17		97	60	51
	Nonmembers	24	42	89	63	43

* Entries in the table are the proportion of the sample agreeing with the policy statement.

† The first two of the Norwegian issues were asked of the Rogaland sample. The other four were asked of the nationwide sample. In the latter case, the respondents are divided into those who identified themselves as members of one of the Norwegian parties and those who stated an intention to vote for a particular party although they were not party members.

‡ The strong Liberal group in the nationwide sample was too small to justify inclusion.

TABLE 13-3 (continued)

| | United States | | |
Issue	Party Identification	Democrats	Republicans
Government has concerned itself too much with world problems	Strong Weak	29 18	16 21
Government has given too much economic aid to poor countries	Strong Weak	30 24	21 27
Government has gone too far in keeping soldiers overseas	Strong Weak	9 8	8 9
Government has given too much help to neutralist nations	Strong Weak	21 17	18 19
Government has been too friendly with other countries	Strong Weak	15 13	8 10
Government has not been tough enough in dealing with Russia and China	Strong Weak	38 26	25 28
Government has not gone far enough in guaranteeing full employment	Strong Weak	39 22	12 16
Government has not done enough to help build more schools	Strong Weak	44 37	28 32
Government has not done enough to help provide low-cost medical care	Strong Weak	48 32	21 29
Government is going too far in leaving electricity and housing to private businessmen	Strong Weak	15 15	5 9
Government is not doing enough to see that Negroes get fair treatment in jobs and housing	Strong Weak	22 22	16 20
Government is not doing enough to control business influence on government	Strong Weak	37 27	10 19
Government is not doing enough to control union influence on government	Strong Weak	21 20	19 19

TABLE 13-3 (continued)

Issue	Party Identification	United States	
		Democrats	Republicans
Government has not done enough to cut taxes	Strong	34	13
	Weak	24	16
Government has not gone far enough in firing suspected Communists	Strong	19	15
	Weak	10	15
Government has concerned itself too much with racial integration of schools	Strong	22	12
	Weak	23	22

is no consistent pattern across the party continuum, although the Laborites and Conservatives hold the extreme positions.

(b) Strong and weak identifiers of the Norwegian parties do not differ significantly in their issue positions. Only in the Conservative Party is there a consistent tendency for the strong identifiers to take a more strongly partisan position than the weak identifiers.[10]

(c) None of the issues presented to the American sample divides the followers of the two parties as sharply as the Norwegian sample is divided. Questions relating to various domestic economic policies bring out moderate differences between Democrats and Republicans that conform to the general posture taken by the leadership of the two parties, but questions relating to foreign affairs and civil rights result in generally small and inconsistent party differences.

(d) In general strong Democrats are most likely and strong Repub-

[10] It is not clear why the policy attitudes of the strong and weak identifiers of the Norwegian parties do not differ more sharply than they do. In the case of the nationwide sample it is possible that the division of the voters for the various parties into members and nonmembers does not catch the quality of party attachment that we assumed. This is suggested by the fact that when we divide the voters in this sample into those who were politically active beyond simply voting and those who did no more than vote, the actives were consistently more likely to support the policy positions of the party they voted for than were the voters-only. It is unfortunate for this aspect of our analysis that a clearer measure of strength of party identification was not obtained from the nationwide sample.

licans least likely to criticize the policies of the government (which was Republican at the time of the study). The differences between strong and weak partisans are small or nonexistent on issues which do not divide the two parties, but they are relatively large when the party differences are large, particularly in the case of the economic welfare policies.

In general, we may conclude that the Norwegian parties differ not only in their publicly declared positions but in the positions held by their rank and file. The one issue on which there is not coincidence of viewpoint between the party leadership and the party followers is instructive. The question of national defense has not in fact been a partisan issue in Norway during recent years; all parties in the Storting, except the Communists, have supported the defense budget. Traditionally, however, the Conservative and Agrarian Parties have been most favorable to a strong defense program; before the Second World War the Labor Party was generally resistant to defense expenditures. Despite the fact that the Labor Party has been in power throughout the postwar period and has been responsible for the development of the present defense program of Norway, public attitudes on this issue appear to reflect strong convictions carried over from the prewar period.

It seems very likely that the relatively small differences found between Democrats and Republicans in the United States are also carried over from the depression period of the 1930's. The only issues on which partisan differences are appreciable are those which relate to the New Deal ideology and the early Roosevelt period. The strong identification of the Democratic Party with various forms of welfare legislation that came into American politics as a result of the economic distress of the 1930's was probably less clear in 1956 than it had been twenty years earlier, but reverberations of that period still persist.

4. *Identifiers of the Norwegian parties will be more likely to vote in accordance with their identification than will identifiers of the American parties.* If the Norwegian electorate sees greater differences among their parties than the Americans do between theirs, we should expect it to be more difficult for a Norwegian voter to shift his vote from one party to another than it would be for voters in the United States. We can test this hypothesis in two ways: first by comparing the lifetime voting record of the samples in the two countries, and, second, by comparing the votes of party groups in certain recent elections. Reports of votes over a period of many years are obviously subject to errors of memory, but if we assume that this type of error is no greater in one country than another we find that the Norwegians do

TABLE 13-4

Party Regularity in Voting in Norway and the United States *
(in per cent)

	Strength of Identification	
	Strong	Weak
Norway:		
Have you always voted for the same party at Storting elections, or have you voted for different parties?		
Labor	83	77
Liberal	74	63
Christian †	17	22
Agrarian	81	72
Conservative	70	44
United States:		
Have you always voted for the same party or have you voted for different parties for President?		
Democrats	67	45
Republicans	65	44

* Entries in the table are the proportion of each group who say they have always voted for the same party.

† The Christian Party was founded in 1935 and has drawn its membership primarily from the Liberal and Labor Parties.

in fact have a more consistent record of party regularity than the Americans (Table 13-4). In both countries the strong party identifiers are more dependable in their party loyalty than the weak identifiers.[11]

[11] The substantial difference in the voting history of the present followers of the Labor and Conservative Parties raises an interesting question as to the character of political movement in a party system having as strong a "left-right" quality as the Norwegian system has. We have seen that the Conservative partisans as a group are considerably older than the Labor partisans, a difference which suggests the commonplace observation that people tend to grow more conservative as they grow older. We also find when we compare the first vote reported by these people with their present party preference that there has been considerably more movement from left to right on the party scale than in the other direction. The Conservative Party at the extreme of this scale apparently profits from these life-cycle changes and

The vagaries of memory and the ambiguities of comparing a Storting election to a presidential election are considerably reduced when we look at the reported votes of the Norwegian party groups in the Storting election of 1957 and the American party groups in the congressional election of 1958. Table 13-5 again shows the Norwegian voters to be less likely to cross party lines than the American voters and the strong partisans in both countries to be most likely to vote their party's ticket.

Discussion

The evidence we have presented supports our general expectation that identification with the Norwegian parties would be associated with greater demographic and political distinctiveness than would identification with the American parties. Although we have been able to compare only two nations, we think it likely that similar results would be obtained from the comparison of any pair of stable multiparty and two-party systems.

It is apparent, as various scholars have observed, that in a two-party system one party draws away from the other in its position on important policy issues at the risk of losing adherents in the center who now find themselves closer to the opposition party.[12] In such a situation considerations of self-preservation tend to hold the two parties close to each other, so close in the American situation that large segments of the electorate cannot distinguish any clear policy differ-

---

counts a larger proportion of erstwhile members of other parties in its numbers than does the Labor Party from which the movement mainly comes. If this exchange of personnel were the only change in the constituency of the parties, the Conservative Party would obviously increase its relative strength over the long run. Other facts at least as important, however, are the additions to the electorate of the young voters and the subtractions of those who die, a continuing process of replacement which benefits the party with the greatest appeal to youth, in Norway the Labor Party.

There is some reason to believe that a similar balance of exchanges occurs between the American parties, although there is so much movement from one party's presidential candidate to that of the other for reasons having very little ideological quality that such life-cycle increases in conservatism as do occur are entirely obscured in the totals given in Table 13-4. We would not in any case expect to find as large a life-cycle shift in partisanship in the United States as we would in a country having strongly differentiated liberal and conservative parties.

[12] We have reviewed the vagaries of spatial representations of party competition in Chapter 10.

TABLE 13-5

Vote of Party Groups in Norway and the United States
(in per cent)

1957 Storting Election Vote	Norwegian Party Identification									
	Labor		Liberal		Christian		Agrarian		Conservative	
	Strong	Weak	Strong	Weak	Strong	Weak	Strong	Weak	Strong	Weak
Communist	1	2					2			
Labor	97	95		2						
Liberal	1	1	96	92	8	20	3			2
Christian		1	4	6	92	80	3	4		
Agrarian							94	90		
Conservative	1	1						4	100	98
Total	100	100	100	100	100	100	100	100	100	100
(N)	(120)	(130)	(26)	(67)	(35)	(21)	(34)	(46)	(27)	(41)

1958 Congressional Election Vote	United States Party Identification			
	Democratic		Republican	
	Strong	Weak	Strong	Weak
Democratic	96	86	11	32
Republican	4	14	89	68
Total	100	100	100	100
(N)	(187)	(173)	(149)	(120)

ences between the parties. In a multiparty system, the parties typically develop as the expression of special interests within the electorate and they seek to associate themselves with specific appeals to these special segments of the electorate. As Duverger remarks, "Each tries to emphasize the differences of detail which distinguish it from its nearest rivals, instead of drawing attention to their profound similarities." [13]

The question of why a two-party system develops in one country and a multiparty system in another is not illuminated by the evidence from our studies. We can only surmise from a knowledge of the political histories of Norway and the United States the sequence of forces which gave rise to the different party systems we find in the two countries at the present time. Our studies do give us some insight, however, into

[13] M. Duverger, *Political Parties*, London: Methuen, 1959, p. 388.

the manner in which the characteristics of a party system are maintained or modified once it has been established.

In the American situation, the major cohesive force which gives the party system stability and continuity is the psychological attachment of the electorate to the parties. In the absence of strong class identification and class-associated programs of political action, the parties themselves serve as the significant source of political direction for the electorate. The parties do not represent themselves as spokesmen of special social classes and do not develop strong ideologies to express special class interests. In their appeal to the electorate, they tend to emphasize broad party virtues, the righteousness of party heroes, past and present, and the general ineptitude, if not wickedness, of the opposition. As the electorate's major source of political education, they create a public image of politics as a competition between parties per se rather than a choice between alternative policies. In such a situation, politics tends to lose its ideological character: the public is not stimulated to inform itself regarding specific policies; its political role becomes one of deciding who shall manage the government, not what shall the government do. For the bulk of the electorate, this decision is determined by long-established party loyalties, loyalties to parties which, in their effort to stay close to what they take to be the political center, have reduced policy differences between themselves to a minimum.

The strength of these party attachments and the general weakness in the American electorate of ideological interest both serve to maintain the two-party system. The failure of various attempts to launch third parties appealing to the special interests of the farmers or the urban working class reflects the conserving force of these two attributes of the American party system. Deriving from the two-party system, they have become important factors in its preservation.

The party system which took shape in Norway after the First World War was an extremely polarized one, and the conflict between the working-class movement and the parties in the center and to the right was at times so violent as to endanger the basic constitutional framework. Electoral statistics suggest that during the years since the depression there has been a significant decline in the intensity of this status polarization, associated with the rise to power of the Labor Party, the experience of the all-party government-in-exile during the war, and the post-war growth of the "new middle class" and other intermediary groups in the social structure. The system is still highly polarized, however, and, as we have seen, the fit between class status and party preference is marked. The Norwegian electorate has learned to structure politics in terms of party representation of class interests, and despite the softening of interparty and interclass conflict in recent years its expectations regarding the interests which the different parties represent are still much clearer than comparable expectations in the United States.

In a party system having a close relationship between the parties and the social classes, it is difficult to isolate the independent influence which party identification itself has on the electorate. The Norwegian labor union member who is a member of the Labor Party may display a strong party attachment, but one wonders if this does not merely express in different form his basic identification with the working class. Certainly it appears that this conjoining of party identification with more basic loyalties is more significant in Norway than it is in the United States. Because the party-class relationship is so weak in the United States, the voters are freer to move from one party to the other in successive elections and the parties are freer to exploit such opportunities as arise to induce them to do so. An examination of the history of American elections would demonstrate the frequency with which the parties have relied on outstanding personalities and contemporary embarrassments of the party in power to achieve political advantage and would reveal the extent to which the electorate has responded to these largely nonideological appeals.

It is a paradox that because of these facts the weakly organized American parties may exert a greater independent influence on political attitudes and votes than do the highly organized and more clearly class-related parties of Norway. To a voter who has not learned to interpret political events in terms of an ideology of social class, the party is likely to be the most important source of political direction available. In contrast, when a self-conscious segment of the electorate comes to see its party as the instrument for the implementation of its policy aspirations, it may exert at least as much influence on the party as the party does on it.

CHAPTER 14

Politicization of the Electorate in France and the United States

Philip E. Converse and Georges Dupeux

The turbulence of French politics has long fascinated observers, particularly when comparisons have been drawn with the stability or, according to one's point of view, the dull complacency of American political life. Profound ideological cleavages in France, the occasional threat of civil war, rather strong voter turnout, the instability of governments and republics, and the rise and fall of "flash" parties like the R.P.F. in 1951, the Poujadists in 1956, and the U.N.R. in 1958 have all contributed to the impression of a peculiar intensity in the tenor of French political life.

It is a sign of progress in the study of political behavior that such symptoms no longer seem to form a self-evident whole. We feel increasingly obliged, for example, to take note of the level in the society at which the symptoms are manifest. Most of our impressions of the French scene reflect only the behavior of French political leadership. Growing familiarity with survey data from broad publics has schooled us not to assume perfect continuity between the decision-making characteristics of a leadership and the predispositions of its rank and file. The extremism of the military elite in Algeria or ideological intransigence in the French National Assembly are in themselves poor proof that the shipyard worker in Nantes has political reflexes which differ from those of the shipyard worker in Norfolk.

This chapter appeared originally in the *Public Opinion Quarterly*, 26 (Spring 1962).

We feel increasingly obliged, moreover, to discriminate between some of these well-known symptoms of turbulence, for they no longer point in a common direction as clearly as was once assumed. Two signs which unquestionably reflect mass electoral behavior in France provide a case in point. Turnout levels in France are indeed high relative to those in the United States,[1] suggesting that, in the politically indifferent strata of the electorate where nonvoting is considered, political motivations are more intense. On the other hand, we now doubt that the rise and fall of "flash" parties are parallel symptoms of intense involvement. Rather, it seems likely that such episodes represent spasms of political excitement in unusually hard times on the part of citizens whose year-in, year-out involvement in political affairs is abnormally weak.[2] Obviously, for France and the United States, the basic traditions of a two-party or a multiparty system affect the likelihood that the flash party phenomenon will occur. But other things being equal, it seems that such phenomena are hardly signals of long-term public involvement in politics but betray instead a normal weak involvement. The durably involved voter tends toward strong partisan commitments, and his behavior over time stabilizes party fortunes within a nation.

Other less direct indicators add doubt as to the high involvement of the broad French public. Demographically, French society differs from the American in its lesser urbanization and lower mean formal education. Intranational studies have persistently shown higher political involvement among urban residents and, more strongly still, among people of more advanced education. While cross-national extrapolation of such data may be precarious, it does leave further room to question our intuitive impressions.

We intend in this paper to examine comparative data on the French and American publics in an effort to determine more precisely the locus of Franco-American differences in these matters.[3] We shall con-

[1] They are not, of course, outstanding against the backdrop provided by other Western European nations.

[2] For a fuller discussion see *The American Voter* (New York: John Wiley and Sons, Chap. 15).

[3] The French data were gathered in three waves of a national cross-section sample in the fall of 1958, during the constitutional referendum launching the Fifth Republic and the ensuing legislative elections, and are reported in G. Dupeux, A. Girard, and J. Stoetzel, "Une enquête par sondage auprès des electeurs," *Le Referendum de Septembre et les Elections de Novembre 1958*, Cahiers de la Fondation Nationale des Sciences Politiques (Paris: A. Colin, 1960, pp. 119–160). The study was jointly supported by the Conseil Supérieur de la Recherche Scientifique, the Rockefeller Foundation, and the Fondation Nationale des Sciences Politiques. The

sider the locus in qualitative terms, covering an extended series of political characteristics which run from expressions of involvement, acts of participation, and information seeking to orientations whereby the voter links party alternatives to the basic ideological issues in the society. We shall throughout maintain an interest as well in a vertical locus of differences. That is, we shall think of the two electorates as stratified from persistent nonvoters at the bottom, through the large middle mass of average voters, to citizens who engage in some further partisan activity, and thence by extrapolation to the higher leadership whose highly visible behavior is so frequently the source of our cross-national impressions. Such extrapolation is necessary, of course, because it is unlikely that the handful of "activists" whom we can distinguish at the top layer of both national samples include more than one or two persons who have ever had any direct hand in a leadership decision of even a parochial party organization or political interest group.

Involvement, Participation, and Information Seeking

Although a relatively large number of comparisons may be drawn with regard to simple manifestations of political involvement in the two countries, these comparisons vary widely in quality. Broad differences in institutions and political practices in the two societies can serve to channel public interest in different directions. The French political poster, often a full-blown campaign document, is addressed to other goals than the American political billboard, and hence the reading of such posters in the two societies is in no sense comparable activity. Similarly, the national control of the domestic airwaves in France means that two media of communication are given a totally different cast than in the United States. This fact, coupled with reduced access to radio or television sets in France, renders the attention paid by the two publics to such political broadcasts fundamentally incomparable. Or, in a different vein, certain manifestations of involvement are known to vary widely in their frequency within a nation from one type of election to another, or for the same type of election between periods of crisis and troughs of routine politics. While an

American studies were conducted by the Survey Research Center. Informal cross-national collaboration prior to the 1958 French study led to a French interview schedule permitting more rigorous comparative analysis than unrelated studies usually offer.

extended American time series has provided some useful norms, these were more difficult to find for the French data. In general, then, we shall elaborate upon only a few of the most solid comparisons, referring summarily to the flavor conveyed by other, looser comparisons.

Given the broad institutional differences between the two societies, it might seem useful to draw contrasts between self-estimates of psychological involvement between the two nations, however differently institutions might channel the ultimate behavioral expressions of such interest. While the data permit a number of matches between questions on political interest, posed at comparable times with comparable wording and with superficially comparable alternatives, one hesitates at comparisons which depend on crude "amount words" such as "very," "fairly," and the like. Cautiously, however, it may be observed that Americans gauge their interest in their elections at a rather higher level than do the French. Two to five times as many French respondents indicated that they were "not at all" interested in the 1958 elections as is the tendency for Americans with regard to their presidential elections; three to four times as many Americans say that they are "very" interested. Distributions from France in the more normal political year of 1953 show slightly higher levels of expressed interest, but even this distribution fails to approach the most unenthusiastic American distributions collected at the time of off-year congressional elections. For what it is worth, then, it is relatively hard to get French citizens to confess much interest in their elections.

More solid are comparisons of reported acts of political participation selected as involving comparable motivation in the two systems: membership in political organizations, attendance at political rallies, and attempts to influence the political choice of others through informal communications.[4] As Figure 14-1 suggests, the cross-national similarities on these items are impressive. Furthermore, we can examine such additional points as the number of meetings attended by those French and Americans who do attend political gatherings. Graphs of the frequency of attendance by attender are almost indistinguishable

[4] Of these three pairings, the first is technically the weakest. The American item asks about membership in "any political club or organization," whereas the French item focuses directly on political party membership, although the term "party" may be rather broadly construed in France. Furthermore, there were a substantial number of refusals to answer this membership item in France. These refusals have simply been removed from the calculations, since such treatment leaves the gross rate on the upper side of the range that informed estimates have suggested for total party membership in France, after realistic appraisal of the memberships claimed by the parties.

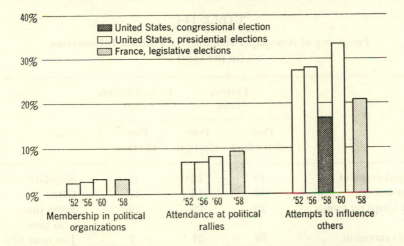

Figure 14-1. Rates of several forms of political participation, France and the United States.

between the two countries. The mean number of meetings attended among those who attend at all is in both cases a slight fraction over two. In sum, it is hard to imagine that any slight divergences in rates of attendance are crucial in any dramatic differences between the two systems.

Data were collected in both countries as well with regard to dependence on the mass media for political information. Here one of the most excellent bases for comparison which the data afford is provided by reports of the regularity with which political news about the elections was followed in daily newspapers. Although the structured alternatives again involve "amount words," there is a more tangible standard for responses implicit in the rhythm of newspaper production. "Regularly" or "never," when applied to readership of daily papers, has a common meaning in any language. Furthermore, we find empirically that responses to the newspaper questions show much higher stability for individuals over time than the direct interest questions. It is clear that we are dealing here with stable habits which are reliably reported.

When we compare distributions from the two countries (Table 14-1), there seems little doubt of higher American devotion to newspapers as a source of political information. Furthermore, the French citizen appears also to monitor other media for political information less. Thus, for example, he is less likely to have a television or radio

TABLE 14-1

Frequency of Newspaper Reading for Political Information
(in per cent)

	France, 1958		United States, 1960	
	Post-referendum	Post-election	Post-election	
Regulièrement	19	18	44	Regularly
Souvent	12	10	12	Often
De temps en temps	25	29	16	From time to time
Très rarement	19	21	7	Just once in a great while
Jamais	25	22	21	Never
	100	100	100	

set than his American counterpart; but even among those French who possess sets, attention to political broadcasts is markedly less than for comparable Americans. As we have observed, these latter differences are not in themselves proof of lesser French motivation, since the choices offered through the airwaves are not comparable cross-nationally. But such facts, along with further comparisons as to magazine reading, indicate that lower French attention to political material in the newspapers is not compensated for from other sources. Since elite political competition in France, even when reduced to simplest terms, is considerably more complex than two-party competition in the United States, it is ironic that the French voter exposes himself less faithfully to the flow of current political information.

Education being a strong determinant of all these information-seeking activities, it is of interest to control the substantial Franco-American differences in level of formal education. For Figure 14-2 we have applied a simple integer scoring to the five response categories of Table 14-1 and extracted means within education categories, the latter having been carefully tailored on the American side to match French intervals with regard to simple number of years of formal education. While the two curves do not match precisely, the main departures lie at the extremes, where case numbers are lowest, and hence where

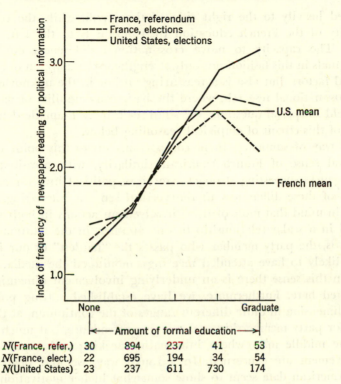

Index of frequency of newspaper reading for political information

— — France, referendum
------- France, elections
——— United States, elections

3.0

U.S. mean

2.0

French mean

1.0

None   Graduate

|←— Amount of formal education —→|

N(France, refer.)	30	894	237	41	53
N(France, elect.)	22	695	194	34	54
N(United States)	23	237	611	730	174

Figure 14-2. Frequency of newspaper reading for political information in France and the United States, by education.

sampling error is bound to disperse results.[5] Where more than 200 cases are available from both sides, the estimates show a most remarkable convergence.

As we see, there are strong cross-national differences in total distribution of regularity of newspaper reading (as represented by the distance between the horizontal lines in Figure 14-2). But these differences very nearly disappear (the general proximity of the two slopes, and their essential identity when case numbers are sufficient), with education controlled. The gap in total news reading for the two electorates comes about, then, simply because the American cases are

[5] The decline in reading among the most educated French citizens approaches statistical significance and is currently unaccounted for. We have been able to show that these people are not substituting political reviews and weekly magazines for daily news reading. The educated elite which follows the reviews also reads the newspapers faithfully; the remainder which fails to attend to the newspapers ignores political magazines as well.

loaded heavily to the right side of the graph, while the center of gravity of the French education distribution is to the left, or low, side. The capacity to move cross-national differences out to the marginals in this fashion not only strengthens presumption of common causal factors, but also is a reassuring anchor in the unknown waters of cross-national research, where the basic comparability of data must be held to special question. We shall see a more dramatic demonstration of this circuit of empirical reasoning below.

By way of summary, then, comparisons up to this point create a general sense of Franco-American similarity, with occasional mild divergences suggesting stronger American political involvement. The locus of these differences in the vertical sense is interesting. Let us bear in mind that most of these involvement actions in both societies stand in a scalar relationship to one another, in the Guttman sense. That is, the party member who passes the "hardest" of our items is very likely to have attended meetings, monitored the media, and so on. In this sense there is an underlying involvement dimension represented here. Furthermore, we have established cutting points on this dimension in quite different ranges of the continuum, at the high end for party membership and meeting attendance, but much deeper in the middle mass where information seeking and expressions of involvement are concerned. In a rough way, we may observe that the American data seem to show somewhat higher motivation in the middle ranges, with cross-national differences narrowing near the very top, and perhaps even showing a slight French advantage. Interestingly enough, this pattern would describe as well the cumulative frequency distributions expressing differences in years of formal education in the two countries. This identity is, of course, no proof that education accounts for the involvement divergences. But it does remind us that these patterns, if they differ cross-nationally at all, may partake of the sharper discontinuities in France between a tiny elite and the remainder of the population that one suspects for a variety of characteristics, and can readily demonstrate for education.[6]

[6] We shall not treat Franco-American differences in vote turnout, save to observe that they are probably more institutional than motivational. American registration requirements in many states are such that an American is persistently confronted by an institutional barrier which is rarely erected in France. It can be argued most strongly that the act of getting somewhere to register demands higher political motivation than getting to the polls on election day. Indeed, over half the Americans who fail to vote in major elections blame such registration barriers as change in residence, failure to renew on time, etc. If such reports are credited, the registration toll in the United States would easily make up the apparent Franco-American differences.

Partisan Orientations

The gross similarities between the two publics in apparent political interest do not, to be sure, remove the possibility that the Frenchman in his interested moments may respond to politics in much different terms than his American counterpart. Actually, when we consider the character of partisan ties felt by citizens in the two countries, we strike upon some contrasts of great magnitude.

We have seen that when Americans are asked to locate themselves relative to the American party system, 75 per cent classify themselves without further probing as psychological members of one of the two major parties, or of some minor party. In France, somewhat before the elections, less than 45 per cent of those who did not refuse to answer the question were able to classify themselves in one of the parties or splinter groups, while another 10 to 15 per cent associated themselves with a more or less recognizable broad *tendance* ("left," "right," a labor union, etc.). The cross-national differences of 20 to 30 per cent are sufficiently large here to contribute to fundamental differences in the flavor of partisan processes in the two electorates. For a long time, we wrote off these differences as products of incomparable circumstances or of reticence on the part of the French concerning partisanship, most of which was being expressed not as refusal to answer the question, but as some other evasion. As we grew more familiar with the data, however, these differences took on vital new interest.

The hypothesis of concealed partisanship was very largely dispelled by a close reading of the actual interviews. It is undeniable that nearly 10 per cent of the French sample explicitly refused to answer the question, as compared with a tiny fraction in the United States. However, we have already subtracted this group from the accounting. Beyond the explicit refusals, the remarks and explanations which often accompanied statements classified as "no party," or as "don't know which party," had a very genuine air about them which made them hard to read as hasty evasions. No few of these respondents were obviously embarrassed at their lack of a party; some confessed that they just hadn't been able to keep track of which party was which. The phrase "je n'y ai jamais pensé" was extremely common. Others indicated that they found it too hard to choose between so many parties; some indicated preferences for a specific political leader but admitted that they did not know which party he belonged to or, more often, had no interest in the identity of his party, whatever it might be. Others, forming a tiny minority of the nonparty people, rejected the notion of parties with some hostility.

It became clear, too, that people reporting no party attachments were distinct on other grounds from those who willingly classified themselves as close to a party. On our vertical involvement dimension, for example, they tended to fall in the bottom stratum of the least involved, just as the paper-thin stratum unable to choose a party in the United States consists heavily of the least involved. Demographically, these nonparty people were disproportionately housewives, poorly educated, young, and the other familiar statuses which tend to be uninformed and uninvolved.

Among actual party identifiers in France there was further interesting variation in the character of the party objects to which reference was made. A very few linked themselves with small new ideological splinter groups which had developed during the political crises of 1958. For these people, it was not enough to indicate that they felt closest to the Radical-Socialists, for example: they had to specify that they were Mendesists or anti-Mendesists, Valoisiens, and the like. Most identifiers suffered no difficulty in seeing themselves as "Radical-Socialists," completely shattered though the party was. Others, perceiving the system even more grossly, linked themselves only with a broad *tendance*. On involvement measures these groupings showed the expected differences: the grosser the discrimination, the lower the involvement.

In other ways as well it was clear that the extreme ideological fractionation of parties in France has few roots in the mass population, members of which simply pay too little attention to politics to follow the nicer discriminations involved. When asked whether the number of parties in France was too great, about right, or too few, 97 per cent of those responding said there were too many parties, and less than 1 per cent said there were too few. In response to an ensuing question as to the desirable number of parties, the mean of the number seen as optimal was 3.5 for the handful of adherents of the new ideological splinters, 3.0 for the partisans of the traditional mass parties, and less than 2.8 among those who had formed no party attachments. Perhaps the most apt expression of the problem of partisan fractionation and discrimination came from the naïve respondent who opined that France should have two or three parties, "enough to express the differences in opinion."

The fact that large proportions of the French public have failed to form any very strong attachments to one of the political parties should not be taken to mean that these people are totally disoriented in the French party system. In particular, a sensitivity to the gulf separating the Communist Party from the remainder of French parties does pervade the mass public. There seems to be less confusion as to the identity of the Communist Party than for any of the other parties; and for the bulk of non-Communists, the Communist Party is a pariah. There are some nonidentifiers who appear to shift from Communist to non-Communist votes with abandon, and were all of these votes to fall to the Communists in the same election, the Party would undoubtedly exceed its previous high-water mark in its proportion of the French popular vote. At the same time, however, one cannot help but be impressed by the number of respondents who, while indicating they were not really sure what they were in partisan terms, indicated as well at one point or another in the interview that they were not only non-Communist but anti-Communist. In other words, were the descriptions of party adherents to proceed simply in terms of a Communist, non-Communist division, the proportion of ready self-classifications would advance considerably toward the American figure, and would probably exceed that which could be attained by any other two-class division in France.

Nevertheless, the limited party attachments outside the Communist camp in France retain strong theoretical interest, as they seem so obviously linked to a symptom of turbulence which is clearly not an elite phenomenon alone—the flash party. With a very large proportion of the electorate feeling no anchoring loyalty, it is not surprising that a new party can attract a large vote "overnight," or that this base can be so rapidly dissolved. Furthermore, there is a problem here that is peculiarly French, in that the low proportion of expressed attachments cannot simply be seen as a necessary consequence of a multiparty system per se. As we have seen in the preceding chapter, fairly comparable data from Norway, where six parties are prominent, show party attachments as widespread as those in the two-party United States.

The French sample was asked further to recall the party or *tendance* which the respondent's father had supported at the polls. Here the departure from comparable American data became even more extreme (Table 14-2). Of those Americans in 1958 having had a known father who had resided in the United States as an American citizen, thereby participating in American political life, 86 per cent could characterize his partisanship, and another 5 per cent knew enough of his political behavior to describe him as apolitical or Independent. Among comparable French respondents, only 26 per cent could link fathers with any party or with the vaguest of *tendances* (including such responses

TABLE 14-2

Respondent's Characterization of Father's Political Behavior,
by Country, 1958
(in per cent)

	France	United States
Located father in party or broad *tendance*	25	76
Recalled father as "independent," "shifting around," or as apolitical, nonvoting	3	6
	—	—
Total able to characterize father's political behavior	28	82
Unable to characterize father's political behavior	68	8
Father did not reside in country or was never a citizen		3
Did not know father; question not asked about father surrogate	4	6
Refused; other		1
	—	—
	100	100
(*N*)	(1,166)	(1,795)

as "il a toujours voté pour la patrie"), and another 3 per cent could describe the father's disposition as variable or apolitical. In other words, among those eligible to respond to the question, 91 per cent of Americans could characterize their father's political behavior, as opposed to 29 per cent of the French.

It goes without saying that differences of this magnitude rarely emerge from individual data in social research. And they occur at a point of prime theoretical interest. We have long been impressed in the United States by the degree to which partisan orientations appear to be passed hereditarily, from generation to generation, through families. It has seemed likely that such transmission is crucial in the stability of American partisan voting patterns. Therefore, we find it startling to encounter a situation in which huge discontinuities seem to appear in this transmission.

What do the French responses concerning paternal partisanship really mean? As best we can determine, they mean what they appear to

mean: the French father is uncommunicative about his political behavior before his children, just as he is more reserved in the interviewing situation than Americans or Norwegians. It seems highly unlikely, for example, that Franco-American differences in recall represent
French concealment: large numbers of the French willing to speak
of their own party preference are unable to give the father's preference
of a generation before, and explicit refusals to answer, while attaining
10 per cent or more where own partisanship is at stake, are almost
nonexistent for paternal partisanship.

Furthermore, we have come to reject the possibility that the bulk
of the Franco-American difference is some simple consequence of the
more fluid and complex French party system. Responses to a similar
question in the Norwegian multiparty system look like our American
results, and not like the French. Nor is there reason to believe that the
Frenchman has trouble finding comparable modern terms for the party
groupings of a generation ago. As we have observed, the respondent
was invited to give a rough equivalent of his father's position in terms
of *tendance*. Moreover, where there are any elaborations of "I don't
know" captured in the interview, the consistent theme seemed to be
that the respondent did not feel he had ever known his father's position
("je n'ai jamais su"; "je ne lui ai jamais demandé"; "il ne disait rien
à ses enfants"; "il n'en parlait jamais"). Finally, if special problems
were occasioned on the French side by the changing party landscape
over time, we should certainly expect that older French respondents
would have greater difficulty locating their fathers politically than
would younger respondents. They do not: the tabulation by age in
France shows only the slightest of variations attributable to age, and
these lend no support to the hypothesis (e.g., slightly less knowledge of
father's position for children under thirty) and are variations which
may be found in the comparable American table as well.

If we accept the proposition, then, that there are basic discontinuities
in the familial transmission of party orientations in France, all of our
theory would argue that weaker party attachments should result in
the current generation. The data do indeed show a remarkable association between the two phenomena, once again involving differences of
30 per cent or more. Both French and Americans who recall their
father's partisanship are much more likely themselves to have developed
party loyalties than are people who were not aware of their father's
position. Of still greater importance are the more absolute Franco-
American similarities. Setting aside those people whose fathers were
noncitizens, dead, apolitical, or floaters, or who refused to answer the
question, we can focus on the core of the comparison (in per cent):

	Know Father's Party		Do Not Know Father's Party	
	France	U.S.	France	U.S.
Proportion having some partisan self-location (party or vague *tendance*)	79.4	81.6	47.7	50.7
Proportion that these are of total electorate	24.0	75.0	63.0	8.0

Where the socialization processes have been the same in the two societies, the results in current behavior appear to be the same, in rates of formation of identification. The strong cross-national differences lie in the socialization processes. In other words, we have come full circle again: we have encountered large national differences but have once again succeeded in moving them to the marginals of the table. This is our best assurance that our measurements are tapping comparable phenomena.

Partisan attachments appear therefore to be very weakly developed within the less politically involved half of the French electorate. While undoubtedly a large variety of factors, including the notoriety which the French parties had acquired in the later stages of the Fourth Republic, have helped to inhibit their development, more basic discontinuities of political socialization in the French family appear to be making some persisting contribution as well.[7] Of course, similar lack of

[7] Among other factors, an alleged paucity of voluntary associations acting vigorously to mediate between the mass of citizens and centralized authority in France has often been cited as a crucial differentium in the quality of the political process between France and the United States. See William Kornhauser, *The Politics of Mass Society* (Glencoe, Ill.: Free Press, 1959). If such differences do exist, they may well have some bearing on the prevalence of partisan attachments, for it is clear intranationally, at least, that high rates of participation in nonpolitical voluntary associations and strong partisan attachments tend to co-occur at the individual level (although it is much less clear whether this represents a causal progression or two aspects of the same stance toward community life). In other contexts, however, it has been argued that ostensibly nonpolitical associations of mass membership in France tend to play more vigorous roles as parapolitical agents than do comparable associations in the United States, which so often tend to regard political entanglement with horror. Both views have some appeal on the basis of loose impressions of the two societies, and are not in the strictest sense contradictory. However, their thrusts diverge sufficiently that a confrontation would seem worthwhile if either can be borne out by any systematic evidence. Where grass-roots participation in expressly political associations is concerned, we have seen no notable differences between the nations in either membership rates or rates of attendance at political gatherings.

party attachment does occur among people indifferent to politics in the American and Norwegian systems as well; but the strata of unidentified people are thinner in these systems and do not extend greatly above that layer of persistent nonvoters which is present in any system.

The link between an electorate heavily populated with voters feeling no continuing party attachments and a susceptibility of "flash" parties is an obvious one. It must be recognized at the outset, of course, that such phenomena arise only under the pressure of social, political, or economic dislocations occurring in some segment of the population, thereby generating an elite which wishes to organize a movement and a public which is restive. This means that even a system highly suscep- tible to such phenomena is not likely to experience them when it is functioning smoothly: their prevalence in postwar France cannot be divorced from the severe dislocations the society has been undergoing. Once misfortunes breed discontent, however, the proportions of parti- sans in an electorate is a datum of fundamental significance. One can- not fail to be impressed by the agility with which the strong partisan can blame the opposing party for almost any misfortune or deny the political relevance of the misfortune if some opposing party cannot conceivably be blamed. Hence, where partisans are concerned, mis- fortunes do relatively little to shift voting patterns. Independents, however, have no stake in such reinforcements and defenses and move more massively in response to grievances. In France, the institutions which conduce to a multiparty system make the organization of new party movements more feasible from an elite point of view than it is likely to be under two-party traditions. At the same time, the presence of a large number of French voters who have developed no continuing attachments to a particular party provides an "available" mass base for such movements. This available base is no necessary con- comitant of a multiparty system, but is rather a peculiarity of the current French scene.

Parties and Policy Controversy

Whatever differences exist in partisan orientations, no assessment of politicization would be complete without consideration of the man- ner in which ideological conflict is worked out through the party system. If parties are recognized at all in the classical view of demo- cratic process, they are relegated to a distinctly secondary position: they are means to policy ends, and should be judged by the citizen accordingly. In this light, the number of Americans with strong party loyalty and a poor sense of what either party stands for in policy terms represents a distinct perversion of the democratic process. In this light, too, weaker partisan orientations in the French populace might simply mean a relegation of party to second rank, with a primary focus on policy goals.

At an elite level, of course, there are distinct Franco-American differences in the phrasing of the means-end relation between party and policy, and these contrasts weigh heavily in our impressions of differences in quality of political process between the two systems. That is, while French political elites are not insensitive to party formations as instruments toward policy goals, the fact remains that parties are split and reshaped with relative freedom in order that the party may be the purest possible expression, not only of the politician's position on a single basic issue dimension, but of the total configuration of positions adopted on cross-cutting issue dimensions. On the American side, remarkable policy accommodations are made to preserve the semblance of party unity, and party competition for votes "in the middle" leads to a considerable blurring of interparty differences on policy. The crucial role of basic political institutions in stimulating either multipartite or bipartite trends has often been discussed, and whether French elite activities would survive long under American ground rules is a moot point. We may consider, however, whether the ideological clarity or intransigence associated with French political elites and the policy compromise or confusion which characterizes the American party system reflect properties of their mass publics.

Data have been collected in both countries concerning reactions to a variety of issues confronting the two systems. While both sets of items must be regarded as only the crudest samplings of hypothetical issue universes, selection on both sides was performed in an attempt to tap some of the most basic controversies of the period. In France, three items were devoted to the classic socio-economic left and right, with one concerning the role of labor and the other two the relative roles of government and private enterprise in housing; two more involved the clerical question; a sixth item had to do with military expenditures and national prestige; a seventh concerned the freedom of the press to criticize the government. Of eight American questions, two dealt with social-welfare legislation and a third with the relative role of government and private enterprise in housing and utilities, covering the classic right and left; two more dealt with the government's role in racial matters (FEPC and school desegregation); and three others were concerned with the internationalist or isolationist posture of the government in foreign affairs. All questions were in Likert scale form.[8]

We shall focus upon three properties of these issues which we can more or less crudely measure in the two countries: (1) the degree to which public opinion is sharply crystallized on each issue; (2) the degree to which opinion within the two publics is polarized on each; and (3) for each issue, the degree to which individual opinion is associated with partisan preference.[9] Assuming the items do give fair coverage to most primary issue dimensions in the two nations, we are interested to see if opinion in France at a mass level appears more sharply crystallized or polarized, and to assess the manner in which policy concerns are linked with party preference. As before, we shall distinguish layers of both populations in terms of partisan involvement. At the top, we isolate as political "actives" those people who were either party members or reported attending two or more political rallies in the respective election campaigns, a group which amounts to 5 to 7 per cent within each population and hence is sufficiently large for analysis. We also continue to distinguish between party identifiers (three-quarters of the American population, but half of the French) and nonidentifiers.

In both nations, the issue items were asked again of the same respondents after an interval of time. We take as a measure of crystallization of opinion the rank-order correlation between the two expressions of opinion. There is a good deal of internal evidence to suggest that "change" in opinion between the two readings is almost

---

8 These questions are included in the list presented in Table 14-3.

9 Of these three properties, polarization is most dependent on question wording. It is measured by the standard deviation of the response distribution, after the five steps of the scale have been assigned simple integer scores. The statistic takes high values (e.g., over 1.50) only when the distribution of opinion is relatively U-shaped. Party-relatedness is measured by a rank-order correlation between the respondent's partisan position and his issue position. In the United States, the Democratic Party was presumed to be the more liberal on domestic issues and the more internationalist in foreign affairs, and respondents were arrayed from a Democratic to a Republican pole on the basis of party loyalty for identifiers, or patterns of 1956–1958 vote for nonidentifiers. In France, a panel of expert observers arranged the many parties or fractions thereof on a socio-economic left-right continuum and again on a continuum from clerical to anticlerical. The second was used to array respondents for the two religious issues; the first was used for the other five issues. Once again, nonidentifiers were located on the basis of reports of 1956 and 1958 votes. All rank-order correlations, including those used for the crystallization measure discussed in the text, are tau-betas, based on tables of equal rows and columns. See H. M. Blalock, *Social Statistics* (New York: McGraw-Hill, 1960, pp. 321 ff.).

never a matter of true conversion, but rather represents haphazard reactions to items on which the respondent has never formed much opinion. With minor exceptions, there is no significant change in the marginal distributions of the tables, despite the high turnover of opinion. There is a persistent relation between the proportions of people who confess they have no opinion on any given issue and the amount of turnover shown by those who do attempt an opinion. As one might expect, too, there is a tendency for high crystallization, high polarization, and high party-relatedness to co-occur, despite intriguing exceptions. Clearly both publics are more likely to have arrived at stable prior opinions on some items than on others, and this degree of crystallization has an obvious bearing on the vitality of the role the issue dimension may play in partisan choice.

Unfortunately, the magnitude of these turnover coefficients may not be compared cross-nationally, since the interval between tests averaged little more than a month on the French side but ran twenty-six months on the American side.[10] Nevertheless, as Table 14-3 indicates, the level of these coefficients is by any standard remarkably low in both populations. Taken as test-retest reliability coefficients, they would send the psychologist in search of a better measuring instrument. After all, on an item where the stability seems relatively high (freedom of the press), less than eight Frenchmen in ten take the same side of the issue twice in a five-week period, when five out of ten would succeed in doing so by making entirely random choices. On the other hand, while more routine measurement error certainly imposes a rather constant ceiling on these coefficients which may not greatly exceed .8, the further incapacity of the two publics to respond reliably to these items must be considered a substantive datum of the first water. For if these items, reduced to an unusually simple vocabulary, fail to touch off well-formed opinions, the remoteness of both publics from most political and journalistic debate on such dimensions is

---

[10] In American panel studies we are beginning to fill in a picture of the manner in which these coefficients erode over time. For example, coefficients after four years show almost no decline from their two-year levels, and it seems likely that, in the infrequent instances where opinions on these issues are truly crystallized, they are subject to little change. As the test-retest interval changes, we may suppose that the coefficient declines very rapidly in the brief period in which respondents forget their previous answers and hence are obliged to "guess again," and then stabilizes at a hard core of well-formed opinions. The French interval was so brief, however, that it is hard to imagine that the coefficients had yet dropped to their stabilized level. We would hazard the loose judgment that the French coefficients lie about where one would expect were they destined to decline to American levels in a comparable period of time.

TABLE 14-3

Selected Issue Characteristics in France and the United States

	Crystallization		Polarization		Party-relatedness			
	Total Sample	Actives	Total Sample	Actives	Actives	Non-South Actives	Identifiers	Unidentified
France:								
State support of religious schools	.65	.74	1.54	1.62	.58		.39	.32
Strikes by government employees	.52	.69	1.60	1.70	.59		.31	.22
Current threat posed by clergy	.47	.80	1.32	1.64	.56		.34	.19
Freedom of press	.47	.68	1.50	1.60	.39		.22	.13
State responsibility for housing	.42	.34	1.39	1.45	.38		.13	.08
Level of military expenditures	.34	.46	1.36	1.56	.33		.18	.17
Private responsibility for housing	.28	.35	1.26	1.60	.37		.22	.04

(For the United States, the fifth column reports Total Sample Actives; the last three columns report the Non-South figures: Actives, Identifiers, Unidentified.)

	Crystallization		Polarization		Total Sample Actives	Non-South		
	Total Sample	Actives	Total Sample	Actives		Actives	Identifiers	Unidentified
United States:								
Federal school integration action	.42	.47	1.69	1.72	.00	.12	.07	-.06
Federal guarantees of employment	.35	.49	1.45	1.55	.16	.30	.19	.03
Federal FEPC	.34	.34	1.41	1.55	.00	.14	.06	.01
Federal aid to education	.34	.54	1.09	1.60	.16	.29	.21	.16
General isolationism-internationalism	.33	.25	1.48	1.48	.16	.06	.03	.04
Deployment of U.S. forces abroad	.28	.10	1.23	1.25	.07	.04	.05	-.02
Government vs. private enterprise in power and housing	.25	.41	1.37	1.45	.21	.27	.18	.21
Foreign aid	.24	.31	1.36	1.38	.11	.10	.02	-.05

obvious. It is not as though the items presented new controversies on which opinion had not yet had time to develop. With few exceptions, they have been the basic stuff of political disagreement for decades or generations. Opinions still unformed are unlikely to develop further.

In this light, then, it is interesting to compare the stability over time of reactions to parties with the stability of responses to these "basic" controversies shown in the first column of Table 14-3. This assessment is rather difficult on the French side in view of the frequent indeterminacy of party locations; however, it seems that, in a comparable period of time, affective reactions to the parties are more stable than issue reactions even in France. In the United States, we know that partisan reactions show dramatically greater stability than the issue responses. Most important, perhaps, is the failure of data in Table 14-3 to support an image of the mass French public as remaining aloof from party sentiments while hewing dogmatically to ideological goals. Beyond the political actives, stability of issue opinion seems unimpressive, and, for the majority of French voters without party attachments, the articulation of party choice with any of the issue dimensions covered here is slight indeed (Table 14-3, final column).

While the instability of opinion in both nations is of primary interest in Table 14-3, several further comparisons may be summarized. The major cross-national contrast comes in the party-relatedness column, where French actives and partisans show much higher coefficients than their American counterparts. The most obvious American phenomenon which blunts interparty policy differences is the disparity between the southern and non-southern wings of the Democratic Party. While setting aside the southern Democratic rank and file does not remove the perceptual problem posed for northern Democrats who may find the top leaders of their party at odds on many issues, we complete this exercise in Table 14-3 to show that, even for actives, this regional limitation does not begin to bring the American coefficients up to the French level. While the higher French coefficients are no statistical necessity, it is likely that in practice, closer party-relatedness is inevitable in the multiparty system. The interparty differences in opinion among French *partisans* appear to lie in about the same range as those found in Norway. However, as we have seen, party attachments are more prevalent in Norway than in France; when the unidentified enter the French electorate in an actual vote, it is likely that individual issue opinions receive less clear expression across the electorate as a whole than is the case in Norway.

Beyond this primary contrast, Table 14-3 is impressive for its cross-national similarities. Actives in both countries show more highly crystallized opinions, and usually more polarized opinions as well, although American actives differ less sharply and consistently from their mass public than do French actives. In neither country do identifiers differ reliably from nonidentifiers with regard to crystallization or polarization of opinion. In both countries, however, there are quite reliable differences in party-relatedness, not only between actives and the remaining 95 per cent of the population, but between identifiers and nonidentified. In other words, while the partisan manner of relating to the political process makes little difference in basic opinion formation save for the extremely active, the translation of these attitudes to some kind of party choice seems increasingly haphazard as party attachments become weaker.

Throughout these comparisons, however, we may remain struck by the fact that the "slope" is steeper on the French side: the differences between actives and mass are large relative to those in the United States. From the upper end of this steep slope, one might wish to extrapolate to the sharp and rigid cleavages on policy matters for which French elites are noted; for our purposes, it is sufficient to observe that these cleavages blur rapidly and lose their tone in the mass of the French electorate.

Finally, it should be observed that the issues seem to sort themselves into two rough categories in both nations: (1) emotional-symbol issues involving some of the more gross group conflicts within the two societies (racial in the United States, religious in France, along with items which touch in a direct way upon labor as an interest group), which show relatively high crystallization and polarization; and (2) more complex questions of relations between the state and private enterprise which, along with all foreign policy issues, tend to be less crystallized.

These differences in crystallization are scarcely surprising, as the objects and means involved in the second group of issues are clearly more remote from the common experience of the man-in-the-street. Yet the pattern is ironic, for the issues which show a stronger resonance in both mass publics tend to be those which both elites make some attempt to soft-pedal, in favor of direct debate over such more "ideological" matters as arrangements between state and private enterprise. The more resonant issues are not dead, of course, and are used for tactical advantage by elites in both countries. Calculations of vote gain are made in the United States on the basis of the religion of the nominee, and the clerical question in France has been resuscitated repeatedly as a handy crowbar to split apart government coalitions. At the same time, however, there is genuine elite effort to keep such cleavage issues in the background: the American public is told that religion is not a proper criterion for candidate choice, and the battleground for elite debate on the racial issue is usually displaced quite notably from race itself in the modern period. Similarly, much sophisticated French opinion has for some time argued that even the secondary role which the clerical question has been playing in elite debate exaggerates its importance.

Given this common background, the different manner in which the two types of controversy weave into partisan choices in the two countries is fascinating. In France, there is fair coincidence between the ordering of issues in terms of party-relatedness and the ordering on the other two properties. The clerical questions, for example, are highly crystallized and polarized, and show high levels of party-relatedness as well. The structure of party competition is such that, elite values notwithstanding, these emotional cleavages achieve prominent partisan expression. Such is not the case in the United States: there is little coincidence between the party-relatedness of issues and the other two properties. Indeed, the racial issue finds little clear party expression, while the "elite" issue concerning government and private enterprise, one of the least crystallized issues, is at the same time one of the most party-related across the full electorate.

Where mass or elite control of issue controversy is concerned, then, the two systems have rather paradoxical outcomes. By conception, the French party system is geared to elites, encouraging them to a multifaceted ideological expression which is too complex for most of the public to encompass. At the same time, the multidimensional clarity of party positions serves to return a measure of control to part of the public, for the more involved citizens can single out certain dimensions to reduce the system to manageable simplicity. These reductions are naturally made in terms of issues which are more resonant in the public, even if these are not the dimensions which the elites might wish to stress. The American system is less elite in conception; it is sufficiently simple in its gross characteristics that it is easier for the common citizen to follow it with only limited attention. But this simplification requires great blurring of party differences across most of the universe of possible issues, and the differences which are maintained are those which the competing elites select as battlegrounds. Hence, control of controversy which can be given partisan expression is, paradoxically, more nearly in elite hands.

Conclusions

We have attempted to sort through a number of those characteristics of French politics which add up to vague impressions of intense

French politicization, in order to identify more precise loci for Franco-American differences. It appears likely that the more notable of these differences stem from the actions of elites and require study and explanation primarily at this level, rather than at the level of the mass electorate. While certain peculiarities reminiscent of French political elites are visible in the most politically active twentieth of the French population, these peculiarities fade out rapidly as one approaches the more "representative" portions of the broad French public.

It is unlikely that the common French citizen devotes any greater portion of his attention to politics than does his American counterpart, and he may well give less. His behavior is constrained within a much different set of political institutions, and these differences have important consequences for the character of his political behavior, including the opportunity of closer articulation between any crystallized opinions he may hold and an appropriate party instrument. However, the data give no striking reason to believe that the French citizen, either through the vagaries of national character, institutions, or history, is predisposed to form political opinions which are more sharply crystallized or which embrace a more comprehensive range of political issues than do comparable Americans. On both sides, opinion formation declines as objects and arrangements become more remote from the observer; and much of politics, for both French and Americans, is remote. Hence the proliferation of choices offered by the multiparty system is itself a mixed blessing: it is capitalized upon only by the more politically interested segments of the electorate, and appears to represent "too much" choice to be managed comfortably by citizens whose political involvement is average or less.

Over the range of characteristics surveyed, only one striking difference at the level of the mass public was encountered which seemed more uniquely French than the multiparty system itself. There is evidence of a widespread absence of party loyalties, a phenomenon which can be empirically associated with peculiarities in the French socialization process. This characteristic has obvious links with the major symptom of French political turbulence, which is based on the behavior of the mass population rather than that of elites—the current availability of a mass base for flash party movements under circumstances of distress.

CHAPTER 15

De Gaulle and Eisenhower:
The Public Image of the Victorious General

Philip E. Converse and Georges Dupeux

Among students of human affairs, the political scientist has perhaps the clearest right to despair at the complexity and particularity of his materials. While history, we are told, is a storehouse of lessons for future generations, any intensive study of its riches leads readily to disillusionment. The configuration of events at any point in time is clearly unique, and the unfolding of political history depends so obviously upon the peculiar pattern of conditions just past that any attempt to sift out useful generalizations seems doomed to failure at the outset. These difficulties are compounded where specific personalities have come to dominate a political epoch in the life of a nation. For personalities, like broad historical conditions, impress us with their infinite variety, and the interaction of the commanding personality with his unique times seems thereby to lie at a double remove from orderly analysis.

Of course, in modern western society the application of democratic concepts has served to hedge about the role which the single personality can play in the shaping of his nation's history. Yet it is clear that from time to time, even in the older democracies, a political leader is endowed by the voters with such an extraordinary measure of personal support at the polls that his latitude for personal decisions becomes

An abridged translation of this chapter appeared under the title "Eisenhower et de Gaulle: Les Généraux devant l'Opinion," in the *Revue Française de Science Politique*, **XII**, No. 1 (March 1962).

rather large. If he chooses to exercise the power proffered him, he may leave a strong and unique imprint on the course of national events.

Such transcendent public support is not entirely common in the electoral history of western democracies. Yet at least two figures—De Gaulle in France and Eisenhower in the United States—have clearly achieved this kind of popular response in recent years. Once beyond their common military background, it would be hard to imagine two more sharply contrasting personalities. De Gaulle has been cold and aloof, autocratic, and rigidly single-minded in pursuit of national goals which he himself erected. Eisenhower was warm, gregarious, inarticulate, and indecisive. There is no better measure of the temperamental difference in the two men than the use to which they have chosen to put their immense popularity. De Gaulle has consistently converted it to support for marked changes he wished to make in the direction of French policy; Eisenhower was content to enjoy his personal popularity, letting public policy proceed under its own momentum in channels largely carved before he came to office. If we knew no more than this, it would be difficult indeed to understand how two such polar figures could excite what appears to be the same public adulation. Yet it is obvious that both figures have partaken of processes as old as recorded history: the acclaim which a populace reserves for its conquering generals.

No one can be surprised that a victorious general wins the admiration of the public which he has prominently served to defend. Somewhat more surprising, however, is the fact that the military hero can transfer his credit with the public to votes for civil office. Furthermore, as we have noted earlier, a recent study by Sellers suggests that the harvest of votes which a victorious general can win may be rather unique. Searching for characteristic voting patterns which emerge when a candidate draws personal support far beyond his party's expectations, Sellers has combed through United States voting records dating back to the founding of the Republic, picking out those elections which fit this description. He identifies six elections which betray this unusual personal support for a candidate, and all six are elections in which the fortunate candidate was a prominent victorious general before his presidential candidacy.[1] It is important to note that major military achievements cannot be said to guarantee an overwhelming reception by the public at the polls, or even a presidential

[1] Charles G. Sellers, Jr., "The Equilibrium Cycle in Two-Party Politics," *Public Opinion Quarterly*, 29 (Spring 1965).

victory in the American case. Prominent generals have, in rare instances, suffered defeat. But the fact remains that the capacity to draw transcendent popular support seems, across 44 American presidential elections, the particular domain of the military hero.

Therefore, although the peculiar temperaments brought to high office by figures like De Gaulle or Eisenhower may be part of the incalculable uniqueness of history, it is an equally significant fact that they were granted popular consent to dominate their respective epochs as figures of civil politics, and this fact is considerably less fortuitous. It is natural to wonder what common elements in public perceptions compound to create such a reliable response.

We are fortunate to have sample survey data of remarkable comparability, drawn from the national cross sections of the American and French electorates, described in the previous chapter. Comparable open-ended questions were asked of the respective publics concerning perceptions of Eisenhower and De Gaulle. These questions make it possible to construct the qualitative images held of these leaders by their electorates, as well as to examine the affect felt toward each by various segments of the electorates. It is our intention to consider these two bodies of data side by side. Although we cannot be sure on the basis of these two comparisons alone that common elements in the public response to these different figures are necessary and generic regularities, it is our assumption that the political cultures in which each has operated are sufficiently distinct that discovery of common elements in the public response will shed some initial light on the recurrent phenomenon of the victorious general in civil politics.

The French and American Backgrounds

It is useful before approaching the data to take a brief inventory of differences in the historical and political situations that Eisenhower and De Gaulle faced, over and above the obvious differences in temperament. First, it cannot be overlooked that Eisenhower was running directly for office himself, and the public was called upon to judge him by name on the ballot. On the French side, De Gaulle was not directly involved as nominal object of the vote in either the constitutional referendum or the ensuing legislative elections.[2] In

---

[2] This difference is responsible for some differences in wording of the questions used to draw positive and negative perceptions of the two leaders on the two sides of the Atlantic. In 1952 and 1956 the American questions followed the form, "Is

the actual situation, however, this difference is less profound than might appear. There was little doubt in the fall of 1958 that De Gaulle's leadership in an executive role was at stake in the referendum results. Dupeux has shown that 40 per cent of the French public, when asked before the referendum whether they would be voting on the proposed constitution or on the personality of De Gaulle himself, confessed to a personality vote.[3] Since this was clearly not the "proper" political response, one can be sure that many others felt the same way but concealed the fact. As we shall see below, reactions to De Gaulle as a person lent shape to public reactions to the ensuing elections every bit as potently as did the attractiveness of the Eisenhower candidacy in the United States. If there is a lack of comparability in the political role the two men were playing at the time of the studies, a more serious problem is probably posed by the fact that Eisenhower was paired as a candidate against Stevenson whereas De Gaulle, as a shadow candidate, stood alone. It is true that the interview materials involving Eisenhower were focused directly upon him as a person and did not demand comparisons between him and Stevenson. Nevertheless, it must be recognized that in a two-man race of this sort, the image of each man is almost sure to be modified by the perception of his opponent. This difference cannot be controlled.

A second difference has to do with the social role which each leader was playing at the time of the surveys. We are intensely interested in this discussion in public perceptions as a popular hero *shifts his role* from the military sphere to that of civilian politics. From this point of view the surveys were taken at points in time which were not comparable. The 1952 materials on Eisenhower were drawn from a public which had known the General only as a general and never as a leader in civil politics. The 1956 materials were drawn at a time when the Eisenhower military role had been superseded by four years of civil leadership. The 1958 materials on De Gaulle were drawn at a time when the French leader, thanks to his role in the early days of the Fourth Republic, had been visible to the French people in a civil capacity for longer than had Eisenhower in 1952, but for a time considerably more brief than that which Eisenhower had served by 1956. Thus whether we look at reactions to Eisenhower in 1952 or

there anything in particular about Eisenhower that might make you want to vote *for (against)* him?" while the 1958 French questions took the form, "Parlant du General de Gaulle, qu'est-ce qui vous plait et vous deplait en lui?"

[3] G. Dupeux, A. Girard, and J. Stoetzel, "Une enquête par sondage auprès des electeurs," *Le Referendum de Septembre et les Elections de Novembre 1958,* Cahiers de la Fondation Nationale de Sciences Politiques, Paris: A. Colin, 1960, p. 132.

1956, the salience of the military as opposed to the civilian role cannot be directly equated with that to be supposed for De Gaulle. Once this lack of comparability is recognized, however, we shall find it fortunate that the single reading of the public pulse on De Gaulle is in these terms "bracketed" between the two readings for Eisenhower.

Finally, the most striking difference in the situation surrounding the two leaders has to do with the gravity of the era in which they operated. It is true that there are some surprising resemblances between the terms of the 1952 American election and the 1958 French election. There is no doubt, for example, that the American public was more deeply upset about the political situation in 1952 than in any other post-war election. Quite apart from the Eisenhower candidacy, there was strong indignation at the evidence of corruption in office, along with a sense of deep frustration at a small but humiliating overseas war which the national power, to public dismay, could not bring to a successful conclusion. Disgust with behavior in government had some of the ring of 1958 French *antiparliamentarisme*, and there were obvious parallels between the struggles in Korea and in Algeria. Nevertheless, it is entirely obvious that the French crisis of 1958 was far more profound than the problems felt by the American people in 1952. Algeria posed not only the aggravations of the interminable war, but its very purpose was held in dispute, and civil war loomed. French *antiparliamentarisme* was not a simple matter of disgust at a party in power, but rather ran to the fundamental ground rules of the system itself. Whatever the parallels in kind of problem, the intensity of the problems can bear no comparison.

The Popular Image of the Two Generals

With these differences in background recognized, let us consider the images which the two publics held of their military heroes. The technique of open-ended questions, while it suffers some drawbacks, has advantages which are critical for the problem under study. The respondent is free to react in any terms which he desires, expressing whatever is salient for him, expanding on his commentary at will. Such freedom provides some assurance that responses are not artificially directed either by the author of the questionnaire or by the interviewer.[4]

---

[4] Among drawbacks of open-ended questions which are important in a study of this sort is the fact that the brevity or length of responses does not depend ex-

Most respondents in both countries had explicit reactions to their respective leaders. Closer analysis of the nonresponses on the French side showed a handful of people who gave incomprehensible responses which the interviewer failed to probe further (1 per cent of the sample) and a slightly larger group (2 per cent) who refused to commit themselves. However, the vast bulk of the nonresponses is made up in nearly even proportions of (1) people who indicated that they found nothing either attractive or unattractive about De Gaulle, and (2) people who did not know what to respond, specifying in a surprising number of cases that they did not know much, or knew nothing at all, about him. The American nonresponses, while not analyzed in this detail, seem to rest on the same bases. Nonetheless, 90 per cent of the American respondents and 85 per cent of the French respondents had some intelligible reactions on the questions.

The freedom permitted and the large number of respondents naturally lead to a flood of responses of the greatest diversity. These references were coded into categories representing major themes and subdivisions thereof. Wherever possible, code categories were made identical for positive and negative reactions. Since the Eisenhower image has been reported in detail elsewhere,[5] we shall focus initially on some specific aspects of the De Gaulle image. The broadest response classes were as follows:

—Responses in generalities, expressing either an incapacity to give a more precise perception ("j'aime bien cet homme-là," "je le trouve bien," "tout me plait en lui," "tout me déplaît"), or pure trust ("digne de confiance," "on peut compter sur lui"), or distrust, or a single phrase which from the respondent's point of view needs no expansion ("le seul possible," "le seul capable de nous sortir de peine," "le seul qui essaie de sauver la France").

---

clusively upon the intensity of feeling entertained by the respondent. Some respondents are timid, others more bold; some are articulate, others quite inarticulate. Moreover, there may be some variation in the fullness of responses which reflects the relative diligence of various interviewers. This source of variation is probably controlled with greater care in the American studies, where intensive probing and accuracy of recording open-ended materials are a key part of interviewer training. Lengthy examination of properties of responses volunteered over the years has provided considerable assurance that some measures of intensity of feeling based on the number of responses give data of remarkable coherence and regularity. However, the French interviewers were unaccustomed to this mode of interviewing and were not trained to probe as intensively as their American counterparts. These facts should be kept in mind as we consider below the numbers of responses made to the questions.

5 A. Campbell, P. E. Converse, W. E. Miller, and D. E. Stokes, *The American Voter*, John Wiley and Sons, 1960, pp. 42–63.

—Responses directed at personal virtues or defects, some of which are very vague in character ("il est formidable," "il est sympathique," "c'est quelqu'un," "sa forte personnalité," "pas très sympathique," "sa personnalité a moins de valeur qu'auparavant") and still others which are most incisive, as we shall see below.

—Responses directed at leadership abilities or defects ("capacités de chef," "vrai chef de gouvernement," "homme d'Etat," "énergie," "courage," "autorité," "prestige," "clairvoyance politique," "expérience," "trop autoritaire," "dictateur," "manque de fermeté").

—Responses concerning De Gaulle's past record, such as his role in 1940 or in the Liberation, or to his retirement to Colombey.

—Responses concerning his more recent role and return to power in 1958.

—Responses concerning the future, including the hopes and fears which his presence created.

—Political responses, dealing with positions taken by the general on major issues of the day, particularly the Algerian problem.

—Social responses, relating the general to the welfare of certain population groups or classes.

The simple distribution of positive and negative responses in these broad categories gives some immediate flavor of the public response and is shown in Table 15-1.

Thus there were in absolute numbers four times as many positive references as negative, indicating the overriding esteem in which De Gaulle was held by the French public. Responses to Eisenhower typically ran two-to-one positive in the United States. This is a very favorable image, yet it falls visibly short of the four-to-one ratio enjoyed by De Gaulle. We shall attempt to account for this difference in the two images at a later point.

The general color of the French reactions to De Gaulle were, at an intuitive level, so similar to those gathered in the United States concerning Eisenhower that it was relatively simple to establish a coding which would lend itself to cross-national comparisons. With only a slight regrouping of the categories given above, we can observe these gross similarities in public response (Figure 15-1). In both countries evaluations turn much more frequently on the personal image created by the two generals than on more political themes. Although policy positions taken by the leader bulk larger in negative references than in positive responses on both sides, it is true that these stands on issues were rarely evoked in either country.

TABLE 15-1

The De Gaulle Image

	Positive References		Negative References	
	N	%	*N*	%
General references	118	9	11	3
Personal image	652	47	116	34
Leadership capacities	241	18	45	13
Record around Second World War	198	14	45	13
Recent record	62	4	17	5
Hopes (fears) for future	50	4	50	15
Policy positions	46	3	50	15
Group references	7	1	7	2
	1,374	100	341	100

Virtually no importance was attached in either country to the leader's position vis-à-vis social groups in the population. An occasional Frenchman liked De Gaulle's "neutralité vis-à-vis des diverses classes sociales," or indicated that "il travaille pour l'intérêt général," just as an occasional American felt that Eisenhower was "good for all the people" and gave "no special privileges." Some few others saw these leaders as favoring the underprivileged. A French worker perceived that De Gaulle "s'occupe de la classe ouvrière," and the wife of a white-collar worker commented that "il défend le peuple." As infrequently, Americans saw Eisenhower as "good for the working class (common people)." On the negative side, the group references all go in the same direction in both countries. De Gaulle was criticized as hostile to the working class, a friend of the "capitalistes" or, more frequently, the "gros." Eisenhower attracted some criticism, particularly by 1956, as too helpful to "big business." However, we must keep in mind that such references are remarkable on both sides primarily for their extreme infrequency.

One of the major differences in the gross images presented in Figure 15-1 arises from the greater salience of "policy positions" for American respondents in both 1952 and 1956. Subdividing this category on both sides into questions of domestic as opposed to foreign policy concern, it is easy to pin down the difference. Both Frenchmen and Ameri-

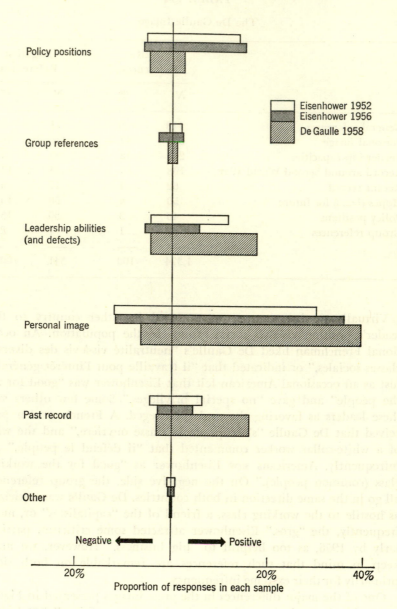

Policy positions

Eisenhower 1952
Eisenhower 1956
De Gaulle 1958

Group references

Leadership abilities
(and defects)

Personal image

Past record

Other

Negative ← → Positive

20%   20%   40%

Proportion of responses in each sample

Figure 15-1. Comparison of popular images of De Gaulle (1958) and Eisenhower (1952 and 1956).

cans, in the rare instances where the leader's broad political philosophy (left or right, conservative or liberal) was called into question, commented very negatively and in roughly the same frequency. Positions on highly specific domestic issues were brought up about as often on both sides, and on both sides the balance of reaction was mildly positive. It is in the area of foreign policy that sharp differences emerge between the two populations.[6] Specific references to De Gaulle's posture in foreign policy were rarely made, and the balance of these responses were mildly negative. Eisenhower was much more frequently linked to foreign policy concerns by the American public, and these references showed five-to-one and fifteen-to-one favorable balances in 1952 and 1956, respectively. It is apparent that the weight of the cold war was more salient for Americans and, in a sense, presented a more focused issue area than that experienced by the French in 1958. French troubles in 1958 were simply more broad and diffuse, and while there were occasional references to the role De Gaulle might play in the cold war, these were rare and not optimistic. Even the references to a De Gaulle solution of the Algerian problem were infrequent, although it is clear that such problems were implied along with other domestic concerns in many of the broad perceptions of De Gaulle as a leader who could salvage the nation from its woes.

On the French side, the role which De Gaulle played in the Second World War, as well as his actions in the crises of 1958, were more salient for the French public and were evaluated in more unconditionally positive terms than were comparable aspects of Eisenhower's past public record.

The "personal image." The fact remains, however, that the center of gravity of both images, as well as their strong positive balance, lies in the area which we have designated the "personal image." These responses may be subdivided into three broad classes which communicate more incisively the meaning of the term. First, there are the references to the leader's attributes as a public figure, aside from questions of leadership initiative per se. For both populations, these attributes include sincerity and integrity, conscientiousness as a public servant, patriotism, characteristics as a public speaker, and general popularity or prestige. Second, there are positive and negative references to what might be called "personal background characteristics," that is, the individual's intelligence, his religious background or prac-

---

[6] At the risk of inciting an international incident, we took the liberty to class references to Algeria in the "foreign policy" category. Perhaps "overseas military operations" would have described this category as well.

tice, his physical vigor, and the type of training which initially formed him. Finally, a third broad class of responses is directed at more ineffable aspects of personality, leading to the vague, highly generalized statements of attraction or identification mentioned above, or to comments on the warmth or coldness of the leader's personality and the like.

The distribution of references, both in terms of content and in terms of affect, is remarkably similar for the two nations *within* each of these three broad classes of response. Thus, for example, the large majority of "public virtue" references in both countries have to do with the leader's sincerity and integrity, and these are, of course, almost all positive. About half of the sparse negative references in this first category have to do with complaints about the leader's public speaking, although even the speaking references are more frequently positive than negative. Personal background characteristics drew a much more affectively varied response in both countries, with primary attention being devoted to intelligence or educational background and the question of military background, although in both instances some people were favorably disposed to the General because of his religious devotion.

Between these three broad subcategories, however, there are rather sharp national differences. Over 60 per cent of the personal image references in France are devoted to the public virtues (Class I), as opposed to only 25 to 40 per cent in the two American samples. The differences are sharpest with regard to "patriotism," with 15 per cent of De Gaulle's personal image references being of this order, as opposed to only 2 per cent in the Eisenhower samples. Correspondingly, American emphasis is displaced more toward comments on personal background or, to a lesser extent, toward vague personality reactions. The French emphasis on public virtues associated with De Gaulle is of no small interest, as in the context of 1958 *antiparliamentarisme,* it is clear De Gaulle was in a sense seen as running against a group of corrupted legislators.

The "military man." References to personal background warrant our particular attention, for it is here that we find the most direct evaluations of the fact that the leader comes from a military environment. It must be recognized that in a subtle sense, the past military splendor of the conquering hero diffuses through a wide variety of references which make up these images—patriotism, past record, leadership, capacities in dealing with foreign problems, etc. Yet it is precisely this subtle diffusion which seems to be of prime theoretical importance, for it indicates a lack of subjective barriers or compartments in the respondents' minds between the world of the military and civil politics. We asked at the outset how a military hero manages to transfer his popular credit with such ease to the arena of civil affairs, an arena in which he is more or less a stranger and, in terms of much normative democratic theory, a dangerous stranger. In both France and the United States there are clear cultural values favoring the insulation of civil politics from religious and military intrusion. These values have remained somewhat more controversial in France than in the United States, particularly where religion is concerned. Nonetheless, it was often maintained before 1958 that the French population, due to a peculiar history stretching back through Boulanger and McMahon to Bonaparte, was exceptionally allergic to the threat of a military man in civil government. It is likely that liberal French elites were more intensely alarmed by the return of De Gaulle in 1958, particularly under the compromising circumstances, than were comparable American elites by the Eisenhower candidacy in 1952.

But the "weight of history" of this sort is likely to rest more heavily on the thinking of educated elites for whom the past is vivid than on the reflexes of a mass electorate. The popular reception accorded De Gaulle in 1958 does not in itself disprove the proposition that the French public had previously abhorred military leaders in civil affairs. In extremis even reluctant elites came to feel that De Gaulle was the only answer, and one can ascribe some part of the warm public reception to the pressure of the immediate situation. But what part? There is little flavor of the reluctant or the conditional in the reaction to De Gaulle captured in these data—much less, certainly, than would have been found in a proper sampling of civil political leaders in this period. Under other circumstances, the mass response would have been less sweeping, to be sure. Yet at the same time it is easy to imagine that in the years prior to 1958 the real barrier to the civil ascendancy of a military leader lay not in a mass public which adored its military heroes *in their proper sphere alone,* but lay rather in the elites of civil politics with their high sensitivity to boundaries between the military and the civil.

In this sense, then, queries as to the nature of the transfer of popularity from military exploits to political support are unrealistic, for they presuppose that some transfer is necessary. For many people in both the French and American publics there was a sense of passage from one order to another; but for many other people—a majority—there was not. It is in this regard that the De Gaulle and Eisenhower images are striking. In the minds of some respondents these images rest explicitly on past military achievements or on leadership attributes which are military in tone. But these themes are relatively faint. The modal themes are those of a more generalized worship, that is, vague, affective attraction or the ascription of attributes which ignore civil-military bounds, such as conscientiousness, sincerity, and integrity. No one can doubt that this worship owes its genesis to initial military achievement, for in this regard the historical record is clear. But what remains significant is the effortless generalization from military virtues to "virtue."

It is with particular interest, therefore, that we approach the minorities within both French and American samples for whom the military background of the victorious general remained a very salient fact in later evaluations. These respondents subdivide into two polar types: individuals who tended toward a positive evaluation of the leader because he was a military man ("un militaire"), and those who resisted the leader on precisely the same grounds.

The two American samples provide an interesting profile of change in this regard. For observers sensitive to the problem, the initial period of transition is the critical one. The military hero who, after some time in public office, has not sought to perform a coup d'etat, or to pull down barriers between civil and military authority, or to pursue a policy of militarism, has served to allay some of the grosser fears which may have been harbored about him before he had had any experience in high civil office. Therefore, it is against the new arrival that reservations about military background will be most strongly felt, and these reservations should decline in salience after a period in civil office. If we can assume on the other hand that most individuals desiring a military man in high civil office are looking for a certain strength of authority and a military sense of priorities in public policy rather than for a coup d'etat or some other of the more dramatic outcomes, then we would expect the years a military man passed in civil office would have less effect on positive evaluations than in the alleviation of negative feelings.

This pattern emerges clearly when we compare the 1952 and 1956 Eisenhower images. In 1952 military references made up 14 per cent of all references and were made by one-third of all respondents. The anti-military reaction here outnumbers the pro-military reaction by more than two to one. By 1956, however, after four years of Eisenhower civil leadership, the picture shifted dramatically. On one hand, positive references were themselves reduced by more than one-third, but on the other, negative references to Eisenhower's military background were cut to one-seventh of their former prominence (whether measured in references or respondents). Thus the overall salience of the

TABLE 15-2

"Military Man" References to Eisenhower in 1952 and 1956
and to De Gaulle in 1958

		Military Man		
		Positive Evaluations	Negative Evaluations	Total
Eisenhower	Proportion of 1952 respondents	10.0%	22.0%	32.0%
	Proportion of 1956 respondents	6.0	3.0	9.0
De Gaulle	Proportion of 1958 respondents	3.0	4.5	7.5

	Eisenhower		De Gaulle
	1952	1956	1958
Proportion of military man references that are negative	70.0%	35.0%	62.0%

military question declined very sharply, and by 1956 the more durable positive reactions outnumbered the negative in five-to-three proportions.

These comparisons provide a useful backdrop in considering French reactions to De Gaulle's military background. As we have noted, De Gaulle, unlike Eisenhower in 1952, had already played a role in civil politics before 1958. Even if the French response to the "military man" were to spring from attitudes identical to those in the American population, then, we would not expect a 1958 French image precisely like that from the United States in either 1952 or 1956 but rather something in-between. Table 15-2 conveys much of this impression.[7]

---

[7] For the purposes of Table 15-2, only the first three positive references and the first two negative references made by American respondents have been taken into consideration, as a means of taking into account the fact that probing was less on the French side and coding was restricted to these five references. Actually, this change makes virtually no difference in the American figures, since most references occur within these limits in any event. The shift produced in the balance of affect by this cutting is entirely negligible, and the necessarily systematic decline in the proportion having made such references is quite regularly of the order of 2 per cent.

The proportion of Frenchmen evaluating De Gaulle negatively because he is "un militaire" was much lower than that for Eisenhower in 1952, but slightly higher than that for Eisenhower in 1956. The balance of responses was somewhat less negative in France than in America in 1952 but much more negative than the American balance in 1956. It is clear that the De Gaulle response falls closer to the 1952 Eisenhower reading on one measure and closer to the 1956 Eisenhower reading on the other, simply because positive evaluations of De Gaulle's military background are fewer than those in either Eisenhower year. Whether this difference is to be read most fruitfully as a heightened American enthusiasm for a military man or as a lower overall salience of the military background per se for the French respondents cannot be determined from the data. However, it might be well to remember that two points at which French responses visibly exceeded their American analogues were the exclusively positive evaluations of De Gaulle's patriotism and his past military achievements. If these "excess" French comments were read as functional equivalents of American praise of Eisenhower as a military man, the similarities between the two images would loom large even in this regard.

Our brief focus here on respondents who remained intensely aware of the military background should not obscure the fact that such citizens seem in a rather profound minority. In one sense, the data document the fact that in both cultures, some resistance is felt to the entrance of a military man into high civil office. Indeed, for Eisenhower in 1952 and for De Gaulle in 1958, the military man criticism appeared by count more frequently than any other negative theme which was coded. In both instances, for example, it received mention more often than the sum of negative criticisms directed at all of the policy orientations of the leader put together.

But the question remains as to whether this frequency of mention is, by other lights, large or small. If a military man had to seek office solely *qua* military man, both populations might well reject him, for the balance of affect toward the military attribute per se is negative. Were we to give these publics an hypothetical question on the subject, it would not be surprising if a majority of both were to reject *in the abstract* the notion of a military man wielding high civil power. But when the concrete situation presents itself, it seems that the vast majority of both populations are swept on into a highly generalized belief in the leader's virtue which ignores any perceptual barriers between the military and the political order.

Differences in Image by Social Category

Another way to develop some understanding of the phenomena at hand is to consider the character of differences which emerge between images held by diverse segments of these populations. These divergences may appear in either the qualitative detail of the images, or in the balance of positive and negative affect which the leader elicits in various population groups. Let us focus first on some of the more qualitative differences.

Qualitative differences: sex. We might note at the outset that in both the American samples and in the French case, women are less likely to be able to respond to the open-ended questions than are men. Anywhere from 2 per cent to 5 per cent more women than men had nothing to say to open questions concerning De Gaulle and Eisenhower. It is clear within the French sample that whereas there were no sex differences in expressions of disinterest in the problem, explicit refusals to respond were more numerous among women (4 per cent for men, 9 per cent for women). Since such refusals occurred more frequently when respondents were invited to make negative responses, it may be that they sprang from fear of expression or doubt as to the anonymity of the survey. However, it is also true that refusals came disproportionately from poorly educated people, and they may well conceal an ignorance of the subject.

The number of references also varies somewhat by sex. While differences are sharper in France than in the United States, men in both cases show more disposition to talk than women, with the discrepancy clearest where negative references are concerned (Table 15-3). In general, fullness of response depends in part on political involvement, and in both countries men are more politically involved than women, although sex differences tend to be sharper in France in this regard, apparently as a result of more recent accession of women to political roles.

While women tend to make fewer references, certain types of response are characteristically feminine. In the French sample only women talk in terms of De Gaulle's fundamental warmth, kindness, and generosity ("il a du coeur," "brave homme," "il agit selon son coeur," "il est bon," "il a été généreux en toutes circonstances"). It occurs only to women to comment on De Gaulle's religious convictions ("il est très croyant," "c'est un chrétien," "un très grand catholique"), al-

TABLE 15-3 *

Average Number of References Made to De Gaulle and Eisenhower, by Sex

	Eisenhower 1952		1956		De Gaulle 1958	
	Posi-tive	Nega-tive	Posi-tive	Nega-tive	Posi-tive	Nega-tive
Men	1.71	0.85	1.94	0.90	1.24	0.40
Women	1.83	0.73	1.94	0.62	1.19	0.22

* The primary comparison in this table is intended to be the discrepancy in average number of responses within each sample for men and women. Two other phenomena—the higher levels of response and the closer balance between numbers of positive and negative references on the American side—are discussed elsewhere in the text.

though in the French case these responses are due exclusively to nuns of the Church. Other responses which tend to be feminine refer to "l'expérience de l'âge," or, in more political terms, to De Gaulle as the force which can unify a divided France, a man of peace and a man of order.

When components of the Eisenhower image are similarly divided according to the sex ratio of respondents making various types of comments, the two most feminine responses are (1) appreciative references to Eisenhower as a religious man; and (2) references to his kindness and warmth. The parallels here with the French case are perfect.

On both sides the specific image components that are clearly masculine—that is, that are mentioned disproportionately by men—are fewer in number than those which are clearly feminine. The French sample includes an occasional male who comments positively upon De Gaulle's military bearing—his "prestance," his "maintien,"—or the manner in which he wears the military uniform. Similarly, men are more likely to appreciate De Gaulle's self-discipline, the absence of personal political ambition, and, among leadership characteristics, his keen political insight ("grande valeur politique," "réaliste," "sa clairvoyance politique," "le sens clair de sa vue," "voit les choses avec exactitude"). With regard to past events, men are more likely to comment that De Gaulle had already saved the Republic or to praise his refusal to be dictated to by the other Western powers. In short, then, men tend toward responses which are somewhat more political in content than are those of women.

To the degree that American men have characteristic responses, they tend to fall in areas which concern policy positions. Most notably, men much more than women were likely to focus on Eisenhower's broad political philosophy, and other types of issue concerns were more often reflected in male responses. In both populations, then, the male evaluations tended to show some vestige of political content whereas female evaluations were more heavily affective or emotional in tone.

However, it should be recognized that in both samples, differences between the sexes are extremely slight across most aspects of the positive image. The notable discrepancies recorded above occur principally in a few fringe categories such as religious or policy outlook, which are at the most sparsely populated. The mainstream of responses shows little variation by sex. In the French case, for example, the predominance of women in two or three specific categories subsumed under the "personal image" heading does not mean that all told women give more personal image responses than men. Indeed, French men devote 50 per cent of their responses to personal qualities of De Gaulle, as opposed to only 45 per cent of the female responses. In the American case, where vague affective responses to the Eisenhower personality are more prominent in the personal image class, women appear slightly more frequently in this broad class as a whole, although once again differences are not significant.

The negative side of both the American and French images is filled in disproportionately by men for, as we have seen, women on both sides were less likely to criticize the General than men. Forty per cent of French men, and 48 per cent of French women indicated in so many words that they could find no fault in De Gaulle, figures that give some indication of the degree of esteem in which the General was held. Furthermore, while there were many expressions of sweeping approval or complete trust in De Gaulle, comparable statements of complete distrust or displeasure were extremely rare (3 per cent of male respondents, 2 per cent of female respondents). De Gaulle's critics in the French public had rather specific complaints.

The strongest sex differences emerge in connection with criticisms of De Gaulle's public record around the time of the Second World War. Men were much more likely to express irritation at De Gaulle's retirement from public life in 1946 ("A la Libération, il aurait dû prendre les rênes et ne pas se laisser renvoyer"; "son échec en 1945, il est parti en disant que tout était en ordre, c'était un mensonge") and his long seclusion at Colombey ("il aurait dû faire plutôt ce qu'il fait aujourd'hui"; "il n'aurait pas dû attendre jusqu'à maintenant, il nous aurait évité des jours sombres"). While these responses class as negative reactions, it is clear that they do not come from citizens who are reluctant to accept De Gaulle's leadership. Less frequently, men tend as well to criticize De Gaulle's management of affairs surrounding the Liberation. Pétainists complain that De Gaulle failed to bring about a proper reconciliation of factions in 1944, anti-Communists complain at his acceptance of Thorez and incorporation of Communists in his government. We might add too that three male respondents believed that De Gaulle was the author of the Constitution of the Fourth Republic (1946–1958), and hence, that its woes were to be blamed on him. All of these criticisms have to do not only with the record but are heavily political in tone, and it is not surprising that over three-quarters of these responses come from men.

In 1952 in the United States Eisenhower had very little in the way of a past political record, but it is interesting that the most masculine of the broad negative categories is the one which concerns the past record, just as in France. By 1956 male predominance in this category increased further, relative to 1952, but in the latter year its masculinity was matched by another broad category, criticism of Eisenhower's attributes as a leader. Since most of these comments were clearly precipitated by Eisenhower's leadership record, 1952–1956, this finding undoubtedly is part and parcel of the same phenomenon.

Despite the male trend toward political content, negative reactions to the leaders' policy positions present a much more mixed picture in both samples than was found in the case of positive reactions. In France and in the United States in 1952, there are simply no overall sex differences in negative policy reactions. By 1956 in the United States there has come to be a slight male preponderance in this general category, but it is far from marked.

If we look at detailed references within this broad category, however, a coherent pattern of difference suggests itself. In France, for example, men tend to question De Gaulle's republican sympathies, to accuse him of being a rightist ("un réactionnaire invétéré," says one, "un clérical" says another) of dictatorial aspirations or, more simply, of indifference toward programs of social amelioration. Women, on the other hand, criticize specific domestic policies, some of which involve mistaken perceptions ("il refuse l'augmentation des salaires," "il a mis de nouveaux impôts") or question De Gaulle's specific policies toward colonial problems ("il ne veut pas arrêter la guerre en Algérie," "il est trop faible dans ses mesures contre le F.L.N."). It is clear that these criticisms are not of the same order. Men tend to challenge De Gaulle's underlying political philosophy; women are more concerned with concrete measures and immediate events.

One sees somewhat the same sex lines on the American side. Within the broad category of policy criticisms the most clearly masculine comments are those that attack Eisenhower's underlying political philosophy ("too conservative") in 1952. (By 1956 such comments are so rare that they afford no sex comparison.) In 1952 women restore the sex balance by disproportionate concern with specific and short-term foreign policy criticisms which generally reflect concern over war; by 1956, however, with "hot war" less imminent, women have shifted out of these categories to some degree.

On the French side, criticisms of the recent past, fears about the future, and derogations of De Gaulle's leadership capacity tend to turn, in a rather confused way, on two distinct themes:

The threat of a coup d'etat and dictatorship ("le soutien moral donné à la rébellion des colonels") or army control, which brings into question De Gaulle's sources of support in the 1958 crisis. There are no sex differences in these responses.

The fear of De Gaulle's naïveté in politics or the fear that he will fall under the control of the parties or the officials of the Fourth Republic, so that no good will come of the new republic. This theme is quite clearly masculine.

In addition, there are some further responses that reflect a fear of war ("certains disent qu'il veut la guerre," "il ne pense qu' à la guerre," "il ne refusera jamais une guerre," "pourvu qu'il ne nous apporte pas la guerre"). These responses, rather like the concern of American women with foreign policy in 1952, all come from women.

The negative references to the personal image show rather comparable sex differences between countries as well. Women again focus on the "feeling tone" of the personality, criticizing coldness and aloofness as readily as appreciating "warmth and kindness." In France such feminine complaints extend not only to De Gaulle's stiffness and coldness ("il a l'air sévère," "il a le regard un peu froid") but also to De Gaulle's vanity, a trait not perceived in Eisenhower ("son moi," "sa façon de dire 'moi, De Gaulle' "). On those rare occasions when De Gaulle's or Eisenhower's fundamental integrity was called into question the criticism tended strongly to be masculine ("il graisse son bifteck et celui de ses pareils"). French men also criticize De Gaulle's background ("ne vient pas du peuple," "son mépris du peuple") and especially certain aspects of his behavior, such as his speaking style and his taste for the grandiloquent and theatrical.

Finally, in the criticisms of these figures as military men, one finds no sex differences for France or for the United States in 1952. When this response became much less salient in the United States in 1956, there was a tendency for men to retain a suspicion of the military background longer than women.

Qualitative differences: age. One of the most obvious hypotheses which might be investigated is that the youngest cohort of Americans in 1952, or the youngest French cohort in 1958, should be more likely to indicate an ignorance of the two generals than would older members of the two populations. Among women on the French side there is no sign that this is so. Among men, however, ignorance is expressed most frequently (6 per cent) by the youngest and oldest cohorts whereas French men of middle age (30 to 54) confess ignorance of De Gaulle only rarely (1 per cent). Within the 1952 American sample the proportions who can say nothing at all about Eisenhower are clearly highest in the very youngest age category (60 cases 23 years of age or less show 13 per cent nonresponse, as opposed to 7 to 8 per cent in middle age), and after age 55 the nonresponse rate climbs back toward that of the very young. Since the same pattern occurs in the 1956 sample, however, after four years of the Eisenhower Presidency, these differences may reflect life cycle changes in political interest more than historical generations.

In general, there is little in the way of important age differences in the broad lines of the leader images in either sample. This absence of findings is quite clear in one area where there might be reason to expect strong differences, references to the past. Among women in both samples there is no increase in the frequency of these responses with age, as had been expected. Among men in the French sample these references show a slight increase from the category 21 to 29 years (10 per cent of such references) to that of 30 to 44 (13 per cent) and 45 to 54 (17 per cent), but then there is a decrease: 15 per cent in the group 55 to 64, with 13 per cent among those over 65. These differences are too weak to give us much confidence in the hypothesis, and a similar progression of responses concerning Eisenhower's role in the Second World War among men in the United States (1956) is even weaker. Even criticisms of De Gaulle's retirement to Colombey are given as frequently by the young (21 to 29 years) as by others, despite the fact that these respondents were less than 16 years old at the time of the event.

There are some mild differences in details of the image which emerge on the French side. We have already noted that references to De Gaulle's patriotism are frequent. For both sexes, it is particularly the younger respondents (under 45) and the oldest group (over 65) who give this type of response. It seems as though two generations are represented here, one of which had its patriotism forged in the First World War, the other during the Resistance. Furthermore, there is some progression of interest in De Gaulle's policy positions by age. Such references are rarely made by the young, somewhat more often by middle-aged persons, and more often still by the oldest respondents. Most characteristic of the young, however, is antimilitarism: 30 per cent of the negative references of young men and 22 per cent of young women protest De Gaulle's military background.

There is no comparable increase of interest in Eisenhower's policy positions with age, nor are there more hostile references to his military background among the young. However, as we have seen, there was a stronger concern over foreign policy questions on the American side quite generally, and the youngest age group (21 to 29) gives a disproportionate number of these responses. There may be some common concern here among the youngest cohort in both countries prompted by the possibility of military service.

Qualitative differences: status level. It is when one considers measures of status that one finds, on the French side alone, a strong and rather curious pattern. The only notable differences in image of De Gaulle by education—beyond the obvious fact that more poorly educated people are less likely to know much about De Gaulle—emerge with even greater strength across the occupational status hierarchy: (1) the higher the status, the more frequent the mention of aspects of personal image, and (2) the higher the status, the fewer the mentions of past events as bases for evaluation. These tendencies seem almost the inverse of what one might have expected. Yet they are very strong tendencies, particularly for men arrayed by occupation. Among professional men 68 per cent of positive references have to do with the personal attributes of the General; for higher managerial people the proportion is 59 per cent; for white-collar workers it is 55 per cent; it falls to 44 per cent for artisans, to 18 per cent for farmers, and to 12 per cent for farm laborers. Within the working class the same progression appears, although the incidence of such references starts again at a high level. Seventy-three per cent of responses given by foremen are of the personal order, dropping to 54 per cent for skilled workers, 47 per cent for the semi-skilled, and 44 per cent for the unskilled laborers. At the same time, in counterpoint, farm laborers are most likely to evaluate De Gaulle in terms of past events, then semi-skilled and unskilled, then artisans and farmers. In general, there is a high negative correlation between the two types of responses across the occupation categories, and the ordering of categories in terms of relative strength of the two types of responses comes very close to a traditional status array.

There is no such pattern visible in the American responses, despite great similarities between the two bodies of data on other counts. There is some mild tendency for lower-status people to make more references to the achievements of Eisenhower in the Second World War period. The gradient of references is regular across the status divisions, but rather weak. And there is no sign whatever that higher-status responses flow instead into discussions of personal qualities of Eisenhower. The sole progression of responses positively correlated with status has to do with reactions to Eisenhower's policy positions. Quite as one would expect, more educated people are more likely to evaluate the leader in terms of policy expectations.

What then may be made of the remarkable correlation on the French side? It seems that the better-educated, higher-status people tend to evaluate De Gaulle by asking themselves: "Is he the man we need? Does he have the capacities which will be demanded by his role in government?" On the other hand, less well-educated people lower in the hierarchy are more willing to base their decisions on what they know of the historic role of De Gaulle. In a sense, these are the most obvious events which might be attached to his name. Anyone evaluating De Gaulle's personal characteristics with some familiarity would surely recognize his role during the Second World War and take it for granted; the fact that someone remembers that it was De Gaulle who was so prominent in the Second World War does not assure us that he has a very clear image of De Gaulle as the current political leader. The same phenomenon occurs in the United States, but here the tendency of lower-status people to hark to major past events is much weaker, in part perhaps because these past events (Second World War) had a much slighter personal impact in the United States. Thus lower-status people in France seem to be basing their decision on their own past experience rather than on the character of the problems which confront the nation in the immediate future.

The Balance of Positive and Negative Feeling toward the Generals

Beyond attention to the qualitative content of references made to the two generals, it is possible as well to summarize these materials by arraying respondents on an affective continuum running from negative through neutral to positive. An individual can be given a score which simply represents the algebraic sum of his positive and negative references. For example, an individual making three positive references and no negative references would receive a score of +3. A person with one positive reference and two negative references would receive a score of −1. The score of 0 represents a midpoint of indifference or neutrality, reserved for individuals making no references or a balance of positive and negative references.

Any category of persons (e.g., males 21 to 29 years old, women of college education, farm laborers, etc.) can be assigned a position on the continuum simply by calculating the mean of individual scores involved. However, to take into account differences in mean which might be attributable solely to the fact that members of one category were more loquacious than those of another, we shall make a practice of dividing this mean by the standard deviation of scores in the category.

In these terms the mean attitudes toward Eisenhower in the two American samples from 1952 and 1956 are +0.46 and +0.55, respectively. This is a relatively minor difference between the two years. While these figures are very significantly skewed to the positive side of the zero point, the French sample shows an even more unconditionally favorable figure of +0.89. And in neither sample is the balance of favor entirely similar across social categories.

Quantitative differences: sex. As we have already seen, women are about as likely to volunteer positive references as are men in both countries but are less likely to express criticism of the leaders. This difference is expressed by our attitude measure as shown in Table 15-4.

Although the sex differences are not of startling magnitude, they

TABLE 15-4

Balance of Attitude toward De Gaulle and Eisenhower, by Sex

	Eisenhower		De Gaulle
	1952	1956	1958
Men	0.39	0.46	0.81
Women	0.52	0.62	0.95
Difference	0.13	0.16	0.14

are extremely regular across the three tests. In both France and the United States, negative evaluations of the generals tend to rest more frequently than do positive references on political content. As we have seen, even in positive responses, women tend less than men to bring political content to bear on their evaluations. Therefore, they find less to criticize in such a figure than do men.

Quantitative differences: age. As we move from a simple dichotomization of the samples to finer subdivisions, it must be remembered that differences of increasing magnitude can occur simply as a function of heightened sampling error. Therefore, we shall restrict our attention to large differences occurring in significant patterns across categories in the data. The differences in affect which emerge as a function of age are in both countries so slight and irregular (Table 15-5) that one can reasonably consider age a negligible factor in the response to the two generals.

Quantitative differences: education. A rather different picture is presented when one considers attitudinal differences associated with differences in formal education. On the American side, a very strong pattern asserts itself in both years, however, with the mean attitude toward Eisenhower becoming rapidly more favorable for both sexes with increasing education (Table 15-6). With the exception of the row referring to people with no education, and especially where these people are further subdivided by sex, case numbers for the Eisenhower cells are all quite adequate. On the French side, one finds the first three steps of a comparable pattern, which holds within sex as well as for the sample as a whole. But the gradient is reversed among the French respondents with the most advanced education. While case

TABLE 15-5

Balance of Attitude toward De Gaulle and Eisenhower, by Sex and Age

Age	Eisenhower, 1952			Eisenhower, 1956			De Gaulle, 1958		
	Men	Women	Total	Men	Women	Total	Men	Women	Total
21–29	0.35	0.60	0.47	0.39	0.66	0.54	0.72	0.92	0.83
30–44	0.30	0.45	0.38	0.47	0.60	0.54	0.88	0.96	0.91
45–54	0.47	0.58	0.53	0.41	0.56	0.49	0.88	0.85	0.87
55–64	0.57	0.57	0.57	0.54	0.79	0.66	0.72	0.80	0.76
Over 65	0.43	0.48	0.46	0.50	0.62	0.56	0.73	1.29	1.03

TABLE 15-6

Balance of Attitude toward De Gaulle and Eisenhower,
by Sex and Education

Education	Eisenhower, 1952			Eisenhower, 1956			De Gaulle, 1958		
	Men	Women	Total	Men	Women	Total	Men	Women	Total
None	0.09	0.26	0.21	0.05	0.58	0.31	0.56	0.40	0.46
	0.17	0.21	0.18	0.38	0.42	0.40	0.82	0.93	0.88
	0.39	0.57	0.48	0.39	0.52	0.46	0.87	1.27	1.08
	0.65	0.67	0.66	0.55	0.77	0.66	0.74	0.74	0.74

numbers in this row in France are quite weak (66 males, 20 females, total 86 cases), the total column in particular should be of adequate size to assure that the failure of the gradient to continue upward is not attributable to sampling error.

To shed any light on such a discrepancy, it is necessary to consider why any relationship emerges at all between education and these attitudes. We know that education is one way of measuring social class level, and that by and large in both countries rightist party sympathies are associated with higher class level. Furthermore, although both leaders avoided taking clear-cut issue positions, both were considered essentially rightist in outlook, not only by expert observers, but by the occasional respondents in both samples who concerned themselves with such matters. Given these facts, we might expect favorable attitudes toward these leaders to increase with education in both countries, less because of education per se, than because education reflects a certain enduring bias in party location, and people sympathizing with rightist parties would be more likely to evaluate a rightist candidate more favorably. As we shall consider the role of party directly in a moment, however, we shall postpone further consideration of the relationship until we have examined the impact of partisanship in these evaluations.

Quantitative differences: occupation. Congruent with the education differences, there is a clear correlation between the urban occupation status hierarchy and attitudes toward De Gaulle or Eisenhower (Figure 15-2). This association is much stronger in the United States in 1952 than in France in 1958. Actually, a comparable graph for 1956 in the United States shows a pattern which is somewhat weaker than

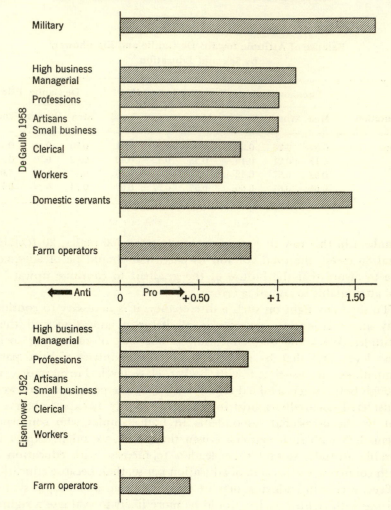

Figure 15-2. Attitudes toward De Gaulle and Eisenhower by occupation.

that for 1952 but which remains visibly stronger than the correlation on the French side.[8]

Beyond the basic status relationship, a few other details command attention. First, it is not surprising that the group most favorable to De Gaulle is that of military personnel and their wives. Although it is impossible to isolate comparable military personnel for the 1952

[8] The phenomenon of status depolarization, occurring in the United States in this period, is discussed in detail in Campbell et al., *op. cit.*, Chap. 13.

American sample, this distinction can be drawn for 1956, and one finds immediately that the response to Eisenhower registered by this group departs nearly as remarkably from the remainder of the sample as it does in the French case.

The decline in enthusiasm about De Gaulle with declining status is dramatically interrupted by the category of female domestic workers. Although these women are extremely low in the status hierarchy, their attitude toward De Gaulle is extremely favorable.[9]

There is an accumulation of reasons which underlie this result. In the first place, this occupation category is by definition exclusively female, and we know that women in general show relatively favorable attitudes toward De Gaulle. Against a backdrop of women from other occupational milieus these domestic workers would appear somewhat less extreme in their attitudes.[10]

Furthermore, it seems to be the rule in the French sample that within occupation categories, women who are themselves active in the labor force are quite markedly more positive toward De Gaulle than either men of the same occupation *or their wives*. Indeed, by and large, the wives from occupation to occupation look very much like their working husbands in affect toward De Gaulle. It is the active women who stand apart. The data suggest that housewives are more likely to give equivocal answers, balancing positive and negative carefully whereas working women take more sharply defined positions. Perhaps activity outside the home stimulates stronger political commitments for women which housewives can avoid. However, there is no comparable phenomenon in the American case.

Nonetheless, the fact that these domestic workers are women and active in the labor force still could not be said to account completely for their warm reaction to De Gaulle. However, there are more interesting aspects of the life situation of these people which are likely to affect their attitudes. It has often been observed that domestic workers, cut off from others of their own status and bound up in an environment

[9] While this deviation would reduce the overall correlations between status and attitudes toward De Gaulle, it must be remembered that female domestic workers, even in France, are a small group relative to other workers, who fit the trend well.

[10] Sex differences affect Figure 15-2 at one other point as well. Although the "artisan and small business" category appears to be as favorable to De Gaulle as the professional category, it is *not* once the sex factor is controlled. Women are disproportionately represented in the small business ("commerçant") grouping. To the degree that cases suffice for comparisons, professional men, women active in professional occupations, and the wives of professional men are all in an absolute sense more favorable to De Gaulle than are their counterparts within the artisan and commerçant grouping.

of much higher status than that of their origin tend to take on higher-status attitudes and values.[11] We can shed light on this hypothesis if we consider the class identifications of women who serve in these capacities.

Both French and American respondents were asked to locate themselves in a social class. As we would expect from the occupation materials, there is, in general, a positive relationship between self-assigned status and attitudes toward De Gaulle or Eisenhower (Figure 15-3). In both samples, the most favorable and least favorable attitudes are held by those respondents—constituting a large majority of both samples—who place themselves in the middle or the working class. But female domestic workers, along with some other smaller groups like farm laborers who show the same apparent combination of low status and high regard for De Gaulle, also show unusually high proportions unable to identify with a social class. These people, lacking the anchors provided by an identification with the working class, seem to have succumbed more readily to the Gaullist tide.

It is important to note that while the French correlation between occupation and attitude toward De Gaulle seemed weaker than that in the United States (Figure 15-2), there do not seem to be great discrepancies between the two countries in the magnitude of the subjective class relationship. Subjective class does not, of course, correspond perfectly to social class as it might be objectively determined by occupation. The lower white-collar group, for example, is quite divided in its loyalties; in both countries members of this category favor the working class over the middle class in a 53–47 ratio. In both countries, too, a visible portion (13 per cent in France, 19 per cent in the United States) of workers identify with the middle class.

Despite occupational homogeneity these groups do not react to the leader in the same fashion. Table 15-7 permits us to evaluate the interplay of objective and subjective class in the direction of these attitudes by comparing the difference in attitude means associated with each. In the American case, for example, we note that two broad changes occur between 1952 and 1956: the general level of means increases, reflecting the increased favor toward Eisenhower in the latter year; and the status polarization of these attitudes is weaker in 1956 than in 1952. Despite these shifts, however, the ratio of mean

[11] M. Lipset, P. F. Lazarsfeld, A. Barton, and J. Linz, "The Psychology of Voting: An Analysis of Political Behavior," in Gardner Lindzey, *Handbook of Social Psychology*, Reading, Mass.: Addison-Wesley, 1954, p. 1140.

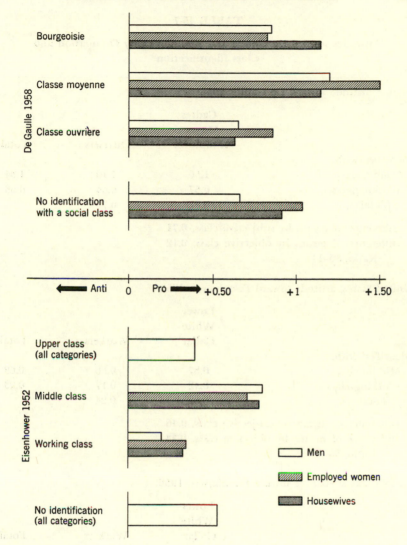

Figure 15-3. Attitudes toward De Gaulle and Eisenhower by subjective class identification.

differences associated with each factor remains constant, giving us some assurance that we are dealing with a rather stable property and a stable statistic.

When we look at the French case, however, this ratio is strikingly different. We must bear in mind here that we are not examining the full range of objective class variation on either side. We are

TABLE 15-7

Attitudes toward De Gaulle and Eisenhower by Occupation and Class Identification

France, attitude toward De Gaulle, 1958

Identified with:	Cadres Moyen, Employés	Ouvriers	Total
Middle class	1.50	1.10	1.34
Working class	0.57	0.66	0.63
Total	0.82	0.70	

Difference of means by subjective class, 0.71
Difference of means by objective class, 0.12
　　Ratio, 86–14

United States, attitude toward Eisenhower, 1952

Identified with:	Lower White Collar	Workers	Total
Middle class	0.87	0.56	0.69
Working class	0.42	0.17	0.23
Total	0.62	0.24	

Difference of means by subjective class, 0.46
Difference of means by objective class, 0.38
　　Ratio, 55–45

United States, attitude toward Eisenhower, 1956

Identified with:	Lower White Collar	Workers	Total
Middle class	1.00	0.66	0.78
Working class	0.55	0.41	0.43
Total	0.75	0.46	

Difference of means by subjective class, 0.35
Difference of means by objective class, 0.29
　　Ratio, 55–45

looking only at an abbreviated section of the class hierarchy, and therefore we are reducing the total explanatory power of the objective class factor. Within this section, however, it is clear that it is far more important *in France* to know an individual's class orientation than to know simply whether he is a blue-collar or white-collar worker.[12] Even in the United States were it necessary to choose, we would prefer to know the subjective term as well, but the difference is slight. In France, the role of class orientations is much stronger vis-à-vis these attitudes. The French employé who went out of his way to identify with the working class resisted De Gaulle even more firmly than the worker himself.

Among the social factors we have considered, then, it is the factor which is most psychological and most political which appears to have the clearest bearing in both samples on attitudes toward these leaders. All things considered, it must be admitted that the responses to De Gaulle and to Eisenhower do not show a strong degree of social patterning. It seems to be part of the phenomena surrounding these figures that their appeal is very general across their electorates, ignoring social boundaries. The only significant exception is the heightened resistance in certain lower-status milieus where there appears to be some political and class awareness. Since it is obvious that this resistance follows ancient party lines, let us consider the impact of the party system on the development of these attitudes toward the leaders in both countries.

The Two Generals and the National Party Systems

It is a matter of no small significance that the weight of the *positive* public image of the General has to do with personal characteristics and past achievements whereas the weight of the *negative* image is more policy oriented. The service which the victorious general has performed for his society cannot be seriously disputed before the public, and this

[12] It might be maintained that the stratum of "cadres moyen et employés" (e.g., white-collar workers) in France has long been maintained in more of a "working class" situation than in the United States, so that the objective status range in France is foreshortened relative to that in the United States. If this were true, it would not be surprising that objective differences predict less well for France than subjective differences. Let us reiterate, however, that the French "employé" chooses a working class identification with no greater frequency than his American counterpart (53 per cent in France, 52 per cent and 54 per cent in the United States, 1952 and 1956). We feel that the differences portrayed are no mere artifactitious discrepancies.

credit appears to remain strong despite the shift from a military to a political role. However, entrance to the political arena places the general in a position where his judgments are matters of public controversy. The most dramatic symbol of this entrance into controversy comes at the point where the hitherto nonpartisan military leader is forced to adopt a posture toward the normal party competition of the ongoing system.

The classical strategy of the victorious general is, of course, to avoid controversial commitment as long as possible, either as to party or to policy. If mass electorates fulfilled the ideal of democratic theory, failure of the candidate to indicate clearly the policy directions he intends to pursue in office would be fatal. However, it is clear that this is not the case. As a result, the victorious general, unlike the common politician who has no treasury of noncontroversial credit in the public mind, has much to lose and little to gain by partisan or policy commitment.

At the same time, these strategies are necessarily constrained by the political institutions of the society in which the general is operating. Both Eisenhower and De Gaulle were able to remain quite vague about policy intentions. But Eisenhower was constrained to choose one of the two major parties over the other whereas De Gaulle was able to maintain a position "above the parties." Of course, Eisenhower postponed his choice of party so successfully that for a considerable period of time Democratic Party leaders maintained hopes that they, rather than the Republicans, would be able to present him for office. Yet ultimately, given the deeply imbedded two-party tradition in the United States, Eisenhower was forced to reveal a partisan choice. In the French case, however, the fluid state of the multiparty system in 1958, the attacks which it had undergone, and the fact that De Gaulle was not himself a nominal candidate all conspired to permit him to stand aloof from the party system. What were the consequences of these differences for the public response?

The Eisenhower case. Evidence is strong that Eisenhower's forced choice of a party ticket had a deep effect on his public image. Let us sketch in briefly what has been learned of these processes. Although data are lacking as to the public image of Eisenhower before he adopted the Republican Party, there is no reason to believe that admiration for him had followed any lines of political or social cleavage. Therefore it is noteworthy that our first measurements of public response to Eisenhower drawn *after* his commitment to the Republican Party showed a popular image quite strongly correlated with the individual's own partisan attachment. The stronger the loyalty the voter felt for the

Republican Party, the more unconditional his respect for Eisenhower; Democrats were much less enthusiastic, and where sense of identification with the Democratic Party was strong enough, evaluated Eisenhower negatively.

There is, of course, a question of causal ordering here. It might be argued, for example, that attitudes toward Eisenhower form the prior term, and that people who originally disliked Eisenhower for whatever reason shifted their political allegiance to the Democrats when Eisenhower's candidacy became clear, and that strong admirers of the General became strong Republicans. We have seen the evidence, however, indicating that party loyalties in the American system remain stable for long periods of time. Therefore, it seems indisputable that with very few exceptions, partisanship antedated and profoundly modified the reactions to Eisenhower. In other words, had Eisenhower chosen instead the Democratic Party, we may assume the relationship would have rotated in the opposing direction: strong Republicans would have decided they disliked Eisenhower.

This loss of enthusiasm in one part of the electorate was, then, the price which Eisenhower was forced to pay in public support as a result of the fact that the ongoing system required him to choose a party. He paid some further price for choosing the Republicans rather than the Democrats, since it is demonstrable that the Democrats in the modern period enjoy a strong majority of public loyalties. Therefore, Eisenhower would have alienated a smaller fraction of the electorate and heightened the enthusiasm of a larger portion, had he run on the Democratic ticket.

Two further observations must be drawn to complete the picture of Eisenhower's passage before a partisan electorate. While his partisan choice led to a strong correlation between voter partisanship and affective reaction to him, the fact remained that his general public image remained very positive. That is, while weak Democrats were less enthusiastic about Eisenhower than Independents, and much less enthusiastic about him than weak Republicans, on balance they were still positively disposed toward him. Only the strongest Democratic adherents showed a net reaction which was negative. The partisan reaction to a partisan object is, of course, entirely to be expected. What is unusual here, and what seems peculiar to the figure of the victorious general, is the fact that despite a strong partisan influence on the image, the public response remains heavily skewed to the positive side. Although in 1952 the American public felt other strong short-term aggravations with the Democratic Party, it is beyond dispute that the marked skewing of the Eisenhower image in a positive direction contributed in a major way to the seduction of many Democrats across party lines to vote for the General, thereby fashioning the strong personal groundswell which characterized the election totals surrounding the victorious general.

Finally, we must keep in mind that the tide toward Eisenhower was a transient one which was registered in votes rather than in shifts of underlying party loyalty. Democrats who had voted for Eisenhower in 1952 and 1956 went on considering themselves Democrats, voting Democratic in off-year elections and even in some measure voting Democratic at lower levels after a presidential vote for Eisenhower. This phenomenon underscores once again the role of the personal popularity of the general in electoral patterns. Despite his capacity to lure weaker Democrats to vote for him, more recent data have shown beyond doubt that Eisenhower's final imprint on the partisanship of the American public was most negligible. He drew personal votes but failed to convert his Democratic admirers to his party.[13]

The case of De Gaulle: similarities. We have already suggested that De Gaulle was subjected to fewer constraints from the French party system than was Eisenhower in the United States. Before we survey the differences in public response which were reflected as a result, let us consider the similarities which the French data show, by way of establishing points of reference.

Although De Gaulle placed himself above the party structure and avoided policy commitment, he could not escape all links with political controversy. His earlier tour in civil politics had, for example, located him vaguely as center-right in orientation. More important, while he could refuse to choose between the parties, he could not prevent the parties from reacting toward him and thereby endowing him with some political coloration. Now there is obviously a complex interaction between perception by party leaders that a potential political figure is a popular hero and the position which the party is likely to adopt toward him. If the victorious general pays some price in popularity by align-

---

[13] This absence of a more permanent effect on partisan tendencies may once again be entirely peculiar to the candidate who has enjoyed status as a popular hero before entering realms of public controversy. In the United States, for example, Franklin Delano Roosevelt and Theodore Roosevelt would classify as two political leaders who rose to prominence largely through political party channels and later stimulated a tremendous public response as "charismatic" Presidents. It is likely that these leaders left a more profound imprint on partisan loyalties than is normal for the victorious general. While certain types of nonpolitical acclaim can be converted into votes, it seems that the public retains some fundamental dissociation between this popularity and the party which is the later instrument of the hero.

ing himself with a political party, so a party may undergo some loss of support if it opposes too directly a popular hero. The Democrats in the United States strenuously avoided direct attacks on Eisenhower the man, choosing to aim their criticism instead at the people around him, the policies of the Republican Party, and the like. Similarly, there were strong forces on the French parties, generated in part by the gravity of the situation but also by De Gaulle's fundamental popularity, not to oppose the General too vigorously. Nevertheless, some spectrum of party reactions from positive to negative toward De Gaulle did emerge, and we can use these reactions to analyze the role of the party system in the public response.

At a simple level, it is clear from Figure 15-4 that the net affect felt toward De Gaulle by different groups of party adherents in the early autumn of 1958 were quite distinct. These differences by party are much sharper than any which were discovered in connection with social boundaries. Whether party assignment is made to the voter on the basis of his report of 1956 vote or his statement of party identification as of the time of the interview (and the turnover between the two is higher than one might expect), the correlation between partisanship and attitude toward De Gaulle is very apparent.

One aspect of the figure deserving special attention is the bar representing people with "no party attachment" in the fall of 1958. This group excludes the 10 per cent of the French population who refused to reveal their party attachment, if any. It remains, however, a very substantial contingent, since one-third of the respondents said that they felt close to no party or could not decide what party they found most attractive.[14] Therefore we must keep in mind that when American data involving differences in party loyalties are displayed we are talking of 90 to 95 per cent of the American electorate whereas

[14] There is no doubt but that the distinction between "refusal" and "no party attachment," although coded carefully from the remarks made by the respondent, is not entirely pure. That is, some respondents "refused" to give a party attachment in order to hide the fact that they had none, and others said they had none to hide an existing attachment. Exhaustive internal study has assured us, however, that most of the people who said they had no attachment in fact felt none. As a group, they are disinterested about politics and have difficulty responding to questions of sheer information about the parties and current politics which would in no way reveal their own orientations. Often, they indicated embarrassment at their ignorance of political affairs, or excused themselves on grounds of total indifference. Actually, the group which "refused" shows some of the same characteristics, although to a less marked degree, and represents undoubtedly a mixture of people embarrassed by lack of relation to politics and people who are covert militants, particularly those of the Communist Party, drastically underrepresented in the sample.

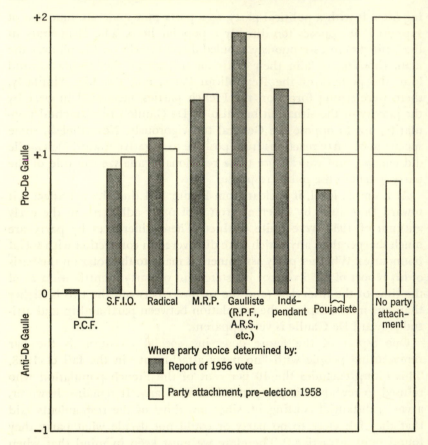

Figure 15-4. Attitudes toward De Gaulle by party choice of respondent. The height of each bar indicates the mean attitude toward De Gaulle expressed by respondents indicating support for or attachment to the party group. In each case the mean attitude for a party group has been divided by the standard deviation of the attitude for the group, thereby reducing differences in the means that are attributable solely to differences in the number of references to De Gaulle, rather than to the relative partisanship of these references. Most Poujadist voters in 1956 indicated no attachment to this faction by the fall of 1958, so that there are entirely too few cases in the sample to represent a second reading for Poujadists, and the first (1956) bar has few enough cases to be of substantial reliability. However, it is true as the figure suggests that 1956 Poujadists who showed no support for the faction by 1958 were respondents with somewhat positive attitudes toward De Gaulle, while those who remained with the Poujadists were lest sympathetic to the General (see text). The category labeled "No Party Attachment" includes those respondents who reported in the early fall of 1958 that they felt close to "none of the parties," or who indicated that they did not know to which party they felt closest. Excluded from the figure entirely are respondents (1) who reported feeling close to some party grouping so vaguely described as to be unidentifiable; (2) who identified themselves

French data refer only to the half of the French electorate comparable in the presence of some party identification (see Chapter 14).

Finally the patterns of partisan difference in Figure 15-4, and particularly those representing party attachments in the fall of 1958, are obviously related to the positions taken by the various parties toward De Gaulle prior to the survey. To examine this relationship more closely, it is desirable to employ an ordering of the parties not on a rough left-right continuum, as in Figure 15-4, but specifically with regard to the positions which they had adopted toward De Gaulle in this period. The two orderings were not, of course, perfectly correlated. The leadership of the S.F.I.O., for example, was more warmly disposed toward De Gaulle than might be expected for a leftist party and indeed was warmer than some factions normally located to its right. Such departures from the basic left-right rankings demand consideration. With this end in view, then, we commissioned a panel of French judges to rate the positions of a variety of major parties and splinter groups on several policy dimensions, including reactions of faction leadership to De Gaulle in the relevant period.[15]

[15] The advantages of introducing such an ordering are numerous. It is obviously desirable, for example, to locate people who identify themselves with small dissident splinters at a position appropriate to the positions of their factions. Most identifiers of course align themselves only with some gross, traditional party-object, like "the Socialists" or "the Radicals." However, there are occasional militants for whom internal factions or dissident groups have great salience. Thus, in the period of the survey, a person might not think of himself crudely as a "Radical," but rather as a *Mendesiste* or an *anti-Mendesiste;* or again, was not a Socialist, but rather an adherent of the P.S.A., or a more orthodox Socialist, etc. Where faction attitudes toward De Gaulle are concerned, it obviously would be crude indeed to associate these people with their gross traditional parties. Therefore, the judges ranked small factions as well as gross, traditional party-objects, so that various dissidents could be properly located in the spectrum of attitudes.

Another obvious advantage is the fact that when case numbers are too few to support necessary statistics for a small party grouping, its numbers can be filled out by collapsing the ordering of parties to fewer categories, still respecting the important distinctions between parties on attitudes toward De Gaulle.

---

with some broad *tendance,* such as *centre-droite;* or (3) who refused to reveal their party attachment. Respondents reporting an identification with a tendance show a variation in attitude toward De Gaulle as one moves from left to right which has the same form as the party adherents. Respondents who refused to indicate their party show a mean attitude toward De Gaulle as one moves from left to right which has the same form as the party adherents. Respondents who refused to indicate their party show a mean attitude toward De Gaulle which is less favorable than the 1956 Poujadists. It is undoubtedly true that this group contains a disproportionate number of the covert Communists known to exist in the sample.

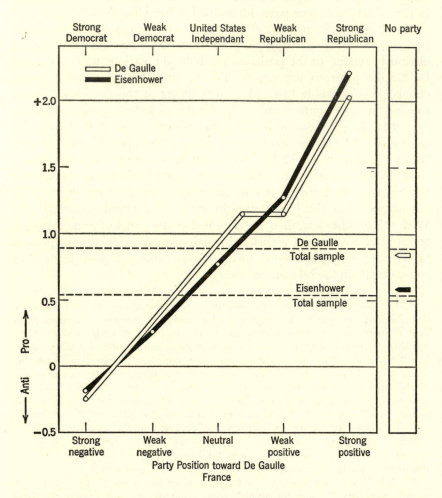

Figure 15-5. Respondent attitude toward De Gaulle/Eisenhower as a function of party choice. The data points show the mean attitude toward De Gaulle or Eisenhower for the party grouping indicated. In the case of data from both countries, attitude means have been normalized by use of standard deviations as in Figure 15-4. Party grouping is determined in both cases by reports of party attachment made prior to the respective national elections (for the United States, early fall of 1956; for France, the early fall of 1958). A comparable slope computed for Eisenhower in 1952 differs only negligibly from that of 1956. The groups labeled "No Party" are defined in Figure 15-4 for France, and comparably for the United States.

The two slopes lie in such striking proximity that it is important to review briefly the decisions made concerning the location of data points in the plane. The form of data organization used for the Eisenhower slope follows that employed in Campbell et al., *The American Voter, op. cit.,* Chap. 19, considerably before the French study had been conceived. No changes whatever have been introduced in the

This array of parties allows us to study in "pure" form the relationship between the respondent's own attitude toward De Gaulle and the position of his chosen party. Furthermore, since it may be presumed that the Republican and Democratic Parties in the United States represent comparable positive and negative poles of party attitude toward Eisenhower, we can draw direct comparisons between the character of affect toward these victorious generals by party grouping in both systems (Figure 15-5). In both cases, party location is assigned not by

methods. The French data have been treated as carefully as possible to replicate these methods and, where the scoring of individual attitudes toward De Gaulle are concerned, no new decisions whatsoever were required. The only new decisions which had to be made concerned the correspondence establishd between the party arrays for the two countries. Since it had long been established that simple integer scoring of the five-step party identification continuum in the United States generated linear relationships with other relevant attitudes, this scoring was considered fixed. The French judges had been asked to array the French parties and factions on a continuum "de l'hostilité totale (−4) à la fidelité inconditionnelle (+4) (envers De Gaulle) pendant la période 1er sept.–23 nov. 1958." Implicit in the instructions, in the light of more detailed specifications for other dimensions, was the fact that +0 should be the midpoint of neutrality.

Thus, the United States array had traditionally been scored (−2, −1, 0, +1, +2), while the French scoring of the parties was on a continuum separated from the United States scoring only by the most obvious of linear transformations, the doubling of the U.S. scores. The implications of this correspondence for the cutting points to be established on the French continuum, in order to match the U.S. continuum, left no room for arbitrary decision.

Beyond this point, only one problem remained. The mechanical application of cutting points had produced an awkward distribution of individual cases for the five French categories. Only three respondents fell in the "weak negative" interval. Obviously, these would have to be combined with the strong negative group (or ignored—the difference in the slope attributable to the handling of these three cases would be negligible indeed), and the location of the strong negative group shifted slightly to the right along the continuum to represent their incorporation. Secondly, while the weight of the cases within each interval usually centered around the midpoint of the interval, as it should do if the data point is to be located at the midpoint of the interval, this condition was dramatically violated in the case of the "neutral" category in the center. Here, the cases to be included were those respondents identifying with parties rated by the judges in the range −1 to +1. However, only one tiny splinter, represented by another trio of cases, turned out empirically to have been located to the negative side of zero. Furthermore, the heavy weight of cases—flowing largely from the Radical-Socialists—lay just short of the +1 cutting point. Hence location of this data point at 0, rather than at the empirical mean of the cases in the interval (+.87) seemed inadvisable. Quite generally, therefore, the French data point has been located within its interval not at the midpoint of the interval, but at the empirical mean of the scores allotted the cases falling in the interval. Actually, this decision does not greatly affect the sense of "fit" between the two slopes, as simple inspection will show. In any event, it seems by far the most logical disposition of the problem, quite aside from the character of these data.

ultimate vote in the election, but by party attachment as reported in the weeks before the respective elections (for France the legislative elections in November; for the United States the 1956 presidential election).

We see that the salient features of the Eisenhower phenomenon in the United States are very remarkably duplicated in France for De Gaulle. In the first place, the slope of the two lines starts to suggest a comparable linkage between partisanship and reaction to the leaders in the two countries. More important still is the displacement of the two slopes to the positive side of the point of neutrality in personal attitude toward the leaders. In France we see that it takes a strongly negative party position toward De Gaulle before the balance of adherent opinion moves at all to the negative side of the neutral point; and where party position is relatively neutral, adherent attitudes are already strongly positive.

Another important point of comparison lies in the distance between the two horizontal dotted lines in Figure 15-5. It has constantly been apparent earlier in this discussion that although the Eisenhower image was strongly positive in 1952 and 1956, it was not as unconditionally positive as the French view of De Gaulle in 1958. References to Eisenhower in both years ran between two- and three-to-one favorable. References to De Gaulle in 1958 exceeded a four-to-one positive ratio. The distance between the dotted lines in Figure 15-5, although calculated for net individual reactions rather than for total references, captures this difference in the response of the two publics. It is of great interest to see, then, that when party position is controlled this difference vanishes, and the two slopes nearly coincide. The net positive Eisenhower response is lower because the majority of the American respondents fall in the Democratic space at the *left* of the figure. The net De Gaulle response is higher because the bulk of the large parties fall to the *right* or positive side of the neutral point. Therefore the figure suggests some of the price in popularity which Eisenhower paid in aligning himself with a political minority.

It is apparent that the party array employed in Figure 15-5 has some conceptual differences for the two countries. Discrimination along the American continuum is achieved by measuring the strength of identification with the two polar parties. We would naturally expect such differences in identifications to be operating in France and to produce conceptually analogous results within party groups, even though such distinctions are not taken into account in Figure 15-5. That is, we would expect strong adherents of parties reacting negatively to De Gaulle to be more strongly negative in their personal reactions to the

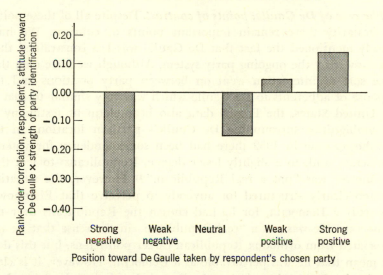

Rank-order correlation, respondent's attitude toward De Gaulle × strength of party identification

Position toward De Gaulle taken by respondent's chosen party

Figure 15-6. Relationship between respondent's attitude toward De Gaulle, and his strength of party identification, as a function of his chosen party's position toward De Gaulle. The message of this figure is perhaps simpler than appears. In brief, strong adherents to parties which had taken negative positions toward De Gaulle were more negative in their personal attitudes toward De Gaulle than were weaker adherents of the same parties. On the other hand, strong adherents of parties which had taken strongly positive positions toward De Gaulle were more positive in their personal attitudes toward De Gaulle than were weaker adherents of the same parties. Therefore, strength of party identification is positively related to agreement with the chosen party's position on the leader, as in the United States (Figure 15-5). The grouping of party adherents, as well as the rough spacing of the bars along the horizontal line, follows the rationale described for Figure 15-5. Strength of party identification is measured by items tapping the respondent's determination to vote for his party despite drawbacks such as a poor candidate, feeble chance of party success, and the like.

general than weaker adherents of the same parties. Or, on the other hand, we would expect strong adherents of parties reacting positively to De Gaulle to be more strongly positive in their personal reactions than weaker adherents of such parties. Figure 15-6 serves to confirm these simple expectations, thereby completing the survey of correspondences between the two bodies of data.[16]

[16] The gradient of correlations represented by the bars in Figure 15-6 confirms the basic prediction. However, the reader will note that the gradient "crosses" the zero point to the positive side of the neutral position, and the correlation for adherents of strong positive parties departs less far from zero than the correlation for strong negative parties. This lack of symmetry was not unexpected, although

The case of De Gaulle: points of contrast. Despite all of these points of similarity there remain important points of contrast. We have already mentioned the fact that De Gaulle was less constrained than Eisenhower by the ongoing party system. Although we have seen that some sort of interaction went on between party positions and the response of adherents to De Gaulle which was very similar to that in the United States, the French data also bear eloquent testimony to the ambiguities surrounding De Gaulle's partisan location. In the Eisenhower case in 1952 there had been some tendency for voters— Democrats, and, to a slightly lesser degree, Republicans—to feel that Eisenhower was "not a real Republican." [17] However, the situation was too clearly structured for anybody to perceive that Eisenhower was truly a Democrat, for he had chosen the Republicans over the Democrats. He was not a "real Republican" in the sense that he was dissociated from orthodox Republican career politicians, but this does not mean that he was perceivable as a Democrat. However, it is clear that in the few weeks prior to the French legislative elections, there was substantial public confusion as to the party representing views closest to those of General De Gaulle (Table 15-8). This ambiguity was very sharply diminished in the period of time in which the two election *tours* were held, with public perception that the U.N.R. was the party closest to De Gaulle taking much clearer shape. But on the eve of the first tour it appears that more than half of the electorate was unable to locate De Gaulle at all, and among those who tried, there was no astonishing consensus.

Perceptual relocation of De Gaulle himself. Locations of De Gaulle relative to the party system made before the first tour by different partisan groups in the population provide a case study in all the mechanisms of perceptual distortion which arise when external conditions are sufficiently ambiguous. First, it may be observed that persons with no partisan attachment themselves found it most difficult to specify a party close to De Gaulle, and among that quarter who tried, the

---

the reasons are somewhat subtle. It will become clear later in the discussion that a general process was operative in this period whereby strong admirers of De Gaulle were drifting toward parties positively disposed to the general, either from prior locations in parties less warmly disposed, or from positions of no prior attachment. Therefore, these people represented by definition individuals of weak party attachments but strong positive reactions to De Gaulle, and, in piling up at the right end of the continuum, tend to attenuate the relationships between party position and strength of party identification on that side.

[17] A. Campbell, G. Gurin, and W. E. Miller, *The Voter Decides,* Evanston, Ill.: Row, Peterson, 1954, pp. 63–64.

TABLE 15-8

**Party Perceived Closest to De Gaulle Before and After the
Legislative Elections, 1958**

"A votre avis, quel est le parti dont les objectifs correspondent le mieux à ceux
du général de Gaulle?"

	Before the First Tour (Nov. 3–22)	After the Second Tour (Dec. 15–31)
Do not know	51%	28%
All parties	3	1
No parties	4	3
The right	7	3
The center	3	1
The Indépendants	3	1
The U.N.R., R.P.F., A.R.S., or simply "Gaullists"	14	57
The M.R.P.	4	2
The Socialists	6	3
Other parties	5	1
	100%	100%

guesses show an unusual dispersion (Table 15-9). Partisans who were most likely to have a perception were the adherents of the two party groups whose positions were most polarized (Gaullists and Communists). For adherents of parties whose positions lay more in the middle ground there were vaguer responses, along with a strong tendency for partisans of several stripes to lay claim to De Gaulle as their own. Among respondents of any specifiable partisanship at all 91 per cent of the responses linking the Socialist Party to De Gaulle were made by Socialists, 59 per cent of the responses linking the M.R.P. to De Gaulle were made by adherents of the M.R.P., and 62 per cent of all responses linking the Indépendants with De Gaulle were made by people identified with this party group. Furthermore, it is apparent that the tendency to locate De Gaulle perceptually in one's own party or in some opposing party is a simple function of personal reactions to De Gaulle, as we see in the Socialist case (Table 15-10).

TABLE 15-9

Perceptions of the Party Closest to De Gaulle, by Own Partisan Attachment

	P.C.F.	S.F.I.O.	Rad.	M.R.P.	U.N.R., Gaull- iste	Indé- pend- ant	No Party Attach- ment
No specific perception (all parties, no parties, don't know which parties)	36%	45%	52%	42%	39%	56%	73%
Right	30	4	5	8	4	3	6
Center	8	2				3	1
Indépendants	2	1	5	1	1	12	2
U.N.R., Gaulliste, etc.	8	8	16	19	47	20	10
M.R.P.	4	1	5	26	4	3	3
Socialist	6	35	3		1		1
Other parties	6	4	14	4	4	3	4
	100%	100%	100%	100%	100%	100%	100%

This ambiguity is apparent in the attenuation of the relationship between voters' attitudes toward De Gaulle and the positive or negative reactions to De Gaulle on the part of their respective parties. Among those respondents whose perceptions were "accurate," in that they judged the Gaullist groups to be closest to De Gaulle's objectives, a correlation coefficient for this relationship is .55. Among pople who saw no party (or "all parties") as being closest to De Gaulle, a comparable coefficient is .33. Among those partisans of non-Gaullist groups who claimed that their own party was closest to De Gaulle, there is no significant correlation at all between own party's position toward the General and individual attitudes toward him.[18] It should be noted that the fact there is a moderate correlation for people who did not

[18] Unfortunately, these coefficients cannot be made comparable to the American data, due to the strong departure from normality of the distribution of cases on the "natural" French continuum forming the abscissa of Figure 15-5. This poses no problems for the simple entry of means, but makes correlation comparisons impossible. The correlation coefficients cited here are based on a collapsing of this distribution to approximate a normal distribution, and are internally comparable.

TABLE 15-10

Socialist Perception of Party Closest to De Gaulle, by Personal Attitude toward De Gaulle

Attitude toward De Gaulle	Parties Located Closest to De Gaulle		
	Those Right of Center	"All," "None," or "Don't Know"	Socialists
Positive +++	0%	3%	21%
++	13	26	25
+	52	29	33
Neutral 0	20	36	21
Negative −	13	6	0
	100%	100%	100%
Number of cases	15	31	24

attempt to cite any specific party as closest to De Gaulle reflects a more generalized location perceived for the General toward the right, with the responses simply denying any specific party links.

All of these data converge to underscore the degree to which De Gaulle as a political figure was focal during this period. Apparently a sense of dissonance between one's own attitudes toward De Gaulle, whether warm or cool, and the position of De Gaulle relative to one's chosen party was a matter of some psychological discomfort. Where such dissonance was experienced, steps were taken to reduce it. Logically, there were three possible means of accomplishing this. First, where De Gaulle's own party location was sufficiently ambiguous the individual could perceptually "move" the General into a party location less dissonant, as we have seen above. Such a process would have two rather differing political effects. In any personal plebiscite, or referendum perceived as such, the voter could support or repudiate the General directly as he saw fit with no sense of conflict with his partisanship. On the other hand, such distorted perceptions in a normal legislative election would have the effect of conserving the existing partisan divisions, for the individual could continue to vote for his normal party while feeling that he was responding appropriately to the General who was then dominating the political scene.

The second and third steps which the individual might take to remedy the felt discrepancies would be to change party to one in more appropriate relationship to the General; or to change one's personal attitude toward the General to fit the attitudes of own party. As we have suggested, in the American case the party location of the General was too ambiguous for much perceptual distortion, so that change centered in the second and third types. While there was much change in attitudes toward Eisenhower to fit partisanship, there was also important *temporary* change in party (in vote, but not shift of basic loyalty) to fit attitudes toward Eisenhower.

Change in attitudes toward De Gaulle to fit own party. In addition to the strong trends toward perceptual relocation of De Gaulle himself, it appears that the second and third types of change were occurring frequently in France during this period as well.

First, prior partisanship apparently biased 1958 attitudes toward De Gaulle in the same sense that it did for Eisenhower attitudes in 1952; reactions were turned on a partisan axis, but the center of gravity of popular opinions were more positive than party positions. It is doubtful, for example, that much of the choice of parties which voters made in 1956 was in any reasonable sense "caused" by prior attitudes toward De Gaulle; yet, as Figure 15-4 suggests, there was a substantial correlation (r of .24) between the partisanship of votes cast two years earlier and the reactions to De Gaulle voiced by the public in 1958.

Change in party to fit attitudes toward De Gaulle. Figure 15-4 also suggests that there was a somewhat stronger correlation (r of .33) between 1958 partisanship and attitudes toward De Gaulle in the fall of 1958. In other words, there were changes in partisanship between the 1956 vote and the pre-election 1958 statements of party attachment, and these changes were acting strongly to bring the individual to parties more appropriate to his attitudes toward De Gaulle. The only real doubt left by the data has to do with the transience or permanence of partisan change when it occurred.

This partisan change to accommodate prior attitudes toward De Gaulle can be most clearly illustrated with reference to the Communists (Table 15-11). Although cases are very few, the patterns are sharp and repeat themselves between two different time intervals. It seems clear that the diminution of Communist strength at the polls in 1958 reflected in no small part the departure of former sympathizers who happened to feel warmly toward De Gaulle. Naturally, the clarity of the Communist position on De Gaulle made it particularly difficult to misconstrue and was sufficiently extreme to create discomfort for adherents who liked De Gaulle. We can ask, however, the more general

TABLE 15-11

Relation of Partisan Shifts from Communist Party toward Parties More
Warmly Disposed to De Gaulle to Personal Attitudes toward De Gaulle

	1956 Communist Voters Who, in 1958 Pre-election Statement of Party Attachment . . .		Pre-election 1958 Communist Identifiers Who, by Post-election Report of 1958 First Tour Vote . . .	
	Remained Communist	Shifted to Party More Favorable to De Gaulle	Remained Communist	Shifted to Party More Favorable to De Gaulle
Net Affect toward De Gaulle:				
Positive ++	5%	30%	0%	40%
+	14	60	7	20
Neutral 0	39	10	48	0
−	33	0	33	20
Negative − −	9	0	12	20
	100%	100%	100%	100%
Number of cases	43	10	27	5

question as to whether other of the many signs of party shifting observed over three waves of the sample in 1958 similarly followed lines of personal attitude toward De Gaulle.

For each point in time—1956 vote, 1958 pre-election party attachment, and 1958 vote—we have split the ordering of parties as to position on De Gaulle as finely as cases will sustain. For the two time intervals we have taken all partisans whose parties at the beginning of the interval were of a particular disposition toward De Gaulle and subdivided them according to whether they shifted toward a party more warmly disposed to De Gaulle than the party of origin, less warmly disposed, or remained at the same position (in the case of the extremely positive and negative groups, of course, only one direction of departure is possible, as in Table 15-11). We then have noted the degree of correlation between party shift and personal balance of attitudes toward De Gaulle. That is, a correlation for a particular range of the party continuum is positive if people who shifted out of the range toward parties more favorable to De Gaulle had more positive attitudes toward the General than did people who remained; and also if people shifting out of the range toward parties less favorable to the General had personal attitudes less favorable to him than did those who failed to change parties. A set of positive correlations, then, would help to document the proposition that party shifting which went on in this period followed lines of personal reaction to De Gaulle.

Although case numbers are few enough that *individual* correlations should not be taken too literally, the total pattern in Table 15-12 leaves little room for dispute. Nine of the twelve comparisons afforded showed positive correlations of .10 or better; only two slip barely into a negative range. The table has interest from several points of view. First, it seems to show higher coefficients at both extremes, with reduced coefficients in the middle. It is likely that the greater ambiguity of positions taken toward De Gaulle by parties in the middle range,

TABLE 15-12 *

Relation of Partisan Change to Personal Attitudes toward De Gaulle

| | | Position Taken toward De Gaulle of Party Chosen at t_1 | | | | | |
| | | Negative | | | | | Positive |
t_1————————→t_2		$--$	$-$	0	$+$	$++$	$+++$
1956 vote	1958 pre-election party attachment	.59 (53)	−.03 (61)	−.01 (71)	.20 (123)	.10 (67)	.36 (9)
1958 pre-election party attachment	1958 1st tour vote	.20 (32)	.15 (48)	.13 (48)	.03 (80)	.15 (45)	.20 (17)

* The cell entry in each case is a rank-order correlation between personal attitudes toward De Gaulle and the direction of departure on the continuum of party positions toward De Gaulle. Number of cases involved in each comparison are indicated in parentheses. It should be noted that not all party shifting contributes to this table, since if a person shifted between two parties who were ranked as having the same position toward De Gaulle, the move would not be recorded. These cases are, however, rare.

already noted in connection with Table 15-9, results in partisan shifts in this range which follow less clearly the structure supposed by the organization of the data.

Second, the implications of the second row of the table must be emphasized. In this case there can be no doubt that attitudes toward De Gaulle were an antecedent factor, for these attitudes were measured in the pre-election period, and it was only after this time that the individuals involved decided to change their party choice, at least for purposes of the 1958 legislative vote, to groups whose positions on De Gaulle corresponded more closely with their own feelings toward the General. Finally, the table is useful in revealing a flow to partisan change in this period which was only partially evident in the vote returns. That is, the tremendous success of the U.N.R. in the 1958 election gave immediate proof of the groundswell of popular support for De Gaulle himself. But it is also true that many other shifts were occurring which did not involve the U.N.R.[19] The data indicate that these shifts, no less than those directly to the U.N.R., were often motivated and foreshadowed by personal reactions to De Gaulle, occasionally negative reactions as well as the flood of positive responses.

One of the most interesting patterns of change not entirely involving the U.N.R. is that which surrounded the Socialists and the Radicals. Changes in vote totals between 1956 and 1958 showed that the Socialist Party maintained its own, while the Radicals suffered mortal losses. It was easy to suppose that a large mass of former supporters of the Radicals moved directly to the U.N.R., while the Socialists, having taken a position more strongly favorable to De Gaulle, forestalled losses of this sort. Neither opinion is entirely accurate, if the fragmentary data supplied by limited cases in the survey samples may be trusted. There was a rather broad dispersion of former Radical supporters, and a substantial group of erstwhile Radicals did indeed move directly to the U.N.R. But a stream of equal importance moved instead toward the Socialists, who failed to gain support on balance because numerous of their own adherents were shifting onward toward the U.N.R.

In this interchange it seems likely that perceptions of the relationship of De Gaulle to the party system were crucial. We have already seen that it was far easier to perceive the Socialists as close to De Gaulle

[19] See Dupeux, *op. cit.*, p. 146, or A. Girard and J. Stoetzel, "Le Comportement Electoral et le Mécanisme de la Décision," *Le Referendum de Septembre et les Elections de Novembre, 1958,* Cahiers de la Fondation Nationale de Sciences Politiques, Paris: A. Colin, 1960, p. 180.

than it was to perceive the Radicals in this position, even though these locations fly in the face of the traditional left-right ordering. Our data give intriguing hints as to some of the problems which were created by this disruption of normal left-right relations. In brief, early attitudes toward De Gaulle seem to have coalesced to conform to left-right expectations, and later adjustments had to occur to take account of the fact that the Socialists had broken more strongly for De Gaulle than their left-right position seemed to warrant. Thus, for example, partisans arrayed according to 1956 vote in Figure 15-4 show the Radical supporters more pro-De Gaulle than the Socialists. However, the gap is narrowed where party is measured by party attachment reported before the election in 1958. The drain on Radical ranks had already started, drawing off former supporters more favorable to De Gaulle, and the losses and gains of support by the Socialists was showing a net increase in De Gaulle enthusiasm. This evolution continues in the later stages of the interviewing, so that after the election the Socialist supporters actually show a warmer response to De Gaulle than the core of remaining Radicals.[20] Thus an initial correlation between the left-right ordering and personal attitudes toward De Gaulle was slowly being modified throughout this period away from the left-right ordering and toward the new ordering of parties in positions toward De Gaulle.

All of these processes are analogous to the tides which swept Democrats to cast Republican votes in the United States when Eisenhower headed the ticket. While we have dealt here primarily with the half of the French electorate which related itself most closely to the party system, Girard and Stoetzel have heavily documented the fact that less politically involved voters (and this includes heavily the voters missing from our analysis as having "no party attachment") were even more susceptible to the Gaullist tide.[21] Evidence from the United States shows an analogous increase in susceptibility to party shifts toward Eisenhower among the less involved.[22]

[20] It might be noted that the bend in the middle point of the slope referring to De Gaulle in Figure 15-5 springs directly from the temporary warring of the normal left-right expectations with the new ordering produced by party positions on De Gaulle. The middle point, which departs to the high side, contains the Radicals who are more favorable to De Gaulle than the party positions would warrant; while the next point to the right includes the Socialists, who are slightly less favorable than might be expected. The process discussed above had the effect, at a later stage, of ironing out this irregularity.

[21] Girard and Stoetzel, *loc. cit.*

[22] Campbell et al., *op. cit.*, pp. 111 and 264.

Finally, American data have been striking in their indication that the Eisenhower tide had had no lasting effect on partisan loyalties. It would be interesting, by way of conclusion, if we might determine whether the De Gaulle tide is of similar transience. We suspect that it is, but we must wait for any definitive evidence. However, the 1958 survey does provide one suggestive fragment of information.

After the two tours of the legislative election voters were asked once again not only how they voted but also what party attachment they felt. Now the second question as to party attachment was worded in a way to discourage responses as to long-term, underlying loyalties and to encourage the transitory current feelings about the parties, which would naturally reflect more closely than we would like the vote just cast.[23] However, if we consider the correlations of party shift and personal attitude toward De Gaulle in the format of the time comparisons of Table 15-12 where t_1 is the pre-election statement of party attachment and t_2 is now the post-election statement, we find our first visible negative correlations:

Position toward De Gaulle of Party Chosen
before the Election

$--$	$-$	0	$+$	$++$	$+++$
.57	.14	.04	.15	−.07	−.17
(13)	(26)	(22)	(36)	(20)	(7)

While it must be emphasized that case numbers here are painfully small, the emergence of negative correlations at the right end of the continuum hints at the recession of the De Gaulle tide. It can be argued that people so strongly attracted to De Gaulle that they had already shifted to a more Gaullist party before the elections, were, by the time of the post-election interviews, starting to drift back toward their more normal positions in less Gaullist parties. Of course, this evidence is comprised of the weakest of fragments, and the case will not become clear until future surveys. However, if the De Gaulle case continues to parallel the Eisenhower case, we would have to expect such developments.

[23] The question posed after the election was "Quel est *maintenant* le parti ou tendance dont vous vous sentez le plus proche?" [italics ours]. It is the "maintenant" which gives the question a much more current cast than comparable post-election items on party identification asked in the United States, which showed Democrats having just voted for Eisenhower still considering themselves "in general" Democrats.

The post-election "recession of the De Gaulle tide" should not be construed in any way to mean that the public was necessarily disillusioned with De Gaulle himself. American Democrats who defected to vote for Eisenhower in 1952 and then returned to their normal voting habits were as eager to vote for him again and did so at the first opportunity. What we mean rather is that voters—even those deeply impressed by De Gaulle— may return to more normal partisan patterns when De Gaulle himself is not the key electoral figure. Therefore, if this premise were correct, De Gaulle might leave no more personal imprint on French partisanship than did Eisenhower in the United States.

Conclusion

This discussion has attempted to assess some aspects of the electoral response to the prominent general. Whether this response occurs in the setting of a referendum or a competitive election, it seems to show many common traits. By and large, the transfer of military prominence to civil popularity is readily made; although there is evidence of cultural values against a military man at the top of civil government, in the concrete case the majority of electors make little distinction between the two spheres. The military hero is not revered specifically for his military contribution to the society, nor is he praised for his personal military virtues. He is rather seen as a man of integrity and sincerity. The vagueness of his policy aims are for some few disconcerting; for the vast majority, if it matters at all, it is as much an asset as a liability; he is thereby "above politics."

The victorious general has an appeal which largely transcends social boundaries; he is truly a "national hero." To the degree that socially patterned differences in response can be observed at all, they tend to be between enthusiastic approval and tempered approval rather than between approval and disapproval. The most effective instrument for the creation of disapproval is the political party. But the political party can mold a segment of the population which is on balance negative toward the military figure only among its strong adherents, only with the effort of a determined and unequivocal negative position and at the price of at least a temporary loss in electoral strength. The strategy often followed by the general of avoiding or minimizing party commitment is very fruitful for him. But where such strategy is impossible, the victorious general alone among political aspirants appears to have the potential of maximizing the electoral strength of his own party to its very limit while achieving some inroads among parties unequivocally opposed to him and large inroads among parties who hesitate. Party elites opposed in principle to the ascendancy in civil politics of a military hero may well act more efficaciously at the elite levels to discourage the emergence of the military figure in political circles. Once he has emerged before the public in a candidate or quasi-candidate role, the situation passes beyond what is, for the parties, the realm of the manipulable.

IV

Institutional Analysis

That behavioral research has nothing to offer the study of institutions was said so often of the early survey studies of political behavior that it came to be generally believed. However, the idea owed much of its currency to the fact that interview research on politics had been used first to study electorates. Since the voter is far removed from most arms of the state and plays a political role that is at best a simple one, it was easy to think of the new research as cut off from the study of institutions.

This doctrine of separation has steadily weakened, however, as behavioral research has broadened its scope. Even the description of voting has aided the understanding of certain political institutions, and electoral research, once it had lifted itself from a total immersion in problems of individual decision-making, began to consider the place of voting in a wider institutional framework. In particular, it took up the questions of how the party system influences electoral behavior and of how such behavior sustains or modifies the party system itself.

As we have just seen, the entry of research on public opinion and voting into comparative studies has further sensitized it to institutional factors. No one was likely to examine political attitudes in two or more nations at once without paying the closest attention to the institutional settings in which electorates act. Since the legal arrangements of voting vary mainly between nations, comparative studies could disclose the impact of electoral law on mass behavior. Likewise, cross-national comparisons could overcome the absence of variation within a single country in the study of voting under two-party and multi-party systems.

Yet it was the extension of interview surveys to other political actors than the voter that did most to remove doubts as to their institutional relevance. When the legislator, for example, became the object of these studies, their value to the analysis of institutions was convincingly apparent. Reporting their four-state legislative survey, an innovative study of this kind, John Wahlke, Heinz Eulau, William Buchanan, and Leroy Ferguson observe that:

The attempt to study institutions by looking primarily at behavior will seem paradoxical to anyone accustomed to think of "institutional" and "behavioral" approaches to the study of government as fundamentally antithetical to each other. But a major methodological theme of this book is that the two are, in fact, interdependent. . . .[1]

Only the most hardened skeptic could finish their remarkable book and not agree.

A last development that has harnessed the behavioral survey for institutional analysis has been the appearance of complex survey designs involving two or more populations whose members play related roles within the structure of some political institution. Once again, the legislative arena affords a principal example. In all western nations the representation of mass publics in legislative bodies is a critical means of legitimizing political authority. This institutional relationship involves two classes of actors, constituents and representatives, each of whom has authority to take a given type of decision. By assembling comparable information on the attitudes, motives, and perceptions of legislators and those they represent, the interview survey has brought under empirical examination an institutional problem that has been a familiar topic of speculative theory.

As survey studies strive for a complexity adequate to the institutions they explore, they inevitably draw on data other than those produced by interviews. The interview may produce data that can be had in no other way, yet it does not by any means displace the data sources that other types of institutional analysis have used. This sort of amalgam may be seen in the chapters of this book. The integration of interview data with records of roll-call votes in the Congress and a variety of classical economic, demographic, and political characteristics of constituencies, for example, has made possible new approaches to the study of legislative representation.

The advantages to be gained from unified designs of this sort are especially promising in studies of the communication networks that are intrinsic to all political institutions. The interview—or even the

---

[1] J. C. Wahlke, H. Eulau, W. Buchanan, and L. C. Ferguson, *The Legislative System: Explorations in Legislative Behavior*, New York: John Wiley and Sons, 1962, p. 4.

questionnaire—may be an exceedingly useful means of disclosing the frequency, direction, and content of messages in such networks, and it may be the indispensible means of discovering perceptual and motivational factors that influence the encoding, transmission, and reception of messages. But the investigator may want other data as well, including records of contact between political actors and the content of messages. Such a medley of information has been used most successfully in studies of political power and decision-making in the local community but there is not any significant type of institutional interaction in politics that could not be susceptible to this approach. Survey projects whose design matches the intricacy of institutional struture and incorporates as appropriate a variety of other data hold obvious promise for the study of political institutions.

CHAPTER 16

Constituency Influence in Congress

Warren E. Miller and Donald E. Stokes

Substantial constituency influence over the lower house of Congress is commonly thought to be both a normative principle and a factual truth of American government. From their draft constitution we may assume the Founding Fathers expected it, and many political scientists feel, regretfully, that the Framers' wish has come all too true.[1] Nevertheless, much of the evidence of constituency control rests on inference. The fact that our House of Representatives, especially by comparison with the House of Commons, has irregular party voting does not of itself indicate that Congressmen deviate from party in response to local pressure. And even more, the fact that many Congressmen *feel* pressure from home does not of itself establish that the local constituency is performing any of the acts that a reasonable definition of control would imply.

[1] To be sure, the work of the Federal Convention has been supplemented in two critical respects. The first of these is the practice, virtually universal since the mid-19th Century, of choosing Representatives from single-member districts of limited geographic area. The second is the practice, which in our own century has also become virtually universal, of selecting party nominees for the House by direct primary election.

This chapter appeared originally in the *American Political Science Review,* 57 (March 1963).

Constituency Control in the Normative Theory of Representation

Control by the local constituency is at one pole of *both* the great normative controversies about representation that have arisen in modern times. It is generally recognized that constituency control is opposite to the conception of representation associated with Edmund Burke. Burke wanted the representative to serve the constituency's *interest* but not its *will,* and the extent to which the representative should be compelled by electoral sanctions to follow the "mandate" of his constituents has been at the heart of the ensuing controversy as it has continued for a century and a half.[2]

Constituency control also is opposite to the conception of government by responsible national parties. This is widely seen, yet the point is rarely connected with normative discussions of representation. Indeed, it is remarkable how little attention has been given to the model of representation implicit in the doctrine of a "responsible two-party system." When the subject of representation is broached among political scientists the classical argument between Burke and his opponents is likely to come at once to mind. So great is Burke's influence that the antithesis he proposed still provides the categories of thought used in contemporary treatments of representation despite the fact that many students of politics today would advocate a relationship between representative and constituency that fits *neither* position of the mandate-independence controversy.

The conception of representation implicit in the doctrine of responsible parties shares the idea of popular control with the instructed-delegate model. Both are versions of popular sovereignty. But "the people" of the responsible two-party system are conceived in terms of a national rather than a local constituency. Candidates for legislative office appeal to the electorate in terms of a *national* party program and leadership, to which, if elected, they will be committed. Expressions of policy preference by the local district are reduced to endorsements of one or another of these programs, and the local

---

[2] In the language of Eulau, Wahlke, et al., we speak here of the "style," not the "focus," of representation. See their "The Role of the Representative: Some Empirical Observations on the Theory of Edmund Burke," *American Political Science Review,* 53, 742–756 (September 1959). An excellent review of the mandate-independence controversy is given by H. F. Pitkin, "The Theory of Representation" (unpublished doctoral dissertation, University of California, Berkeley, 1961). For other contemporary discussions of representation, see A. de Grazia, *Public and Republic* (New York, 1951), and J. A. Fairlie, "The Nature of Political Representation," *American Political Science Review,* 34, 236–48, 456–66 (April–June 1940).

district retains only the arithmetical significance that whichever party can rally to its program the greater number of supporters in the district will control its legislative seat.

No one tradition of representation has entirely dominated American practice. Elements of the Burkean, instructed-delegate, and responsible party models can all be found in our political life. Yet if the American system has elements of all three, a good deal depends on how they are combined. Especially critical is the question whether different models of representation apply to different public issues. Is the saliency of legislative action to the public so different in quality and degree on different issues that the legislator is subject to very different constraints from his constituency? Does the legislator have a single generalized mode of response to his constituency that is rooted in a normative belief about the representative's role or does the same legislator respond to his constituency differently on different issues? More evidence is needed on matters so fundamental to our system.

An Empirical Study of Representation

We have described briefly in Chapter 11 the design of the study in which the Survey Research Center interviewed the incumbent Congressman, his nonincumbent opponent (if any), and a sample of constituents in each of 116 congressional districts, which were themselves a probability sample of all districts.[3] These interviews, con-

[3] It will be apparent in the discussion that follows that we have estimated characteristics of whole constituencies from our samples of constituents living in particular districts. In view of the fact that a sample of less than two thousand constituents has been divided among 116 districts, the reader may wonder about the reliability of these estimates. After considerable investigation we have concluded that their sampling error is not so severe a problem for the analysis as we had thought it would be. Several comments may indicate why it is not.

To begin with, the weighting of our sample of districts has increased the reliability of the constituency estimates. The correct theoretical weight to be assigned each district in the analysis is the inverse of the probability of the district's selection, and it can be shown that this weight is approximately proportional to the number of interviews taken in the district. The result of this is that the greatest weight is assigned the districts with the largest number of interviews and, hence, the most reliable constituency estimates. Indeed, these weights increase by half again the (weighted) mean number of interviews taken per district. To put the matter another way: the introduction of differential weights trades some of our sample of congressional districts for more reliable constituency estimates.

How much of a problem the unreliability of these estimates is depends very much on the analytic uses to which the estimates are put. If our goal were case analyses of particular districts, the constituency samples would have to be much larger. Inducted immediately after the congressional election of 1958, explored a wide range of attitudes and perceptions held by the individuals who play the reciprocal roles of the representative relation in national government. The distinguishing feature of this research is, of course, that it sought direct information from both constituent and legislator (actual and aspiring). To this fund of comparative interview data has been added information about the roll-call votes of our sample of Congressmen and the political and social characteristics of the districts they represent.

Many students of politics, with excellent reason, have been sensitive to possible ties between Representative and constituent that have little to do with issues of public policy. For example, ethnic identifications may cement a legislator in the affections of his district, whatever (within limits) his stands on issues. And many Congressmen keep their tenure of office secure by skillful provision of district benefits ranging from free literature to major federal projects. In the full study of which this analysis is part we have explored several bases of constituency support that have little to do with policy issues. Nevertheless, the question of how the representative should make up his mind on legislative issues is what the classical arguments over representation are all about, and we have given a central place to a comparison of the policy preferences of constituents and Representatives and to a causal analysis of the relation between the two.

In view of the electorate's scanty information about government it was not at all clear in advance that such a comparison could be made. Some of the more buoyant advocates of popular sovereignty have regarded the citizen as a kind of kibitzer who looks over the

---

deed, for most case analyses we would want several hundred interviews per district (at a cost, over 116 districts, of several small nuclear reactors). However, most of the findings reported here are based not on single districts but on many or all of the districts in our sample. For analyses of this sort the number of interviews per district can be much smaller.

Our investigation of the effect of the sampling variance of the constituency estimates is quite reassuring. When statistics computed from our constituency samples are compared with corresponding parameter values for the constituencies, the agreement of the two sets of figures is quite close. What is more, by adapting procedures which have arisen in psychological testing to adjust for attenuation of correlation due to the unreliability of measures (see, for example, H. Gulliksen, *Theory of Mental Tests,* New York: John Wiley and Sons, 1950, pp. 101–104) it is possible to restore the relationships between our constituency estimates and other variables to the values they could be expected to have had if the constituency measures had been based on complete censuses rather than on limited samples of constituents. The nature of this adjustment is described in detail in W. E. Miller and D. E. Stokes, *Representation in the American Congress* (Englewood Cliffs, N.J.: Prentice-Hall, in press).

shoulder of his Representative at the legislative game. Kibitzer and player may disagree as to which card should be played, but they were at least thought to share a common understanding of what the alternatives are.

No one familiar with the findings of research on mass electorates could accept this view of the citizen. Far from looking over the shoulder of their Congressmen at the legislative game, most Americans are almost totally uninformed about legislative issues in Washington. At best the average citizen may be said to have some general ideas about how the country should be run, which he is able to use in responding to particular questions about what the government ought to do. For example, survey studies have shown that most people have a general (though differing) conception of how far government should go to achieve social and economic welfare objectives and that these convictions fix their response to various particular questions about actions government might take.[4]

What makes it possible to compare the policy preferences of constituents and Representatives despite the public's low awareness of legislative affairs is the fact that Congressmen themselves respond to many issues in terms of fairly broad evaluative dimensions. Undoubtedly policy alternatives are judged in the executive agencies and the specialized committees of the Congress by criteria that are relatively complex and specific to the policies at issue. But a good deal of evidence goes to show that when proposals come before the House as a whole they are judged on the basis of more general evaluative dimensions.[5] For example, most Congressmen, too, seem to have a

[4] See A. Campbell, P. E. Converse, W. E. Miller, and D. E. Stokes, *The American Voter*, John Wiley and Sons, pp. 194–209.

[5] This conclusion, fully supported by our own work for later Congresses, is one of the main findings to be drawn from the work of D. MacRae on roll-call voting in the House of Representatives. See his *Dimensions of Congressional Voting: A Statistical Study of the House of Representatives in the Eighty-First Congress* (Berkeley and Los Angeles: University of California Press, 1958). For additional evidence of the existence of scale dimensions in legislative behavior, see N. L. Gage and B. Shimberg, "Measuring Senatorial Progressivism," *Journal of Abnormal and Social Psychology*, 44, 112–117 (January 1949); G. M. Belknap, "A Study of Senatorial Voting by Scale Analysis" (unpublished doctoral dissertation, University of Chicago, 1951), and "A Method for Analyzing Legislative Behavior," *Midwest Journal of Political Science*, 2, 377–402 (1958); two other articles by MacRae, "The Role of the State Legislator in Massachusetts," *American Sociological Review*, 19, 185–194 (April 1954), and "Roll Call Votes and Leadership," *Public Opinion Quarterly*, 20, 543–558 (1956); C. D. Farris, "A Method of Determining Ideological Groups in Congress," *Journal of Politics*, 20, 308–338 (1958); and L. N. Rieselbach, "Quantitative Techniques for Studying Voting Behavior in the U. N. General Assembly," *International Organization*, 14, 291–306 (1960).

general conception of how far government should go in the area of domestic social and economic welfare, and these general positions apparently orient their roll-call votes on a number of particular social welfare issues.

It follows that such a broad evaluative dimension can be used to compare the policy preferences of constituents and Representatives despite the low state of the public's information about politics. In this study three such dimensions have been drawn from our voter interviews and from congressional interviews and roll call records. As suggested above, one of these has to do with approval of government action in the social welfare field, the primary domestic issue of the New Deal-Fair Deal (and New Frontier) eras. A second dimension has to do with support for American involvement in foreign affairs, a latter-day version of the isolationist-internationalist continuum. A third dimension has to do with approval of federal action to protect the civil rights of Negroes.[6]

Because our research focused on these three dimensions, our analysis of constituency influence is limited to these areas of policy. No point has been more energetically or usefully made by those who have sought to clarify the concepts of power and influence than the necessity of specifying the acts *with respect to which* one actor has power or influence or control over another.[7] Therefore, the scope or range of influence for our analysis is the collection of legislative issues falling within our three policy domains. We are not able to say how much control the local constituency may or may not have over *all* actions of its Representative, and there may well be pork-barrel issues or other matters of peculiar relevance to the district on

[6] The content of the three issue domains may be suggested by some of the roll call and interview items used. In the area of social welfare these included the issues of public housing, public power, aid to education, and government's role in maintaining full employment. In the area of foreign involvement the items included the issues of foreign economic aid, military aid, sending troops abroad, and aid to neutrals. In the area of civil rights the items included the issues of school desegregation, fair employment, and the protection of Negro voting rights.

[7] Because this point has been so widely discussed it has inevitably attracted a variety of terms. Dahl denotes the acts of *a* whose performance *A* is able to influence as the *scope* of *A*'s power. See R. A. Dahl, "The Concept of Power," *Behavioral Science*, 2, 201–215 (July 1957). This usage is similar to that of H. D. Lasswell and Abraham Kaplan, *Power and Society* (New Haven: Yale University Press, 1950, pp. 71–73). D. Cartwright, however, denotes the behavioral or psychological changes in *P* which *O* is able to induce as the *range of O's* power: "A Field Theoretical Conception of Power," *Studies in Social Power* (Ann Arbor: Research Center for Group Dynamics, Institute for Social Research, The University of Michigan, 1959, pp. 183–220).

which the relation of Congressman to constituency is quite distinctive. However, few observers of contemporary politics would regard the issues of government provision of social and economic welfare, of American involvement in world affairs, and of federal action in behalf of the Negro as constituting a trivial range of action. Indeed, these domains together include most of the great issues that have come before Congress in recent years.

In each policy domain we have used the procedures of cumulative scaling, as developed by Louis Guttman and others, to order our samples of Congressmen, of opposing candidates, and of voters. In each domain Congressmen were ranked once according to their roll-call votes in the House and again according to the attitudes they revealed in our confidential interviews. These two orderings are by no means identical, nor are the discrepancies due simply to uncertainties of measurement.[8] Opposing candidates also were ranked in each policy domain according to the attitudes they revealed in our interviews. The nationwide sample of constituents was ordered in each domain, and by averaging the attitude scores of all constituents living in the same districts, whole constituencies were ranked on each dimension so that the views of Congressmen could be compared with those of their constituencies.[9] Finally, by considering only the constituents in each district who share some characteristic (voting for the

[8] That the Representative's roll-call votes can diverge from his true opinion is borne out by a number of findings of the study (some of which are reported here) as to the conditions under which agreement between the Congressman's roll call position and his private attitude will be high or low. However, a direct confirmation that these two sets of measurements are not simply getting at the same thing is given by differences in attitude-roll call agreement according to the Congressman's sense of how well his roll call votes have expressed his real views. In the domain of foreign involvement, for example, the correlation of our attitudinal and roll call measurements was .75 among Representatives who said that their roll call votes had expressed their real views fairly well. But this correlation was only .04 among those who said that their roll call votes had expressed their views poorly. In the other policy domains, too, attitude-roll call agreement is higher among Congressmen who are well satisfied with their roll call votes than it is among Congressmen who are not.

[9] During the analysis we have formed constituency scores out of the scores of constituents living in the same district by several devices other than calculating average constituent scores. In particular, in view of the ordinal character of our scales we have frequently used the *median* constituent score as a central value for the constituency as a whole. However, the ordering of constituencies differs very little according to which of several reasonable alternatives for obtaining constituency scores is chosen. As a result, we have preferred mean scores for the greater number of ranks they give.

incumbent, say) we were able to order these fractions of districts so that the opinions of Congressmen could be compared with those, for example, of the dominant electoral elements of their districts.

In each policy domain, crossing the rankings of Congressmen and their constituencies gives an empirical measure of the extent of policy agreement between legislator and district.[10] In the period of our

[10] The meaning of this procedure can be suggested by two percentage tables standing for hypothetical extreme cases, the first that of full agreement, the second that of no agreement whatever. For convenience, these illustrative tables categorize both Congressmen and their districts in terms of only three degrees of favor and assume for both a nearly uniform distribution across the three categories. The terms "pro," "neutral," and "con" indicate a relative rather than an absolute opinion. In Case I, full agreement, all districts relatively favorable to social welfare action have Congressmen who are so too, etc.; whereas in Case II, or that of no agreement, the ordering of constituencies is independent in a statistical sense of the ranking of Congressmen: knowing the policy orientation of a district gives no clue at all to the orientation of its Congressman. Of course, it is possible for the orders of legislators and districts to be *inversely* related, and this possibility is of some importance, as indicated below, when the policy position of nonincumbent candidates as well as incumbents is taken into account. To summarize the degree of congruence between legislators and voters, a measure of correlation is introduced. Although we have used a variety of measures of association in our analysis, the values reported in this article all refer to product moment correlation coefficients. For our hypothetical Case I a measure of correlation would have the value 1.0; for Case II, the value 0.0. When it is applied to actual data, this convenient indicator is likely to have a value somewhere in between. The question is where.

Case I: Full Policy Agreement
Constituencies

Congressmen	Pro	Neutral	Con	
Pro	33	0	0	33
Neutral	0	34	0	34
Con	0	0	33	33
	33	34	33	100%

Correlation = 1.0

Case II: No Policy Agreement
Constituencies

Congressmen	Pro	Neutral	Con	
Pro	11	11	11	33
Neutral	11	12	11	34
Con	11	11	11	33
	33	34	33	100%

Correlation = 0.0

The values of the coefficients expressing the relationships between constituency

research this procedure reveals very different degrees of policy congruence across the three issue domains. On questions of social and economic welfare there is considerable agreement between Representative and district, expressed by a correlation of approximately .4. This coefficient is, of course, very much less than the limiting value of 1.0, indicating that a number of Congressmen are, relatively speaking, more or less "liberal" than their districts. However, on the question of foreign involvement there is a good deal less agreement: the corresponding coefficient was less than .2. Apparently it made little difference to the internationalism of the Congressman whether he represented an internationalist or isolationist district. It is in the area of civil rights that the rankings of Congressmen and constituencies most nearly agree. When we took our measurements in the late 1950's the correlation of congressional roll call behavior with constituency opinion on questions affecting the Negro was about .65.

The description of policy agreement that these three simple correlations give can be a starting point for a wide range of analyses. For example, the significance of party competition in the district for policy representation can be explored by comparing the agreement between district and Congressman with the agreement between the district and the Congressman's nonincumbent opponent. Alternatively, the significance of choosing Representatives from single-member districts by popular majority can be explored by comparing the agreement between the Congressman and his own supporters with the agreement between the Congressman and the supporters of his opponent. Taking *both* party competition and majority rule into account magnifies rather spectacularly some of the coefficients reported here. This is most true in the domain of social welfare, where attitudes both of candidates and of voters are most polarized along party lines. Whereas the correlation between the constituency majority and congressional roll call votes is nearly +.59 on social welfare policy, the correlation of the district majority with the nonincumbent candidate is −.44. This difference, amounting to slightly more than 1.0, between these two coefficients is an indicator of what the dominant electoral element of

attitude and congressional behavior have been adjusted to remove the attenuation of correlation due to the sampling unreliability of constituency measures based on limited samples, as mentioned in footnote 3 above. Since this adjustment had not been applied to the correlations originally reported in the *American Political Science Review*, the values reported here differ somewhat from those carried in the original article.

the constituency gets on the average by choosing the Congressman it has and excluding his opponent from office.[11]

These three coefficients are also the starting point for a causal analysis of the relation of constituency to Representative, the main problem of this paper. At least on social welfare and Negro rights a measurable degree of congruence is found between district and legislator. Is this agreement due to constituency influence in Congress, or is it to be attributed to other causes? If this question is to have a satisfactory answer the conditions that are necessary and sufficient to assure constituency control must be stated and compared with the available empirical evidence.

The Conditions of Constituency Influence

Broadly speaking, the constituency can control the policy actions of the Representative in two alternative ways. The first of these is for the district to choose a Representative who so shares its views that in following his own convictions he does his constituents' will. In this case district opinion and the Congressman's actions are connected through the Representative's own policy attitudes. The second means of constituency control is for the Congressman to follow his (at least tolerably accurate) perceptions of district attitude in order to win re-election. In this case constituency opinion and the Congressman's actions are connected through his perception of what the district wants.[12]

These two paths of constituency control are presented schematically in Figure 16-1. As the figure suggests, each path has two steps, one

[11] A word of caution is in order, lest we compare things that are not strictly comparable. For obvious reasons, most nonincumbent candidates have no roll call record, and we have had to measure their policy agreement with the district entirely in terms of the attitudes they have revealed in interviews. However, the difference of coefficients given here is almost as great when the policy agreement between the incumbent Congressman and his district is also measured in terms of the attitudes conveyed in confidential interviews.

[12] A third type of connection, excluded here, might obtain between district and Congressman if the Representative accedes to what he thinks the district wants because he believes that to be what a Representative *ought* to do, whether or not it is necessary for re-election. We leave this type of connection out of our account here because we conceive an influence relation as one in which control is not voluntarily accepted or rejected by someone subject to it. Of course, this possible connection between district and Representative is not any the less interesting because it falls outside our definition of influence or control, and we have given a good deal of attention to it in the broader study of which this analysis is part.

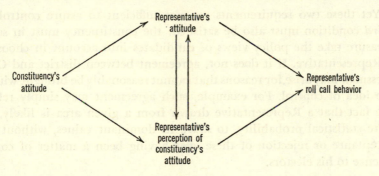

Figure 16-1. Connections between a constituency's attitude and its Representative's roll-call behavior.

connecting the constituency's attitude with an "intervening" attitude or perception, the other connecting this attitude or perception with the Representative's roll call behavior. Out of respect for the processes by which the human actor achieves cognitive congruence we have also drawn arrows between the two intervening factors, since the Congressman probably tends to see his district as having the same opinion as his own and also tends, over time, to bring his own opinion into line with the district's. The inclusion of these arrows calls attention to two other possible influence paths, each consisting of *three* steps, although these additional paths will turn out to be of relatively slight importance empirically.

Neither of the main influence paths of Figure 16-1 will connect the final roll call vote to the constituency's views if either of its steps is blocked. From this, two necessary conditions of constituency influence can be stated: *first,* the Representative's votes in the House must agree substantially with his own policy views or his perceptions of the district's views, and not be determined entirely by other influences to which the Congressman is exposed; and, *second,* the attitudes or perceptions governing the Representative's acts must correspond, at least imperfectly, to the district's actual opinions. It would be difficult to describe the relation of constituency to Representative as one of control unless these conditions are met.[13]

---

[13] It scarcely needs to be said that demonstrating *some* constituency influence would not imply that the Representative's behavior is *wholly* determined by constituency pressures. The legislator acts in a complex institutional setting in which he is subject to a wide variety of influences. The constituency can exercise a genuine measure of control without driving all other influences from the Representative's life space.

Yet these two requirements are not sufficient to assure control. A *third* condition must also be satisfied: the constituency must in some measure take the policy views of candidates into account in choosing a Representative. If it does not, agreement between district and Congressman may arise for reasons that cannot reasonably be brought within the idea of control. For example, such agreement may simply reflect the fact that a Representative drawn from a given area is likely, by pure statistical probability, to share its dominant values, without his acceptance or rejection of these ever having been a matter of consequence to his electors.

Evidence of Control: Congressional Attitudes and Perceptions

How well are these conditions met in the relation of American Congressmen to their constituents? There is little question that the first is substantially satisfied; the evidence of our research indicates that members of the House do in fact vote both their own policy views and their perceptions of their constituents' views, at least on issues of social welfare, foreign involvement, and civil rights. If these two intervening factors are used to predict roll call votes, the prediction is quite successful. Their multiple correlation with roll call position is .67 for social welfare, .56 for foreign involvement, and .86 for civil rights; the last figure is especially persuasive. What is more, both the Congressman's own convictions and his perceptions of district opinion make a distinct contribution to his roll call behavior. In each of the three domains the prediction of roll call votes is surer if it is made from both factors rather than from either alone.

Lest the strong influence that the Congressman's views and his perception of district views have on roll call behavior appear somehow foreordained—and, consequently, this finding seem a trivial one—it is worth taking a sidewise glance at the potency of possible other forces on the Representative's vote. In the area of foreign policy, for example, a number of Congressmen are disposed to follow the administration's advice, whatever they or their districts think. For those who are, the multiple correlation of roll call behavior with the Representative's own foreign policy views and his perception of district views is a mere .2. Other findings could be cited to support the point that the influence of the Congressman's own preferences and those he attributes to the district is extremely variable. Yet in the House as a whole over the three policy domains the influence of these forces is quite strong.

The connections of congressional attitudes and perceptions with actual constituency opinion are weaker. If policy agreement between district and Representative is moderate and variable across the policy domains, as it is, this is to be explained much more in terms of the second condition of constituency control than the first. The Representative's attitudes and perceptions most nearly match true opinion in his district on the issues of Negro rights. Reflecting the charged and polarized nature of this area, the correlation of actual district opinion with perceived opinion is greater than .7 and the correlation of district attitude with the Representative's own attitude is nearly .5 as shown by Table 16-1. But the comparable correlations for foreign involvement are much smaller. And the coefficients for social welfare are also smaller, although a detailed presentation of findings in this area would show that the Representative's perceptions and attitudes are more strongly associated with the attitude of his electoral *majority* than they are with the attitudes of the constituency as a whole.

Knowing this much about the various paths that may lead, directly or indirectly, from constituency attitude to roll call vote, we can assess their relative importance. Since the alternative influence chains have links of unequal strength, the full chains will not in general be equally strong, and these differences are of great importance in the relation of Representative to constituency. For the domain of civil rights Figure 16-2 assembles all the intercorrelations of the variables of our system. As the figure shows, the root correlation of constituency attitude with roll call behavior in this domain is .65. How much of this policy congruence can be accounted for by the influence path involving the Representative's attitude? And how much by the path involving his percep-

TABLE 16-1

Correlations of Constituency Attitudes

Policy Domain	Correlation of Constituency Attitude with	
	Representative's Perception of Constituency Attitude	Representative's Own Attitude
Social welfare	.17	.26
Foreign involvement	.25	.32
Civil rights	.74	.50

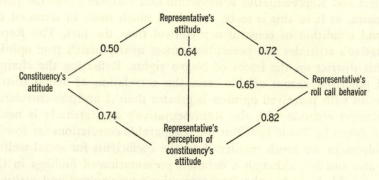

Figure 16-2. Intercorrelations of variables pertaining to civil rights.

tion of constituency opinion? When the intercorrelations of the system are interpreted in the light of what we assume its causal structure to be, it is influence passing through the Congressman's perception of the district's views that is found to be preeminently important.[14] Under

[14] We have done this by a variance-component technique similar to several others proposed for dealing with problems of this type. See especially H. A. Simon, "Spurious Correlation: A Causal Interpretation," *Journal of the American Statistical Association*, 49, 467–479 (1954); H. M. Blalock, Jr., "The Relative Importance of Variables," *American Sociological Review*, 26, 866–874 (1961); and the almost forgotten work of S. Wright, "Correlation and Causation," *Journal of Agricultural Research*, 20, 557–585 (1920). Under this technique a "path coefficient" (to use Wright's terminology, although not his theory) is assigned to each of the causal arrows by solving a set of equations involving the correlations of the variables of the model. The weight assigned to a full path is then the product of its several path coefficients, and this product may be interpreted as the proportion of the variance of the dependent variable (roll call behavior, here) that is explained by a given path. A special problem arises because influence may flow in either direction between the Congressman's attitude and his perception of district attitude (as noted above, the Representative may tend both to perceive his constituency's view selectively, as consistent with his own, and to change his own view to be consistent with the perceived constituency view). Hence, we have not a single causal model but a whole family of models, varying according to the relative importance of influence from attitude to perception and from perception to attitude. Our solution to this problem has been to calculate influence coefficients for the two extreme models in order to see how much our results could vary according to which model is chosen from our family of models. Since the systems of equations in this analysis are linear, it can be shown that the coefficients we seek have their maximum and minimum values under one or the other of the limiting models. Therefore, computing any given coefficient for each of these limiting cases defines an interval in which the true value

the least favorable assumption as to its importance, this path is found to account for more than twice as much of the variance of roll call behavior as the paths involving the Representative's own attitude.[15] However, when this same procedure is applied to our social welfare

---

of the coefficient must lie. In fact these intervals turn out to be fairly small; our findings as to the relative importance of alternative influence paths would change little according to which model is selected.

The two limiting models with their associated systems of equations and the formulas for computing the relative importance of the three possible influence paths under each model are given below.

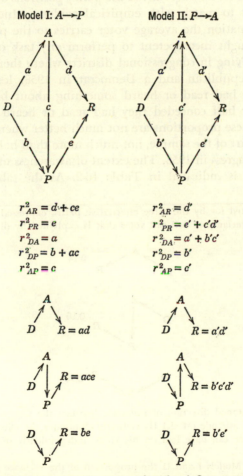

Model I: $A \rightarrow P$

$$r^2_{AR} = d + ce$$
$$r^2_{PR} = e$$
$$r^2_{DA} = a$$
$$r^2_{DP} = b + ac$$
$$r^2_{AP} = c$$

$$R = ad$$
$$R = ace$$
$$R = be$$

Model II: $P \rightarrow A$

$$r^2_{AR} = d'$$
$$r^2_{PR} = e' + c'd'$$
$$r^2_{DA} = a' + b'c'$$
$$r^2_{DP} = b'$$
$$r^2_{AP} = c'$$

$$R = a'd'$$
$$R = b'c'd'$$
$$R = b'e'$$

data, the results suggest that the direct connection of constituency and roll call through the Congressman's own attitude is the most important of the alternative paths.[16] The reversal of the relative importance of the two paths as we move from civil rights to social welfare is one of the most striking findings of this analysis.

Evidence of Control: Electoral Behavior

Of the three conditions of constituency influence, the requirement that the electorate take account of the policy positions of the candidates is the hardest to match with empirical evidence. Indeed, given the limited information the average voter carries to the polls, the public might be thought incompetent to perform any task of appraisal. Of constituents living in congressional districts where there was a contest between a Republican and a Democrat in 1958, less than one in five said they had read or heard something about both candidates, and well over half conceded they had read or heard nothing about either. And these proportions are not much better when they are based only on the part of the sample, not much more than half, that reported voting for Congress in 1958. The extent of awareness of the candidates among voters is indicated in Table 16-2. As the table shows, even

---

behavior accounted for by the three alternative paths, expressed as proportions of the part of the variance of roll call votes that is explained by district attitude, are these:

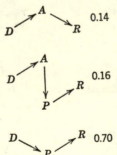

Inverting the assumed direction of influence between the Congressman's own attitude and district attitude (Model II) virtually eliminates the effect that the Representative's attitude can have had on his votes, independently of his perception of district attitude.

[16] Under both Models I and II the proportion of the variance of roll call voting explained by the influence path involving the Representative's own attitude is twice as great as the proportion explained by influence passing through his perception of district attitude.

TABLE 16-2

Awareness of Congressional Candidates among Voters, 1958

		Read or Heard Something About Incumbent *		
		Yes	No	
Read or Heard Something	Yes	24	5	29
About Nonincumbent	No	25	46	71
		49	51	100%

* In order to include all districts where the House seat was contested in 1958 this table retains ten constituencies in which the incumbent Congressman did not seek re-election. Candidates of the retiring incumbent's party in these districts are treated here as if they were incumbents. Were these figures to be calculated only for constituencies in which an incumbent sought re-election, no entry in this four-fold table would differ from that given by more than two per cent.

of the portion of the public that was sufficiently interested to vote, almost half had read or heard nothing about either candidate.

As we have seen in Chapter 11 what the voters "knew" was confined to diffuse evaluative judgments about the candidate: "he's a good man," "he understands the problems," and so forth. Of detailed information about policy stands not more than a chemical trace was found. Among the comments about the candidates given in response to an extended series of free-answer questions, less than 2 per cent had to do with stands in our three policy domains; indeed, only about three comments in every hundred had to do with legislative issues of *any* description.

This evidence that the behavior of the electorate is largely unaffected by knowledge of the policy positions of the candidates is complemented by evidence about the forces that *do* shape the voters' choices among congressional candidates. The primary basis of voting in American congressional elections is identification with party. In 1958 only one vote in twenty was cast by persons without any sort of party loyalty. And among those who did have a party identification, only one in ten voted against their party. As a result, something like 84 per cent of the vote that year was cast by party identifiers voting their usual party line. What is more, traditional party voting is seldom connected with current legislative issues. As the party loyalists in a nationwide sample of voters told us what they liked and disliked about the parties in 1958, only a small fraction of the comments (about 15 per cent) dealt with current issues of public policy.

Yet the idea of reward or punishment at the polls for legislative stands is familiar to members of Congress, who feel that they and their records are quite visible to their constituents. Of our sample of Congressmen who were opposed for re-election in 1958, more than four-fifths said the outcome in their districts had been strongly influenced by the electorate's response to their records and personal standing. Indeed, this belief is clear enough to present a notable contradiction: Congressmen feel that their individual legislative actions may have considerable impact on the electorate, yet some simple facts about the Representative's salience to his constituents imply that this could hardly be true.

In some measure this contradiction is to be explained by the tendency of Congressmen to overestimate their visibility to the local public, a tendency that reflects the difficulties of the Representative in forming a correct judgment of constituent opinion. The communication most Congressmen have with their districts inevitably puts them in touch with organized groups and with individuals who are relatively well informed about politics. The Representative knows his constituents mostly from dealing with people who *do* write letters, who *will* attend meetings, who *have* an interest in his legislative stands. As a result, his sample of contacts with a constituency of several hundred thousand people is heavily biased: even the contacts he apparently makes at random are likely to be with people who grossly overrepresent the degree of political information and interest in the constituency as a whole.

But the contradiction is also to be explained by several aspects of the Representative's electoral situation that are of great importance to the question of constituency influence. The first of these is implicit in what has already been said. Because of the pervasive effects of party loyalties, no candidate for Congress starts from scratch in putting together an electoral majority. The Congressman is a dealer in increments and margins. He starts with a stratum of hardened party voters, and if the stratum is broad enough he can have a measurable influence on his chance of survival simply by attracting a small additional element of the electorate—or by not losing a larger one. Therefore, his record may have a very real bearing on his electoral success or failure without most of his constituents ever knowing what that record is.

Second, the relation of Congressman to voter is not a simple bilateral one but is complicated by the presence of all manner of intermediaries: the local party, economic interests, the news media, racial and nationality organizations, and so forth. Such is the lore of American politics, as it is known to any political scientist. Very often the Representative reaches the mass public through these mediating agencies, and the information about himself and his record may be considerably transformed as it diffuses out to the electorate in two or more stages. As a result, the public—or parts of it—may get simple positive or negative cues about the Congressman which were provoked by his legislative actions but which no longer have a recognizable issue content.

Third, for most Congressmen most of the time the electorate's sanctions are potential rather than actual. Particularly the Representative from a safe district may feel his proper legislative strategy is to avoid giving opponents in his own party or outside of it material they can use against him. As the Congressman pursues this strategy he may write a legislative record that never becomes very well known to his constituents; if it doesn't win votes, neither does it lose any. This is clearly the situation of most Southern Congressmen in dealing with the issue of Negro rights. By voting correctly on this issue they are unlikely to increase their visibility to constituents. Nevertheless, the fact of constituency influence, backed by potential sanctions at the polls, is real enough.

That these potential sanctions are all too real is best illustrated in the election of 1958 by the reprisal against Representative Brooks Hays in Arkansas' Fifth District.[17] Although the perception of Congressman Hays as too moderate on civil rights resulted more from his service as intermediary between the White House and Governor Faubus in the Little Rock school crisis than from his record in the House, the victory of Dale Alford as a write-in candidate was a striking reminder of what can happen to a Congressman who gives his foes a powerful issue to use against him. The extraordinary involvement of the public in this race can be seen by comparing how well the candidates were known in this constituency with the awareness of the candidates shown by Table 16-2 above for the country as a whole. As Table 16-3 indicates, not a single voter in our sample of Arkansas' Fifth District was unaware of either candidate.[18] What is more, these

---

[17] For an account of this episode see C. Silverman, "The Little Rock Story," Inter-University Case Program series, reprinted in E. A. Bock and A. K. Campbell, editors, *Case Studies in American Government* (Englewood Cliffs, N.J., Prentice-Hall, 1962, pp. 1–46).

[18] The sample of this constituency was limited to twenty-three persons of whom thirteen voted. However, despite the small number of cases the probability that the difference in awareness between this constituency and the country generally as the result only of sampling variations is much less than one in a thousand.

TABLE 16-3

Awareness of Congressional Candidates among Voters in Arkansas
Fifth District, 1958

		Read or Heard Something About Hays		
		Yes	No	
Read or Heard Something	Yes	100	0	100
About Alford	No	0	0	0
		100	0	100%

interviews show that Hays was regarded both by his supporters and his
opponents as more moderate than Alford on civil rights and that this
perception brought his defeat. In some measure, what happened in
Little Rock in 1958 can happen anywhere, and our Congressmen ought
not to be entirely disbelieved in what they say about their impact at the
polls. Indeed, they may be under genuine pressure from the voters even
while they are the forgotten men of national elections.[19]

Conclusion

Therefore, although the conditions of constituency influence are not
equally satisfied, they are met well enough to give the local constituency
a measure of control over the actions of its Representatives. Best satisfied is the requirement about motivational influences on the Congressman: our evidence shows that the Representative's roll call behavior is
strongly influenced by his own policy preferences and by his perception

[19] In view of the potential nature of the constituency's sanctions, it is relevant to
characterize its influence over the Representative in terms of several distinctions
drawn by recent theorists of power, especially the difference between actual and potential power, between influence and coercive power, and between influence and
purposive control. Observing these distinctions, we might say that the constituency's
influence is *actual* and not merely *potential* since it is the sanction behavior rather
than the conforming behavior that is infrequent (Dahl). That is, the Congressman
is influenced by his calculus of potential sanctions, following the "rule of anticipated
reactions" (Friedrich), however oblivious of his behavior the constituency ordinarily
may be. We might also say that the constituency has *power* since its influence depends partly on sanctions (Lasswell and Kaplan), although it rarely exercises *control*
since its influence is rarely conscious or intended (Cartwright). In the discussion
above we have of course used the terms "influence" and "control" interchangeably.

of preferences held by the constituency. However, the conditions of influence that presuppose effective communication between Congressman and district are much less well met. The Representative has very imperfect information about the issue preferences of his constituency, and the constituency's awareness of the policy stands of the Representative ordinarily is slight.

The findings of this analysis heavily underscore the fact that no single tradition of representation fully accords with the realities of American legislative politics. The American system *is* a mixture, to which the Burkean, instructed-delegate, and responsible-party models all can be said to have contributed elements. Moreover, variations in the representative relation are most likely to occur as we move from one policy domain to another. No single, generalized configuration of attitudes and perceptions links Representative with constituency but rather several distinct patterns, and which of them is invoked depends very much on the issue involved.

The issue domain in which the relation of Congressman to constituency most nearly conforms to the instructed-delegate model is that of civil rights. This conclusion is supported by the importance of the influence-path passing through the Representative's perception of district opinion, although even in this domain the sense in which the constituency may be said to take the position of the candidate into account in reaching its electoral judgment should be carefully qualified.

The representative relation conforms most closely to the responsible-party model in the domain of social welfare. In this issue area, the arena of partisan conflict for a generation, the party symbol helps both constituency and Representative in the difficult process of communication between them. On the one hand, because Republican and Democratic voters tend to differ in what they would have government do, the Representative has some guide to district opinion simply by looking at the partisan division of the vote. On the other hand, because the two parties tend to recruit candidates who differ on the social welfare role of government, the constituency can infer the candidates' position with more than random accuracy from their party affiliation, even though what the constituency has learned directly about these stands is almost nothing. How faithful the representation of social welfare views is to the responsible-party model should not be exaggerated. Even in this policy domain, American practice departs widely from an ideal conception of party government. But in this domain, more than any other, political conflict has become a conflict of national parties in which constituency and Representative are known to each other primarily by their party association.

It would be too pat to say that the domain of foreign involvement conforms to the third model of representation, the conception promoted by Edmund Burke. Clearly it does in the sense that the Congressman looks elsewhere than to his district in making up his mind on foreign issues. However, the reliance he puts on the President and the administration suggests that the calculation of where the public interest lies is often passed to the executive on matters of foreign policy. Ironically, legislative initiative in foreign affairs has fallen victim to the very difficulties of gathering and appraising information that led Burke to argue that Parliament rather than the public ought to hold the power of decision. The background information and predictive skills that Burke thought the people lacked are held primarily by the modern executive. As a result, the present role of the legislature in foreign affairs bears some resemblance to the role that Burke had in mind for the elitist, highly restricted *electorate* of his own day.

Index

Group(s), *see also* Community; Region
common interest of members, 107
conflict, 99
intergroup contact, 122
legitimacy of intervention, 111
loyalty, 99
membership, 100
memberships of the candidates, 123, 124
minority, 76
relations, 107
primary and secondary, 107
sense of proximity, 107
structure of intragroup correlations, 110
voting, 14
Group Influence in Voting Behavior, 110
Gulliksen, Harold O., 354
Gurin, Gerald, 45, 334
Guttmann, Louis, 152, 357

Handbook of Social Psychology, 320
Harding, Warren G., 212
Hartley, Eugene L., 222
Hays, Brooks, 369, 370
Homans, George, 251
Hoover, Herbert, 61, 74
Hotelling, Harold, 162, 168
How to Predict Elections, 10, 181
Human Group, The, 251
Hume, David, 245

Identification, community, 109
ethnic, 166
meaning of, 216
racial, 166
religious, 166
strength of, 264
with the Catholic community, 108
Ideology, 76, 171, 253, 289
character of politics, 267
cleavages, 270
concepts, 166
content, 166
dimensions, 174
focus, 176, 177
fractionation, 278
intransigence, 284
issues, 271

Ideology, position views of party leadership, 259
splinter group, 278
structure, 175
Immigrants, 230
contribute to turnout, 230
Republican coloration, 230
Income, 46, 52
Independents, 44, 67, 68, 89, 283, *see also* Vote; Voters; Voting
dropout rate, 197
Influence, and coercive power, 370
and power, 356
and purposive control, 370
scope of, 356
of statewide contests on House races, 203
through informal communication, 272
Information, 123, 136, 143, 144, 147, 148, 150, 151, 152, 153, 156, 174, 198, 368
about House candidates in 1958, 204
about policy, 367
about the congressional candidates, 142
about the policy positions, 209, 367
and interest in the constituency, 368
and normative theory of representation, 194
flow, 143, 155
the government has and government by responsible parties, 195
intake, 145
level, 141
needs for, 152
political, 144
seeking, 271
the average voter carries, 366
to the nineteenth century, 152
Institute for Social Research in Oslo, 249
Interaction among party leaders, 247
Interest, 42, 46, 47, 73, 126, 147, 150
Involvement, 22, 23, 24, 53, 59, 108, 117, 118, 137, 139, 140, 144, 145, 155, 270, 271, 276, 278, 285, 291, 307, 342
associational, 106, 107
asymmetry of, 25, 34